PAUL, HIS LETTERS, and ACTS

PAUL, HIS LETTERS, and ACTS

Thomas E. Phillips

LIBRARY OF PAULINE STUDIES

Stanley E. Porter, *General Editor*

Paul, His Letters, and Acts
© 2009 by Hendrickson Publishers Marketing, LLC
P. O. Box 3473
Peabody, Massachusetts 01961-3473

ISBN 978-1-59856-001-5

Printed in the United States of America

First Printing — October 2009

Cover Art: Bassano, Francesco (1549–1592), Saint Paul Preaching. Oil sketch.
Location: Musei Civici, Padua, Italy
Photo Credit: Cameraphoto Arte, Venice / Art Resource, N.Y.

Library of Congress Cataloging-in-Publication Data

Phillips, Thomas E.
     Paul, his letters, and Acts / Thomas E. Phillips; Stanley E. Porter, general
     editor.
          p. cm. — (Library of Pauline studies)
     Includes bibliographical references and indexes.
     ISBN 978-1-59856-001-5 (alk. paper)
     1. Paul, the Apostle, Saint. 2. Bible. N.T. Acts—Criticism, interpretation,
etc. 3. Bible. N.T. Epistles of Paul—Criticism, interpretation, etc. I. Porter,
Stanley E., 1956– II. Title.
     BS2506.3.P45 2009
     227'.06—dc22
                                        2009022567

To George Lyons,
from whom I learned
the best and the most

TABLE OF CONTENTS

ABBREVIATIONS

AB	Anchor Bible
ABD	*Anchor Bible Dictionary.* Edited by David N. Freedman. 6 vols. New York: Doubleday, 1992
AGJU	Arbeiten zur Geschichte des antiken Judentums und des Urchristentums
AJT	*American Journal of Theology*
ANRW	*Aufstieg und Niedergang der römischen Welt*
BAFCS	Book of Acts in Its First Century Setting
BAIAS	*Bulletin of the Anglo-Israel Archeological Society*
BETL	Bibliotheca ephemeridum theologicarum lovaniensium
Bib	*Biblica*
BJRL	*Bulletin of the John Rylands University Library of Manchester*
BNTC	Black's New Testament Commentaries
BW	*The Biblical World: A Dictionary of Biblical Archaeology.* Edited by C. F. Pfeiffer. Grand Rapids, 1966
BZ	*Biblische Zeitschrift*
BZNW	Beihefte zur Zeitschrift für die neutestamentliche Wissenschaft
CBET	Contributions to Biblical Exegesis and Theology
CBQ	*Catholic Biblical Quarterly*
CBR	*Currents in Biblical Research*
ETL	*Ephemerides theologicae lovanienses*
ExpTim	*Expository Times*
FRLANT	*Forschungen zur Religion und Literatur des Alten und Neuen Testaments*
HTR	*Harvard Theological Review*
ICC	International Critical Commentary
Int	*Interpretation*
JBL	*Journal of Biblical Literature*
JQR	*Jewish Quarterly Review*
JR	*Journal of Religion*
JSNT	*Journal for the Study of the New Testament*
JSNTSup	Journal for the Study of the New Testament: Supplement Series

KEK	Kritisch-exegetischer Kommentar über das Neue Testament
LNTS	Library of New Testament Studies
LPS	Library of Pauline Studies
NCBC	New Century Bible Commentary
NICNT	New International Commentary on the New Testament
NIDNTT	*New International Dictionary of New Testament Theology.* Edited by C. Brown. 3 vols. Grand Rapids: Zondervan, 1971
NIV	New International Version
NovT	*Novum Testamentum*
NovTSup	Novum Testamentum Supplements
NTM	New Testament Monographs
NTS	*New Testament Studies*
OBT	Overtures to Biblical Theology
PEGLBS	Proceedings of the Eastern Great Lakes Biblical Society
PEGLMBS	Proceedings of the Eastern Great Lakes and Midwest Biblical Societies
PRSt	*Perspectives in Religious Studies*
RB	*Revue biblique*
SBLDS	Society of Biblical Literature Dissertation Series
SBLSP	Society of Biblical Literature Seminar Papers
SBLSymS	Society of Biblical Literature Symposium Series
SJT	*Scottish Journal of Theology*
SNTSMS	Society for New Testament Studies Monograph Series
TAPA	*Transactions of the American Philological Association*
WBC	Word Biblical Commentary
WUNT	Wissenschaftliche Untersuchungen zum Neuen Testament
ZNT	*Zeitschrift für Neues Testament*
ZNW	*Zeitschrift für die neutestamentliche Wissenschaft und die Kunde der älteren Kirche*

PREFACE

PAUL IS so inherently interesting that anyone who writes about Paul should feel an appropriate sense of intimidation, lest one's words detract from the writings and accomplishments of Paul himself. The immense body of secondary literature on Paul can also become daunting—one sometimes wonders, what more can be said? As I compose this volume, my hope is not to offer the last word—or even many truly original words—on Paul. My hope is merely to introduce some aspects of Paul's life that intersect in Paul's letters and in Acts, and secondarily to expose the reader to some of the intriguing scholarly discourse surrounding those aspects of Paul's life.

As with any project of similar size, several people have supported my research, writing, and reflection. I have been unusually blessed with a host of supportive friends and colleagues. I owe a particular debt of gratitude to Robin Ottoson, the former director of the library at my own former institution, and to the many skilled librarians in the Ryan Library at Point Loma Nazarene University (PLNU), where I now teach. Additionally, I wish to thank the Wesleyan Center at PLNU for its financial support of my research time.

Many colleagues have contributed to the discourse behind this volume, notably, Brad E. Kelle, John W. Wright, Robert Smith, Mark Bilby, and Sam Powell at PLNU. My appreciation for PLNU extends to all of the students, faculty, staff, and administration who have prompted, questioned, and otherwise supported me in my research and writing. As I sit in my new office overlooking the Pacific Ocean, I am especially grateful to the Smee family, whose generosity provided the office where I now sit.

Finally, I end this preface where the original idea for the volume began, with Stanley E. Porter and Shirley Decker-Lucke. Their invitation to contribute to this series came when I was privileged to cochair the section on Acts at the Society of Biblical Literature. It is, therefore, fitting to begin this printed work with a note of gratitude to them for their kind patience while waiting to see the finished work.

INTRODUCTION

HAVING LIVED and worked on both coasts of North America, in Boston on the east coast and San Diego on the west coast, I am drawn to maritime metaphors. If the vast and varied field of Pauline studies can be likened to a sea of scholarly discourse that extends even beyond the horizon of any particular scholar and writer, then the Library of Pauline Studies is designed to provide a chart by which to navigate all—or nearly all—of that sea. As for this particular volume, however, the cartographical agenda is much smaller, comparable perhaps to the charting of a single bay and its accompanying terrain. That bay, the overlap between the Paul of the letters and the Paul of Acts, is, however, particularly interesting. It is the place where the Paul of the narrative of Acts meets the Paul of the discourse in Paul's letters. It is a bay of brackish waters where one cannot always discern what has entered from the river of Acts and what has entered from the sea of Paul's letters. Although both the river of Acts and the sea of Paul's letters are rich and productive environments, each nurtures different species of flora and fauna. To the casual observer, the blending of these environments can be so subtle as to produce the illusion of one continuous and undifferentiated environment. To the more astute observer, however, the differences between the saline sea waters and the fresh river water are profound and clearly discernible. But the brackish waters—where the waters meet, intermingle, and become one—present a challenge to even the most skilled observers.

This volume will explore those brackish waters where the Paul of Acts meets the Paul of the letters. What can be distinguished as belonging only to Paul's letters? What can be distinguished as belonging only to Acts? What belongs to both or to neither? *To what degree are the Paul of Acts and the Paul of the letters the same character, and to what degree are the Paul of Acts and the Paul of the letters two distinct—and perhaps incongruous—characters?* These are the questions that drive this volume.

To some readers, the very idea of distinguishing between the Paul of Acts and the Paul of the letters will be new and surprising. For many such readers, the two Pauls have often been uncritically blended and seldom clearly distinguished. To many other readers, the Paul of Acts and the Paul of the letters will have long ago been separated. For some within this second group of readers, the two Pauls are so deliberately cordoned off from one another that they have never been compared in a careful and disciplined way. It seems to me that many readers—both scholarly and lay—have erred in their reflections about Paul. *The central project of this volume, therefore, has two distinct, but related, aspects. First, this book will seek to help interpreters to understand—and perhaps establish for themselves—the lines of demarcation between the Paul of Acts and the Paul of the letters. Second, this volume will help interpreters to compare the "Paul" on each side of these lines of demarcation.*

Of course, this volume is not oblivious to the many complexities involved in both aspects of its central project. Some readers will be troubled by the notion of dividing what has often been viewed as a single habitat (Acts and Paul's letters) and as a single person (Paul) within the ecosystem of the church. Other readers will be equally troubled by the potential for creating artificial points of comparison between what is perceived to be two very different characters. Such diversity of opinion, both in interpreters' initial assumptions and in their eventual conclusions, is neither easily overcome nor wisely ignored. In fact, such diversity of opinion is inevitable in the brackish waters where the Paul of Acts meets the Paul of the letters. After surveying the evidence in this book, some readers will be left with a strong sense of having met two different Pauls. After surveying the same evidence in this same volume, other equally perceptive readers will be left with an equally strong sense of having met the same person in two different literary settings.

As I have already acknowledged, this volume cannot span the entire sea of Pauline studies, but it will seek to suspend a bridge between the two primary environments that Paul inhabits in Scripture: the habitat of Paul's letters and the habitat of Acts. This bridge will provide a bird's-eye view both of where these two habitats intersect and of the degree of similarity and difference between the Paul who resides in each habitat. This bridge between the habitats is suspended from two observation towers that provide the framework for this volume and that orient its development. Those twin towers are the recognition of *Paul's split personality* within contemporary biblical scholarship and the importance of *the apostolic conference in Jerusalem.*

The first two chapters of this volume view Pauline scholarship from the vantage point of the first observation tower and explore the phenomenon of Paul's split personality within contemporary New Testament scholarship. More narrowly, the first chapter of this book reviews two recent volumes on Paul's life and offers those two books as examples of the divided state of contemporary scholarly work on Paul's life. This first chapter illustrates how critical scholars often promote two different images of Paul, one that leans in the direction of Acts and one that leans away from Acts. Although I argue that both images of Paul are plausible, I also observe that the image of Paul that leans away from Acts is becoming increasingly prominent in critical scholarship and that critical scholars are increasingly emphasizing the presence of two different "Pauls" within Scripture—the Paul of the letters and the Paul of Acts. The second chapter explores the origin and scope of the contemporary scholarly trend to separate the Paul of Acts from the Paul of the letters by briefly chronicling the major writings of the nineteenth- and twentieth-century scholars whose work established this trend. In tandem, these first two chapters explain the nature and origin of the contentious relationship that the Paul of the letters has with the Paul of Acts in much contemporary New Testament scholarship. Having accomplished this agenda, the second chapter will also lay out the agenda for the rest of the volume, explaining the approach this volume will use to compare the data sets in Acts with the data sets in Paul's letters in regard to Pauline chronology, Pauline social location, and Pauline relationships.

The next four chapters of the book, chapters three through six, view the Paul of Acts and the Paul of the letters using the Jerusalem Conference as their primary observation tower. The third chapter makes the Jerusalem Conference a central focus of its investigation by asking the most basic question about Paul's life: what do Acts and Paul's letters each teach us about the chronology of Paul's life? As the chapter seeks to answer this question, the timing and significance of the Jerusalem Conference becomes the central interpretive issue for comparing the chronological data in Acts and Paul's letters. The Jerusalem Conference remains in the background, but plays a less central role in the fourth chapter, which looks at Paul's social location within the Greco-Roman world. The particular points of comparison in this chapter are Paul's family of origin, his educational background, his pre-Christian religious background, his vocation, and his political orientation as depicted in Acts and Paul's letters.

Although the Jerusalem Conference fades to the sidelines in the fourth chapter, the conference again moves to center stage in the fifth and sixth chapters that examine Paul's relationships with other early Christians. The fifth chapter considers the people who were reported as participants in the conference, and the sixth chapter considers the early Christians whom Acts or Paul's letters report as active in Paul's ministry, but not as present at the Jerusalem Conference.

Both observation towers, the timing and significance of the Jerusalem Conference and prominence of Paul's split personality within contemporary scholarship, share equal prominence in the conclusion to the volume as I offer my own critical reflections upon both the state of contemporary scholarship on Paul and the role of the Jerusalem Conference for understanding the relationship between the Paul of Acts and the Paul of the letters.

ᐱ 1 ᐱ

THE PLURALITY OF PLAUSIBLE PAULS

WHILE THE vineyard of biblical scholarship has seen many good years for Pauline studies, 2004 was an exceptionally good year for Paul. It produced two books with extraordinary bouquet and flavor, *Rabbi Paul* by Bruce Chilton[1] and *In Search of Paul* by John Dominic Crossan and Jonathan Reed.[2] Both books follow on the heels of the same authors' widely acclaimed volumes on the historical Jesus. In many ways, it seems altogether fitting that these distinguished authors should continue their explorations into Christian origins with a sampling from the Apostle. With the singular exception of Jesus, no figure within the first century of Christianity has sustained a more robust body of theological reflection than the Apostle Paul.

The Apostle's role as a catalyst to the church's ongoing theological reflection is hardly surprising, given his frenetic energies and contentious personality. While some personalities are sated with small accomplishments and minor victories, the Apostle's ambitions demanded grand accomplishments and unqualified victories. Paul's inhibitions and fears seem few; his daring and innovations, many. By all indications, Paul's passions provoked debate wherever he went, inspiring admiration from some, and disdain from others. In the first century, this persecutor turned preacher could be doubted—or even rejected—but never ignored.

Nor has Paul's demand for attention been quenched by the passing centuries. Even in the twenty-first century, the Apostle confronts saints and scholars with the same contentious demand for engagement. The Christian canon not only preserves Paul's own literary output (at least seven letters) but also offers up a list of Paul's premier first-century interpreters (as many as six

---

[1] Bruce Chilton, *Rabbi Paul: An Intellectual Biography* (New York: Doubleday, 2004).

[2] John Dominic Crossan and Jonathan L. Reed, *In Search of Paul: How Jesus's Apostle Opposed Rome's Empire with God's Kingdom* (San Francisco: HarperSanFrancisco, 2004). Among the scores of volumes which addressed Paul either directly or indirectly in 2004, two additional volumes deserve honorable mention: Robin Griffith-Jones, *The Gospel according to Paul: The Creative Genius Who Brought Jesus to the World* (San Francisco: HarperSanFrancisco, 2004); and Jerome Murphy-O'Connor, *Paul: His Story* (Oxford: Oxford University Press, 2004).

pseudonymous letters of Paul) and a cache of secondary sources in the Acts of the Apostles.

With such a rich canonical investment in Paul, it is hardly surprising that Paul's theological heirs have been blessed with a frustrating wealth of dividends from Paul's interpreters. With so many raw materials provided by Paul and Paul's canonical interpreters, the versions of "Paul" offered up by contemporary Pauline scholars often bear little resemblance to one another. Even the most competent interpreters can arrange the tessarae of the canonical Paul into quite varied—though perhaps equally faithful—mosaics of Paul. Such is the case with the skilled artisans behind *Rabbi Paul* and *In Search of Paul*. Each reconstruction of "Paul" is plausible, but neither looks much like the other. Let me introduce each of these two "plausible Pauls" in turn.

I. Chilton's Plausible Paul

Chilton's "intellectual biography" of Paul provides the narrative of a man whose life, thought, and energies were punctuated and shaped by two dramatic events: his conversion to Christianity and his rejection by the Jerusalem church. Accordingly, Chilton divides Paul's life into three phases: (1) Paul's Jewish devotion until his baptism and sojourn into Arabia, (2) Paul's Christian missionary activity until James's rejection of Paul's gospel, and (3) Paul's subsequent quest for reunion between his Gentile Christians and James's Jewish Christians. Paul's conversion marks the transition between the first and second phases of his life and his rejection by the Jerusalem church marks the transition between the second and third phases of his life.

Like any astute biographer, Chilton recognizes the need for scrutiny of his sources—even primary sources like Paul's letters. He cautions that Paul's letters, like any other writing, sometimes reflect the self-interest of their author. Chilton warns that Paul's letters are "as limited as Paul was," and they inevitably contain lapses, omissions and biographical glosses. For Chilton, therefore, "What Paul does not say makes the Book of the Acts of the Apostles an extremely valuable resource in any attempt at biography." Chilton even suggests that a secondary source, like Acts, may reveal what Paul wished to conceal: "Sometimes there is good reason to infer that Paul keeps *a self-interested silence* that Acts breaks."[3]

Although Chilton dates Acts "around 90 c.e.," he is confident that some of the traditions in Acts owe their origin to one or more of Paul's traveling partners, most likely and notably Timothy.[4] Even though these accounts from Timothy have been edited by the author of Acts, according to Chilton they

---

[3] Chilton, *Rabbi Paul*, xv, emphasis added.

[4] Ibid., xv. Chilton warns: "That doesn't make Acts more reliable than Paul's letters, but it does mean that what Acts says should be assessed, not simply rejected." Also see p. 149.

retain significant value as independent reports from a contemporary of Paul—and he intends to draw upon those assets.

In keeping with Chilton's commitment to employ Acts as a source for his biography of Paul, the material for reconstructing the opening phase of Paul's life is drawn almost entirely from Acts. Chilton's Paul, although a loyal Jew, is emphatically a child of the pagan city of Tarsus; he has even been influenced by Tarsus's festivals to the pagan god Tarku.[5] Chilton's Paul is a child of Tarsus's privileged and wealthy class. Chilton assures us that Paul's family "could afford real mansions with courtyards, space for the extended family, and servants' quarters."[6] According to Chilton, Paul's "persistent traits of attitude and temperament derived from his home city. He was a Cilician, a Stoic, a tent-maker, and—by deliberate ambition—a Pharisee."[7]

Even though he was reared as a Diaspora Jew and child of Tarsus, Chilton's Paul was not reluctant to accept change. According to Chilton, in the four-year period between 28 and 32 C.E., Paul left Tarsus, abandoned his Hellenistic name (Paul), adopted a Hebrew name (Saul), and committed himself to study in Jerusalem under Gamaliel, the leading rabbi of Paul's time.[8] Although Gamaliel maintained a studied indifference to the emerging Christian movement, Paul broke with his policy. In 32 C.E., Paul began participating in the violent persecution of Christianity. Through his admittedly minor role in the stoning of Stephen, Paul established a clear divide between himself and his former mentor.[9]

Shortly after this break with Gamaliel, Paul's life saw even more profound change when he experienced a series of four interrelated events: an apocalyptic vision, a bout of blindness, healing from that blindness, and Christian baptism. Chilton labels these aggregate events Paul's "conversion."[10] In obvious reliance upon Acts, Chilton explains how Paul saw a light "that changed his life."[11] Even though Chilton acknowledges that Paul probably did not see a literal shaft of light, he argues that the event nonetheless did leave Paul physically blind.[12] (Chilton attributes this physical impairment to herpes zoster, a disease common to Paul's homeland of Tarsus.[13]) Whatever

---

[5] Ibid., 11.

[6] Ibid., 13.

[7] Ibid., 27.

[8] Ibid., 28–35.

[9] Ibid., 43.

[10] In spite of many scholars' reluctance to speak of any "conversion" in Paul's life, Chilton is quite comfortable with this language and religious construct (*Rabbi Paul*, e.g., 55, 62, 64, 66, 69). For a recent assessment of the call versus conversion discussion, see Ron Elsdon, "Was Paul 'Converted' or 'Called'? Questions of Methodology," *Proceedings of the Irish Biblical Association* 24 (2001): 16–48.

[11] Chilton, *Rabbi Paul*, 50.

[12] Chilton sees no reason to interpret this event as Paul's literal observation of a heavenly light, choosing instead to interpret the light in Acts as an apocalyptic vision in the mode of Daniel's apocalyptic visions. See *Rabbi Paul*, 55.

[13] Chilton, *Rabbi Paul*, 60–61.

the exact nature and origin of Paul's blindness, according to Chilton, the affliction was healed when Ananias baptized Paul; thus, "Paul's baptism was also a moment of healing."[14]

This first phase of Paul's life concludes with a series of ironies: Paul receives a heavenly vision, but is blinded by it; Paul receives Christian baptism, but is shunned by the Christian community; Paul had committed himself to a very restrictive sect of Judaism, but is called to be a witness to the Gentiles. As the first phase of his adult life drew to a close and the second opened before him, the prospects must have seemed discouraging. Paul was driven by the conviction that "the God of Israel was extending his promises to humanity as a whole,"[15] but the seed of his conviction seemed to be falling upon hard soil. His fellow Christians in Jerusalem feared him; his Jewish family in Tarsus disowned him; and his would-be converts in Nabataea rejected him. His ideas could find no home. Adding injury to insult, the newly converted, but no longer family-funded, Paul found himself reduced to his previously neglected vocation of tentmaking.[16]

After three years of apparently unsuccessful missionary activity in Nabataea (32–35 C.E.),[17] Paul ventured back to Jerusalem "to claim the mantle of an apostle . . . but it was a rocky start."[18] For Chilton, the tension between Paul and the Jewish Christians is epitomized in Acts by the competing—and thrice recounted—visions of Peter and of Paul. On the one hand, Paul's vision had called him to take the gospel to *all Gentiles.* On the other hand, Peter's vision—and his experience with the God-fearer Cornelius—had taught him to accept *God-fearing Gentiles* into the Christian community.[19] In theory, these two visions should have been compatible, and Peter's vision should have prepared him for Paul's proclamation of a Gentile-inclusive people of God. In reality, however, after only fifteen days in Peter's Jerusalem, Paul "was shipped unceremoniously out of Jerusalem" and back to Tarsus. According to Chilton, Peter was unwilling to accept Paul's claim that "Gentiles should be offered the realization of God's promises to humanity *without accepting the Law of Judaism.*"[20] Peter and Paul split over the issue of whether Gentiles must first convert to Judaism before converting to Christianity. Peter could accept Gentiles who came to Christianity via Judaism, that is, as God-fearers, but not Gentiles who came to Christianity apart from Judaism. Peter's vision had not prepared him for "the direct approach to Gentiles without conversion to

---

[14] Ibid., 60.
[15] Ibid., 76.
[16] Ibid., 66.
[17] "Paul does not say what happened in Nabatea, and Acts skips any reference to this three-year stay. There is a simple reason for the silence: Paul's sojourn there was a failure." Ibid., 76.
[18] Ibid., 80.
[19] Ibid., 95–98.
[20] Ibid., 84, emphasis Chilton's.

Judaism that Paul's vision demanded."[21] This incompatibility of visions left Paul with "no welcome in Jerusalem" and prompted his return to Tarsus.[22]

In addition to providing Paul with a setting in which he could nurture "the entrepreneurial side" of his personality, Paul's stay in Tarsus provided him with the "intellectual isolation" needed for sustained theological reflection. During this period in his hometown of Tarsus (35–40 C.E.), Paul developed the "social definition of the body of Christ" that shaped and sustained the rest of his ministry.[23] According to Chilton, Paul adapted the Stoic idea of "the Roman Empire as a single body animated by reason" to the needs of the church. When wed to the Christian practice of the Eucharist, this distinctive understanding of the body of Christ became the core of his mature theology. The Eucharist was the mystic experience by which "all disciples everywhere were marshaled into a single body."[24]

While Paul was chipping away at these theological constructs, things were also changing in Jerusalem. James was gaining ascendancy over Peter, and Peter's commitment to a gospel for God-fearers was losing favor. Eventually, Peter retreated to Antioch where he and Barnabas began to think about the distant Tarsus-bound Paul as "a potential asset." Peter dispatched Barnabas to retrieve Paul from his unceremonious exile. According to Chilton, then, Paul's famed missionary career began from Antioch around 40 C.E. at the initiative of Peter and under the supervision of Barnabas.[25] For Chilton, "without the influence of Barnabas, Paul would in all probability have died in idiosyncratic anonymity in Tarsus."[26]

During Paul's stay in Antioch, his distinctive vision of Gentile inclusion became a contentious issue within the emerging Christian discourse, gathering both advocates and detractors. As tensions rose, the leaders ("prophets") of the Christian community in Antioch encouraged Barnabas to take Paul, "his junior colleague," on a road show to field test Paul's gospel in Barnabas's homeland of Cyprus.[27] While on the road, Paul's gospel continued to attract attention, in the forms of both acceptance and resistance. The heightening tensions within the church over the role of Gentile converts appeared to reach a climax when James and the Jerusalem elders decided to meet with Paul.[28] According to Chilton, the resulting meeting in Jerusalem was significant for Paul not only because of his earlier chilly relations with the Jerusalem believers,

---

[21] Ibid., 83.

[22] Ibid., 87.

[23] Ibid., 87. Chilton apparently sees no irony in an intellectually isolated Paul creating a social definition of the body of Christ.

[24] Ibid., 93.

[25] Ibid., 99. Paul's "vision had called him, but Peter's vision as interpreted by Barnabas gave him a job."

[26] Ibid., 100.

[27] Ibid., 113.

[28] Although Chilton uses "Paul" throughout his volume, he notes that "Saul" changed his name to "Paul" during this period after his encounter with Sergius Paulus. Ibid., 116.

but also because "in his own time, James's stature was dominant; the Book of Acts says so plainly and Paul openly admits the fact."[29] According to Chilton, on account of his need for approval from the trio of Peter, James, and John, Paul "said nothing" about the incongruity between his vision and Peter's.[30]

This Jerusalem Conference offered the strategically silent Paul "an endorsement Paul could barely have hoped for."[31] The Jerusalem elders had clearly agreed with Paul's insistence that Gentiles were to be accepted into the church. Yet, Paul's tongue-biting silence at the conference revealed an underlying tension. Would Gentiles enter the church under the vision of Peter or of Paul? Was the Christian message open to all Gentiles (Paul's vision) or only to Gentile God-fearers (Peter's vision)? The conference, though successful in the eyes of all participants, left a key issue open to interpretation. For his part, Barnabas interpreted the Jerusalem decision as an endorsement of "Peter's mission as defined in Galatians—to Jews and God-fearers—not Paul's." For his part, Paul interpreted the decision as an endorsement of his own efforts to convert "Gentiles fresh from the raw state of their natural idolatry." This difference of interpretation ensured that the foremost missionary team of the first century "would never work together again."[32]

According to Chilton, the Jerusalem Conference was a mixed blessing for Paul. On the one hand, it had endorsed the Gentile mission and had given "Paul new authority." On the other hand, it had cost him the partnership of his senior colleague and mentor, Barnabas. Barnabas abandoned Paul and his vision in favor of Peter and his vision. With Barnabas no longer interested in promoting Paul's vision, Paul was placed both under the authority of the Jerusalem elders and under "the constant surveillance of Silas." This newly created team was quickly instructed to redirect its mission further west.[33] While traveling with Silas, and in keeping with the wishes of the Jerusalem cadre, Paul performed Timothy's circumcision. According to Chilton, in an act that "cut to the core of Israelite identity, and therefore Christian identity[,] . . . Paul himself wielded the knife that cut off Timothy's foreskin."[34] Chilton is fully cognizant of many interpreters' reluctance to place this flint blade in Paul's hands, but he insists that in regard to Timothy's circumcision "Acts is right."[35]

If Chilton's Paul subjected Timothy to circumcision—a practice that Chilton's Paul could justify on the basis of Timothy's Jewish maternal ancestry—one would expect Paul to have gained immunity from further outbreaks of Jewish Christian opposition. But Paul acquired no such immunity. He was soon plagued by resentment from both his newly appointed theological mentor, Silas, and his newly circumcised colleague, Timothy. In their minds, Paul

---

[29] Ibid., 135.
[30] Ibid., 144.
[31] Ibid., 143.
[32] Ibid., 145.
[33] Ibid., 147.
[34] Ibid., 148.
[35] Ibid., 149.

had overstepped his Jerusalem-sanctioned mission when he took the message of Christ "outside of synagogues and into the pagan populace of patriotic cities in Macedonia."[36] By the time Paul reached Athens, he alone was faithful to his vision of unrestricted Gentile inclusion. All of his colleagues chose faithfulness to Peter's vision of a more restricted Gentile inclusion. In spite of the relative success of Paul's subsequent missionary activity in Corinth, the nagging incongruity between his vision and Peter's continued to raise problems. With Silas already back in Antioch reporting Paul's apparent violations of Peter's vision, Paul wisely sensed the need to preempt the forthcoming blows from his Petrine detractors. He opted to parry the expected onslaught by proving that he—if not his converts—was a loyal Jew. Accordingly, he decided to place himself under a Nazirite vow and planned to return to Jerusalem with an offering for the poor saints.[37]

As politically astute as it may have seemed, this tactic of moving himself—but not his converts—to the religious right of his more centralist critics accomplished little, because it evaded the real issue: Paul's total rejection of the law's authority over Gentiles. Paul's strategy didn't work. James insisted that some aspects of ritual purity remained incumbent even upon Gentiles; Peter and Barnabas fell in line with James; and Paul was "a minority of one . . . effectively an excommunicant from his own movement."[38] All of the influential leaders of early Christianity—except Paul—accepted James's reservations about Gentile Christians practicing complete freedom from the law. Although Gentile circumcision was never explicitly advocated by James, Paul equated all Gentile obedience to the law with circumcision and dismissed it *en masse.* The Paul who had earlier kept silent was replaced by the Paul who would not compromise. The earlier silent Paul had won approval from the leaders of the Jerusalem church; the later uncompromising Paul was excommunicated by many of the same people in Antioch.

The trauma of excommunication brought the second phase in the life of Chilton's Paul to a close. The rejection of his message occasioned a transitional period for Paul that was as difficult and life-altering as was his former transition from persecutor to preacher. According to Chilton, Paul's departure from Antioch in 53 C.E. "involved neither a hopeful mission nor even a strategic retreat. It was a rout."[39] A vision even more restrictive than Peter's—to say nothing of Paul's—had won the day. After losing his converts in Galatia to "his apostolic opponents" in Antioch, Paul needed "a soft landing," and he found it in Ephesus—thanks to Priscilla and Aquila.[40] In Ephesus, Paul planted his apostolic crops in the soil already broken by his fellow tentmakers. After a few tense months, Paul made virtue out of necessity and "at last figured

---

[36] Ibid., 157.
[37] Ibid., 167–68.
[38] Ibid., 170.
[39] Ibid., 173.
[40] Ibid., 174–75.

out that, if you really believed you were the Israel of God, then you did not need the approval of local synagogues. If they bother you, rent a hall."[41] In Ephesus, Chilton's Paul gained a tremendous reputation among Gentiles as an exorcist.[42]

The growth of Paul's Gentile congregation in Ephesus prompted Paul to rethink his assumptions about the people of God, and eventually "he redefine[d] what 'Israel' means in terms of the Spirit. Spirit, received in baptism, takes the place of circumcision as the measure of who the people of God are."[43] This altered identification of the people of God enabled Paul to boldly go where no Christian leader had gone before: he began to insist that Jewish believers should disregard traditional dietary laws in order to participate in fellowship with Gentile Christians. Paul came to view the law as "provisional" and no longer binding upon any Christian (Jewish or Gentile) in the wake of the Christ event.[44] According to Chilton, these insights brought Paul success on a previously unimaginable scale and "something he had never dreamed of: a base of power."[45]

From the comfort of his Ephesian acceptance, Paul wrote his Letter to the Galatians as a bid to win those converts back from James. But not even the power of Paul's newfound insights regarding Israel and the law could reverse James's ascendancy in Galatia. Further west, however, Paul was moderately successful in reestablishing authority over his Corinthian converts.[46] In the meantime in Ephesus, Paul encountered a new problem: opposition from pagans. His preaching stirred up resistance from the business sector. Paul's preaching and his converts' fiery displays of dissatisfaction with magic and idols were disrupting the futures market in idols. The local artisans responded with violence, and Paul was forced to leave the city.[47]

With Ephesus thus added to the Apostle's list of inhospitable cities, Paul decided to revive his efforts at reunion with James and the Jerusalem Christians. Paul understood that reunion with Jerusalem would not be easy; nonetheless, he "plotted a triumphant return to the holy city, bringing with him another collection for the Nazirites of James's circle, greater than his previous gifts, together with his new reputation as a zealous activist against idolatry."[48] Paul planned to gain money for the offering from his Corinthian and Macedonian congregations before going east to Jerusalem and then back

---

[41] Ibid., 181.

[42] Ibid., 181–85.

[43] Ibid., 190.

[44] Ibid., 192.

[45] Ibid., 193.

[46] Ibid., 198–219.

[47] "A single verse in Acts . . . provides everything we need to know to understand why—despite all his success—he had to depart from the city, and why he never returned (Acts 19:19): 'A large number of those who had practiced charms brought together the books and burned them in front of all, and they estimated their prices and hit upon fifty thousand silver drachmas.'" Ibid., 216.

[48] Ibid., 218.

west to Rome, the heart of the Gentile world.[49] In preparation for his upcoming journeys and as a cloak for his blatant financial appeals, Paul engaged in a period of significant literary activity, producing his two longest letters, Romans and 1 Corinthians.

In his correspondence with the Christians in the capitol of the empire, Paul was compelled not only to lay out his gospel for their inspection, but also to address his sometimes troubled relationship with Rome. In Romans, Paul took a rather optimistic stand toward the empire (the very empire that had previously imprisoned him and that would eventually execute him), suggesting that "earthly rulers are divine ministers 'for the good.'"[50] Although some interpreters are tempted to doubt the sincerity of Paul's words at this point, Chilton insists that Paul "could take this position because he knew that obedience to any political authority was as temporary as this world."[51] According to Chilton, otherworldly apocalypticism created a Stoic indifference in Paul regarding the claims of the Roman Empire.

Chilton's Paul demonstrated a corresponding lack of reforming zeal in matters of slavery and gender equality. Paul wrote to Philemon during this period and requested that Philemon overlook the former wanderlust of his slave, Onesimus. Even though Chilton's Paul exhibited tremendous affection for the frightened slave, he never viewed Onesimus as anything other than Philemon's property.[52] Such inattention to Onesimus's servitude may seem harsh by contemporary standards, but it is typical of Chilton's Paul, who demonstrated a similar disregard for the plight of women in the world of the Roman *pater familias*. Paul may have sensed the need for the Corinthians' money and for Jerusalem's approval, but he apparently felt no need for women's voices. In the midst of his admonitions to the Corinthian believers, Chilton's Paul insisted that "women in the churches will keep silent" (1 Cor 14:34). According to Chilton, these disputed words belong to the Apostle. "The phrasing is Paul's, the sentiment typically Pauline, the arrogance unmistakable."[53]

However, as Paul was collecting funds around the Aegean (largely through a now canonical letter-writing campaign), the situation on the far side of the Mediterranean in Jerusalem was changing. The social and religious tensions between Jews and Christians were taking their toll on James, and he "was struggling to maintain his position as a pious Nazirite in the Temple and as Jesus' preeminent disciple."[54] The pressure was particularly acute for James because he was the knot that tied together the loose threads of Gentile baptism and Jewish temple devotion.

---

[49] Ibid., 218–33.
[50] Ibid., 233.
[51] Ibid., 233–34.
[52] Ibid., 241–42, 262.
[53] Ibid., 215.
[54] Ibid., 237.

According to Chilton, Paul and James never reached a genuine consensus on the future shape of Christianity. James allowed for the inclusion of Gentiles who were willing to practice at least token adherence to the law; Paul insisted that Gentiles were to be included in the people of God without regard for the law. Nevertheless, in the spring of 57 C.E., both men believed that a Pauline sacrifice in the temple could shore up support with their respective constituencies. Chilton explains: "In practical terms they could both claim victory if Paul agreed to enter publicly into the Temple in order to participate in the Nazirite vow with some of James's disciples. God would decide finally how to redeem all his people, whether it was through Israel preeminent among the nations or Israel stretching its boundaries to include pagans who believed in Jesus. Either way, James and Paul would start the process by offering in the Temple together."[55]

Events did not proceed according to plan. Paul's entry into the temple was met with violence; his death at the hands of a temple-defending mob was stopped only by Roman intervention. Paul's Roman citizenship saved him,[56] but he was quickly abandoned by James and the Jerusalem Christians. Only Timothy, the half-Jew circumcised by Paul's own hand, remained.[57] Timothy traveled with the indicted Paul to Rome (and left his travel diary behind, which became a source for the book of Acts), but "the two men obviously parted soon after their arrival in Rome."[58] James's death in Jerusalem in that same year (62 C.E.) "quashed any hope of mounting another collection to offer on behalf of Gentiles in the Temple. Paul's prose output, in letters designed largely to make that collection happen, simply dried up with his plans for travel."[59] Paul was beheaded two years later.

No light as bright as Paul's could be snuffed by the mere swing of an executioner's ax. For Chilton, glimmers of the Pauline genius continued to glow into the late first century through the work of his protégé, Timothy, who collected and supplemented many of Paul's existing writings. According to Chilton, as Paul's letters were being collected in the late first century, it was probably the aging Timothy who "consolidated and arranged the fragments that make up 2 Corinthians" and who penned Colossians and Ephesians in Paul's name.[60] Later, other pseudonymous writers took on Paul's name and provided the Pastoral Epistles (Titus and 1–2 Timothy) for the church. This collection, portions of which "at first sight [look] so un-Pauline," is actually "a derivative version of the apostle's message for a new and desperate

---

[55] Ibid., 238.
[56] Ibid., 239–40.
[57] Ibid., 241.
[58] Ibid., 246.
[59] Ibid., 248.
[60] Ibid., 254. Timothy tips his hand as a pseudonymous author in Colossians and "cleans up the apostle's image by having him [Paul] say (Colossians 2:5): 'Because I am absent in the flesh, yet I am with you in spirit, rejoicing and seeing your order and the firmness of your faith in Christ.'"

time."[61] According to Chilton, "these works trim down Paul's theology more than they continue Paul's thought: they run parallel to his letters, dealing with levels of organization and theological disputes outside of Paul's own experience."[62] Chilton is sensitive to the criticisms often leveled against these presumably post-Pauline books, but warns that Paul "tacitly endorses" many of the claims (particularly regarding women, slaves, and ecclesiastical authority) that these later letters explicitly (and, in today's world, controversially) advocate.[63]

Chilton's Paul is related to the Paul of the undisputed letters, but not identical with that Paul, for he also has great affinity with the Paul of Acts and the Paul of the disputed Pauline letters. He is from Tarsus, possesses family wealth, studies under Gamaliel, enjoys the privileges of Roman citizenship, encounters a converting light on the road to Damascus, is baptized by Ananias, suffers from herpes zoster, participates in the gender inequalities of the Roman world, advocates a Stoic acceptance of existing social structures (like slavery), promotes an apocalyptic disregard for life under empire, gains a reputation as a flamboyant preacher and flashy exorcist, takes a series of Nazirite vows, and circumcises Timothy. Perhaps most importantly, the mission of this Paul is defined in terms of his relationships to the other apostles and the Jerusalem elders, whose approval he desired but ultimately failed to acquire.

Chilton's Paul has significant resonance with the Paul often found in contemporary proclamation. This Paul is plausible, but he is not the only Paul of Scripture. Let me now introduce another "plausible Paul."

II. Crossan's and Reed's Plausible Paul

Crossan and Reed sculpt their Paul using Reed's archaeological chisel and Crossan's exegetical mallet. They seek to forge a true-to-life Paul from the archaeological ruins of the first century and the seven undisputed letters of Paul. Their plausible Paul is an apostle shaped by "the Roman imperial world that surrounded him, the Jewish covenantal religion that formed him, and the Christian faith that enthralled him."[64] Crossan and Reed are uninterested in excavating a Paul with any particular resemblance to the Paul of Acts because their "book is about the actual and historical Paul, about the radical apostle who was there before the reaction, revision, and replacement began."[65]

Crossan and Reed view Luke's Acts as one of the most influential revisions of Paul, warning that Luke "adds some details better taken as enthusiasm rather than as history." They regard Acts' accounts of Paul's Roman and

---

[61] Ibid., 258.
[62] Ibid., 260–61.
[63] Ibid., 262–63.
[64] Ibid., x.
[65] Ibid., xiii–xiv.

Tarsian citizenship, of his education under Gamaliel, and of his pre-Christian Jerusalem studies as "Lukan upgrading of Paul's status."[66] Acts' insertion of a blinding light into its account of Paul's Damascus Road experience "is a superb example of Luke's literary imagination."[67] Crossan and Reed "imagine instead a vision in which Paul both *sees* and hears Jesus as the resurrected Christ, the risen Lord."[68]

For Crossan and Reed, not only the events of Paul's life in Acts are suspect; more importantly, the relationships in Paul's life in Acts are equally suspect. They warn that "Luke emphasizes certain elements with regard to Christians, pagans, Jews, and Roman authorities that reflect his own, much later views rather than Paul's much earlier experiences." For Crossan and Reed, Acts is "a most ambiguous source for understanding Paul's life and work, mission and message."[69] However, these ambiguities do not arise from Luke's lack of historically significant Pauline information. They arise from Luke's tendency toward anachronism. According to Crossan and Reed, "Luke's Acts was written in the 80s or 90s, several decades after Paul's time, and Luke gives him an overall interpretation from within his own geographical situation, historical understanding, and theological vision. In the Acts of the Apostles, Paul becomes a Christian not of his own time and place, but of Luke's."[70]

According to Crossan and Reed, Acts distorts Paul's historical relationships in several key areas. Acts subordinates Paul to the original apostles, implying that he "could never be the one thing Paul always insisted that he was, namely, an apostle sent by God through a revelation of the risen Lord. . . . At stake is not just name but status, not just title but authority."[71] According to Crossan and Reed, Acts minimizes any disturbances caused by the Christian message under the pretense that "any problems, disputes, or even riots are the fault not of Christians, but of pagans or Jews."[72] For example, Paul's demeaning exodus from Damascus in a basket provides "an example of how Lukan fiction must be distinguished from Pauline fact even about the same incident." The Pauline account in 2 Corinthians names the Nabataean ruler Aretas IV as the source of Paul's problems, while Luke characteristically blames the Jews, "a scenario . . . all but impossible in an Arab-controlled city."[73] From their analysis of this episode, Crossan and Reed develop "a paradigmatic warning, be careful to distinguish between Luke's *information* about Paul and Luke's

---

[66] Ibid., 5. They reject only Paul's citizenship in Tarsus, not his origin and early residence there.
[67] Ibid., 6.
[68] Ibid., 8, emphasis Crossan's and Reed's.
[69] Ibid., 16.
[70] Ibid., 28.
[71] Ibid., 29.
[72] Ibid., 30.
[73] Ibid., 31. The authors note that this incident provides the only Pauline derived date for Paul's life (37–39 C.E.).

interpretation of Paul, and be very careful to discern where Luke's *interpretation* becomes Luke's *information* about Paul."[74]

As Crossan and Reed read Paul, one key Lukan revision of Paul's relationships lies in the realm of the Roman response to Paul. In Acts, Paul is dressed in "apologetic garments" in order to validate Luke's insistence that Roman officials should "allow Christianity 'without hindrance.'" Acts takes pains to conceal the constant tension between the historical Paul and the Roman Empire. The historical Paul of Crossan's and Reed's account was "as the Roman authorities knew full well, . . . an ideological danger without ever being a violent threat." Crossan and Reed suspect that Luke was aware of Paul's turbulent relationship with Rome, but was also eager to gloss over it. According to Crossan and Reed, "Luke both reveals and conceals, admits and denies, that there were constant troubles between Paul and Rome."[75]

In keeping with their profound suspicions about Luke's version of Paul's interaction with Rome, Crossan and Reed reject Luke's account of Paul's trial before Gallio in Corinth. Because Acts reports that "Gallio paid no attention to any of these things" (Acts 18:17), the historicity of Paul's appearance before Gallio is dismissed as part of Luke's fictitious effort to reconcile Paul's message with Roman authority. The Lukan trial before Gallio is interpreted "as a Lukan symbol of the appropriate response of Rome to Paul." Crossan and Reed explain that Paul's appearance before Gallio is "much more likely Lukan parable than Pauline history. It is, indeed, Luke's first and most paradigmatic combination of Jewish accusation, Pauline innocence, and Roman dismissal."[76]

According to Crossan and Reed, much of the confusion that surrounds Paul's relationships in Acts stems from an incongruity between the religious categories presupposed by Luke and by Paul. On the one hand, Luke places non-Christians in three categories: Jews, pagans, and God-fearers. For Luke, God-fearers were, in spite of their Gentile ancestry and partial obedience to the law, essentially Jewish by means of their participation in the synagogue. Paul, on the other hand, views all non-Christians as either Jews or pagans. Paul had no special category for "God-fearers" because he "would not have accepted a form of semi-Judaism or semipaganism. He understood faith and unfaith, but would never have understood semifaith."[77] Accordingly, Paul viewed these God-fearers as essentially *pagan* and under his evangelistic mandate as the apostle to the Gentiles. This clash of categories is important for Crossan's and Reed's understandings of both the historical Paul and the Paul of Acts.

According to Crossan and Reed, both the historical Paul and the Lukan Paul concentrated much of their evangelistic efforts on these God-fearers. However, because Paul and Luke understood the status of this target audience

[74] Ibid., 32, emphasis Crossan's and Reed's.
[75] Ibid., 33.
[76] Ibid., 34.
[77] Ibid., 38.

very differently, Luke misinterprets Paul's activity in synagogues. Crossan and Reed are emphatic that they "do not accept that Paul always went first to the synagogue and tried to convert *Jews* to Jesus as the Messiah."[78] Of course, Paul did go to synagogues and preach about Christ, but according to Crossan and Reed, Paul was seeking converts among the God-fearers in the synagogue, not, as Luke portrays, among the Jews themselves.

For Crossan and Reed, Luke's affinity with these God-fearers (perhaps he was converted from their ranks) explains "why he himself was at the same time so familiar with Judaism, and yet opposed to it, as well as so conversant with Romanism, and yet reconciled with it."[79] This understanding of Luke as reconciled to the values of Roman society stands in sharp contrast to Crossan's and Reed's view of the historical Paul as engaged in a "clash" with Rome over "alternative visions of world peace." Rome's vision was "peace through victory"; Paul's vision was "peace through justice." According to Crossan and Reed, since the time of Augustus, the Roman Empire had advanced the idea that global peace would be ushered in by Rome's military victories. This *Pax Romana* was Rome's gift to the world. Paul also offered the world a vision of global peace, but in his vision, global peace came into the world through global justice.[80] In the subsequent chapters, Crossan and Reed begin exploring this Pauline theme of peace through justice by considering the role that equality plays within this justice. They argue that "the historical Paul insisted on equality among Christians over against the hierarchical normalcy of Roman society. First, a *Christian* mistress or master should not and could not have a *Christian* slave. Second, Christian women and Christian men were, *as Christians,* equal in marriage, assembly, and apostolate. How could one be equal and unequal at the same time, since *in Christ* all were equal before God?"[81]

Crossan and Reed insist that later "pseudo-Pauline" traditions "deliberately muted the radicality of Paul's Christian equality back to inequality."[82] According to them, the New Testament has placed Paul within a frame of less radical voices. They explain that on the front side of Paul's letters, "in the New Testament's present sequence, you meet the Lukan Paul before you meet the Pauline or historical Paul. . . . Paul gets colored Lukan."[83] Then, on the back side of Paul's major letters, the pseudo-Pauline letters seek "to sanitize a social subversive, to domesticate a dissident apostle, and to make Christianity and Rome safe for one another."[84]

In their attempt to recover the historical Paul, Crossan and Reed intend to focus primarily on the historical Paul between the frames of Acts and of

---

[78] Ibid., 35, emphasis added. The authors suggest that Luke makes the "theological principle of 'first Jews, then pagans' into a historical pattern for Paul" (p. 34).
[79] Ibid., 41.
[80] Ibid., 74.
[81] Ibid., 75, emphasis Crossan's and Reed's.
[82] Ibid., 75.
[83] Ibid., 105.
[84] Ibid., 106.

the pseudo-Pauline letters. They are, however, also willing to sift through the Lukan frame on Paul in accordance with the principles of "whether Luke disagrees with Paul (omit it), whether Luke adds to Paul but within his own rather than Paul's theology (bracket it), and whether Luke adds to Paul but within Paul's rather than Luke's own theology (keep it)."[85] They entirely bracket the canon's post-Pauline pseudonymous frame on Paul by excluding the six disputed Pauline letters from consideration.[86]

As their recovery of the unframed—historical—Paul proceeds, Crossan and Reed insist that the Pauline Paul espouses equality among Christians, thus prompting him to reject both slavery[87] and gender inequality[88] *within the Christian community.* Those passages that contradict this radical Pauline equality are dismissed either as the work of a "pseudo-Pauline" author or as non-Pauline insertions into Paul's letters.[89] Even the notoriously anti-Jewish comments in 1 Thessalonians are deemed "later interpolations."[90] Crossan and Reed are sensitive to the charge that their Paul anachronistically embodies Enlightenment commitments to "equal creation and inalienable rights," and, accordingly, they emphasize that the ideals of their Paul are "not about abstract and universal principles of freedom and democracy."[91]

Even though Crossan and Reed freely admit that Paul's ethical vision was not developed in dialogue with Enlightenment values, they also insist that *Paul's vision was developed in opposition to Roman values.* Crossan and Reed remind their readers that, in spite of its pro-Roman agenda, even Acts is forced to preserve some of the anti-Roman accusations against Paul (in 16:21). They claim that "those accusations ring true as we read Paul's I Thessalonians," explaining that "one of the most striking aspects of I Thessalonians is the number of Pauline terms that were religio-political." Crossan and Reed offer a list of key Pauline "expressions absolutely guaranteed to prick up Romanized ears and raise Romanized eyebrows."[92] The *ekklēsia*, normally translated "church," "originally meant the citizens of a free Greek city officially assembled for self-governmental decisions."[93] Paul's proclamation of

---

[85] Ibid., 105. The authors accept Romans, 1–2 Corinthians, Galatians, Philippians, 1 Thessalonians, and Philemon as Pauline and regard the remaining six letters as pseudonymous. Chilton also accepts the authenticity of these seven letters and discusses the pseudonymous authorship of the remaining letters with the exception of 2 Thessalonians (which he passes over without mention).

[86] Ibid., 106.

[87] Ibid., 110.

[88] "Paul presumes equality between women and men in the assembly, but absolutely demands that they follow the socially accepted dress codes of their time and place. Difference, yes. Hierarchy, no." Ibid., 114.

[89] Ibid., 110, 116–20.

[90] Ibid., 163. According to Crossan and Reed, 1 Thess 2:14–16 presumes the destruction of the temple and therefore must be post-Pauline.

[91] Ibid., 110.

[92] Ibid., 165.

[93] Ibid., 165–66.

Jesus as *kyrios,* "Lord," co-opted a title normally reserved for the emperor; Paul's designation of Christ's message as *euaggelion,* "good news," reverberated with tones threateningly similar to imperial decrees; and his attribution of "honor, power, and glory" to Christ laid claim to accolades that Roman authorities claimed exclusively for themselves.[94] Even the peace wish in the opening of 1 Thessalonians and the warning against the purveyors of "peace and security" in the letter's body could be interpreted as mockery of imperial pretensions.[95] In fact, the very idea of an eschatological *parousia,* "appearing," challenged Caesar's prestige by adapting the language of a "state visit" to the service of Christ's presence.[96] Crossan and Reed even wonder if the language of *parousia* meant that Christ's "visitation is just like that of the emperor, is greater than that of the emperor, or is the replacement for that of the emperor . . . a calculated anti-*parousia.*"[97]

In a world dominated by the presence of empire, Crossan and Reed see little danger in overinterpreting the political implications of Paul's language. Even when they cannot recover the specific imperial associations in a text, they are confident that such associations exist. For example, they can insist that "regardless of the details," the appropriate interpretive context for understanding the post-Pauline origins of the "lawless one" in 2 Thessalonians "is probably the theology of Roman imperialism and the ideology of emperor worship that, one way or another, lies behind that description."[98]

Of course, Paul's life and thought were not shaped solely by the negative experience of living under empire; they were also shaped by the positive experience of Judaism. As Crossan and Reed explain, the very notion of peace through justice (which is central to their reading of Paul) has its origins in "a *shalom* from the heart of the Jewish tradition."[99] More specifically, in the context of 1 Thessalonians, Paul's revision of the empire's theology of *parousia* was accomplished by drawing upon "Pharisaic Judaism's theology of the general bodily resurrection."[100] Resurrection thus served as an ethical category for Paul. Resurrection implied transformation. Crossan and Reed explain: "To claim that God has already begun to transform this earth into a place of divine justice and peace demands that you can show something of that transformative activity here and now. . . . To see God's transformational process, come and see how we live."[101]

Up to the approximate midpoint in their work, Crossan and Reed say little about Pauline chronology—other than to reject the historicity of Paul's

---

[94] Ibid., 166.
[95] Ibid., 165–67.
[96] Ibid., 170.
[97] Ibid., 171.
[98] Ibid., 170.
[99] Ibid., 129.
[100] Ibid., 173.
[101] Ibid., 174.

Lukan appearance before Gallio in Acts.[102] However, in their chapter on Paul's Letter to the Galatians, they explain that one cannot develop any "precise Pauline chronology, because that can only be done or even attempted by accepted Lukan data, especially about Paul before Gallio at Corinth in 51–52, that is not historical."[103] According to Crossan and Reed, the inconclusive nature of our sources precludes the possibility of developing a chronology of Paul's life. However, interpreters can, in spite of the ambiguity of the evidence, discern

> three divergent strategies behind Paul's three great missions. The first mission, in the 30s C.E., in Arabia, would have been assisted by the fact that the Jews and Arabs had a common ancestor in Abraham and both cultures circumcised their males. . . . The second mission, in the 40s C.E., under Barnabas as leader, . . . focused on converting Jews and God-fearers in the synagogue. The third mission, in the 50s, with Paul as leader, focused on . . . the God-fearers rather than on full Jews or pure pagans.[104]

Since all of Paul's letters come from this third mission[105] and since Crossan and Reed are only interested in the historical Paul, not the "revised" Paul of later tradition, their book cannot be structured chronologically (like Chilton's). Rather, their volume is structured thematically in terms of Paul's moral vision—peace through justice. As Crossan and Reed proceed, they trace Roman responses to Paul's moral vision throughout his letters. In keeping with this agenda, Crossan and Reed find that Paul's Letter to the Galatians reflects the continuing conflict between "Roman imperial theology's peace through victory" and Paul's Christian theology "based on Jewish covenantal theology's peace through justice."[106] According to Crossan and Reed, in the rhetorical context of Galatians, Paul's "opponents had told his Galatian converts that his gospel was all wrong, that their males must still be circumcised, that Paul was nothing but a subordinate missionary (not even an apostle), and that, moreover, he was living and teaching in disagreement with his superiors at Jerusalem and Antioch."[107]

---

[102]Ibid., 33–34.

[103]Ibid., 230.

[104]Ibid., 230. Having *illustrated* their book-by-book approach while discussing 1 Thessalonians, Crossan and Reed *explain* their approach in their subsequent examination of Paul's autobiographical comments in Gal 1–2.

[105]Crossan and Reed argue that Paul's Letter to the Galatians was addressed to the tribes in northern Galatia. They suggest that Paul and Barnabas probably engaged in a joint mission to Cyprus and south Galatia (as recorded in Acts 13–14, but not in Paul) but that Paul proceeded to northern Galatia alone when Barnabas returned to Jerusalem ahead of Paul (Acts 14:21–28). Because the southern cities of Galatia had been introduced to the Christian faith while Paul and Barnabas were colleagues on this journey, Paul ceded authority over these cities to Barnabas when he and Paul parted ways. See *In Search of Paul,* 200, 230–31.

[106]Ibid., 183.

[107]Ibid., 215.

Crossan's and Reed's Paul sought to overcome the Galatians' potential rejection of his authority—and more importantly, of his gospel—by clarifying his eschatological (and ethical) vision of an egalitarian community. This Pauline conception of the emerging Christian community challenged both Jewish election and Roman hierarchy by developing Isaiah's imagery of "the Great Final Banquet on Mt. Zion."[108] In Paul's mind, Isaiah had looked forward to a time when Gentiles would convert to Judaism and would join Jews in a great banquet. Since Isaiah said nothing about circumcision in relation to this event, Paul reasoned that circumcision was unnecessary for the Gentiles who participated in this eschatological gathering. Such reasoning was, according to Crossan and Reed, compelling to even the Jewish Christians in Jerusalem. Therefore, at Paul's urging, "James and all the others decided that . . . male pagan converts did not need to be circumcised in this climatic moment."[109]

According to Crossan and Reed, these issues were crucial for Paul because they explain "why Paul's vocation was so important."[110] Paul became convinced both that "the eschatological climax was to be an age and not just an instant, a process in time and not just an end of time" and that he was the agent—the apostle to the Gentiles—through whom God was accomplishing this great feat. Therefore, according to Crossan and Reed, to doubt Paul's gospel and apostleship was to doubt the work that God began in the resurrection of Christ. Accordingly, Crossan and Reed are not surprised by Paul's outrage over "the Antioch problem." When Jewish Christians in Antioch began to withdraw from their common meals with uncircumcised Gentiles, Crossan's and Reed's Paul interpreted their withdrawal as tantamount to a rejection of God's fulfillment of divine promises.[111] They were denying that Christ's resurrection had ushered in a new age of eschatological fulfillment, an age characterized by an equality previously unknown between Jews and Gentiles, between males and females, and between slave and free (in fact, between all people who follow Christ). Because of his radical egalitarian claims, Paul encountered resistance from both Jews (who regarded his thought as a threat to their election) and Romans (who regarded his thought as a threat to their empire). According to Crossan and Reed, this motif of eschatological fulfillment empowered Paul's ethics and "helps us to understand how Paul ever conceived of a program of radical egalitarianism in Christ. It was simply his understanding of life in the community of apocalyptic consummation, his interpretation of community in the eschatological instant-become-era, his application of utopian equality to utopia already begun."[112]

Crossan and Reed surmise, therefore, that Paul's opposition to both circumcision and the Roman Empire stemmed from his "apocalyptic rhap-

---

[108] Ibid., 217. See Isa 25:6–8.
[109] Ibid., 218.
[110] Ibid., 218.
[111] Ibid., 219.
[112] Ibid., 234.

sody" over the resurrection of Christ and from the resulting "program of radical egalitarianism in Christ."[113] Further, Paul's Jewish opponents in Galatia opposed him for essentially the same reason that Roman Gentiles opposed him: they rejected his eschatological and ethical vision of radical equality within the Christian community. Romans saw Paul's message as a threat to their domination and privilege; Jews saw Paul's message as a threat to their election and privilege. In spite of the subsequent hostilities to his message, according to Crossan and Reed, at least some Galatians had initially been drawn to Paul's vision. This initial acceptance of his message was fortunate for Paul, because during his initial visit to Galatia, he had experienced a bout of malaria that had left him temporarily incapacitated.[114] Had the early stages of his relationship with the Galatians been as tumultuous as his later relations (as reflected in the Letter to the Galatians), Crossan's and Reed's Paul may never have lived to continue his missionary career.

Having completed their analyses of the other brief Pauline letters, Crossan and Reed move to Philippians and Philemon, letters that they deem to share a common origin during Paul's conjectured imprisonment in Ephesus. According to these authors, the essential point for understanding these letters is an appreciation of Paul's mysticism. They ask and answer their own rhetorical question: "Does Paul think, therefore, that only mystics can be Christians or that all Christians must be mystics? In a word, yes."[115]

For Crossan's and Reed's Paul, the mystical experience of being "in Christ" was central to Christian self-definition and identity, and Crossan and Reed interpret even this mysticism as a challenge to the empire. The empire promoted being "in Rome" as the ultimate source of self-definition and identity; Paul offered the mystic alternative of being "in Christ" as the ultimate source of self-definition and identity.[116] Paul's mysticism was profoundly ethical, and the ethical content of being in Christ is provided in the kenotic hymn of Phil 2. For Crossan and Reed, this hymn presented an "obvious challenge" to Roman expectations of how one "with the 'form of God' should act."[117] They see the kenosis and the cross as a rejection of the theology of empire: "Paul would have insisted that the cross was not just slow, terrible, or humiliating suffering, but also official, legal, and formal Roman public execution. That [event] displayed unmistakably in Christ that clash of gods and gospels between Jewish covenantal justice and Roman imperial normalcy."[118] Thus, for Crossan and Reed, Paul, the Roman prisoner, continued his campaign for peace through justice even as Rome had him chained to its vision of peace through victory.

---

[113]Ibid., 234.
[114]Ibid., 232–33.
[115]Ibid., 280.
[116]Ibid., 280.
[117]Ibid., 289.
[118]Ibid., 290.

Crossan and Reed believe that Paul's Corinthian correspondence was also profoundly shaped by his ongoing conflict with the values of the empire. They suggest that the fractured Christian communities in Corinth were reluctant to accept and embody Paul's egalitarian gospel. They explain: "At Corinth, Paul and his vision encountered more forcefully than ever before the full normalcy of high-powered Roman patronage backed, of course, by Roman imperial theology. What, after all, was a divine emperor but a supreme patron?"[119] The divisions within the community over wisdom, wealth, status, and personal loyalties were, according to Crossan and Reed, sparked by thinly veiled allegiances to the patronage system of the empire. Paul desired a Christ-like "kenotic community," but some Corinthians insisted upon a Roman style "patronal community." Crossan and Reed insist that "*a kenotic community begets equality, a patronal community begets inequality; kenosis begets cooperation, patronage begets competition.*"[120] The problems in Corinth, according to Crossan and Reed, derived from the Corinthians' commitment to the values of the empire, primarily the values associated with patronage. Both the animosities between Paul and the Corinthians and the animosities within the Corinthian church itself originated from frustrations over breaches of the patronage system. In the Corinthian correspondence, Paul sought to reverse the divisive and competitive effects of the patronage system both by rejecting gifts from the elite in the Corinthian community (which placed Paul outside the elite's self-serving patronage system) and by insisting that the Corinthian church establish an egalitarian community (which placed the entire community outside of the hierarchal patronage system).

For Crossan's and Reed's Paul, the answer to the Corinthians' divisiveness and competitiveness was found in a deeper understanding of the effects of Christ's resurrection. Paul wanted the Corinthians to appreciate that Christ's resurrection had inaugurated the general resurrection and had ushered in "an end to this evil aeon."[121] For Crossan's and Reed's Paul, "the term *resurrection* meant one thing and only [one] thing at that time—it meant the general bodily resurrection as God finally began the great cleanup of the world's mess."[122] Paul saw the Corinthian church as plagued by mistaken loyalties to a patronage system that the resurrection had rendered obsolete. For Crossan and Reed, to truly believe in the resurrection was to decisively reject the empire's hierarchical patronage system.

Like their readings of Paul's other letters, Crossan's and Reed's reading of Romans places Paul's vision of peace through justice at the center of the document's detailed arguments. They choose to read Romans "as a sweeping theology of human history seen by Paul as God's desire to create one world under global *justification* (*making just*), under, in other words, the divine

---

[119] Ibid., 333.
[120] Ibid., 334, emphasis Crossan's and Reed's.
[121] Ibid., 342.
[122] Ibid., 343, emphasis Crossan's and Reed's.

equity of distributive justice rather than under the divine threat of retributive justice."[123] For Crossan and Reed, this global justification brings transformation to human society through participation in Christ. Paul's vision of justice is achieved as God brings moral transformation into the world.[124] Even though Crossan and Reed explicitly reject a substitutionary interpretation of Pauline atonement, they insist that Paul's "theology would not be the same if Christ had simply died in his bed and been raised thereafter by God. Jesus did not simply die; he was publicly, legally, officially executed by the contemporary authority of the Roman Empire, that is, by the normalcy of civilization's permanent violence in his own time and place. It was not simply death and resurrection. It was execution by *Rome* and therefore resurrection against *Rome.*"[125]

The closing of Romans provides Crossan and Reed an opportunity to bring Paul's letters into significant dialogue with Acts for the second time. In Paul's appeal for his Jerusalem offering, Crossan and Reed find

> the second major case . . . when it is absolutely necessary to *combine* Paul's letters and Luke's Acts, and the reason is the same. Our first chapter on the God-worshipers showed how Paul never mentions them, but Luke does so repeatedly. In this present chapter on the collection, we have the reverse, Acts never mentions that collection, but Paul does so repeatedly. Still, in both cases, each has material that only makes sense by adding in the other's data.[126]

According to Crossan and Reed, "we know from Paul, about the collection, but only from Acts about its delivery."[127] Crossan's and Reed's Paul fears that the Jerusalem Christians will reject his offering, or that the non-Christian Jerusalem Jews will oppose him, or both—and, in keeping with the narrative in Acts, both probably occurred. Paul's ensuing imprisonment and martyrdom in Rome was prompted by a coalition of those with a vested interest in the status quo, by an array of forces opposed to his message of eschatological equality.[128] Since Crossan's and Reed's Paul was not a Roman citizen, he was not "executed by a privileged beheading with the sword," but rather his death was "hidden among all those deaths described in the *Annals* of Tacitus."[129] With his death at the hands of the empire that he so vehemently—but nonviolently—opposed, Paul's story closes for Crossan and Reed.

By design, this Paul has little affinity with the Paul of Acts and the Paul of the disputed letters because that Paul has allegedly been revised and domesticated by later interpreters. Crossan's and Reed's Paul believes that a new eschatological age was inaugurated by the resurrection of Christ. His vision of peace through justice stands in unflinching opposition to the values

---

[123] Ibid., 355, emphasis Crossan's and Reed's.
[124] Ibid., 382–84.
[125] Ibid., 384, emphasis Crossan's and Reed's.
[126] Ibid., 398, emphasis Crossan's and Reed's.
[127] Ibid., 398.
[128] Ibid., 399–400.
[129] Ibid., 401.

of the Roman Empire. This Paul boasts of his own weakness, rejects Rome's hierarchal and patronal systems, promotes a radical equality between genders and ethnicities among Christians, renounces the claims of slavery within the Christian community, refuses to circumcise Timothy, and suffers from malaria. This Paul never benefits from Roman citizenship, never studies under Gamaliel, never takes a Nazirite vow, and never mentions the human agent of his baptism. This Paul is an apostle sent by God to the Gentiles with divine authority that cannot be questioned by any human authority, including the other apostles. This Paul is plausible, but he is not the only Paul of Scripture.

III. Reflecting upon the Plurality of Plausible Pauls

In spite of some shared forms and features, the mosaics that emerge from *Rabbi Paul* and *In Search of Paul* depict very different Pauls. Undoubtedly, scholarly discourse will continue to debate with each of these Pauls for years to come. However, before engaging in direct discourse with one or the other of these Pauls, it may be interesting to engage these two Pauls in imaginary dialogue with each other. Imagine that it is a few months before Nero ordered the death of Crossan's and Reed's Paul. Imagine that Chilton's Paul overhears Crossan's and Reed's Paul preaching to some God-fearers in Rome and that these two Pauls strike up a conversation during the coffee hour after the service. What would they think of one another? Would they see a mirror image of themselves in the other's eyes or would each look upon the other as a grotesque parody of himself?

At first glance, the family resemblance between these two apostles would no doubt be striking. Both are Christian missionaries and letter writers whose identity is defined in terms of Gentile mission. They have visited the same cities, shared common prison cells, and even penned the same seven letters. Each has a background in Pharisaic Judaism, but also troubled relations with the Jewish Christians in Jerusalem and Antioch. In many significant ways, there is uncanny resemblance. Upon closer inspection, however, differences also become noticeable. Both are from Tarsus, but only Chilton's Paul is a citizen of Tarsus and of Rome; and both give significant thought to the Roman Empire, but their assessments of the empire's ideology are radically incongruent.

Imagine the outrage of Crossan's and Reed's Paul if Chilton's Paul were to explain that the Christian community was a single body animated by the Spirit like the Roman Empire, or if he were to describe how he had personally circumcised Timothy, or if he were to seek to justify his demand that women remain silent during Christian worship. Or imagine the astonishment on the part of Chilton's Paul if he were to learn that Crossan's and Reed's Paul had never studied under Gamaliel, had never been a citizen of Rome, and had never stood trial before Gallio. What would Chilton's flamboyant exorcist think when Crossan's and Reed's Paul boasted of his weakness? Could Crossan's and Reed's Paul even comprehend why Chilton's Paul would subordinate himself to the apostles and elders in Jerusalem? Would the two Pauls ever be able to reconcile their differences on issues of Christian equity between the genders or between slaves and free?

Even more importantly, the two figures would probably be unable to discover a common framework for discussing their differences. Philosophical and theological categories? Chilton's Paul thinks in terms inherited from Stoicism; Crossan's and Reed's Paul thinks in terms inherited from Jewish covenantal theology. Apocalypticism? For Crossan's and Reed's Paul, apocalypticism fuels ethics and calls for an end to the inequitable structures of this world; for Chilton's Paul, apocalypticism defuses ethical energies and leads to a nonchalant acceptance of existing inequities. Their approach to ministry? Chilton's Paul understands himself as a powerful exorcist; Crossan's and Reed's Paul understands himself in contrast to the powerful religious showmen of his day.

These Pauls take very different shapes, certainly due in part to the complexity of interpreting ancient texts. Indeed, the distinctive lines and contours of each image arise from the cumulative effects of scores of exegetical and historical judgments, none of which is beyond question. Undoubtedly, as scholarly reflection proceeds, each artisan's image of Paul will garner its share of criticism, but in the end, neither reconstruction will consistently be judged careless, naive, or irresponsible. Each of these Pauls is plausible and worthy of careful scrutiny. In this chapter, however, I do not yet wish to engage in that scrutiny. I wish only to offer one observation about these plausible Pauls and then to introduce a research agenda that proceeds from that observation: *The most important differences between Chilton's Paul and Crossan's and Reed's Paul develop from the respective authors' decisions about the role that the book of Acts will play as evidence in their reconstructions of Paul.*

In theory, both images of Paul are crafted from the same raw materials: the seven undisputed letters of Paul and a critical appropriation of Acts. In practice, however, Chilton draws upon Acts much more frequently and positively than do Crossan and Reed. Consequently, Chilton's Paul shares many characteristics with the Paul of Acts. Chilton is convinced that Acts' secondary sources about Paul can—when critically considered—provide important insights that even the most cautious reading of Paul's letters will leave undetected. Chilton believes his Paul has significant continuity with the Paul of Acts because Luke's Paul did, in fact, resemble the historical Paul in significant ways. Therefore, in light of this overarching judgment about Acts, when Chilton faces an exegetical or historical judgment, his interpretation of the letters *leans toward Acts.*

In contrast, Crossan and Reed severely restrict their use of Acts as a source for reconstructing Paul's life, and the resulting Paul does, by design, look significantly different from the Paul of Acts. Crossan and Reed believe that a secondary source like Acts is far less significant for understanding Paul than are the primary sources of Paul's letters. Crossan and Reed believe that their Paul has significant discontinuity with the Paul of Acts because Luke's Paul was, in fact, at variance with the historical Paul in significant ways. Therefore, in light of their overarching judgment about Acts, when Crossan and Reed face an exegetical or historical judgment, their interpretation of the letters *leans away from Acts.*

This rapid survey of these expertly crafted volumes well illustrates the current shape of Pauline scholarship. Paul has a dual personality within contemporary biblical studies. For some scholars (like Crossan and Reed), the Paul of Acts bears very little or no resemblance to the historical Paul. For other scholars (like Chilton), the Paul of Acts bears tremendous resemblance, or is even identical, to the historical Paul. Of course, individual scholars frequently seek to distinguish their particular Paul by adding some unique brush strokes of their own, but the resulting images seldom manage to escape this basic duality. In nearly every case, the Pauline personality that emerges is largely shaped either by its conformity to or by its contrast with the Paul of Acts. The Pauls in contemporary scholarship are either consciously leaning into or away from Acts. For contemporary reconstructions of Paul's life and thought the first question is, therefore, *the role that Acts will play in one's reconstruction.*[130]

Even though this first question of Pauline studies is not always asked and answered in a conscious, straightforward fashion, any sustained investigation of Paul will inevitably convey—sometimes overtly, sometimes covertly—a host of assumptions about Acts. The danger is that in the absence of a well-conceived and clearly articulated understanding of Acts' role in the study of Paul, Pauline scholarship can be tempted to draw upon the book of Acts haphazardly, accepting one bit of data about Paul from Acts while simultaneously rejecting another without any clearly defined rationale. Acts can become a literary boneyard where scholarly vultures are free to forage for appealing Pauline morsels. On the one hand, some scholars find almost nothing of

---

[130]Two other preliminary questions are, of course, (1) the authorship of the six disputed letters of Paul and (2) their relationship to the historical Paul. These issues, although equal in importance to the question about the role of Acts, are beyond the scope of this volume. On the possibility that Acts and the Pastoral Epistles share common authorship, see Jean-Daniel Kaestli, "Luke-Acts and the Pastoral Epistles: The Thesis of a Common Authorship," in *Luke's Literary Achievement: Collected Essays* (ed. C. M. Tuckett; JSNTSup 116; Sheffield: Sheffield Academic Press, 1995), 110–26.

In order to avoid any confusion of the issue at hand, this volume will consider only the seven undisputed letters when considering Paul's thought. On the image of Paul in the Pastoral Epistles, see James W. Aageson, *Paul, the Pastoral Epistles, and the Early Church* (LPS; Peabody, Mass.: Hendrickson, 2008). On the image of Paul in Ephesians and Colossians, see Gregory E. Sterling, "Images of Paul at the End of the First Century," *ZNW* 99 (2008): 74–98. For surveys of the images of Paul in the entire New Testament, see Leander E. Keck, "Images of Paul in the New Testament," *Int* 43 (1989): 341–51; and J. Christiaan Beker, *Heirs of Paul* (Minneapolis: Fortress, 1991). For a brief but cogent survey of the scholarly quest to interpret and appropriate those images, see Victor Paul Furnish, "On Putting Paul in His Place," *JBL* 113 (1994): 3–17.

appeal in Acts and dismiss the Paul of Acts as compromised, domesticated, or otherwise revised. Conveniently, then, whatever is found unappealing in Paul's letters can also be interpreted as corruptions on the basis of their resonance with the supposed distortions of Paul in Acts. On the other hand, other scholars are attracted to much or almost everything within Acts as Pauline and privilege the Paul of Acts as helpful, clarifying, or otherwise supplementary to Paul's letters. Conveniently, then, in this scenario, whatever is found to be disturbing, provocative, or idiosyncratic in Paul's letters can be reinterpreted in light of the secondary materials in Acts. In either case, an underdeveloped theoretical framework for the employment of Acts as a source for understanding Paul's life and thought enables even an otherwise evenhanded interpreter to pull off all manner of exegetical slights of hand.

Accordingly, the research agenda of this volume is to examine the Paul of Acts and the Paul of the undisputed letters and to provide a disciplined approach for their comparison and employment in Pauline studies.[131] This volume will provide suggestions for appropriate ways to approach comparative studies of the Paul of Acts and the Paul of the letters and will offer and employ a disciplined method for limited testing of the plausibility of claims about the relationship between the Paul of Acts and the Paul of the letters.

---

[131] Without addressing the question of the authenticity of the disputed Pauline letters, this volume will set those letters aside in order to focus upon the relationship between the Paul of the undisputed letters and the Paul of Acts. On the significance of challenging and rethinking the scholarly consensus about the disputed Pauline letters, especially the Pastoral Epistles, see Stanley E. Porter, "Pauline Authorship and the Pastoral Epistles: Implications for Canon," *Bulletin for Biblical Research* 5 (1995): 105–23. On the broader issue of pseudonymity and the Christian canon, see Kent D. Clarke, "The Problem of Pseudonymity in Biblical Literature and Its Implications for Canon Formation," in *The Canon Debate* (ed. Lee Martin MacDonald and James A. Sanders; Peabody, Mass.: Hendrickson, 2002), 440–68.

~ 2 ~

PAUL, LET ME INTRODUCE YOU TO PAUL

THE SPLIT personality that we have observed within the Paul of critical scholarship emerged gradually over the last two centuries, but took two discernible strides. The first step occurred when Paul came under the scrutiny of F. C. Baur and the Tübingen school in Germany. In the mid-nineteenth century, Baur's *Paul, the Apostle of Jesus*[1] appealed for complete and uncompromising separation of the Paul of Acts from the Paul of the letters. Although fidelity to Baur's appeal became a hallmark of the Tübingen school over several decades, his appeal was not widely heeded outside of that narrow sector of scholarship. A second step was necessary in order to bring Paul's split personality into prominence within scholarship. That second step occurred with the work of two twentieth-century scholars: John Knox and Philipp Vielhauer. Although Knox and Vielhauer reached conclusions that were similar to Baur's in many respects, they arrived at those conclusions on the bases of significantly different (and, in the eyes of many scholars, more plausible) methodological and historiographical assumptions.

Of course, the scholarly traditions that have split Paul's personality between the Paul of the letters and the Paul of Acts are much larger than the legacy of these three scholars and these two eras. However, a preliminary understanding of the story of how Paul came to have a split personality within contemporary scholarship can be acquired by considering the legacy of these three scholars. Therefore, this chapter will first briefly sketch the claims promoted by Baur in the nineteenth century. It will then examine the later—though similar and more widely accepted—claims advanced by Knox and Vielhauer in the twentieth century. Finally, by drawing upon a critical appropriation of the methods promoted by Knox and Vielhauer, this chapter

---

[1]Ferdinand Christian Baur, *Paul, the Apostle of Jesus: His Life and Work, His Epistles and His Doctrines: A Contribution to the Critical History of Primitive Christianity* (2 vols.; London: Williams & Norgate, 1873; repr., Peabody, Mass.: Hendrickson, 2003); trans. of *Paulus, der Apostel Jesu Christi: Sein Leben und Wirken, seine Briefe und seine Lehre. Ein Beitrag zu einer kritischen Geschichte des Urchristenthums* (2 vols.; Stuttgart: Becher & Müller, 1845). For appreciative introductions to Baur's reading of Paul, see Robert Morgan, "Biblical Classics: II. F. C. Baur: Paul," *ExpTim* 90 (1978): 4–10; and Joseph B. Tyson, "The Legacy of F. C. Baur and Recent Studies of Acts," *Forum* 4 (2001): 125–44.

will offer a model for reconsidering the relationship between the Paul of Acts and the Paul of the letters.

I. The Story of Paul's Estrangement from Paul

Baur considered himself an historian of early Christianity and, for him, understanding Paul's life and thought was essential for understanding the history of earliest Christianity. In fact, Baur regarded Paul's thought as the central creative force beneath the rise of Christianity. He insisted: "That Christianity, in its universal historical acceptation, was the work of the Apostle Paul is undeniably an historical matter of fact."[2] For Baur, Paul's preeminence within earliest Christianity ensured that his theology merited "a most careful and accurate inquiry" of the Pauline traditions in both Acts and the Pauline letters.[3] Such ideas were common among his nineteenth-century peers, but Baur insisted upon a new approach for investigating Pauline traditions. He argued that the Paul of the letters had to be distinguished from the Paul of Acts because the Pauline traditions in Acts were historically unreliable. He explained: "It is true that one would think that in all the cases where the accounts in the Acts do not altogether agree with the statements of the Apostle the latter would have such a decided claim to authentic truth that the contradictions in the Acts would scarcely be worth attention, but this rule, which would seem to spring from the nature of the case, has not up to this time been so much followed as it deserves."[4]

Baur suggested that most of his peers inappropriately merged the historically suspect traditions in Acts with the historically accurate traditions in Paul's letters and were, as a consequence, misled in their reconstructions of earliest Christianity. According to Baur, when the traditions in Acts and the letters are harmonized, "not only is historical truth set in a false light, but the justice and impartiality which are due to the Apostle in the investigation of his life and labours cannot be thoroughly employed."[5] Baur sought to address this perceived loss of the historical Paul with an unflinching methodological commitment. Comparing the differences between the Paul in Acts and the Paul in the letters to the differences between the Jesus in John and the Jesus in the synoptic gospels, Baur insisted that the differences between these Pauls were so pronounced that "historical truth can only belong to one of them."[6] In contrast to the tendency of his times, Baur claimed that "the Paul of the Acts is manifestly quite a different person from the Paul of the Epistles." Baur saw the recovery of the historical Paul in moral terms and argued that "the

---

[2] Baur, *Paul,* 1:3.
[3] Ibid., 1:4.
[4] Ibid., 1:4.
[5] Ibid., 1:4.
[6] Ibid., 1:5.

historical character of the author [Luke] can only be maintained at the cost of the moral character of the Apostle [Paul]."[7]

According to Baur, recovery of the historical Paul began with the recognition that the aim of Acts was apologetic.[8] Baur offered two primary arguments for his hostility to interpreting Paul through the lens of Acts. One argument was broadly based upon his comparative reading of Acts and Paul's letters; the other was based upon his understanding of the history of earliest Christianity.[9]

First, in his comparative argument, Baur argued that the first two chapters of Galatians "form a historical document of the greatest importance" for understanding Paul's relationship to the other apostles and that "if these chapters are to be of any value in the interest of the truth of the history, we must first of all free ourselves from the common arbitrary suppositions that generally attend this enquiry, by which the most complete harmony is established between the author of the Acts of the Apostles and the Apostle Paul, and one narrative is used as a confirmation of the other."[10]

Baur argued that attempts to reconcile Paul's travel narrative in Gal 1–2 with the narrative of Acts were "but useless trouble." According to Baur, Acts 9 recorded that Paul traveled to Damascus and then Jerusalem *immediately* after his conversion, but Paul insisted in Gal 1 that after his conversion he *immediately* traveled "into Arabia, and from there again back to Damascus, and then *three years afterwards* traveled to Jerusalem."[11] As Baur interpreted Acts and Galatians "the facts are exactly contrary" and the accounts contain "a contradiction which cannot be got over."[12] Having satisfied himself that Acts was an unreliable source for recovering the sequence of events that immediately followed Paul's conversion, Baur continued his comparison by analyzing Paul's subsequent Jerusalem visits as recorded in Acts 11 and 15 and in Gal 1 and 2. Baur found it impossible to reconcile these accounts, suggesting that perhaps the visit in Acts 11 was "an erroneous statement, a mere fiction."[13]

In light of his comparison of these texts, Baur detected what he regarded as a pattern of historical unreliability in Acts. His comparison concluded with a warning:

> Reasoning from what we have hitherto observed, we have every cause to be distrustful of a statement like that of the Acts of the Apostles, which agrees so little with the Apostle's own account, and the only result possible for us, is to ignore the idea of an identity [between Acts' chronology and Paul's] that does

---

[7] Ibid., 1:11.
[8] Ibid., 1:7–8.
[9] Baur accepted the authenticity of only Romans, 1–2 Corinthians, and Galatians as certain. Ibid., 1:260–381; 2:1–5.
[10] Ibid., 1:109.
[11] Ibid., 1:110, emphasis added.
[12] Ibid., 1:111–12.
[13] Ibid., 1:120.

not exist, and—without any further regard to whether the discrepancies are greater or lesser—*entirely to separate the two statements.*[14]

On the basis of his careful comparison of the narratives in the letters and in Acts, Baur, therefore, issued his appeal for the estrangement of the Paul of the letters from the Paul of Acts. However, Baur's comparative argument was not the only basis of his appeal for separating the Paul of Acts from the Paul of the letters.

Second, Baur developed a more historically sweeping argument to explain the historical distortions he claimed to have discovered through his comparison of the biblical accounts. Baur theorized that the first decades of the Christian movement saw Christianity divided into two competing groups and that Paul and Gentile Christianity stood on one side of this divide, while the original apostles and Jewish Christianity stood on the other. According to Baur, this conflict within earliest Christianity is displayed in Paul's letters as a conflict between Peter and Paul. Baur asserts that Paul "places himself in opposition to Peter, so that we have before us man against man, teacher against teacher, one Gospel against another, one apostolic office against another."[15] According to Baur, the author of Acts was aware of this conflict, but wished "to throw a concealing veil" over such animosities as part of his "apologetic and conciliatory tendency."[16] In Baur's reading, Acts differed from Paul's letters because the author of Acts *intentionally distorted* earliest Christian history in order to conceal historical unpleasantries and significant divisions within earliest Christianity from later Christians. He therefore "represent[ed] the difference between Peter and Paul as unessential and trifling."[17] When viewed through Baur's eyes, the historical Peter and Paul existed in direct competition, but Acts created the anachronistic fiction of a unified church. In Baur's reading of Acts, Acts had developed an Hegelian synthesis between the competing thesis and antithesis of Peter and Paul.[18]

On the bases of these two overlapping literary and historical arguments, Baur rejected any use of the narratives in Acts as a source for reconstructing the sequence of events in Paul's life. Although Baur's Hegelian reconstruction of earliest Christian history has been almost universally rejected by later scholars,[19] his skepticism about the historical reliability of Acts has often been

---

[14] Ibid., 1:120–21, emphasis added.

[15] Ibid., 1:129.

[16] Ibid., 1:134.

[17] Ibid., 1:8.

[18] Baur's commitment to a Hegelian model of thesis (in Peter's Jewish Christianity), antithesis (in Paul's Gentile Christianity), and synthesis (in the Lukan merger of Petrine and Pauline Christianity) is well documented. For a helpful analysis of Hegel's influence upon Baur, see W. Ward Gasque, *A History of the Interpretation of the Acts of the Apostles* (Tübingen: J. C. B. Mohr, 1975; repr., Peabody, Mass.: Hendrickson, 1989), 29–40.

[19] As a contemporary expression of fidelity to Baur's basic historical reconstruction (although with some modifications), see Michael Goulder, *St. Paul versus St. Peter:*

embraced. Baur's effect upon Acts scholarship was profound. Over one hundred years ago, by the turn of the twentieth century, surveys of scholarship already were demonstrating that Acts scholarship was clearly divided into two traditions, a Baur-inspired, largely German, tradition, which had very little confidence in the historicity of Acts and a more conservative, largely British, anti-Baur tradition, which had much greater confidence in the historicity of Acts.[20] Subsequent surveys of scholarship throughout the twentieth century and into the twenty-first have discovered the same divide between Baur-like skepticism about the historicity of Acts and anti-Baur assertions of confidence in the historicity of Acts.[21] Baur's influence lingers on within Acts scholarship to the present time. In their classic histories of Acts scholarship from the mid-nineteenth to mid-twentieth century, W. Ward Gasque and A. J. Mattill well illustrate Baur's role as the most influential figure in nineteenth- and twentieth-century Acts scholarship.[22] Gasque, who profoundly disagreed with Baur, wrote in consistent dialogue with Baur and his Tübingen legacy even while preferring the more historically conservative anti-Baur tradition of Acts scholarship. Mattill, who largely agreed with Baur's skepticism about the his-

---

A Tale of Two Missions (Louisville: Westminster John Knox, 1994). Goulder's attempted revival of Baur's historical reconstruction has not gained much acceptance in contemporary scholarship.

[20] As witnesses to this nineteenth-century division within Acts scholarship, see, e.g., W. C. van Manen, "A Wave of Hypercriticism," *ExpTim* 9 (1898): 205–11, 257–59, 314–19; Arthur Bumstead, "The Present Status of Criticism," *BW* 17 (1901): 355–60; and James Moffatt, "Wellhausen and Harnack on the Book of Acts," *ExpTim* 19 (1908): 250–52.

[21] See, e.g., A. T. Robertson, *Luke the Historian in Light of Research* (New York: C. Scribner's Sons, 1920); W. K. Lowther Clarke, "The Acts of the Apostles in Recent Criticism," *Theology* 4 (1922): 69–81, 314–22; J. W. Hunkin, "British Work on the Acts," in *The Beginnings of Christianity: Part 1. The Acts of the Apostles* (ed. F. J. Foakes-Jackson and Kirsopp Lake; 5 vols.; London: Macmillan, 1920–1933), 2:396–433; A. C. McGiffert, "The Historical Criticism of Acts in Germany," in ibid., 2:363–95; C. K. Barrett, *Luke the Historian in Recent Study* (London: Epworth, 1961); Donald Guthrie, "Recent Literature on the Acts of the Apostles," *Vox evangelica* 2 (1963): 33–49; Martin Rese, "Zur Lukas-Diskussion seit 1950," *Jahrbuch der theologischen Hochschule Bethel* 9 (1967): 62–67; E. M. Blaiklock, "The Acts of the Apostles as a Document of First Century History," in *Apostolic History and the Gospel: Biblical and Historical Essays Presented to F. F. Bruce* (ed. W. Ward Gasque and Ralph P. Martin; Exeter: Paternoster, 1970), 41–54; Robert J. Karris, *What Are They Saying about Luke and Acts?* (New York: Paulist, 1979); Eckhard Plümacher, "Acta-Forschung 1974–82," *Theologische Rundschau* 48 (1984): 105–69; Ferdinand Hahn, "Der gegenwärtige Stand der Erforschung der Apostelgeschichte: Kommentare und Aufsatzbände 1980–85," *Theologische Revue* 82 (1986): 117–90; Mark Allan Powell, "Luke's Second Volume: Three Basic Issues in Contemporary Studies of Acts," *Trinity Seminary Review* 13 (1991): 69–81; Erich Grässer, *Forschungen zur Apostelgeschichte* (WUNT 137; Tübingen: Mohr Siebeck, 2001); and I. Howard Marshall, "Acts in Current Study," *ExpTim* 155 (2003): 49–52.

[22] Gasque, *History*; A. J. Mattill, "Luke as a Historian in Criticism since 1840" (PhD diss., Vanderbilt University, 1959). Although Gasque's work is more widely available, Mattill's work is a less polemical guide to the first century of post-Baur criticism of Acts.

toricity of Acts, preferred the less historically conservative pro-Baur tradition of Acts scholarship and treated the anti-Baur tradition essentially as a reaction to Baur. From the middle of the nineteenth to the middle of the twentieth centuries, whether one agreed or disagreed with Baur's historical skepticism, the conversation about Acts and its historical reliability began with Baur—and it still begins there.[23]

In spite of Baur's profound effect upon Acts scholarship and his creation of an enduring legacy of skepticism about the historicity of Acts, his influence upon Pauline studies was far less significant. Even though Baur had emphatically rejected Acts as a valid source for Paul's life or thought, his skepticism was often dismissed as a product of Baur's misguided commitment

---

[23]In the second half of the twentieth century, the best of the conservative tradition was represented by scholars like F. F. Bruce (*Commentary on the Book of Acts: The English Text with Introduction, Exposition, and Notes* [NICNT; Grand Rapids: Eerdmans, 1954]; *The New Testament Documents: Are They Reliable?* [5th ed.; Downers Grove: InterVarsity, 1960]; "The Acts of the Apostles: Historical Record or Theological Reconstruction?" *ANRW* 25.3:2570–2603; and *The Acts of the Apostles: The Greek Text with Introduction and Commentary* [3d ed.; Grand Rapids: Eerdmans, 1990]), I. Howard Marshall ("Recent Study of the Acts of the Apostles," *ExpTim* 80 [1969]: 4–8; *Luke: Historian and Theologian* [Grand Rapids: Zondervan, 1970]; *The Acts of the Apostles: An Introduction and Commentary* [Tyndale New Testament Commentaries; Grand Rapids: Eerdmans, 1978]; *The Acts of the Apostles* [New Testament Guides; Sheffield: JSOT Press, 1992]; and "Acts in Current Study"), and Colin J. Hemer ("Luke the Historian," *BJRL* 60 [1977]: 28–51; and *The Book of Acts in the Setting of Hellenistic History* [ed. Conrad H. Gempf; WUNT 49; Tübingen: Mohr Siebeck, 1989]), who often followed the earlier work of the British William M. Ramsay (*St. Paul the Traveller and Roman Citizen* [3d ed.; London: Hodder & Stoughton, 1897; repr., Grand Rapids: Baker, 1979]; and *The First Christian Century* [London: Hodder & Stoughton, 1911; repr., Boston: Elibron, 2005]), the American Henry J. Cadbury (*The Making of Luke-Acts* [London: SPCK, 1927]; *The Book of Acts in History* [New York: Harper, 1955]; and *The Making of Luke-Acts* [2d ed.; London: SPCK, 1958; repr., Peabody, Mass.: Hendrickson, 1999], and, to a lesser degree, the German Adolf von Harnack, *Luke the Physician: The Author of the Third Gospel and the Acts of the Apostles;* vol. 1 of *New Testament Studies* [trans. J. R. Wilkinson; Crown Theological Library 20; New York: G. P. Putnam's, 1908]; and *The Date of Acts and of the Synoptic Gospels;* vol. 4 of *New Testament Studies* [trans. J. R. Wilkinson; Crown Theological Library 33; New York: G. P. Putnam's, 1911]). During the same period, the other tradition, which had less confidence in the historicity of Acts, was best represented by Martin Dibelius (*Studies in the Acts of the Apostles* [ed. Heinrich Greeven; trans. Mary Ling; New York: Scribners, 1956]), Hans Conzelmann (*The Theology of St. Luke* [trans. Geoffrey Buswell; San Francisco: Harper & Row, 1960]; "Luke's Place in the Development of Earliest Christianity," in *Studies in Luke-Acts* [ed. J. Louis Martyn and Leander E. Keck; Nashville: Abingdon, 1966; repr., Philadelphia: Fortress, 1980], 298–316; and *Acts of the Apostles: A Commentary on the Acts of the Apostles* [ed. Eldon Jay Epp and Christopher R. Matthews; trans. J. Limburg, A. Thomas Krabel, and Donald H. Juel; Hermeneia; Philadelphia: Fortress, 1987]), and Ernst Haenchen ("The Book of Acts as Source Material for the History of Earliest Christianity," in Martyn and Keck, *Studies in Luke-Acts,* 258–78; and *The Acts of the Apostles: A Commentary* [trans. R. McL. Wilson; Philadelphia: Westminster, 1971]). The best contemporary introduction to the issue of historicity in Acts is Daniel Marguerat, "Wie historisch ist die Apostelgeschichte?" *ZNT* 9 (2006): 44–51.

to an Hegelian model of history. Baur's ideas never created the same clear divisions within Pauline studies that they produced within Acts scholarship. However, a Baur-like skepticism about the value of Acts became established within Pauline studies in the mid-twentieth century through the work of John Knox and Philipp Vielhauer. Vielhauer and Knox made two critical methodological shifts that significantly altered the terms of the debate over the value of Acts for Pauline studies. First, they offered sustained critiques of the reliability of Acts that were free from the taint of Baur's Hegelianism and its overtly anti-Jewish polemic.[24] Second, they separated the question of Paul's life in Acts from the question of Paul's thought in Acts. Knox concentrated his efforts on arguments against using Acts as a source for understanding the chronology of Paul's life. Vielhauer concentrated his efforts on arguments against using Acts as a source for understanding Paul's thought (theology). Through the collective weight of their roughly contemporary publications, Knox and Vielhauer called for a division of the questions Baur had lumped together. In tandem, their work brought Paul's split personality to prominence within biblical studies. Scholars of Paul were forced to address the perceived differences between the Paul of Acts and the Paul of the letters.

Nearly a hundred years after Baur's work appeared in its original German edition, John Knox complained that studies of Pauline chronology were still deeply dependent upon what Knox, like Baur before him, regarded as the historically misleading traditions in Acts. In two closely related journal articles, Knox laid out methodological principles very close to those earlier propounded by Baur. In 1936, Knox asserted:

> It does not need to be said that our principal sources for the life of Paul are the letters generally esteemed authentic and the several sections of Luke-Acts that deal with his career. It is equally unnecessary to add that of these the letters are by all odds the more important and in cases of conflict with Acts, whether explicit or implied, are always to be followed. This is probably obvious enough and yet is often ignored.[25]

Knox expressed very similar convictions again in 1939 when he asserted, "it is my conviction that students of the life of Paul must rigidly hold themselves to using Acts as a secondary source and must be ready to disregard it whenever the letters give the slightest ground for doing so."[26]

[24] On Baur's regrettable anti-Jewish bias, see Joseph B. Tyson, *Luke, Judaism, and the Scholars: Critical Approaches to Luke-Acts* (Columbia: University of South Carolina Press, 1999), 12–29.

[25] John Knox, "'Fourteen Years Later': A Note on the Pauline Chronology," *JR* 16 (1936): 341–49, here 341–42. Over fifty years later in a retrospective on his life's work and his 1936 article in particular, Knox declared that "I have been aware of no changes in my thinking on this particular point." See "Reflections," in *Cadbury, Knox, and Talbert: American Contributions to the Study of Acts* (ed. Mikeal C. Parsons and Joseph B. Tyson; Atlanta: Scholars Press, 1992), 107–13, here 108.

[26] John Knox, "The Pauline Chronology," *JBL* 58 (1939): 15–29, here 23.

Knox's approach was incorporated into the 1940 work of his former professor Donald Riddle,[27] but it was developed and applied most faithfully in 1950 when Knox again picked up his pen to write *Chapters in a Life of Paul*.[28] Although Knox shared much of Baur's skepticism about the value of Acts as a source for understanding Paul, Knox took on a more limited project than did Baur. Baur had sought to completely revise existing understandings of both Paul's life and Paul's thought, but Knox was primarily "concerned with the life of Paul as distinguished from his thought."[29] Knox suspected that the existing scholarly consensus relied too heavily upon Acts for information about Paul, particularly about the chronology of Paul's life. Knox's characterization of his contemporaries' assumptions regarding the Pauline letters and Acts foreshadows his rejection of the existing scholarly consensus. According to Knox, most of his contemporaries assumed that "the letters, rich though they are as sources for the ideas, the personality, and the religious experience of the apostle, have little to tell us about [Paul's] life" whereas "the book of Acts . . . satisfactorily makes up for the autobiographical omissions of the letters."[30] Knox questioned these scholarly assumptions by promoting two ideas. First, he argued that the chronology of Acts should not be uncritically accepted, because the author of Acts "arranged his materials in the order that best suited the purpose of his book."[31] Knox supported this contention both by reminding his readers of Luke's redactional activity in the Gospel of Luke and by rehearsing the widely recognized theological tendencies in Acts.[32] For Knox, Luke did have "in hand important primitive materials," but those materials, like the Jesus materials in Luke's Gospel, were "fragmentary accounts" that could be formed into a coherent narrative only through "a good deal of imagination."[33] Second, and my main concern, Knox sought to demonstrate that Paul's letters provided more information about the chronology of Paul's life than was often acknowledged. Knox laid out a methodological principle similar to that earlier offered in his articles on Paul. Knox suggested:

> the letters remain our only firsthand source for the outer facts [chronology of Paul's life] . . . even though they happen not to say as much about them as Acts

---

[27] Donald W. Riddle, *Paul, Man of Conflict: A Modern Biographical Sketch* (Nashville: Abingdon, 1940). In spite of later widespread suspicions that Knox had adopted his ideas from Riddle, Riddle clearly acknowledged his dependence upon Knox for the "basic perceptions" in his book. See Knox, "Reflections," 108–12; and Riddle, *Man of Conflict*, 9.

[28] John Knox, *Chapters in a Life of Paul* (New York: Abingdon-Cokesbury, 1950). This volume will cite the revised edition, *Chapters in a Life of Paul* (ed. Douglas R. A. Hare; rev. ed.; Macon: Mercer University Press, 1987). For a complete bibliography of Knox's writings with complete references to reviews, see Mikeal C. Parsons, "Bibliography of John Knox," in Parsons and Tyson, *Cadbury, Knox, and Talbert*, 115–30.

[29] Knox, *Chapters*, vii.

[30] Ibid., 4.

[31] Ibid., 11.

[32] Ibid., 4–5, 10–16.

[33] Ibid., 17.

does. The distinction between primary and secondary sources in this case is of such importance that we can justly say that a fact only suggested in the letters has a status that even the most unequivocal statement of Acts, if not otherwise supported, cannot confer. We may, with proper caution, use Acts to supplement the autobiographical data of the letters, but never to correct them.[34]

For Knox, developing a chronology based upon Paul's letters began by dispensing with the idea that Paul's career was composed of "three great missionary journeys." Knox insisted that "this way of visualizing and representing the career of Paul is based entirely upon Acts, with no support from the letters whatsoever."[35] Knox recognized that Paul did journey to Jerusalem on a number of occasions, but he asserted that "these are *visits;* they are not *returns.*"[36] For Knox, these "visits" to Jerusalem were central to any accurate understanding of Pauline chronology, and they demonstrated an important difference between the chronology in Acts and in Paul. Knox explained: "Paul mentions three visits and Luke five. . . . The issue of the number and nature of Paul's contacts with Jerusalem was important from first to last. Paul says there were only three visits and that they had the purposes . . . [of] 'acquaintance,' 'conference' and 'offering.'"[37]

According to Knox, therefore, a chronology of Paul that followed his approach and consistently privileged Paul's letters over Acts would be constructed around Paul's three—and only three—visits to Jerusalem. Knox elaborated:

> If . . . we had only the letters of Paul, we should undoubtedly have something like the following understanding of the course of Paul's career after his conversion: He remained in the neighborhood of Damascus for three years or more. After a visit to Jerusalem to become acquainted with Cephas [the "acquaintance" visit], he returned to Syria (probably to Antioch), then went on (probably soon

---

[34] Ibid., 19. Knox remained committed to this principle throughout his long career. In fact, Knox even seems to have intensified his position with time. In his last published statement about his approach to Pauline chronology, Knox explained: "There was nothing new in my proposal that Paul's own letters were a better source for Paul than Acts could be; I suppose that no one could deny so obvious a fact. Any novelty my proposal could claim lay in my conception of the dimension of the superiority. I argued . . . (a) that the merest hint in the letters is to be deemed worth more than the most explicit statement of Acts; (b) that a statement in Acts about Paul is to be regarded as incredible if it conflicts directly with the letters (as many statement do) and is to be seriously questioned even if a conflict is only suggested; and (c) that statements about Paul in Acts are to be accepted with confidence only if such statements are fully and explicitly confirmed in the letters. In a word, it was argued that we can rely only on the letters for completely assured biographical information." See John Knox, "Chapters in a Life of Paul—A Response to Robert Jewett and Gerd Lüdemann," in *Colloquy of New Testament Studies: A Time for Reappraisal and Fresh Approaches* (ed. Bruce C. Corley; Macon: Mercer University Press, 1983), 341–64, here 342.

[35] Knox, *Chapters,* 27.

[36] Ibid., emphasis Knox's.

[37] Ibid., 35.

afterward) to Cilicia. In the course of the next fourteen years he lived and worked in Galatia, Macedonia, Greece and Asia, and possibly elsewhere. He ran into increasing difficulty with conservative Jewish Christians, probably from Judea, and finally went to Jerusalem to talk with the leaders about the growing rift [the "conference" visit]. This conference ended . . . with their giving him the right hand of fellowship, but with the stipulation of aid for the poor. This aid Paul set about raising. In Romans we see him, the collection completed, ready to embark for Jerusalem [the "offering" visit] to deliver it but apprehensive as to what will happen there.[38]

Knox's "three-visit" chronology was revolutionary for his time. As John McRay's recent volume on Paul accurately asserts, "virtually all studies before the publication of *Chapters in the Life of Paul* by John Knox in 1950 worked essentially from a framework of five Jerusalem visits by Paul in Acts as against a two-visit framework in Galatians."[39] Although Baur had foreshadowed many of Knox's suggestions, Knox's work is often regarded as being without precedent, and as it would be with any new idea, reactions to Knox's chronology varied wildly, ranging from outright rejection to eager acceptance.[40] Ultimately, however, whether one agreed or disagreed with Knox, his work and those who followed in his tradition ensured that subsequent reconstructions of Pauline chronology became increasingly divided between a "letters only" chronology and an Acts chronology.[41] Baur may have called for an estrangement of the Paul in Acts from the Paul in the letters, but Knox brought this estrangement to prominence in twentieth-century studies of Pauline chronology.

At about the same time that Knox's book was gaining an audience in the English-speaking world, Vielhauer published his famous essay "Zum 'Paulinismus' der Apostelgeschichte" and asked "the question whether and to what extent the author of Acts took over and passed on theological ideas of Paul,

---

[38] Ibid., 41–42. Knox, with the consensus of scholarship then and now, assumed that Cephas was the Aramaic form of the Greek name Peter. See Dale C. Allison, "Peter and Cephas: One and the Same," *JBL* 111 (1992): 489–95.

[39] John McRay, *Paul: His Life and Teaching* (Grand Rapids: Baker Academic, 2003), 79. McRay is mistaken in referring to Knox as promoting a Pauline chronology with two visits to Jerusalem. Knox clearly accepts the essential historicity of Acts' account of Paul's final visit to Jerusalem and adds this visit to the two earlier visits mentioned in Gal 1–2. See Knox, *Chapters*, 27, 34–35, 49–52.

[40] For examples of the initial reactions to Knox's book, see Joseph B. Tyson, "John Knox and the Acts of the Apostles," in Parsons and Tyson, *Cadbury, Knox, and Talbert*, 63–67.

[41] The most important followers of Knox's approach have been Gerd Lüdemann, *Paul, Apostle to the Gentiles: Studies in Chronology* (trans. F. Stanley Jones; Philadelphia: Fortress, 1984); and Robert Jewett, *A Chronology of Paul's Life* (Philadelphia: Fortress, 1979). Knox regarded Lüdemann as more faithful to his own work and approach. See Knox, "Chapters," 361–63. More recently, see Gregory Tatum, *New Chapters in the Life of Paul: The Relative Chronology of His Career* (Catholic Biblical Quarterly Monograph Series 41; Washington, D.C.: Catholic Biblical Association, 2006).

whether and to what extent he modified them."[42] Although he acknowledged that Acts made no attempt to present a full-orbed Pauline theology, Vielhauer insisted that Acts portrayed Paul "as a theologian, at least in the speeches." As a German, Vielhauer recognized the residual debates about the "party conflicts" and historical events that dominated the post-Baur work of the Tübingen school, but he sought to avoid those debates by restricting himself "to the elements of the Lukan portrayal of Paul which characterize him as a theologian; that is, we limit ourselves primarily if not exclusively to his speeches and group the theological statements of the Paul of Acts under four headings: natural theology, law, Christology, and eschatology, and compare them with statements on these themes from the letters of Paul."[43] According to Vielhauer, the theology in Paul's letters and the theology attributed to Paul in the speeches of Acts were markedly different in all four of these areas. Vielhauer insisted that "the natural theology has an utterly different function" in Acts and in Paul's letters and that Acts "eliminated Christology" from Paul's message to the Gentiles.[44] In comparing Luke's account of Paul's message to Gentiles with the Gentile message as found in Paul's letters, Vielhauer suggested that "it is no accident that in the Areopagus speech [Acts 17] the concepts of 'sin' and 'grace' are lacking, not only the words, but also the ideas. . . . The 'word of the cross' has no place in the Areopagus speech because it would make no sense there; it would be folly."[45] According to Vielhauer, Luke's portrayal of Paul's attitude toward the law is sometimes historically suspect, but "whether or not the action . . . attributed to Paul is historical, the motivation to which Acts ascribes it is due to the author of Acts."[46] As one example of Luke's misrepresentation of Paul's attitude toward the law, Vielhauer argued that "the circumcision of Timothy stands in direct contradiction to the theology of Paul, but it fits Luke's view that the law retains its full validity for Jewish Christians and that Paul acknowledged this in a conciliatory concession to the Jews."[47] Vielhauer also finds important differences between the christology in Paul's letters and in Acts. According to Paul's letters, "in the cross of Christ salvation is wholly realized," while in Acts "the crucifixion of Jesus is an error of justice and a sin of the Jews." Vielhauer complained that Acts says "nothing of the [Pauline] reality of 'in Christ.'"[48] Also according to Vielhauer, Paul's "eschatology disappears" in Acts only to be replaced by

---

[42] Originally published in German as Philipp Vielhauer, "Zum 'Paulinismus' der Apostelgeschichte," *Evangelische Theologie* 10 (1950–1951): 1–15. The translation referenced in this volume is from "On the 'Paulinism' of Acts," in *Studies in Luke-Acts* (ed. Leander E. Keck and J. Louis Martyn; trans. Wm. C. Robinson Jr. and Victor Paul Furnish; Nashville: Abingdon, 1966; repr., Philadelphia: Fortress, 1980), 33–50, here 33.

[43] Vielhauer, "'Paulinism' of Acts," 33.

[44] Ibid., 36–37.

[45] Ibid., 37.

[46] Ibid., 40.

[47] Ibid., 41.

[48] Ibid., 45.

a "theology of history."[49] On the bases of such assessments, one cannot be surprised by Vielhauer's conclusion that "the author of Acts is in his Christology pre-Pauline, in his natural theology, concept of the law, and eschatology, post-Pauline. He presents *no specifically Pauline idea*. His 'Paulinism' consists in his zeal for the worldwide Gentile mission and in his veneration for the greatest missionary to the Gentiles."[50]

Vielhauer's essay, like Knox's work, has had a profound influence upon Pauline scholarship. In many ways, Vielhauer's essay served a parallel function to Knox's work, bringing to prominence within Pauline studies a Baur-like skepticism regarding the value of even attempting to reintegrate the theology in Acts' Pauline speeches with the theology in Paul's letters. Gasque, one of Vielhauer's harshest critics, begrudgingly acknowledged the influence of Vielhauer's essay in the midst of a bombastic criticism of it. Gasque complained that Vielhauer's essay "is full of unwarranted assumptions, question-begging exegesis, and false inferences. It would, in fact, be difficult to find a better example of a false critical methodology and theological bias. Yet *the amazing thing is the widespread influence that Vielhauer's brief, and one would think, ill-conceived essay has had in the world of New Testament scholarship!*"[51] The obvious rhetorical excesses in Gasque's effort to counter Vielhauer's influence attest to the power that Vielhauer's essay had to frame subsequent debate.

The work of Knox and Vielhauer served as important catalysts for recent scholarship's frequent break with the centuries old precritical pattern of harmonizing the Paul of Acts with the Paul of the letters both historically and ideologically. Although Baur's work had set a precedent for most of their ideas, Knox and Vielhauer provided arguments for separating the Paul of Acts from the Paul of the letters that were free from the lingering specter of Baur's most controversial assumptions and conclusions. Although—and perhaps because—their claims were less grandiose and sweeping in scope than Baur's, Knox and Vielhauer were able to move Baur's major methodological concerns and interpretive approaches from the periphery to the center of scholarly discourse. Of course, both the assumptions behind these works and the conclusions they present remain widely disputed. Yet, in spite of considerable disagreement over the historical accuracy and exegetical merit of their respective arguments, Knox and Vielhauer produced

---

[49] Ibid., 45, 48.

[50] Ibid., 48, emphasis added.

[51] Gasque, *History*, 287, emphasis added. Also see Gasque's "A Fruitful Field: Recent Study of the Acts of the Apostles," *Int* 42 (1988): 117–30, which calls Vielhauer's thesis "gross overstatement of the evidence" (130). The best available brief critique of Vielhauer's theses is Stanley E. Porter, *Paul in Acts* (LPS; Peabody, Mass.: Hendrickson, 2001), 187–206. Also see Armin D. Baum, "Paulinismen in den Missionsreden des lukanischen Paulus: Zur inhaltlichen Authentizität der *oratio recta* in der Apostelgeschichte," *ETL* 82 (2006): 405–36; Werner Georg Kümmel, "Current Theological Accusations Against Luke," trans. William C. Robinson, *Andover Newton Quarterly* 16 (1975): 131–45; and Jacob Jervell, *The Unknown Paul: Essays on Luke-Acts and Early Christian History* (Minneapolis: Augsburg, 1984), 52–67, 68–76.

milestones that continue to mark the path of inquiry for historical and theological journeys into Paul's world. Even when academic travelers stake out different routes for themselves, they are often impelled to orient their alternative routes in relation to the established thoroughfares charted by Knox and Vielhauer.

Critics of the Knox/Vielhauer tradition will undoubtedly notice that the preceding discussion has passed over the many critics of this tradition. This is true. However, the purpose of the preceding discussion has been to understand the origins of Paul's split personality within contemporary scholarship. How did the Paul of Acts become estranged from the Paul of the letters? The combined influence of the Baur and Knox/Vielhauer traditions seems to me the best explanation. The scholars who opposed the Tübingen school in the nineteenth century and the Knox/Vielhauer tradition in the twentieth century are indeed important to the history of scholarship, but they did not create Paul's split personality—they sought to reintegrate it. I will *not* now turn to the objections raised against the Knox/Vielhauer tradition. For my goal has been neither to praise nor to condemn this tradition but first to show its role in establishing Paul's split personality within contemporary scholarship and second to draw upon its methodological insights to develop tools for my own comparison of the Paul of the letters and the Paul of Acts, which I hope to accomplish in the remainder of this chapter.

II. The Recurring Problems

Given Paul's split personality within critical scholarship, Pauline scholars are often tempted to lend their interpretive skills to the promotion of one side or the other of Paul's dichotomous personality. Although the plausibility of the resulting arguments varies according to the skill and acumen of the respective interpreters, few expect that they will heal Paul's split personality. Eventually, all interpreters and would-be reconcilers of Paul's dichotomous personality run into the same problems. Broadly conceived, these problems are the ancient purposes of the sources, the frequent inconsistency within and among the sources, the inherent flexibility of the data within the sources, and the frustrating silences within the sources.

First, both Paul's letters and the book of Acts pose the problem that, as ancient documents, they were never intended to answer the kinds of questions that contemporary interpreters often pose to them. Contemporary efforts to answer questions about the sweeping chronology of Paul's life or about the timeless structures of his theology find themselves working at cross-purposes to the design of these ancient texts. Although Acts and the letters both contain extensive data about Paul's life and teaching, neither Acts nor Paul's letters were designed to serve as an introduction to Paul's life or thought. In the case of Acts, scholars have classified the book as historiography, biography, novel, and epic.[52] Yet, in spite of their disagreements about the precise genre and purpose of Acts, scholars universally recognize that Acts was never designed to function anything like a modern biography.[53] Thus, modern interpreters must seek to bridge the gap between ancient and modern generic expectations and purposes, a gap further widened by the fact that the purpose of Acts has more to do with Jesus than with Paul. As Joseph Fitzmyer has reminded scholarship, Luke's Paul is first and foremost a witness to Christ and only secondarily a witness to himself.[54] When modern readers seek to learn about Paul from Acts, they are both addressing modern questions to an ancient text and exploring a secondary, rather than the primary, concern within that ancient text.

In the case of Paul's letters, the modern historian's struggle over working at cross-purposes to the intent of the documents is even more acute than in Acts. Paul's letters arose from his work as a Christian missionary and were designed to address the specific needs of the particular Christian communities to which they were written. As Albrecht Dihle's classic survey of ancient Greek and Latin literature explained, Paul's letters were really "pastoral care over a distance."[55] Historical, biographical, and ideological data appear in an *ad hoc* fashion and are typically offered in the service of other more immediate Pauline concerns. Paul's letters, as valuable as they are, were designed to answer the questions of their day and not the questions of twenty-first century historians and theologians. Frequently, the questions of greatest concern to modern historians and theologians were either irrelevant or tangential to Paul's first-century concerns. Consequently, if such questions can be answered at all, they can often be answered only by inference or extrapolation.

Second, the inconsistency and diversity within Acts and Paul's letters also pose problems for those seeking to reconstruct Paul's life and theology. Even a casual reading of Acts and Paul's letters reveals that the same events and topics often receive very different treatments. These differences exist not only between Acts and the letters, but also within each individual corpus. Neither Paul's letters nor the book of Acts present a monolithic characterization of Paul's life and theology. For example, in Galatians Paul strongly emphasized that his gospel did not derive from the witness of the Jerusalem apostles. He asserted:

---

[52] For a survey of recent proposals regarding the genre of Acts, see Thomas E. Phillips, "The Genre of Acts: Moving Toward a Consensus?" *CBR* 4 (2006): 365–96.

[53] On the distinction between ancient and modern generic differentiation, see Stanley E. Porter, "The Genre of Acts and the Ethics of Discourse," in *Acts and Ethics* (ed. Thomas E. Phillips; NTM 9; Sheffield: Sheffield Phoenix, 2005), 1–15, esp. 10–12.

[54] Joseph A. Fitzmyer, *The Acts of the Apostles* (AB 31; New York: Doubleday, 1998), 55–60.

[55] Albrecht Dihle, *Greek and Latin Literature of the Roman Empire: From Augustus to Justinian* (New York: Routledge, 1994), 205. Dihle also noted that antiquity offered no "exact parallel to Paul's letters" (205). As the author of pastoral letters, Paul had many subsequent imitators, but no clear predecessor.

For I want you to know, brothers and sisters, that the gospel that was proclaimed by me is not of human origin; for *I did not receive it from a human source,* nor was I taught it, but I received it through a revelation of Jesus Christ. (Gal 1:11–12, emphasis added)

However, in 1 Corinthians Paul seemed to acknowledge his role as a recipient of preexisting traditions when he reminded the Corinthians

of the good news that I proclaimed to you, which you in turn received. . . . For I handed on to you as of first importance *what I in turn had received*: that Christ died for our sins in accordance with the scriptures, and that he was buried, and that he was raised on the third day. . . . (1 Cor 15:1–4, emphasis added)

In both cases, Paul uses the same, seemingly technical, verb (παραλαμβάνω) to describe reception of the gospel. In Galatians, Paul denies any human agency in his reception of the gospel; in 1 Corinthians, Paul celebrates his fidelity to a gospel that he has received from others.[56] Such seeming inconsistency appears in Paul's letters over a wide range of issues. When Paul's letters provide repeated visits to the same topic, his comments are seldom uniform. Scholars often account for this diversity within Paul's letters by appeal to development within Paul's thought, or to Paul's sensitivity to the unique circumstances of each community, or to a distinction between the coherent and contingent elements in Paul's thought, or even to Paul's disinterest in coherence.[57] Regardless of how one accounts for such diversity within Paul's letters, this diversity further complicates efforts to develop a systematic account of Paul's life and theology.[58]

A close examination of Acts reveals similar diversity and inconsistency in that text. For example, Paul's life-altering encounter with Christ on the Damascus road is recounted three times in Acts (9:1–31; 22:3–21; 26:12–23), and each account provides details that are seemingly incongruent with the other accounts. On the most obvious level, Acts can't decide if Paul's traveling companions heard Jesus' words to Paul or not. In the first account of this event, they were confused because "they heard the voice but saw no one" (9:7), while in a subsequent account, those same traveling companions were

---

[56] The most useful introduction to this issue is Jack T. Sanders, "Paul's 'Autobiographical' Statements in Galatians 1–2," *JBL* 85 (1966): 335–43.

[57] Succinct introductions to scholarly approaches to this diversity can be found in N. T. Wright's *The Climax of the Covenant* (Edinburgh: T&T Clark, 1991), 1–15; and J. Christiaan Beker, "Paul the Theologian: Major Motifs in Pauline Theology," *Int* 43 (1989): 352–65.

[58] Throughout this volume, I assume the essential truth of Calvin Roetzel's thesis "that Paul did not begin his apostolic ministry with a developed theology in mind, and that he often did not know what he thought about a given subject until he faced a context that required its discussion, and the composition of a written statement. . . . Paul's theology must be viewed as an emergent theology and not a systematic theology, as an interactive theology rather than just a proclaimed theology, and as a product of a dialogue rather than a monologue" (*Paul: The Man and the Myth* [Minneapolis: Fortress, 1999], 4).

confused because they "did not hear the voice" (22:9). Acts, like Paul in the example above, uses the same term (ἀκούω) to describe both acts of hearing.[59] Although this ambiguity in Acts about who heard what is admittedly superficial, these accounts contain a much more significant incongruity. In the first two accounts, Paul was instructed to enter Damascus where he would learn what Christ wished for him to do (9:6; 22:10), but in the third account, Christ himself immediately gave Paul instructions about his future. This third account recorded no delay between Paul's Damascus road experience and Christ's instructions for his future (26:15–18). In terms of Acts' narrative, the point in each case is simply that Christ told Paul about his future proclamation and suffering, and that the subsequent events of Paul's life came as no surprise to Paul. In relative terms, whether Paul heard the message indirectly through his fellow Christian Ananias or directly through a heavenly vision is insignificant. In terms of social history, however, the origin of Paul's knowledge about his future is extremely important because it speaks to Paul's relationship to those who were Christians before him. Was Paul dependent upon Ananias for instructions about God's will or did Paul believe that he learned about God's will directly from Christ? To what extent was Paul's sense of identity and mission shaped by instruction from other Christians, and to what extent were they shaped by Paul's own sense of the divine? The diversity in Acts leaves such historical questions without compelling answers.

The problems of diversity and inconsistency are multiplied exponentially when Acts and Paul's letters are, with all of their individual diversity and inconsistencies, brought into dialogue. For example, as Knox's work so forcibly demonstrated, Acts recorded Paul making five visits to Jerusalem (9:26; 12:25; 15:2–4; 18:22; 21:15), while Paul's letters recorded only two visits (Gal 1:11–2:10) and implied a third (Rom 15:22–29; 1 Cor 16:1–4).[60] Although such incongruities within and between the texts may not be insurmountable, they do complicate any effort at historical reconstruction.

Third, the accounts in Acts and Paul's letters pose problems because they are flexible enough to allow for a diversity of plausible readings. As in any complex text, the data in Acts and Paul's letters are open to numerous readings. In one widely debated example, Acts casually reported that Paul circumcised Timothy when the pair began their work as co-missionaries (16:3) even though Paul's letters argued that "if you let yourselves be circumcised, Christ will be of no benefit to you" (Gal 5:2). On the face of it, Acts' claim that Paul himself circumcised Timothy appears hopelessly irreconcilable with Paul's explicit prohibition of circumcision in Galatians. However, even in this extreme case, the texts

---

[59] For comprehensive comparisons of these three accounts (with particular attention to the issue of hearing in these scenes), see Charles W. Hedrick, "Paul's Conversion/Call: A Comparative Analysis of the Three Reports in Acts," *JBL* 100 (1981): 415–32; and Daniel Marguerat, "Saul's Conversion (Acts 9, 22, 26) and the Multiplication of Narrative in Acts," in *Luke's Literary Achievement* (ed. Christopher M. Tuckett; JSNTSup 116; Sheffield: Sheffield Academic Press, 1995), 127–55.

[60] Knox, *Chapters*, 32–52.

allow for some flexibility of interpretation. To reconcile Acts and Paul's letters, interpreters often appeal to Paul's other commitments, recalling that Paul
himself declared, "To the Jews I became as a Jew, in order to win Jews" (1 Cor
9:20).[61] On the one hand, perhaps Paul circumcised Timothy "as a Jew" in
order to win Jews. The evidence is flexible enough to allow for the possibility—
but not the necessity—that Paul would have performed Timothy's circumcision under such circumstances. On the other hand, however, the evidence is
flexible enough to allow for the possibility—but not the necessity—that Acts
portrays Paul performing an act that he would never have performed after he
became a Christian.[62] In many cases like this one, the flexibility of the texts
allows for plausible interpretations that run directly contrary to one another.
No amount of scholarly acumen can dissipate such flexibility or the variety
of interpretations that arises from it.

Fourth, the letters and Acts contain frustrating silences. While the first three
problems for modern historians and theologians relate to the available evidence and its interpretation, this final problem relates to what those sources
omit. Examples of such silences abound. Acts mentions nothing of Paul's canonical letters; Paul's letters reveal no knowledge of John the Baptist (cf. Acts
19:3–4). Paul's letters give us no idea of the outcome of his (presumed) final
visit to Jerusalem. Neither Paul's letters nor Acts provide much information
about Paul's family (cf. Acts 23:16), his contact with the Johannine and synoptic Jesus traditions, or the length and scope of his various imprisonments.
Acts says nothing of Paul's sojourn in Arabia, and Paul's letters make only a
passing reference to Arabia (Gal 1:17). Paul's offering for Jerusalem figures
prominently in his letters, but is never explicitly mentioned in Acts. Such
silences in Paul's letters, in Acts, or in both are not easily overcome and offer
ample opportunity for even the most disciplined imagination to run amok.

Given these recurring problems, scholars often begin their discussions
of Paul with a carefully crafted discussion about their "use of sources" in their
reconstructions of Paul's life and thought. As the previous pages have demonstrated, critical approaches to the sources vary widely. Generally speaking,
however, scholars tend to locate themselves on a spectrum ranging from a
complete or nearly complete dismissal of the traditions in Acts to an eagerness
to supplement, or even correct, the traditions in Paul's letters on the basis of
the traditions in Acts.[63] On the one hand, approaches on the Acts-affirming

[61] E.g., Ben Witherington III, *The Acts of the Apostles: A Socio-Rhetorical Commentary*
(Grand Rapids: Eerdmans, 1998), 474–77; Gerd Lüdemann, *Early Christianity according to the Traditions in Acts: A Commentary* (trans. John Bowden; Minneapolis: Fortress,
1987), 173–77; and Luke Timothy Johnson, *The Acts of the Apostles* (Sacra pagina 5;
Collegeville, Minn.: Liturgical, 1992), 288.
[62] E.g., Haenchen, *Acts*, 480–82; Conzelmann, *Acts*, 125; C. K. Barrett, *The Acts of
the Apostles* (2 vols.; ICC; Edinburgh: T&T Clark, 1994–1998), 2:760–62; and Jürgen
Roloff, *Die Apostelgeschichte* (Das Neue Testament Deutsch 5; Göttingen: Vandenhoeck
& Ruprecht, 1981), 240.
[63] In addition to works previously discussed, Udo Schnelle's *Apostle Paul: His
Life and Theology* (trans. M. Eugene Boring; Grand Rapids: Baker, 2003) and Griffith-

end of the spectrum often diminish the difficulty of reconciling the Paul of the letters with the Paul of Acts. On the other hand, approaches on the Acts-dismissing end of the spectrum often leave no room for meaningful dialogue between the Paul of Acts and the Paul of the letters. Therefore, rather than locating this volume on the existing spectrum of Pauline scholarship regarding Acts, I wish to offer a different approach to thinking about the relationship between Paul and Acts.

III. A MODEST METHODOLOGICAL PROPOSAL

Although the recurring problems just discussed cannot be eliminated, they can be addressed. The goal of this chapter is to lay out an approach to the study of Paul in the letters and in Acts that confronts these recurring problems in a manner that enables disciplined and meaningful comparison between the Paul of the letters and the Paul of Acts. Scholars often deviate to the extremes, either underestimating or overestimating the difficulties of comparing the Paul of the letters to the Paul of Acts. Presentations that under-estimate the difficulties tend to gloss over the distinction between the identity of Paul in the letters and the identity of Paul in Acts. They therefore often deny each Paul a fair hearing. Presentations that overestimate the difficulties tend to ignore the substantial areas of convergence between each Paul. They therefore often fail to consider the potential benefit of gaining corroborat-ing or supplemental data from each source. In order to avoid both of these tendencies, this volume will develop a disciplined approach for comparing the Paul of the letters with the Paul of Acts. This approach will operate on the bases of four guiding principles: 1) independent inquiry into Acts and the letters; 2) intentional separation of Paul's life and thought; 3) conscious focus upon lesser data sets; 4) and disciplined comparison moving from the lesser data sets to the greater data sets.

The first two of these four principles were developed in dialogue with the Baur and Knox/Vielhauer traditions. As a positive appropriation of those traditions, the first guiding principle, *independent inquiry into Acts and the letters*, recognizes that Baur's methodological skepticism regarding the reliability of Acts offers the best protection against unconscious blending of the Paul of the letters and the Paul of Acts. Although not all of Baur's conclusions are accepted in this volume, it is assumed that Baur and his successors were wise to insist that the best way to get a clear hearing of both the Paul of Acts and the Paul of the letters is to investigate these two figures in isolation from one another. Premature and undisciplined blending of the Paul of the letters with

---

Jones' *Gospel according to Paul* provide examples of recent volumes which have drawn heavily upon Acts in their depictions of Paul. Calvin J. Roetzel's *Paul: A Jew on the Margins* (Louisville: Westminster John Knox, 2003) and John L. White's *The Apostle of God: Paul and the Promise of Abraham* (Peabody, Mass.: Hendrickson, 1999) provide examples of recent volumes which tend to disregard Acts in their depictions of Paul.

the Paul of Acts can result in a third kind of Paul, a hybrid character who lacks the distinctive elements reflected in Acts and the letters. Therefore, for the sake of clarity, each chapter within this volume will initially investigate the Paul of the letters and the Paul of Acts entirely independently of one another. This approach will initially generate two Pauline data sets, one derived from Paul's letters and one derived from Acts.

The second guiding principle of this volume, *intentional separation of Paul's life and thought*, was developed as a positive appropriation of the Knox/Vielhauer tradition. Although not all of the conclusions of the Knox/Vielhauer tradition will be accepted in this volume, it is assumed that they were wise to separate narrative questions from theological questions in their examinations of Paul.[64] There is no reason to presume that congruence between Acts and Paul's letters in the area of either Paul's life or Paul's thought necessarily implies a symmetrical congruence between Acts and the letters in the other area. Therefore, for the sake of clarity, this volume will separate—as much as possible—questions about Paul's life from questions about Paul's thought and will concern itself primarily with questions about Paul's life and relationships in the data sets of Paul's letters and Acts. Questions about the larger structure of Paul's thought in Acts and Paul's letters (i.e., the questions that most concerned Vielhauer and his successors and critics) are important, but they fall outside the scope of this volume and will have to wait for some other investigation.

By applying these first two guiding principles, therefore, this volume will generate two data sets regarding Paul's life and relationships: a data set from Acts and a data set from Paul's letters. This part of the project is a positive appropriation of the sensitivities of the Baur and Knox/Vielhauer traditions. However, in an effort to move beyond the Baur and Knox/Vielhauer traditions, this volume will also bring those two data sets into conversation with one another in order to establish dialogue between the Paul of the letters and the Paul of Acts.

Whereas the first set of guiding principles was developed in order to avoid underestimating the difficulties of comparing the Paul of the letters with the Paul of Acts, the second set of guiding principles was developed in order to avoid *over*estimating those difficulties. The Baur and Knox/Vielhauer traditions have appropriately cautioned scholars against a premature and facile blending of the Paul of the letters with the Paul of Acts, but that appropriate caution has often resulted in an unwarranted disinterest in cultivating dialogue between these two canonical figures. Accordingly, the third and fourth guiding principles for this investigation were designed to

---

[64] For a helpful example of the value of separating the narrative and discourse in Acts, see Jack T. Sanders, "The Jewish People in Luke-Acts," in *Luke-Acts and the Jewish People: Eight Critical Perspectives* (ed. Joseph B. Tyson; Minneapolis: Augsburg, 1988), 51–75.

bring the two data sets from the letters and Acts into disciplined dialogue with one another.

The third principle, *conscious focus upon the smaller data sets*, was not designed to recover everything that can be known about Paul. In fact, this principle is deliberately restrictive and was designed to limit the range of the exploration to the areas that most likely allow for meaningful comparison without resorting to speculations from silence. In order to impose discipline upon the comparison, this investigation will begin its exploration with data points found within the smaller of the two data sets—the data set from Paul's letters.

Finally, after assembling this smaller data set, this investigation will employ its fourth guiding principle and offer a *disciplined comparison moving from the lesser data sets to the greater data sets*. By allowing the smaller data set to guide and control the comparisons, this investigation will be unable to yield a comprehensive portrayal of Paul's life and relationships. Indeed, many important aspects of Paul's life will not be addressed, but this approach is designed to focus the reader's attention on only those areas within Acts and the letters where the most disciplined and meaningful examination of the relationship between the Paul of the letters and the Paul of Acts can be conducted. The remainder of this volume will, therefore, typically begin by seeking to understand various aspects of Paul's life and relationships as revealed in the smaller data set derived from Paul's letters; then it will consider whether the emergent picture of those aspects of Paul's life and relationships can be reconciled with the much larger data set of Paul's life and relationships in Acts.

∿ 3 ∾

PUTTING PAUL'S LIFE IN ORDER

OF THE writing of chronologies of Paul, the preacher of Ecclesiastes undoubtedly would tell us, there is no end—and he would be right. The preacher would likely also insist that the entire project of Pauline chronology is meaningless—and many would suspect that he was right about that too. Indeed, on one extreme, some scholars have capitulated to the complexities of developing a meaningful chronology of Paul and have insisted that any chronology of Paul's life must necessarily—and inappropriately—presume the historical accuracy of Acts. For example, Crossan and Reed, whose work figured so prominently into the first chapter of this book, rejected all attempts at a "precise Pauline chronology," insisting that such an enterprise "can only be done or even attempted by accept[ing] Lukan data . . . that is not historical."[1] On the other extreme, other scholars have insisted upon the importance—and appropriateness—of developing a Pauline chronology in dialogue with Acts. Some such scholars have even offered polemics against those who would doubt the essential accuracy of the Pauline chronology in Acts. For example, in their recent work on Paul, Martin Hengel and Anna Maria Schwemer have characterized those who doubt the essential historicity of Acts as guilty of "uncritical apologetic," "hypercritical ignorance and arrogance," and "anti-Lukan scholasticism." They complain that rejection of Luke's chronology is common only among those who are "often relatively ignorant of ancient historiography."[2]

By employing the method explained in the previous chapter, this chapter will examine what can be learned about the chronology of Paul from the smaller data set of Paul's letters and will then ask whether the chronological information from that smaller data set can be placed within the larger data set derived from Acts. Before proceeding, however, some comments are in

---

[1] John Dominic Crossan and Jonathan L. Reed, *In Search of Paul: How Jesus's Apostle Opposed Rome's Empire with God's Kingdom* (San Francisco: HarperSanFrancisco, 2004), 230. Also see Dixon Slingerland's important articles "Acts 18:1–17 and Luedemann's Pauline Chronology," *JBL* 109.4 (1990): 686–90 and "Acts 18:1–18, The Gallio Inscription, and Absolute Pauline Chronology," *JBL* 110.3 (1991): 439–49.

[2] Martin Hengel and Anna Maria Schwemer, *Paul Between Damascus and Antioch: The Unknown Years* (trans. John Bowden; Louisville: John Knox Westminster, 1997), 6–7.

order about the danger of relying upon established chronologies. The problem is simple. Even approaches that make no direct appeal to Acts often rely upon existing scholarly consensuses for the dates and order of Paul's letters. Such approaches appear to function independently of Acts until one recognizes that scholarly consensuses about the dates and order of Paul's letters are themselves almost always based, in some measure, upon Acts. Thus, preconceptions about the congruity between the Paul of the letters and the Paul of Acts often make their way into investigations about Paul through the subtle circularity of arguments based on the presumed order of Paul's letters. Because this chapter is intended to examine exactly those preconceptions about the congruity of Acts and Paul's letters, it must exclude all arguments that directly or indirectly draw upon the chronology provided in Acts.[3]

I. THE PAULINE DATA SET

Any attempt to create a chronology of Paul's life is essentially an inquiry about *places* (where did Paul go?), *order* (where did Paul go first?), and *time frames* (what amount of time passed between the respective events?). Answers to these questions are derived from two sources: *direct references* from Paul's letters and *plausible inferences* drawn from those letters. Obviously, direct references are more convincing than even the most well-founded inferences, but not even the most meticulous perusal of Paul's letters can uncover direct references that answer all of these questions. Fortunately, the letters provide a significant (but by no means complete) set of geographical references to the *places* Paul visited (both where he has been and where he wished to go). Unfortunately, however, the letters contain comparatively few direct references to the *order* in which Paul visited the respective places, and the letters relate almost nothing about the *time frames* between his respective visits.

As a warning to the reader who may become overwhelmed by the seemingly endless proliferation of detailed analyses, which seem to lend themselves to an equally profligate number of suspended judgments, let me assert in advance: a detailed Pauline chronology from the letters must depend nearly exclusively on Galatians and Romans. Those who make chronological assertions on the basis of the other letters are forced to do so by relying upon Acts, upon meager inferences from the letters, or upon both. The analysis that follows is designed to ferret out any minor chronological assertions that can be gleaned from the letters.

---

[3] For the best recent treatment of direct and indirect reliance upon Acts among interpreters of Paul, see Heikki Leppä, "Reading Galatians with and without the Book of Acts," in *The Intertextuality of the Epistles: Explorations of Theory and Practice* (ed. Thomas L. Brodie, Dennis R. MacDonald, and Stanley E. Porter; Sheffield: Sheffield Phoenix, 2006), 255–63.

Given the nature of the evidence (significant data about places, far less data concerning order, and very little data regarding time frames), it seems wise to begin with questions about the *places* that Paul visited, then to proceed with questions about the *order* of these visits, and to conclude with questions about *time frames* associated with these visits.[4] For convenience of analysis, the Pauline data set will be divided into three smaller subsets that share common geographical references. We will first consider Philippians and 1 Thessalonians, which share a common concern for travel to and from Philippi and Thessalonica in Macedonia. Following that, we will consider the Corinthian correspondence with its obvious focus upon travel to and from Corinth. Finally, we will consider Galatians and Romans, with their concern for Paul's travels to Jerusalem. (Philemon, which contains no clear geographical references and offers no significant clues for discerning Pauline chronology, will not be considered.[5])

Philippians and 1 Thessalonians

The *places* mentioned in Philippians and 1 Thessalonians and the *order* of visits can be organized into a Pauline itinerary that is easily summarized: *Philippi, Thessalonica, then Athens—and possibly back to Philippi and/or Thessalonica.*[6] Paul claims to have preached in Philippi before Thessalonica (1 Thess 2:1–2), and he states that he was in Athens after he left Thessalonica (3:1–5).[7] Paul expressed his desire (but not firm plans) to return to both Philippi (Phil 1:27) and Thessalonica (1 Thess 3:11) at some unspecified future date. Unfortunately, neither Philippians nor 1 Thessalonians gives any larger *time frame* for this Pauline itinerary. Although none of Paul's other letters specifically mentions Philippi or Thessalonica, 2 Corinthians refers to a Pauline visit to Macedonia, a visit that one may reasonably presume included the Macedo-

---

[4]Over half a century ago, Charles Buck argued that given the ambiguity of the evidence in the letters, a chronology of Paul could be developed only on the basis of one's understanding of the development of Paul's thought. Although many scholars would still agree, I have no confidence in my ability to discern Paul's "earlier" and "later" thought and will, therefore, avoid inferring an order to Paul's letters on the basis of perceived development within Paul's thought. Cf. Charles H. Buck, "The Date of Galatians," *JBL* 70 (1951): 113–22.

[5]A similar approach, using the same Pauline letters, is employed by Tatum, *New Chapters*, 4–5.

[6]Philippi and Thessalonica were about ninety miles apart along the shores of the Aegean Sea in Macedonia. Given their geographical proximity, the overwhelming probability is that Paul would have evangelized and revisited both cities in immediate temporal proximity. On the local geography, see F. F. Bruce, "St. Paul in Macedonia," *BJRL* 61 (1979): 337–54, esp. 344.

[7]Paul speaks in the first person plural ("we") about his experiences in Athens. Although he explicitly states that Timothy left Athens for Thessalonica, he also claims that "we" were left "alone" in Athens after Timothy's departure (1 Thess 3:1). It is quite possible that Silvanus, one of the co-senders of the letter (1:1), could have remained with Paul in Athens. See I. Howard Marshall, *1 and 2 Thessalonians* (NCBC; Grand Rapids: Eerdmans, 1983), 89–90.

nian cities of Philippi and Thessalonica. Paul informed the Corinthians that after a brief stay in Troas, he quickly proceeded to Macedonia (2 Cor 2:12–13; 7:5–7). This visit to Macedonia was also mentioned in the itinerary that Paul had laid out (1 Cor 16:5–6) and revised (2 Cor 1:15–16).[8]

Logically, Paul's discussion of an alteration of the Corinthian leg of this planned itinerary (2 Cor 1:15–2:1) was penned after his discussion of an anticipated visit to Corinth via Macedonia (1 Cor 16:5–6), so it seems safe to infer that at least this part of 2 Corinthians was written after 1 Corinthians.[9] If this inference is sound, then the question arises whether the Macedonian visit in 2 Corinthians records Paul's first visit to Macedonia or a subsequent visit. Paul's letters never explicitly answer this question, but the language of "passing through" (διέρχομαι) Macedonia (twice in 1 Cor 16:5) seems too casual and brief to represent an initial evangelistic effort. Additionally, Paul's plan to visit Macedonia appears in the midst of his financial appeal to the Corinthians, suggesting that Paul also expected financial support from the Macedonians. All of these considerations strongly suggest that the Pauline visit to Macedonia that is discussed in the Corinthian correspondence represents a return visit by Paul to the Thessalonian and Philippian congregations.[10] This inference of *multiple Pauline visits to the Macedonian congregations* is rendered even more likely by the fact that Paul apparently relied upon these congregations for financial support (Rom 15:26; 2 Cor 8:1; 9:2; 11:9).

In addition to offering a brief piece of Pauline itinerary (Philippi, Thessalonica, Athens—and probably back to Macedonia via Troas), these letters also offer two clues for placing that itinerary in the larger temporal framework of Paul's life. First, Paul was imprisoned for a substantial period of time after completing his initial visit to Philippi and Thessalonica. Paul repeatedly mentions the fact that he was imprisoned when he wrote at least portions of Philippians (Phil 1:7, 13–17, 20–26). This imprisonment lasted long enough for word of it to reach the Philippians (1:12–14), long enough for Paul to convert some members of his guard detail (1:13), and long enough for Paul to contemplate the possibility of a death penalty (1:20–26; 2:17). We can't know how long Paul was imprisoned, or even where he was imprisoned, but we can be confident that Paul was imprisoned after his initial visit to Macedonia and that this imprisonment lasted for an extended period of time.[11]

---

[8]The revision of the Corinthian leg of this itinerary will be considered in the subsequent discussion of the Corinthian correspondence.

[9]Second Corinthians is probably a composite letter. Although the history of the Corinthian correspondence is complex, and establishing an order for the various letters is inherently speculative, the conjectures offered here are consistent both with the letters themselves and with scholarly consensus (there is universal agreement that 1 Corinthians was composed before 2 Cor 2 and 7). The integrity of 2 Corinthians will be addressed later in this chapter.

[10]See Gordon D. Fee, *The First Epistle to the Corinthians* (NICNT; Grand Rapids: Eerdmans, 1987), 818–19.

[11]The place of Paul's imprisonment is widely debated, with Rome, Caesarea, and Ephesus the leading candidates. The suggestions of Rome and Caesarea are

Second, Paul was an active missionary for a significant, but undeter-
mined, period of time after his initial visits to the Macedonian cities of Philippi
and Thessalonica. Five pieces of evidence imply the passage of a significant
amount of time and activity after Paul's initial ministry in Philippi and Thessalonica: imprisonment, death, travel, offerings, and nostalgia. As mentioned
above, between leaving Philippi and writing Philippians, enough time passed
both for Paul to become imprisoned and for the Philippians to learn of this imprisonment (Phil 1:12–14). After Paul left Thessalonica, enough time passed
for some of the Thessalonian believers to die (1 Thess 4:13–18). After Paul
left both Philippi and Thessalonica enough time passed for Paul, Timothy,
and Epaphroditus to undertake several trips within Greece and Macedonia (1 Thess 3:1–6; Phil 2:25–30; 4:16–18).[12] The passage of time was also
required for the Macedonian congregations to gain the considerable prominence that they apparently achieved as role models in Paul's ongoing efforts
to raise funds (2 Cor 8:1; 9:2; 11:9; Rom 15:26). Perhaps most important of
all, by the time that he wrote Phil 4,[13] Paul could look back on his evangelism
in Philippi as part of the "early days" of his ministry (v. 15). This nostalgic
look back on his Philippian ministry implies that a significant amount of time
elapsed within Paul's ministry after his initial visits to Macedonia.

Therefore, from Philippians and 1 Thessalonians, we can gain a modest
amount of information about the chronology of Paul: *Philippi, Thessalonica,
Athens, imprisonment—and back to Macedonia via Troas.* We can establish no firm
time frames for these travels and events.

The Corinthian Correspondence

The Corinthian correspondence refers to several of Paul's visits to *places*
across the northeastern Mediterranean. In addition to the previously discussed

---

directly dependent upon Acts, while the Ephesus imprisonment is inferred from 1 Cor
15:32. See Gerald F. Hawthorne, *Philippians* (rev. and enl. by Ralph P. Martin; WBC
43; Nashville: Thomas Nelson, 2004), xxxix–l. In the unlikely event that Paul's reference to "Satan" preventing his travel to Thessalonica (1 Thess 2:18) refers to an
imprisonment, then Philippians and 1 Thessalonians could share a common origin.
On the perplexing reference to Satan in 1 Thessalonians, see Ernest Best, *The First and
Second Epistles to the Thessalonians* (BNTC; London: A & C Black, 1972), 126.

[12]The passage of time is more clearly indicated by Philippians than by 1 Thessalonians, but both documents give evidence that Paul remained active in other areas
long after founding these communities. On the time frames associated with Paul's
activity in Thessalonica, see J. Peter Bercovitz, "Paul and Thessalonica," PEGLMBS
10 (1990): 123–35.

[13]The integrity of Philippians has been questioned by prominent scholars. See,
e.g., Jean-François Collange, *The Epistle of Saint Paul to the Philippians* (trans. A. W.
Heathcote; London: Epworth, 1979), 3–19; *contra* Jeffrey H. Reed, "Philippians 3:1
and the Epistolary Hesitation Formulas: The Literary Integrity of Philippians, Again,"
JBL 115 (1996): 63–90; Hawthorne, *Philippians,* xxx–xxxiv; and Ralph P. Martin, *Philippians* (rev. ed.; NCBC; Grand Rapids: Eerdmans, 1980), 10–21.

references to Macedonia (1 Cor 16:5–6; 2 Cor 1:15–16; 2:12–13; 7:5; 8:1; 9:2; 11:9) and Troas (2 Cor 2:12), Paul also refers to visits and possible visits to Corinth (1 Cor 11:34; 16:3–9; 2 Cor 1:15–16; 1:23–2:1; 12:14; 13:1, 10) and Achaia (1 Cor 16:15; 2 Cor 9:2; 11:10) on the peninsula between the Adriatic and Aegean Seas, Ephesus (1 Cor 15:32; 16:8) and Galatia (1 Cor 16:1) to the east in Asia Minor (modern day Turkey),[14] and Damascus (2 Cor 11:32) and Jerusalem (1 Cor 16:3–4)[15] along the east coast of the Mediterranean.

In spite of—or perhaps because of—the large assortment of evidence to interpret in the Corinthian correspondence, it is difficult to establish a definitive *order* for the visits mentioned in these letters. This difficulty arises from the complex historical background of Paul's correspondence with the Corinthians. Uncertainties abound, but a few things are clear: Paul exchanged several letters with the Corinthians, both sending letters to the community (1 Cor 5:9; 2 Cor 2:3–11; 7:8) and receiving letters from the community (1 Cor 7:1; 2 Cor 10:9–11). In a phenomenon unique to the Corinthian correspondence, Paul even alludes sarcastically to letters the Corinthians had apparently exchanged with other Christian leaders (2 Cor 3:1–3). Although 1–2 Corinthians provide clear references to this ongoing exchange of letters, we no longer possess any of these letters except those that Paul sent to the Corinthians—and even some of those letters are probably lost. To further complicate matters, 2 Corinthians appears to be a composite of two or more letters. Opinions regarding the compositional history of 2 Corinthians vary widely[16] and apart from adherence to some particular theory of this compositional history, only limited determinations can be made regarding the order of Paul's travels.

The most important data point within the Corinthian correspondence is that Paul visited Corinth twice and planned to visit the city a third time. Although Paul apparently altered his travel plans in midcourse, at some point he did accomplish a return trip to Corinth—a visit that seems to have been

---

[14] In 2 Cor 1:8, Paul mentions hardships that he faced in Asia Minor without further clarifying the exact location of these life-threatening hardships. Ephesus is a likely candidate (1 Cor 15:32; 16:8).

[15] In 2 Cor 1:15–16, Paul mentions a planned visit to Judea without further clarifying an exact location within Judea. Jerusalem is the most likely candidate (1 Cor 16:3–4).

[16] J. Paul Sampley, "The Second Letter to the Corinthians: Introduction, Commentary, and Reflections," *The New Interpreter's Bible* 11:5–12; Victor Paul Furnish, *II Corinthians* (AB 32A; Garden City: Doubleday, 1984), 29–55; and Ralph P. Martin, *2 Corinthians* (WBC 40; Waco: Word, 1986), xxxviii–lii, represent the most common scholarly opinions in their discernment of two letters (chs. 1–9 and chs. 10–13) within the canonical 2 Corinthians. Also see Paul Barnett, *The Second Epistle to the Corinthians* (NICNT; Grand Rapids: Eerdmans, 1997), 17–25, who defends the integrity of the canonical 2 Corinthians; and Hans Dieter Betz, *2 Corinthians 8 and 9* (ed. George W. MacRae; Hermeneia; Philadelphia: Fortress, 1985), 129–49; and N. H. Taylor, "The Composition and Chronology of Second Corinthians," *JSNT* 44 (1991): 67–87, who argue that 2 Corinthians is composed of at least five letters or letter fragments.

unpleasant (2 Cor 13:2). In spite of a disagreeable second visit and a previously aborted visit (2 Cor 1:13–2:1), Paul remained committed to completing a third visit to Corinth (2 Cor 12:14; 13:1, 10). Therefore, we may confidently assert that the order of Paul's interaction with Corinth was *his first visit, the composition of 1 Corinthians, his second visit to Corinth, the composition of much or all of 2 Corinthians, and his plan for a third visit to Corinth.* We may also assert that Paul *visited Troas and Macedonia between his first and third visits to Corinth,* that is, between his composition of 1 Corinthians and his composition of much or all of 2 Corinthians (2 Cor 7:2–7).

Additionally, on the basis of the rather safe inference that 1 Corinthians was written before Paul's second trip to Corinth, Paul's Corinthian-derived itinerary can be expanded even further east to Galatia and Ephesus. We can be confident that Paul had visited Galatia before his second visit to Corinth because, while exhorting the Corinthians to participate in an offering, Paul reminded them of the instructions that he had previously given the Galatians (1 Cor 16:1). The delivery of these instructions, whether in person or via a letter, demonstrates the existence of a community of Pauline Christians in Galatia by the time Paul wrote 1 Corinthians. We can likewise be confident that Paul had visited Ephesus at least once before composing 1 Corinthians, because Paul mentioned having battled "wild animals" in Ephesus (1 Cor 15:32).[17] Paul may even have visited Ephesus more than once before composing 1 Corinthians; we may infer this from his plan to "remain in Ephesus until Pentecost" (1 Cor 16:8).[18] This reference almost certainly indicates that Paul was writing from Ephesus. Thus, Paul had clearly visited Ephesus once (and perhaps more than once if the Pentecost and beastly visits were different events) by the time he wrote 1 Corinthians, that is, before his second visit to Corinth.

The problem for understanding the order of Paul's travels lies not in placing at least one visit to both Ephesus and Galatia before Paul's second visit to Corinth, but rather in determining when Paul's second visit to Corinth occurred. In order to place this visit to Corinth in context, one must understand that in 1 Corinthians Paul had anticipated passing through Macedonia *before visiting Corinth.* Paul's itinerary in 1 Corinthians is clear: Ephesus, Macedonia, Corinth (1 Cor 16:5–8). However, from reading 2 Corinthians, we learn that after planning this Ephesus, Macedonia, Corinth itinerary, Paul apparently changed his mind and decided to visit the Corinthians both *before and after visiting Macedonia* (2 Cor 1:16–18). To further complicate matters, it seems that Paul also failed to complete this revised itinerary to the Corinthians' satisfaction (1:17–23). These planned and revised second and third visits to Corinth

---

[17] Although some people have argued that Paul fought literal beasts in the arena at Ephesus, the reference is probably metaphorical. See Robert E. Osborne, "Paul and the Wild Beasts," *JBL* 85 (1966): 225–30.

[18] On Ephesus as the likely place of composition for 1 Corinthians, see Hans Conzelmann, *1 Corinthians: A Commentary on the First Epistle to the Corinthians* (ed. George W. MacRae; trans. James Leitch; Hermeneia; Philadelphia: Fortress, 1975), 4–5.

create several ambiguities, and Victor Paul Furnish is undoubtedly correct to conclude that there are "no certain answers" to the chronological questions that surround Paul's revised itinerary in 2 Corinthians.[19]

In any reconstruction of the order of Paul's travels to Corinth, every-thing hangs on the timing of his second visit to Corinth and, unfortunately, Paul's revisions to his plans in 2 Corinthians make his precise activities un-clear. Part of the problem is that Paul talked about what he wanted to do and what he did not do more than he talked about what he did do. Paul "wanted" (βούλομαι) to make a double visit to Corinth (2 Cor 1:15–16). Paul did not "come again" and "make another painful visit" to Corinth (1:23; 2:1). In the first half of 2 Corinthians, Paul never explicitly stated when—or if—he visited Corinth for the second time.[20] Paul's primary concern was to discuss what he did not do, that is, make "another" visit to Corinth (1:12–2:13). When Paul finally explained what he did do, he made no reference to Corinth, but rather referred to a visit to Troas (a city not mentioned in his original itiner-ary, 1 Cor 16:5–9) and Macedonia (2 Cor 2:12–13). Several interpretations of this evidence are possible.[21] Paul could have abandoned his revised plan to visit Corinth before and after visiting Macedonia and simply reverted to his original plan of visiting Corinth only after Macedonia. Paul could have visited Corinth before Macedonia and then cancelled his post-Macedonian visit to Corinth. Or, if 2 Corinthians is a composite letter, Paul could have revisited Corinth months or even years after his Macedonian visit. In the absence of reliance upon either Acts or a theory regarding the compositional history of 2 Corinthians, one cannot establish a decisive order of Paul's travels.

Therefore, in regard to the order of Paul's travels in the Corinthian correspondence, caution is warranted. We must be ever mindful that Paul apparently made plans, revised those plans, and then failed to complete those revised plans. However, even while employing great methodological caution, on the basis of the Corinthian correspondence we may confidently assert, first, that *Paul visited Ephesus, Galatia, Macedonia (presumably Philippi and Thes-salonica), and Corinth before visiting Corinth the second time.* We can know neither

---

[19]Furnish, *II Corinthians*, 143. In the absence of a theory regarding the compo-sitional history of 2 Corinthians it is impossible to establish where Paul went after his second visit to Corinth or how much time passed between his second visit and his plan for a third visit.

[20]The references which clearly presume Paul's second visit to Corinth all fall in the closing chapters of 2 Corinthians (12:14; 13:1, 10), chapters which are widely believed to derive from a separate letter.

[21]In the most likely reconstruction, Paul completed the first half of his double visit, but the Corinthians were offended by his unanticipated visit. The unpleasant-ness of this second (pre-Macedonian) visit may have then prompted Paul to postpone his third visit in order to avoid "another painful visit" (2 Cor 2:1), forcing Paul to explain both why he had visited them "first" (before going to Macedonia) and why he appeared to be "vacillating" (by not returning to Corinth to complete his double visit) (2 Cor 1:15, 17). See Gordon D. Fee, "ΧΑΡΙΣ in II Corinthians I.15: Apostolic Parousia and Paul—Corinth Chronology," *NTS* 24 (1978): 533–38.

the order of Paul's visits to these places nor exactly what events transpired between his first and his planned third visits to Corinth, but we can confidently assert, second, that *Paul revisited Macedonia (presumably Philippi and Thessalonica) via Troas before his planned third visit to Corinth.*

With both the order of Paul's visits before his second visit to Corinth and the timing of this second visit to Corinth so indefinite, it is impossible to establish any *time frame* for these events on the basis of the letters. Only a few very general observations are possible. *Paul had been a Christian and a missionary for a significant period of time before composing the Corinthian correspondence.* We may infer that Paul had been a Christian (but not necessarily in relationship with the Corinthians) for at least fourteen years before he penned the closing chapters to 2 Corinthians because he boasted of a particularly impressive vision that he had experienced fourteen years earlier (2 Cor 12:2).[22] Paul's lengthy career as a Christian missionary is likewise presumed by Paul's extensive list of hardships. Paul boasted:

> Five times I have received from the Jews the forty lashes minus one. Three times I was beaten with rods. Once I received a stoning. Three times I was shipwrecked; for a night and a day I was adrift at sea; on frequent journeys, in danger from rivers, danger from bandits, danger from my own people, danger from Gentiles, danger in the city, danger in the wilderness, danger at sea, danger from false brothers and sisters. . . . (2 Cor 11:24–26)[23]

Although Paul's list undoubtedly is organized topically and not chronologically, a significant amount of time and travel was needed in order for Paul to experience this list of humiliations, which included several imprisonments (11:23).[24]

The Corinthian correspondence also reflects an extended period of interaction between Paul and the Corinthians, probably several years. Paul claimed to have been the first person to preach in Corinth (2 Cor 10:14), but by the time he composed 1 Corinthians several other prominent ministers had visited Corinth (1 Cor 1:10–3:23). At very least, Peter and Apollos spent time in Corinth after Paul's departure (1 Cor 1:12). When Paul composed 1 Corinthians, he was

---

[22] Apart from an appeal to Acts, there is no way to clarify when this event took place (at the beginning or near the middle of Paul's Christian life) or to speculate upon the content of this vision. However, in spite of Paul's third person reference to "a man," Sampley is undoubtedly correct to assert that "there can be no doubt that the man is Paul." See his "Second Letter to the Corinthians," 162; *contra* Michael Goulder, "Vision and Knowledge," *JSNT* 56 (1994): 53–71.

[23] Paul's letters never clarify when Paul suffered these humiliations. Robert E. Osborne makes the perhaps exaggerated claim that Paul suffered these humiliations before he composed any of his letters and before Barnabas and Paul became missionary partners in Acts 11:25. Even with this extremely restricted time frame, Osborne suggests the passage of eight years is indicated by these verses. See "St. Paul's Silent Years," *JBL* 84 (1965): 59–65.

[24] On Paul's scars as symbols of humiliation, not honor, see Jennifer A. Glancy, "Boasting of Beatings (2 Corinthians 11:23–25)," *JBL* 123 (2004): 99–135.

aware of tensions among the Corinthians over misguided loyalties both to these ministers and to himself. He condemned the resulting divisions within the Corinthian community without criticizing the other preachers (1:10–17). However, by the time that he composed 2 Corinthians, Paul excoriated those whom he called "super-apostles" (2 Cor 11:5; 12:11). Between the composition of 1 and 2 Corinthians, Paul's attitude toward the other preachers changed from a rebuke of the Corinthians for their misguided loyalties to these other preachers to a polemical attack upon the preachers themselves. We cannot know whether these super-apostles included Peter and Apollos or if the super-apostles were a completely separate group of people,[25] but the passage of time can be inferred both from the presence of various other ministers in Corinth and from Paul's change of attitude toward these other ministers.

Few elements in the Corinthian correspondence define the time span of Paul's interaction with the Corinthians or even relate the events in these letters to the other events in Paul's life. *Perhaps the most important elements that link the Corinthian correspondence to Paul's other letters are the references to the offering for Jerusalem* (1 Cor 16:3–4; 2 Cor 1:15–16; 2 Cor 8–9). Paul mentions the offering in both letters, and in 2 Corinthians he even mentions that the Corinthians had an offering on hand "since last year" (2 Cor 9:2). It is impossible to know if this offering was only one of many or if it was the culmination of one long fund-raising campaign, but if all of these references to an offering in the Corinthian correspondence are interpreted as references to a single great offering for Jerusalem (an interpretation the letters favor, but do not require[26]), then the Corinthian correspondence may be inferred to derive from the later stages of Paul's career when the eastern Mediterranean no longer offered him a place for service and he planned to travel further west to Spain after delivering the offering to Jerusalem (Rom 15:22–32).[27]

Also in regard to time frames, the Corinthian correspondence recounts the only event within Paul's letters that can be related to datable events in the Greco-Roman world, the period in which Aretas IV was ethnarch in Damascus (2 Cor 11:32). Although the reference is ambiguous enough to allow for diverse interpretations, this datum, which is sometimes called the "anchor" of Pauline chronology, can confidently be dated in the mid-to-late 30s.[28] Although this date provides no assistance in placing the much later

---

[25] On the plausible interpretations, see Furnish, *II Corinthians*, 502–5.

[26] See Jouette M. Bassler, *God and Mammon: Asking for Money in the New Testament* (Nashville: Abingdon, 1991), 89–115.

[27] On the offering as a decisive and culminating event in Paul's ministry in Romans, see C. E. B. Cranfield, *A Critical and Exegetical Commentary on the Epistle to the Romans* (2 vols.; ICC 32; Edinburgh: T&T Clark, 1975–1979), 2:770–71.

[28] See Douglas A. Campbell, "An Anchor for Pauline Chronology: Paul's Flight from 'The Ethnarch of King Aretas' (2 Corinthians 11:32–33)," *JBL* 121 (2002): 279–302, esp. 298. Although Campbell has demonstrated that the date of 36 C.E. is quite likely, that date is not beyond dispute. Contrast Justin Taylor, "The Ethnarch of King Aretas at Damascus: A Note on 2 Cor 11, 32–33," *RB* 99 (1992): 719–28; and Jewett, *Chronology of Paul's Life*, 30–33, who argue for a date between 37 and 39 C.E.

Corinthian-derived itineraries within any clearly datable context, it provides both an approximate date for Paul's earliest ministry and a date that will help with the subsequent analysis of Galatians.

It is difficult to relate these pieces of Corinthian itinerary (Ephesus, Galatia, Macedonia [presumably including Philippi and Thessalonica], and Corinth before visiting Corinth the second time and a return to Macedonia [presumably including Philippi and Thessalonica] via Troas before his planned third visit to Corinth) to the itinerary derived from Philippians and 1 Thessalonians (Philippi, Thessalonica, Athens, imprisonment—and back to Macedonia via Troas). The only common piece in the itineraries is the Macedonia via Troas piece of the itinerary, and it is unclear in the Corinthian correspondence how this leg of Paul's itinerary and revised itinerary relates to Paul's second visit to Corinth.

Therefore, from the Corinthian correspondence, we can gain a modest amount of information about the chronology of Paul: Paul visited Corinth twice and planned a third visit. He visited Ephesus, Macedonia, and Galatia before his second visit to Corinth and revisited Macedonia (via Troas) between his first and third visits to Corinth. We can establish no meaningful time frame for these travels and events, other than the observation that much or all of the Corinthian correspondence was composed after Paul had been both a Christian and a missionary for several years, at least fourteen years according to 2 Cor 12:2.

Romans and Galatians

The *places* mentioned in Romans and Galatians span a larger geographical area than the ones mentioned in Paul's other letters; Paul refers to places throughout the entire northern and eastern shores of the Mediterranean. An orientation to these places can begin with the extreme southeastern corner of the Mediterranean Basin and move in a counterclockwise direction around the Mediterranean. Along the eastern coast of the Mediterranean, we encounter Arabia (Gal 1:17), Jerusalem and the surrounding area of Judea (Rom 15:25, 26, 31; Gal 1:17, 22; 2:1), and Damascus (Gal 1:17) as well as Antioch and the surrounding area in Syria (Gal 1:21; Gal 2:11). Turning west, along the northern coast of the Mediterranean in modern day Turkey, we have Cilicia (Gal 1:21) and Asia Minor (Rom 16:5). Across the Aegean Sea on the Greek Peninsula, we encounter Macedonia (Rom 15:26) as well as Achaia (Rom 15:26) and Cenchreae (Rom 16:1) to the south. Northeast of the Greek Peninsula, we have Illyricum (Rom 15:19) just across the Adriatic Sea from Rome. Further east, across the Adriatic Sea, we have Rome on the Italian Peninsula (Rom 1:10–11, 15; 15:24) and finally Spain in Western Europe (Rom 15:24, 28).

Unlike the Corinthian correspondence, the Pauline itinerary in these letters is easily reconstructed. In Galatians, Paul insisted that the *order* of his visits was Arabia (1:17), Damascus (1:17), Jerusalem (1:18), Syria and Cilicia (1:21),

Jerusalem again (2:1), and then Antioch (2:11). Throughout these verses, Paul makes no claim to provide an exhaustive account of his travels. However, he does claim to provide a true account ("I do not lie"; 1:20)—and Paul should be trusted in his itinerary for pragmatic reasons. In this rhetorical situation, Paul probably could not afford to get caught in a lie. Even if Paul would have been willing to lie in spite of such a solemn oath,[29] he was undoubtedly aware that his opponents could easily fact-check his story and entirely discredit him if they found any inaccuracies. Because Paul's credibility as an apostle relied upon the accuracy of his claims, his claims can be trusted.[30]

In Romans, the order of Paul's intended travel is also equally clear—even though Romans offers only future travel plans, not a summary of past travels as in Galatians. Of course, we know from the Corinthian correspondence that Paul could change his plans. Nevertheless, Paul was writing from somewhere east of Rome (Rom 15:23), probably Corinth,[31] and was planning to travel first to Jerusalem (15:25) and then to Rome and on to Spain (15:23–24). This trip to Rome was to be his first visit to Rome (1:10–13), but not his first trip to Jerusalem. Paul claims to have proclaimed the gospel from Jerusalem in the east to Illyricum in the west (15:19). Because he desired to preach only where Christ had not already been preached, he believed that he had exhausted his preaching opportunities in "these regions" (15:20–22), and he planned to venture into Spain after his projected trip to Jerusalem. Even though Paul feared a hostile reception in Judea, his projected itinerary was clear. His past travels had taken him from Jerusalem to Illyricum; his future plans were to visit Jerusalem, Rome, and Spain in that order.

The general *time frames* for the pieces of itinerary in Galatians are clearer than are the pieces of itinerary in Paul's other letters. Even though this book undoubtedly leaves significant gaps in Paul's itinerary, Galatians places many events—particularly Paul's first two visits to Jerusalem—in helpful chronological relationships to one another. In Galatians 1–2, after accepting his divine

---

[29] On the forensic background of Paul's claim to truthfulness, see J. Paul Sampley, " 'Before God, I Do Not Lie' (Gal. 1.20): Paul's Self-Defence in the Light of Roman Legal Praxis," *NTS* 23 (1976–1977): 477–82; *contra* Sanders, "Paul's 'Autobiographical' Statements."

[30] Gerd Lüdemann is correct to note that "Paul had to provide absolutely correct information at *one* point in order to retain credibility, namely, when stating the number of visits to Jerusalem." See *Studies in Chronology*, 39 n. 74, emphasis Lüdemann's; *contra* Sanders, "Paul's 'Autobiographical' Statements." On the purpose of Pauline autobiography as persuasive rather than forensic, see George Lyons, *Pauline Autobiography: Toward a New Understanding* (SBLDS 73; Atlanta: Scholars Press, 1985); Beverly Roberts Gaventa, "Galatians 1 and 2: Autobiography as Paradigm," *NovT* 28 (1986): 309–26; and James D. Hester, "Epideictic Rhetoric and Persona in Galatians 1 and 2," in *The Galatians Debate: Contemporary Issues in Rhetorical and Historical Interpretation* (ed. Mark D. Nanos; Peabody, Mass.: Hendrickson, 2002), 181–96. Also see Johan S. Vos, who argues for a mixed genre ("Paul's Argumentation in Galatians 1–2," in Nanos, *Galatians Debate*, 169–80).

[31] On Corinth as the likely place for the composition of Romans, see Joseph A. Fitzmyer, *Romans* (AB 33; New York: Doubleday, 1993), 85–87, 750.

call to be an apostle to the Gentiles (1:13–14), Paul traveled to Arabia and Damascus (vv. 15–17). Then, after three years (or perhaps during the third year),[32] he briefly visited Jerusalem (vv. 18–20)[33] where he claimed to encounter only Peter and James.[34] Unfortunately, we can't know if Paul traveled to Jerusalem three years after his call to the Gentiles or three years after his return to Damascus.[35] In any case, he eventually traveled to Cilicia and Syria (vv. 21–24). In Gal 2, Paul picks up his story fourteen years later, when he again visited Jerusalem and garnered the approval of the leaders of the Jerusalem church (vv. 1–10). Again, unfortunately, we can't be sure when to begin counting these fourteen years.[36] Paul's autobiographical remarks in Gal 2 conclude with his account of a conflict that later took place between himself and Peter in Antioch (vv. 11–14). The amount of time that passed between this confrontation and the composition of Galatians remains unknown, but presumably was not very extensive. Accordingly, Paul's itinerary, including time frames, according to Galatians is as follows: Early in his career, Paul visited Damascus, Arabia and Damascus again, then Jerusalem (with probably no more than three years passing between his first [or second] trip to Damascus and his first trip to Jerusalem, which itself lasted only fifteen days). Then, as early as fourteen years after his life-altering call to preach to the Gentiles or as late as fourteen years after his first journey to Jerusalem, Paul returned to Jerusalem after spending at least some of the intervening years in Syria and Cilicia (but no time at all in Judea between his first [brief] and second [perhaps longer] visits to Jerusalem). At some indeterminate point subsequent to his second trip to Jerusalem, Paul came into conflict with Peter while both were in Antioch (in Syria).

---

[32] Paul may have used an inclusive method of counting in which partial years were counted as complete years, in which case the total elapsed time could have been less than two years. This problem has long been widely recognized (e.g., George S. Duncan, *The Epistle of Paul to the Galatians* [Moffatt New Testament Commentary; New York: Harper & Brothers, 1934], 31).

[33] Jerome Murphy-O'Connor has convincingly argued, against generally held assumptions, that only a small portion of these three years could have been spent in Arabia, given the political and military tension between the Nabataeans in Arabia and the Jews in this period ("Paul in Arabia," *CBQ* 55 [1993]: 732–37).

[34] The text is ambiguous, but it is likely that Paul regarded both Peter and James as apostles. See J. C. O'Neill, "The History and Pre-History of a Text: Gal. 1:19," *Irish Biblical Studies* 21 (1999): 40–45.

[35] In addition to the ambiguity of the event from which to begin counting the three years, dating Paul's first visit to Jerusalem is also complicated by the fact that Gal 1:15 allows for the possibility of a brief period of time between Paul's conversion to Christ and Paul's call to preach to the Gentiles. See John Knox, "On the Meaning of Galatians 1:15," *JBL* 106 (1987): 301–4.

[36] Hans Dieter Betz opts for a seventeen-year reading of Paul's Christian life before his second visit to Jerusalem, but only after admitting that "we are left in the dark whether we should begin counting the 14 years with the last 'then' (1:21, the visit to Syria and Cilicia), with the first journey to Jerusalem (1:18), or with Paul's vision of Christ (1:15)" (*Galatians: A Commentary on Paul's Letter to the Churches in Galatia* [Hermeneia; Minneapolis: Fortress, 1979], 83–84.)

Although Paul's intended itinerary is clear in Romans—he has preached throughout the eastern and northeastern Mediterranean basin, and he intends to visit Rome after leaving his present location in Corinth and returning to Jerusalem—Paul provides no explicit time frames for these travels. Although Romans is generally assumed to be the last of Paul's seven undisputed letters, the book offers little help in establishing Pauline time frames unless one is willing to draw upon Acts. However, given the expanse of the territory that Paul has already covered and his "many years" of previously unfulfilled desires to visit Rome (Rom 1:10–11; 15:23), we may safely infer that Romans was written after Paul had been a missionary for several years. The passage of a significant period is also indicated by the lengthy list of greetings in the closing chapter of Romans.[37] At the very least, Paul planned to visit Rome after he had established converts in Macedonia who were committed enough to Paul to support a Pauline offering for Jerusalem (15:26). Perhaps the strongest evidence that Romans was written toward the end of Paul's life is his comment that there was nowhere left for him to preach "in these regions" (15:23). On the reasonable assumption that Paul wrote Romans from Corinth (Rom 16:23; 1 Cor 1:14), "these regions" probably refers to the eastern Mediterranean from Judea in the southeast to Macedonia in the north central Mediterranean.[38] It is unclear why Paul "no longer" found room to work in these areas,[39] but as James Dunn has noted, by the time that Paul wrote Romans, "for whatever reason, no longer available to us, Paul fixed his sights on Spain."[40]

Summary of the Pauline Data Set

In the absence of the reliance upon Acts, the Pauline data sets offer little hope of creating a definitive chronology of Paul's activities. The data sets sometimes overlap in regard to the *places* Paul visited, but they seldom

---

[37] Even if some of the greetings belonged to Tertius, Paul's scribe, it is still safe to assume that it would have taken a considerable amount of time to become acquainted with such a geographically diverse group of believers. On the status of Rom 16 as an integral part of the letter as Paul conceived it and on the role of Tertius, see Robert Jewett, *Romans* (Hermeneia; Minneapolis: Fortress, 2007), 8–9, 951–55.

[38] For more precise descriptions of the geographical scope of Paul's reference to "these regions," see Cranfield, *Romans*, 2:766–67.

[39] Paul J. Achtemeier has argued that Paul wrote Romans after being forced to move west into Spain by the rejection of his message in the eastern empire ("An Elusive Unity: Paul, Acts, and the Early Church," *CBQ* 48 [1986]: 1–26; and *The Quest for Unity in the New Testament Church: A Study in Paul and Acts* [Philadelphia: Fortress, 1987]). Even if Achtemeier's historical reconstruction is correct, it seems unlikely that a forced departure from the east is something Paul would have acknowledged to the church in Rome—a church that he had never visited and a church from which he desired financial support.

[40] James D. G. Dunn, *Romans 9–16* (WBC 38b; Waco: Word, 1988), 881. Many scholars, including Dunn (881–82), speculate that Paul was rushing to preach the gospel in every nation before the *parousia*. This idea is soundly refuted by Cranfield, *Romans*, 2:767–78.

provide clear overlap in terms of the *order* of Paul's visits to the respective cities. The letters provide even less evidence by which to establish the *time frames* separating Paul's visits to the respective cities. We can, however, glean important bits of information from the letters that will form useful points of comparison with the more extensive chronology of Acts.

In regard to *places*, the data sets from Paul's letters overlap in relation to four places: Damascus, Jerusalem, Corinth, and Macedonia. Unfortunately, none of these overlapping references is decisive in establishing a coherent *order* for Paul's travels. Both 2 Corinthians and Galatians mention Damascus, with 2 Corinthians even providing a roughly datable reference to Aretas IV. However, it is unclear if this visit is the first or second visit to Damascus as implied by Galatians. At most, one can assert that Paul visited Damascus early in his missionary career. Both Galatians and Romans discuss Pauline visits to Jerusalem. However, nothing in the context clearly indicates whether Paul's anticipated visit to Jerusalem in Romans refers to either of his visits to Jerusalem that were so important to Paul's chronology in Galatians. More difficult, Romans places Paul's anticipated Jerusalem visit between visits to Corinth and Rome, while Galatians places Paul's second Jerusalem visit between visits to Syria and Cilicia on the one hand and Antioch (in Syria) on the other hand. Because Paul had already preached in Jerusalem before writing Romans, the Jerusalem visit in Romans cannot be Paul's first visit to Jerusalem as recorded in his Galatians itinerary. Because the itinerary associated with Paul's anticipated Jerusalem visit in Romans does not appear to coincide with Paul's second Jerusalem visit as recorded in Galatians, it seems unlikely that the Jerusalem visit anticipated in Romans should be identified with the second Jerusalem visit in Galatians. Therefore, although it is possible that Paul wrote Romans before his second trip to Jerusalem, the most plausible conclusion is that Romans refers to a later (third?) Jerusalem visit that was planned after the composition of Galatians.

Paul's references to his visits to Corinth and to Macedonia are more likely to correlate to one another than are his references to Damascus and Jerusalem. Again assuming that Paul wrote Romans from Corinth, it is quite possible that this letter was composed as he prepared for his third visit to Jerusalem. Given the late date implied by Romans, it may be reasonably—but not conclusively—inferred that Romans was composed during Paul's third visit to Corinth. Of course, it is also possible that Romans was composed during either an earlier stay in Corinth or an otherwise unknown fourth visit to Corinth. Perhaps the most direct correlation between the pieces of itinerary in Paul's letters can be established in relationship to Macedonia. Both the Corinthian correspondence on the one hand and Philippians and 1 Thessalonians on the other hand refer to a return Pauline visit to Macedonia (via Troas), but even in this case, it remains unclear in the Corinthian correspondence how this leg of Paul's itinerary and revised itinerary relates to Paul's second visit to Corinth.

With the order of Paul's travels so uncertain, it is impossible to establish any meaningful time frames for Paul's travels beyond the somewhat ambiguous information supplied in Galatians 1–2. The biggest obstacle to constructing a Pauline chronology exclusively from the letters is determining whether Paul evangelized Macedonia and Achaia before or after his second visit to Jerusalem (Gal 2:1).[41] On the basis of the letters alone, no definitive answer is possible.[42] At this point, it appears that Crossan and Reed are correct. A definitive Pauline chronology cannot be constructed without the assistance of Acts. However, our concern here is not the creation of a complete Pauline chronology, but merely to discern what pieces of Pauline chronology can be established from Paul's letters and then to compare those pieces with the larger data set from Acts. We now turn to a consideration of that larger data set.

II. The Acts Data Set

The data set in Acts is easily summarized. Since the data in Acts is derived from narrative rather than from the miscellaneous personal references found in Paul's letters, there is no need to distinguish between *places* and *order* as in Paul's letters. Assuming that the narrative order in Acts implies a chronological order, then the order in which the places appear in the narrative conveys the order in which the visits occurred. The question of *time frames* is less straightforward. Although Acts provides significantly more references to datable events from the Greco-Roman world than do Paul's letters, even in Acts, the time frames between events often remain unspecified and imprecise. When read in isolation from Paul's letters, Acts leaves considerable uncertainties regarding time frames. Nonetheless, in keeping with the approach established earlier in this chapter, this examination will begin by chronicling the places and order of events in Acts and will then turn to a separate consideration of possible time frames for these Pauline travels.

In establishing the *places and order* of Paul's travels according to Acts, it is probably not insignificant that Paul first appears in Acts (as the non-Christian "Saul") in Jerusalem (8:1). After receiving a divine call to preach to the Gentiles, Saul traveled to Damascus (9:1–2), Jerusalem (9:26), the coastal city of Caesarea, and—presumably by sea—Tarsus in Asia Minor (9:30). After a brief absence from the narrative, Saul reappears when he and Barnabas traveled from Tarsus to Antioch in Syria (11:25). After visiting Antioch, Saul traveled to Judea (11:29–30), while Peter and James were suffering persecution in Jerusalem (12:1–23). Saul ultimately arrived at ("returned" to) Jerusalem only after

---

[41] On the significance of this problem, see Niels Hyldahl, "Historische und theologische Beobachtungen zum Galterbrief," *NTS* 46 (2000): 425–44.

[42] The best overview and analysis of the two main options for developing a "letters only" chronology remains J. Peter Bercovitz, "Two Letters Chronologies," *PEGLBS* 9 (1989): 178–94. Bercovitz follows John Knox and argues for Paul's missionary activity in Macedonia and Achaia before his second visit to Jerusalem (in spite of the opposite chronology in Acts 15–18). Also see Tatum, *New Chapters*, 123–24.

James's death and Peter's release from prison (12:25). It is difficult to discern whether Acts imagines Saul residing in Jerusalem during this persecution or whether Acts imagines Saul—in keeping with the verb ὑποστρέφω—arriving at Jerusalem, leaving Jerusalem to distribute funds in the surrounding area of Judea, and then returning to Jerusalem again only after completing his "mission" elsewhere in Judea (12:25).[43] In any case, Saul was present in Antioch in the next scene (13:1–3). From Antioch, Saul traveled to Seleucia (13:4), Salamis (13:5) and Paphos on the island of Cyprus (where Saul assumed the name "Paul," 13:6, 9[44]), Perga in Pamphylia (13:13), Antioch in Pisidia (13:14), Iconium (13:51), and Lystra and Derbe in Lycaonia (14:6). Retracing many of his earlier steps, Paul then revisited Iconium and Antioch in Pisidia (14:21), Pamphylia (14:24), Attalia (14:25), and finally Antioch in Syria (14:26).

From there, Paul passed through Phoenicia and Samaria on his way to Jerusalem (15:2–3) before again returning to Antioch (14:22, 30, 35). In rapid narrative succession, Paul then proceeded to visit Syria and Cilicia (15:41), Derbe and Lystra again (16:1), Phrygia and Galatia (16:6), and Macedonia via Troas (16:8–9). On the way to Macedonia, Paul stopped by the island of Samothrace (16:11), and in Macedonia he visited Neapolis (16:11), Philippi (16:12), Amphipolis (17:1), Apollonia (17:1), Thessalonica (17:1), and Beroea (17:10). Paul eventually ended up further south in Athens (17:15), Corinth (18:1), and Cenchreae (18:18). Then, in another sea voyage, Paul traveled to Ephesus (18:19) and Caesarea (18:22) before returning to the land for travel to Jerusalem (18:22), Antioch (18:22), Galatia (18:23), Phrygia (18:23), and Ephesus (19:1). Paul then traveled to Macedonia (20:1), Greece (20:2–3), Philippi, and Troas (20:6) before moving rapidly through a series of cities and sea ports (Assos, Mitylene, Samos, and Miletus) and ultimately to Jerusalem (20:14–16). Paul's journey also continued speedily through Cos, Rhodes, Patara (21:1), Tyre (21:3), Ptolemais (21:7), Caesarea (21:8) and back to Jerusalem again (21:17). From there, Paul was taken back to Caesarea (23:33). Finally, Paul is taken on a long voyage to Rome via Myra in Lycia (27:5), Lasea (27:8), Malta (28:1), Syracuse (28:12), Rhegium (28:13), and Puteoli (28:13). Acts ends with Paul in Rome (28:16–31).[45]

---

[43]This confusion regarding Saul's presence in Jerusalem is reflected in the diverse manuscript traditions associated with this verse. Various texts record Saul returning εἰς or ἐξ or ἀπὸ Ἰερουσαλήμ ("into" or "out of" or "from" Jerusalem). The differences for our present purposes are minor. On the textual variants, see Barrett, *Acts*, 1:595–96. This issue will be revisited when the time frames of Acts are considered below.

[44]The rationale for Saul's name change (e.g., different names in different sources, a desire to impress Sergius Paulus, a desire to reject identification with the biblical King Saul) remains unclear. For a brief summary of contemporary suggestions, see Sean M. McDonough, "Small Change: Saul to Paul, Again," *JBL* 125 (2006): 390–91. The classic study by G. A. Harrer remains valuable ("Saul Who Also Is Called Paul," *HTR* 33 [1940]: 19–33).

[45]The best introduction to the locations, cultures, and relative distances of the cities that Paul is reported to have visited in Acts is found in Eckhard J. Schnabel, *Paul*

As mentioned earlier, Acts is largely silent about *time frames* throughout most of the Pauline narrative (particularly in the early portions of the narrative). Acts provides few substantial clues by which plausible inferences can be drawn regarding time frames for Paul's career before Acts 17. The only exceptions to this early narrative silence regarding time frames appear in Acts 11 and 12 where the narrator mentions that a famine occurred throughout "the whole world" during Claudius's reign (11:28) and that Paul visited Judea (maybe even Jerusalem) during Herod's (Agrippa's) persecution of the church just before Herod's death (12:1, 20–25). Unfortunately, these references to Roman rulers are not of tremendous significance. In regard to Claudius, the issue of dating is complicated by three factors. First, Claudius ruled several years (41–54 C.E.). Second, Acts does not clarify the time span between the *prediction* of the famine and the famine itself. Third, many famines (and food shortages) occurred during and after Claudius's reign.[46] Based upon the references to a severe Judean famine in Josephus's writings (*Ant.* 3.330; 20.51–53), the most widely accepted dates for this famine (but not necessarily for its prediction) fall between 46 and 48 C.E.[47] Even if this range is correct (as it may well be), it provides only a rough time frame for the prophetic event that preceded the famine (11:28–30). One key point remains intact, however: the Christian response to the famine (and thus Paul's visit to Jerusalem) presumably occurred during the famine (11:30; 12:25).

In regard to Herod Agrippa, he ruled from 37 C.E. until his death in 44 C.E., but Acts gives no definitive indication of the temporal relationship between Herod's death and Paul's presence in Jerusalem. In fact, it is possible to read Acts as recording two Pauline visits to Jerusalem in chapters 11 and 12, the first visit occurring immediately after the money was raised for famine relief in nearby Antioch (11:27–30), and the second visit occurring after Herod's death (12:20–25). Indeed, this is the most natural reading of Luke's language of Saul and Barnabas "returning" to Jerusalem (12:25); that is, they immediately delivered their offering to Jerusalem (11:27–30) and then made the rounds of greater Judea before again returning to Jerusalem (12:25). According to this reading, Saul would have arrived in Jerusalem (perhaps to learn where funds were most needed); Herod would have engaged in persecution of the church and died while Saul was delivering aid to

---

and the Early Church (vol. 2 of *Early Christian Mission*; Downers Grove: InterVarsity, 2004), 1031–1292.

[46] Bruce W. Winter notes that most "famines" in the ancient world occurred when local economic and political conditions created local "food shortages." These shortages were largely a matter of distribution, not production. Luke's reference to a worldwide famine is clearly hyperbolic. See "Acts and Food Shortages," in *The Book of Acts in Its Graeco-Roman Setting* (ed. David W. Gill and Conrad Gempf; BAFCS 2; Grand Rapids: Eerdmans, 1999), 59–78.

[47] For arguments in support of the 46–48 C.E. dating, see Fitzmyer, *Acts*, 481–83; Witherington, *Acts*, 372–74; F. F. Bruce, *The Book of Acts* (rev. ed.; NICNT; Grand Rapids: Eerdmans, 1988), 230–31; Conzelmann, *Acts*, 90; and Barrett, *Acts*, 1:562–64.

the communities in Judea; and then Saul would have returned to Jerusalem after Herod's death. Such a reading has the added benefit of explaining both how Saul and Barnabas fulfilled their original commission to help the region of Judea (11:30) and how they "returned into" (ὑπέστρεψαν εἰς) Jerusalem (12:25).[48] Yet neither the acceptance nor rejection of such a double visit to Jerusalem significantly affects the Pauline time frames in Acts 11 and 12. In any case, the time frames remain ambiguous. Nothing in these chapters explains how much time Saul spent traveling or delivering aid to Jerusalem and Judea.[49] The implied time frame could be days, weeks, months, or even years. Saul may or may not have begun his Jerusalem visit before Herod's (Agrippa's) death, but he clearly completed that visit at some unspecified time after Herod's death.[50]

Acts provides a number of these isolated temporal references like Herod's death throughout Paul's ministry. The next notable temporal reference within Paul's ministry occurs during Paul's visit to Corinth. According to Acts, Paul's visit to Corinth began shortly after Claudius expelled all the Jews from Rome (18:1–2), an event that probably occurred in either 41 or 49 C.E.[51] In the first such reference, Acts even clarifies the duration of Paul's

---

[48]Some form of the phrase ὑποστρέφω εἰς appears sixteen times in Luke-Acts. With the exception of an idiom about the resurrected Christ not returning to decay (Acts 13:34), the fifteen other occurrences refer to people returning to a location where they are assumed to have been previously located (Luke 1:56; 2:45; 7:10; 8:39; 11:24; 24:33, 52; Acts 1:12; 8:25; 13:13; 14:21; 21:6; 22:17; 23:32). In several of these occurrences, the narrative presumes, but does not explicitly state, that the persons had been previously located in the place to which this expression has them returning (e.g., Luke 1:56; 7:10; 8:39; 24:33, 52; Acts 1:12; 13:13; 21:6; 22:17; 23:52). To assume that the expression in Acts 12:25 means anything other than that Saul and Barnabas returned to Jerusalem where they had previously been located requires an uncharacteristic use of the expression in this one context.

[49]The strongest argument in favor of this double visit to Jerusalem in Acts 11 and 12 is the solution to the text-critical problem of how to account for the harder reading of εἰς in 12:25, a problem that Mikeal C. Parsons and Martin M. Culy claim "can easily lead text critics to despair" (*Acts: A Handbook on the Greek Text* [Waco: Baylor University Press, 2003], 242). The strongest argument against this double visit to Jerusalem is Saul's presence in Antioch in the next scene in Acts (13:1–2). Admittedly, if Saul departed from, rather than returned into, Jerusalem in 12:25, his presence would be better explained in Antioch in the subsequent verses. However, assuming the harder reading is correct, we should respect Luke's description of Paul returning into, rather than departing from, Jerusalem and at the same time appreciate the fact that Acts often relocates the action of the narrative in a new city with very little transitional material (e.g., from Sharon to Joppa in 9:35–36 and from Joppa to Caesarea in 9:42–10:1).

[50]Barrett wisely notes: "It is mistaken to claim that Luke dates the famine wrongly because 11.27–30 precedes the death of Herod Agrippa I (12.23); what happens in 11:27 is not the famine but a prophecy that there will be a famine" (*Acts*, 1:563–64). *Contra* Conzelmann, *Acts*, 90.

[51]See Peter Lampe, *From Paul to Valentinus: Christians at Rome in the First Two Centuries* (ed. Marshall D. Johnson; trans. Michael Steinhauser; Minneapolis: Fortress, 2003), 11–16.

visit to Corinth, recording that Paul spent eighteen months there,[52] a time span that overlapped (at least in part) with Gallio's service as proconsul in Achaia (18:11–12).[53] Based solely upon the information in Acts—and without concern to harmonize these implied dates with Paul's Corinthian correspondence— this eighteen-month stay in Corinth would likely have occurred between 51 and 53 C.E.[54]

Even though Paul's Corinthian visit can be dated with a fair degree of confidence, efforts to establish a coherent set of time frames for the subsequent events in Acts are immediately frustrated by the complete lack of temporal references for Paul's subsequent journey from Corinth to Jerusalem and back to Ephesus (18:18–19:1). These travels and Paul's activities in these cities could have taken months or years.[55] Upon Paul's eventual arrival in Ephesus,[56] however, Acts again begins providing some specific time spans for Paul's ministry by explaining that he spent three months teaching in the synagogue and two years disputing in the public lecture hall (19:8, 10).[57] Unfortunately, efforts to establish a time frame for the events in Acts are again

---

[52] Eighteen months could refer to the amount of time that Paul spent at the house of Titius Justus (18:7, 11), implying that Paul spent even longer in the city of Corinth. A discrepancy between the amount of time spent in Justus's home and the larger amount of time spent in Corinth would explain why the narrator states very specifically that Paul "stayed there a year and six months" (18:11) only to back away from such specificity a few verses later by noting that Paul left Corinth "after staying there for a considerable time" (18:18, ἡμέρας ἱκανάς). Of course, dual and conflicting traditions could also lie behind these conflicting temporal indicators.

[53] Jerome Murphy-O'Connor argues that Paul "can only have met him [Gallio] in the late summer of AD 51" (*Paul: His Story*, 96). Also see idem, "Paul and Gallio," *JBL* 112 (1993): 315–17; idem, *St. Paul's Corinth: Texts and Archaeology* (3d ed.; Collegeville, Minn.: Liturgical, 2002), 161–69; Bruce W. Winter, "Gallio's Ruling on the Legal Status of Early Christianity (Acts 18:14–15)," *Tyndale Bulletin* 50 (1999): 213–24; and Klaus Haacker, "Die Gallio-Episode und die Paulinische Chronologie," *BZ* 16 (1972): 252–55. As noted earlier, some scholars (e.g., Crossan and Reed, *In Search of Paul*, 33–34, 230) reject the historicity of Paul's appearance before Gallio. Other scholars (e.g., Slingerland, "Acts 18:1–18, the Gallio Inscription, and Absolute Pauline Chronology," *JBL* 110 [1991]: 439–49; "Acts 18:1–17 and Luedemann's Pauline Chronology," *JBL* 109 [1990]: 686–90) doubt the accuracy of the 51–52 date for Gallio's proconsulship.

[54] See Conzelmann, *Acts*, 152–53.

[55] Given the reference to Galatia (Acts 18:23), it may be safely inferred that Paul used a (time-consuming) land route from Judea to Ephesus via Asia Minor.

[56] William H. Malas Jr. suggests that Acts 19:22 marks a major turning point in the narrative with one important indication of this transition being the turn toward clearly defined time spans in Acts after this verse. See "The Literary Structure of Acts: A Narratological Investigation of Its Arrangement, Plot and Primary Themes" (PhD diss., Union Theological Seminary and Presbyterian School of Christian Education, 2001).

[57] Acts later includes a letter which asserts that Paul had previously spent three years in Ephesus (20:31). Although Acts provides no clear indication of when this three-year stay occurred, the letter could be referring back to this stay in Ephesus. Counting partial years as an entire year was common in antiquity, and so a visit of slightly more than two years could legitimately be described as a three-year visit. See Bruce, *Book of Acts*, 366 n. 23.

quickly frustrated when Paul travels through Macedonia for an unspecified time (20:1) before spending three months in Greece (20:2–3). Then Paul took a journey of unspecified duration to Philippi where he remained for five days until the end of the Feast of Unleavened Bread (20:6). As Paul journeyed to Jerusalem, the narrator often provided minor, and largely insignificant, temporal references. Paul stayed in Troas for seven days (20:6), Ptolemais for one day (20:7), and Caesarea for several days (21:10, ἡμέρας πλείους). Although Paul's sea journey lacks any temporal references that could help to determine its duration, Paul is said to have been motivated by a desire to reach Jerusalem by Pentecost (20:16). Consistent with the time span between the Feast of Unleavened Bread and Pentecost, it may be safely inferred that this journey lasted approximately fifty days.[58]

Upon his arrival in Jerusalem, Paul encountered several prominent persons who may help to establish dates for these events. Paul speaks with the high priest Ananias (23:2; 24:1), who served in that capacity 47–59 C.E.[59] Even more importantly, Paul defended himself before the Roman governor Felix after being in Jerusalem for a mere twelve days (24:11). According to Acts, Paul had been in Roman custody under Felix for two years when his governorship expired and Paul was transferred to the custody of Felix's successor, Festus (24:27), who brought Paul's case to King Agrippa (25:13–26:32). Unfortunately, Luke's "several days" (25:14, πλείους ἡμέρας) does little to clarify what amount of time passed between Festus assuming the throne and his presentation of Paul's case to Agrippa, so all dates must remain approximate. While possible dates for this matrix of events range from 55 C.E. to 61 C.E., the most probable date for Festus's ascension to the throne is around 59 C.E. (at the end of Ananias's high priesthood), a date that would establish Paul's arrest around 57 C.E. and his appearance before Agrippa around 59–60 C.E.[60]

In any case, after an unspecified—but seemingly brief—period of time, Agrippa sent Paul on a sea voyage to Rome, a voyage of great difficulty but uncertain duration (27:1–28:15). Parts of the voyage took many days (27:7, ἱκαναῖς ἡμέραις) and saw the loss of "much time" (27:9, ἱκανοῦ χρόνου); a storm consumed fourteen days (27:27, 33), and a friendly reception on the island of Malta consumed another three days (28:7) as did some other unnamed event at Syracuse (28:12); a weather delay stalled progress for a full three months (28:11); and the hospitality of believers in Puteoli prompted a seven-day visit (28:14). Given all of these delays and the difficulty of estimating sailing times in antiquity, no precise time frames can be formulated for

---

[58] Pentecost occurred fifty days after the unnamed Passover, but by the first century, Passover and the Feast of Unleavened Bread were merged into one celebration. See Baruch M. Bokser, "Unleavened Bread and Passover, Feasts of," *ABD* 4:755–65, esp. 763; and Fitzmyer, *Acts*, 232–37. Bruce assumes that these travels took place in 57 C.E. and dates the feast and Pentecost as April 7–14 and May 29, respectively (*Book of Acts*, 383, 387).

[59] See Fitzmyer, *Acts*, 717.

[60] See Joel B. Green, "Festus, Porcius," *ABD* 2:94–95.

Paul's sea journey to Rome. However, the voyage appears to have begun in the autumn of one year and to have ended in the spring of the next year.[61] Once in Rome, Paul was given a hearing after only three days (28:17), but his case remained undecided for "two whole years" (28:30), after which the book of Acts falls silent. If Paul's arrest can be placed around 57 C.E., the book of Acts ends its account of Paul's ministry around 62 C.E.

Summary of the Data Set from Acts

Acts provides an extensive list of places that Paul visited and a pretty clear order for those visits: Jerusalem (before encountering Christ); Damascus; Jerusalem; Caesarea; Tarsus; Antioch in Syria; Judea; Jerusalem; Antioch; Seleucia; Salamis; Paphos on the island of Cyprus; Perga in Pamphylia; Antioch in Pisidia; Iconium; Lystra and Derbe in Lycaonia; Iconium and Antioch in Pisidia; Pamphylia; Attalia; Antioch in Syria; Phoenicia; Samaria; Jerusalem; Antioch in Syria; Cilicia; Derbe; Lystra; Phrygia; Galatia; Troas; Samothrace; Neapolis; Philippi; Amphipolis; Apollonia; Thessalonica; Beroea; Athens; Corinth; Cenchreae; Ephesus; Caesarea; Jerusalem; Antioch; Galatia; Phrygia; Ephesus; Macedonia; Greece; Philippi; Troas; Assos; Mitylene; Samos; Miletus; Cos; Rhodes; Patara; Tyre; Ptolemais; Caesarea; Jerusalem; Caesarea; Myra in Lycia; Lasea; Malta; Syracuse; Rhegium; Puteoli; and Rome.

Acts also provides a few indications for establishing or inferring time frames for Paul's travels, most notably, Paul's eighteen-month stay in Corinth, his (approximately) twenty-seven-month stay in Ephesus, his three months in Greece, seven days in Troas, and finally his four plus years in Roman custody (two years under Felix, a brief time under Festus, several months during his voyage from Jerusalem to Rome, and two years in Rome). Acts also gives clues for dating some key events in Paul's life with relative precision, particularly a visit to Jerusalem during the reign of Claudius around the time of Herod Agrippa's death (46–48 C.E.); a visit to Corinth shortly after Claudius expelled all the Jews from Rome (49 C.E.) and while Gallio was proconsul in Achaia (51–53 C.E.); and Paul's arrest in Jerusalem while Ananias was the high priest and while Felix was governor in Caesarea (ca. 57 C.E.). Acts closes its narrative about four or five years later with Paul under arrest in Rome (ca. 61–63 C.E.).

III. COMPARING THE DATA SETS

Having gleaned the relevant data sets regarding places, order of visits, and time frames of travels from both the smaller data set of Paul's letters and

---

[61] Brian M. Rapske suggests that the journey began in the autumn of 59 C.E. and ended in the spring of 60 C.E. with Paul's three-month winter stopover occurring between November 59 and March 60 ("Acts, Travel and Shipwreck," in *The Book of Acts in Graeco-Roman Setting* [ed. David W. J. Gill and Conrad Gempf; BAFCS 2; Grand Rapids: Eerdmans, 1994], 1–47, esp. 22–24).

the larger data set of Acts, we are positioned to answer the central question of this chapter: *Can the data set from Paul's letters be placed within the data set from Acts?* The answer regarding the *places* referenced in the letters and Acts is simple and affirmative. The book of Acts and Paul's letters both portray Paul as active in essentially the same cities and regions, an area ranging from the southeastern corner of the Mediterranean Sea around the Mediterranean to the north and the west to Rome. In spite of this broad agreement, the itineraries in Acts are significantly more detailed and include references to many more locations than the itineraries in Paul's letters. Most of the unique locations in Acts were logical stops within the itineraries mentioned in the letters (e.g., Caesarea [9:30; 18:22; 21:8–16; 23:23, 33]; Crete [27:7–14]; Cyprus [13:4; 21:2; 27:4]; Miletus [20:15]; Neapolis [16:11]; Pisidia [13:14]) or alternative—often more specific—names for locations mentioned in the letters (e.g., Derbe [14:6, 20]; Lystra [14:5–21; 16:1–5]; Phoenicia [15:3]; Samaria [15:3]). It is interesting, however, to observe that the less detailed itineraries in the letters actually span a larger geographic area. The letters mention Paul spending time during his earliest Christian career in Arabia (Gal 1:17) and planning to travel to Spain, presumably toward the very end of his Christian career (Rom 15:14–28). Spain is clearly further west than Paul's geographical horizons in Acts; Arabia is further south than Paul traveled in Acts (unless Damascus is regarded as part of Arabia).[62] Generally speaking, however, the geographical horizons of Acts and the letters are close enough that few people could find insurmountable discontinuity between the places mentioned in Paul's letters and the places mentioned in Acts. The Paul in Acts may have slightly smaller geographical horizons than the Paul in the letters, but not significantly so—especially given the ambiguities surrounding both Paul's travels to Arabia and his potential travel to Spain.[63]

Answering the question of the congruity between the *order* and *time frames* for Paul's travels as gleaned from his letters and the *order* and *time frames* for those travels as gleaned from Acts requires a more nuanced approach than does answering the question about the places in Acts and the letters. To begin broadly, at many points the itineraries in Paul's letters and in Acts coincide quite closely. For example, both the letters and Acts agree that Paul visited Macedonia via Troas (Acts 16:8–12; 2 Cor 2:12–13; 7:5–7). At other points, however, Paul's letters sometimes—and Acts often—mention places and itineraries that do not appear in the other data set (e.g., Assos [Acts 20:13–14;

---

[62] Regarding the southern extent of Paul's travels, the city of Damascus was temporarily under Arabian (Nabataean) control under Aretas IV, and some scholars have suggested that Paul's reference to Arabia need not refer to any areas significantly south of Judea. On the contrary, however, see Murphy-O'Connor, "Paul in Arabia"; Carsten Burfeind, "Paulus in Arabien," *ZNW* 95 (2004): 129–30; and N. T. Wright, "Paul, Arabia, and Elijah (Galatians 1:17)," *JBL* 115 (1996): 683–92.

[63] Regarding the western extent of Paul's travels, it remains an open question whether Paul actually made it to Spain or whether the emperor's sword put an end to the apostle's planned visit.

Iconium [Acts 13:51–14:5, 21]; Arabia [Gal 1:17]; and Spain [Rom 15:24–28]). Such differences offer no conclusive evidence of the irreconcilability of the chronological information in Acts and the letters. Given that neither Acts nor the letters claim to provide a comprehensive account of Paul's travels, interpreters can quite plausibly argue that one data set is simply more complete than the other. Thus, the accounts may supplement, rather than contradict, one another.

In the previous discussion, we noted that the letters overlap in their discussions of four places: Damascus, Jerusalem, Macedonia, and Corinth. We also noted that the key variable for determining a chronology from the letters was whether one placed Paul's original visits to Macedonia and Corinth before or after his second visit to Jerusalem. The Damascus visit presents no significant problem. Paul's early presence in Damascus is witnessed consistently in both Acts and the letters. Acts also records Paul's visits to Macedonia and Corinth as occurring after his second visit to Jerusalem (Acts 16:9–40; 18:1–17). Acts is clear on these points and easily reconciled with one possible *order* from the letters. It is significant to note, however, that reconciling the order of the Damascus, Corinth, and Macedonia visits in Acts and the letters does not settle the chronological issues. The *time frames* remain problematic. In fact, the questions surrounding the order and time frames for all of these visits become increasingly complicated when the data from Acts is also brought into consideration. The central problem is establishing the order, number, and purposes of Paul's visits to Jerusalem, a problem that has a direct bearing on the time frame of Paul's visits to Macedonia and Corinth.

Initially on the issue of Paul's visits to Jerusalem, it is significant to acknowledge that if the questions of the order and time frames could be completely segregated from one another, then the answers to these questions would be as simple and affirmative as the earlier question about places. Hans Dieter Betz was speaking for much of New Testament scholarship when he applied the hyperbolic label of "hopeless" to the problem of reconciling the evidence from the letters with the evidence from Acts regarding Paul's visits to Jerusalem.[64] Betz's hopelessness arises from the difficulty of making both the order and framework work together. Separately, the order and time frames from Acts and the letters can be reconciled. The thorns poke through the bouquet only when one tries to determine both the order and the timing of Paul's visits to Jerusalem simultaneously.

Yet, in spite of the problems created by integrating these questions of order and time frames, they cannot be segregated. The interrelatedness of the questions of order and time frames was accentuated as far back as 1937 when C. J. Cadoux observed that the creation of a consistent Pauline chronology depended upon two key variables: the sequence of Paul's visits to Jerusalem and the date of Galatians.[65] The eye of the storm for those seeking to correlate the

---

[64] Betz, *Galatians*, 76 n. 191.

[65] C. J. Cadoux, "A Tentative Synthetic Chronology of the Apostolic Age," *JBL* 56 (1937): 177–91. More recently, in regard to his efforts to create a chronology of

Pauline chronologies in Acts and the letters centers on three sets of references to Paul's visits to Jerusalem: (1) According to Acts, Paul visited Jerusalem five times (9:26–29; 11:29–12:25; 15:2–29; 18:22–23; 21:17–23:30). (2) According to Galatians, Paul visited Jerusalem two—and only two—times (1:18; 2:1–10). (3) According to Romans, Paul planned a return visit to Jerusalem (15:25). The third of these references is the least problematic, because nearly all interpreters agree—and wisely so—that the visit to Jerusalem that Paul anticipated in Romans corresponds to his final visit to Jerusalem in Acts, a visit that was planned after the composition of Galatians.

The true epicenter of the problem, therefore, concerns how the two Jerusalem visits in Galatians relate to the first four Jerusalem visits in Acts. The lines of the debate have long been established—so much so that already in 1907, Benjamin Bacon could speak of this issue as "such a well-worn battle-ground of critics that it can be approached only with hesitation and self-distrust."[66] Generally speaking (but with many individual variations), interpreters have divided into two interpretive traditions. On the one hand, those who rely more heavily upon the chronology of Acts for guidance tend to make the simple equation between the first two visits mentioned in Acts (9:26–29; 11:29–12:25) and the two visits mentioned in Galatians (1:18; 2:1–10). Galatians is then generally assumed to have been written before Paul's third visit to Jerusalem as recorded in Acts.[67] On the other hand, those who rely more heavily upon an analysis of the events described in the various visits tend to identify this third visit in Acts (15:2–29) with the second visit

---

Paul, Tatum has likewise noted that "locating Galatians is the crux of the matter" (*New Chapters*, 124). Also see Juan Miguel Díaz Rodelas, "Pablo en Jerusalén: Los Datos de Gálatas," *Estudios bíblicos* 64 (2006): 485–95.

[66] Benjamin W. Bacon, "Acts versus Galatians: The Crux of Apostolic History," *AJT* 11 (1907): 454–74, quoting 454.

[67] The classic defense of this position was offered by F. F. Bruce in a series of articles titled "Galatians Problems" in the *Bulletin of the John Rylands University Library of Manchester* (51 [1969]: 292–309; 52 [1970]: 243–66; 53 [1971]: 253–71; and 54 [1973]: 250–67). Also see F. F. Bruce, *Paul: Apostle of the Heart Set Free* (Grand Rapids: Eerdmans, 1977); idem, *The Epistle to the Galatians: A Commentary on the Greek Text* (New International Greek Testament Commentary; Grand Rapids: Eerdmans, 1982). The same positions have been ably defended by Colin J. Hemer, "Acts and Galatians Reconsidered," *Themelios* 2 (1977): 81–88; *Book of Acts*. Also see Stanley D. Toussaint, "The Chronological Problem of Galatians 2:1–10," *Bibliotheca sacra* 120 (1963): 334–40; George Ogg, *Chronology of the Life of Paul* (London: Epworth, 1968), 72–88; J. N. Sanders, "Peter and Paul in the Acts," *NTS* 2 (1955–1956): 133–43; and Dale Moody, "A New Chronology for the Life and Letters of Paul," *PRSt* 3 (1976): 249–72. With the exception of north/south Galatian theory, the central tenets of this position have remained very similar for over a century (e.g., Willis J. Beecher, "Paul's Visits to Jerusalem," *BW* 2 [1893]: 434–43). With a slightly different nuance, Solomon Zeitlin defended this position by suggesting that Acts 1–15 and Acts 16–28 were originally two distinct documents, each of which recorded two historically accurate visits to Jerusalem. When these documents were combined, they produced four visits to Jerusalem by repeating the same two visits twice, once in Acts 11 and 15 and a second time in Acts 18 and 21 ("Paul's Journeys to Jerusalem," *JQR* 57 [1967]: 171–78).

in Galatians (2:1–10).[68] Both approaches have ardent supporters, but neither approach is without problems.[69]

The first approach has the immediate benefit of simplicity: the two visits in Galatians correspond to the first two visits in Acts. Indeed, equating the visits in Galatians with the first two visits in Acts creates a consistency of order between Acts and the letters, but it also creates three significant problems for reconciling the time frames of Paul's Jerusalem visits. First, the time frames in Galatians do not match the narrative in Acts very well. The time frames in Galatians 1:18 and 2:1 imply both that three years passed between Paul's vision of Christ and his first visit to Jerusalem in Acts (9:26) and that at least eleven and as many as fourteen years passed between Paul's first and second visits to Jerusalem as recorded in Acts (9:26; 11:29–30; 12:24–25). While inclusive counting can reduce the three-year time frame to just over one year, and the fourteen-year time frame to just over twelve years, any further reduction of the temporal framework is impossible without violating the very specific time frames in Galatians. In regard to the time between Paul's encounter with Christ and his first visit to Jerusalem, Paul insisted: "I did not confer with any human being nor did I go up to Jerusalem to those who were apostles before me, but I went away at once (εὐθέως) into Arabia and afterwards I returned to Damascus" (Gal 1:16b–17).[70] According to Paul, it was only "after three years" that he went to Jerusalem (Gal 1:18). According to Acts, Paul spent only "several days" (ἡμέρας τινάς, 9:19) and "some time" (ἡμέραι ἱκαναί, 9:23; cf. 22:12–21) in Damascus before going to Jerusalem.[71] These references do not preclude, but neither do they clearly imply, a three-year time frame.

---

[68] This position was vigorously defended by Knox (*Chapters*) and has been widely followed. See, e.g., Jewett, *Chronology of Paul's Life*; Lüdemann, *Studies in Chronology*; Jerome Murphy-O'Connor, *Paul: A Critical Life* (New York: Oxford University Press, 1996); Jürgen Becker, *Paul: Apostle to the Gentiles* (Louisville: Westminster John Knox, 1993); Schnelle, *Apostle Paul*; James D. G. Dunn, "The Incident at Antioch (Gal 2:11–18)," in Nanos, *Galatians Debate*, 199–234; idem, "The Relationship between Paul and Jerusalem according to Galatians 1 and 2," *NTS* 28 (1982): 461–78; and Alfred Suhl, "Der Beginn der selbständigen Mission des Paulus: Ein Beitrag zur Geschichte des Urchristentums," *NTS* 38 (1992): 430–47.

[69] In an idiosyncratic solution to the problems presented by each of these alternatives, McRay argues for a Pauline chronology with six visits to Jerusalem. Acts 15 is interpreted as Paul's fourth visit to Jerusalem (*Paul*, 60–84). Being consistent with neither the letters nor Acts, this chronology has little to recommend it.

[70] Of course, in regard to the order of Paul's travels, one may plausibly argue that Acts has omitted Paul's travels to Arabia, but the time frames remain difficult to explain. It is possible to read the adverb as describing what Paul *did not immediately do* (i.e., consult with the Jerusalem leadership) rather than what he *immediately did do* (i.e., go to Arabia, as in the NRSV). In any case, Conzelmann is probably correct to assert that the notion of immediacy is a stock feature of call narratives and that its inclusion here emphasizes the immediacy of Paul's reaction to his call (*Acts*, 72).

[71] Mark Harding has correctly pointed out that in spite of the basic agreement between Luke's and Paul's account of his escape from Damascus in a basket, Luke portrays that escape as heroic, while Paul treats the escape as humiliating ("On the

The time frames between Paul's first and second visits to Jerusalem in Acts and Galatians also exist in tension. Acts has Paul spend this entire time (either eleven or fourteen years according to Gal 2:1) in his hometown of Tarsus (Acts 9:30–11:25), but in Galatians 1:21, Paul claims to have spent these years evangelizing in Syria and Cilicia. In spite of the facts that Tarsus was located in Cilicia (where Paul claimed to have engaged in evangelism) and that Acts is primarily concerned with Peter and his activities during the narrative time between Paul's first and second visits to Jerusalem (Acts 9:30–11:25), it remains surprising that Acts records none of Paul's activities in this period. Even though nothing in Acts 9:30–11:25 implies the passage of more than a decade, the next datable event in Acts, the famine under Claudius (11:27–29), likely did occur about a decade later (45–48 C.E.).[72] Admittedly, the time frames associated with Paul's first two visits to Jerusalem in Acts contain several awkward silences and possible conflicts with Galatians, but still the order and time frames of the visits in Acts are not inherently irreconcilable with the order and time frames in Galatians.[73]

Second, in this approach (i.e., equating Paul's first two visits to Jerusalem in Acts with his only two visits to Jerusalem in Galatians), Galatians has to have been written before Paul's third visit to Jerusalem (Acts 15) and even before Acts records Paul having preached in Galatia (16:6). This early date for Galatians has been defended by arguing that the letter was addressed to people in the southern part of the Roman province of Galatia (whom Paul evangelized in Acts 13:4–14:26) and not to the ethnic Galatians to the north (whom Paul subsequently evangelized in 16:1–6).[74] This approach assumes that Luke and Paul had different understandings of the term "Galatians" and that Paul applied the term to the people who lived in Iconium, Lystra, and Derbe in the Roman province of Galatia and that Luke applied the term to the ethnic Galatians further north (Acts 16:6; 18:23). According to this approach, Paul would have written Galatians after evangelizing these "southern

---

Historicity of Acts: Comparing Acts 9.23–5 with 2 Corinthians 11.32–3," *NTS* 39 [1993]: 518–38).

[72] It is important to note that this date, like nearly all of the datable events in Paul's life, is derived from Acts. F. F. Bruce finds nine datable events in Paul's life. Only one comes from Paul's letters (the reference to King Aretas IV). See F. F. Bruce, "Chronological Questions in the Acts of the Apostles," *BJRL* 68 (1986): 273–95. Also see the six dates offered in the older and less optimistic work by Kirsopp Lake, "The Chronology of Acts," in Foakes-Jackson and Lake, *Beginnings of Christianity*, 5:445–74.

[73] It should be noted, however, that dating the famine around 48 C.E. and equating Paul's Jerusalem visit in Acts 11 with the visit in Gal 2:1 imply that Paul was a Christian by 34 C.E. *at the latest* and that Paul was almost certainly a Christian by the time he is depicted as participating in Stephen's martyrdom (Acts 8:1). See Daniel R. Schwartz, "The End of the Line: Paul in the Canonical Book of Acts," in *Paul and the Legacies of Paul* (ed. William S. Babcock; Dallas: SMU Press, 1991), 3–24, esp. 4–8.

[74] See Bruce, "Galatians Problems: 2. North or South Galatia?" *BJRL* 52 (1970): 243–56; and *Commentary on Galatians*, 5–10, 43–45. More recently, see Cilliers Breytenbach, *Paulus und Barnabas in der Provinz Galatien: Studien zu Apostelgeschichte 13f.; 16,6; 18,23 und den Adressaten des Galaterbriefes* (AGJU 38; New York: Brill, 1996).

Galatians" (Acts 14:1–20) and before his third visit to Jerusalem (15:2). Al-though the southern Galatian theory has not been established beyond plau-sible critique,[75] it offers the possibility of reconciling the chronologies in Acts and the letters. However, it is important to note that the notion of Paul writing Galatians before the Jerusalem Conference in Acts 15 raises problems of its own, particularly around the issue of Paul's offering to Jerusalem. The basic problem is that Paul's letters seem to imply a single offering for Jerusalem, the impetus for which originated during Paul's second trip to Jerusalem (Gal 2:10), which Paul then collected from several congregations over a course of years (1 Cor 16:1–4; 2 Cor 1:15–2:1; 8–9) and which he intended to deliver on his third visit to Jerusalem (Rom 15:22–32).[76] This reconstruction is even consistent with the traditions in Acts 20:1–4, which list the persons who ac-companied Paul and the offering on his final visit to Jerusalem. The problem, of course, is that Acts associates this offering with Paul's fifth visit to Jerusalem, not his second visit (as in Galatians). It is possible, of course, to infer two Jerusalem offerings over the course of Paul's career, one *ad hoc* offering from Antioch for famine relief (Acts 11:27–30) and another more organized and theologically significant offering from Paul's Macedonian and Corinthian con-verts (20:1–5; 21:27–36; 24:17). Although nothing in Paul's letters precludes such a double offering, neither does anything in the letters support the notion of two offerings.[77] As with the earlier problem of reconciling the time frames in Acts and Galatians, so also with this problem: Acts and the letters can be reconciled, but only awkwardly. If (and only if) one accepts an early date for

---

[75]Conzelmann quickly dismisses the southern Galatian theory as dependent "upon another hypothesis, the historical reliability of the itineraries in Acts" (*Acts*, 4). Admittedly, the greatest strength of the southern thesis is its ability to reconcile Acts and Galatians, but for a more developed criticism of the theory, see Murphy-O'Connor, *Paul: A Critical Life*, 159–62.

[76]For a dissenting voice to this reconstruction, see A. J. M. Wedderburn, who has recently argued that Galatians 2:10 should not be interpreted as a reference to the offering in Romans and 1–2 Corinthians ("Paul's Collection: Chronology and History," *NTS* 48 [2002]: 95–110).

[77]The seeming incongruity between the letters and Acts has led two of the three major studies of Paul's offering to reject not only the equation between Acts 11:27–30 and Gal 2:1–10, but also the historicity of Paul's involvement in any famine relief project before the composition of Galatians (Stephan Joubert, *Paul as Benefactor: Reciprocity, Strategy and Theological Reflection in Paul's Collection* [WUNT 124; Tübingen: Mohr Siebeck, 2000], 91–93; and Dieter Georgi, *Remembering the Poor: The History of Paul's Collection for Jerusalem* [Nashville: Abingdon, 1965], 43–47). The third major study accepts the historicity of the famine relief project in Acts 11–12 and treats it as an "analogy" for the later Pauline offering discussed in the Corinthian correspondence. This study nonetheless still rejects the accuracy of Luke's chronology by rejecting the historicity of Paul's Jerusalem visit in Acts 9:26 (Keith F. Nickle, *The Collection: A Study in Paul's Strategy* [Studies in Biblical Theology 48; Naperville, Ill.: Alec R. Allenson, 1966], 1–73, esp. 30 n. 61). On the possibility that Luke knows nothing about Paul's offering and that Acts is referring to other events, see David J. Downs, "Paul's Collec-tion and the Book of Acts Revisited," *NTS* 52 (2006): 50–70; and Clayton R. Bowen, "Paul's Collection and the Book of Acts," *JBL* 42 (1923): 49–58.

Galatians, the inference of a double offering for Jerusalem, and the validity of
the "south Galatian" theory, then the order and time frames in Acts are not
irreconcilable with the order and time frames in Paul's letters.[78]

The third—and perhaps most significant—problem with equating Paul's
first two Jerusalem visits in Acts with the two visits in Galatians is the nature
of the visits. Decades ago, John Knox provided a helpful categorization of
Paul's Jerusalem visits in the letters and Acts. Knox argued that the three visits in Paul's letters were best understood as an initial visit for Paul *to establish
an acquaintance* with the original apostles (Gal 1:18–21), as a second visit *to
participate in the Jerusalem Conference* (2:1–10), and as a third visit *to deliver the
offering to Jerusalem* (Rom 15:25–32).[79] Knox's assessment of the purposes of
these three visits to Jerusalem corresponds quite well with the accounts in
Paul's letters. Paul insisted that his first visit was brief (only fifteen days) and
limited to a select group of people, namely Peter and James (Gal 1:18–19).
In fact, Paul insisted that even after this visit he "was still unknown to the
churches of Judea" (1:22). According to Galatians, after this "acquaintance
visit," Paul did not return until fourteen years later when he, Barnabas, and
Titus presented Paul's gospel to Peter, James, and John, the "pillars" of the
Jerusalem church (2:1–2, 9). According to Paul's account, at this "conference
visit," the Jerusalem leaders accepted the validity of Paul's message and sent
him to preach to the Gentiles with the sole provision that he remember the
poor (2:9–10).[80] Subsequent to this conference visit to Jerusalem, Paul and
Peter came into conflict in Antioch when Peter and Barnabas began urging
Gentiles to obey the law ("live like Jews," 2:14).[81]

In Acts, not only the number, but also the nature of Paul's visits appears
different. The depiction of Paul's first visit to Jerusalem in Acts appears more
public and attention-grabbing than in Galatians. According to Acts, after Paul
became a disciple, Barnabas took him to Jerusalem and "brought him to the
apostles, and described to them how on the road he had seen the Lord" (9:27).
This introduction was followed both by Paul's preaching ("speaking boldly,"
9:28) among the Hellenists, who sought to kill him (9:29), and by his deliver-

---

[78] For substantive criticisms of an early (pre-Acts 15) date for Galatians, see
Bercovitz, "Two Letters Chronologies"; and Hyldahl, "Beobachtungen zum Galater-
brief," 425–44.

[79] Knox, *Chapters*, 34–35.

[80] It is important to remember with John M. G. Barclay that Paul's autobiography
in Gal 1–2 is primarily a testimony of God's grace at work in his life and the life of his
community ("Paul's Story: Theology as Testimony," in *Narrative Dynamics in Paul* [ed.
Bruce W. Longenecker; Louisville: Westminster John Knox, 2002], 133–56).

[81] It has been suggested that many first-century Jews regarded Antioch and other
portions of Syria as a part of biblical Israel and not in a separate region, as Paul apparently regarded them. If so, the conflict between Peter and Paul in Antioch may
have been as much about the appropriate boundaries of biblical Israel as it was about
Gentile inclusion. See Markus Bockmuehl, "Antioch and James the Just," in *James the
Just and Christian Origins* (ed. Bruce Chilton and Craig A. Evans; NovTSup 98; Boston:
Brill, 1999), 155–98.

ance from violence by "the believers," who spirited Paul away to Tarsus via Caesarea (9:30). These accounts in Acts of Paul meeting with a collective group of the apostles and of Paul being delivered by a collective group of disciples are difficult to reconcile with Paul's insistence that during his first visit to Jerusalem he met only with Peter and James and that even after this visit, he remained "unknown by sight to the churches of Judea" (Gal 1:22). Additionally, Paul's claim to anonymity in the churches of Judea is difficult to reconcile with the prominence Paul (Saul the persecutor) has in Acts before his encounter with Christ. Acts insists that Paul was present at Stephen's martyrdom *in Jerusalem* (8:1) and was "still breathing threats and murder" against the believers *in Jerusalem* just before his encounter with Christ (9:1). In fact, Paul's encounter with Christ occurred as he was seeking to bring Christians from other places back *to Jerusalem* in chains (9:2). Even Ananias, Paul's Christian benefactor in Damascus, acknowledged that Paul had persecuted "the saints *in Jerusalem*" (9:13, emphasis added). Both the problem of reconciling the time frames (as discussed earlier) and the problem of these inconsistent depictions of Paul's reputation among the Jerusalem Christians before and immediately after his first Christian visit to Jerusalem have led some critics to suggest that Paul's first visit to Jerusalem in Acts is not historically accurate—it is either a Lukan creation or a mischaracterization of a later visit.[82]

Paul's second visit to Jerusalem in Acts is also widely debated. According to Acts, the purpose of this visit was clearly famine relief (11:27–30). In Galatians, Paul reports that the primary agenda of his second Jerusalem visit was to gain the original apostles' approval of his gospel, which he laid before them in a "private meeting" (Gal 2:2).[83] Although the apostles' acceptance of Paul's message was contingent upon his willingness to "remember the poor" (2:10), equating this visit with the offering raises all the problems discussed earlier.[84]

---

[82] E.g., Haenchen, *Acts*, 335. Kirsopp Lake concluded that it was "impossible to see any way of reconciling these two presentments of Paul's movements. No one could ever suppose preaching in Damascus described in Acts ix. was extended over three years. No one could suppose that into this period there must be intercalated a visit to Arabia. Indeed, the natural interpretation of Gal. i. is even further from Acts. . . . The question remains, how far does this affect our confidence in Acts? It seems to me absurd to say that Acts does not suffer. When a witness has been put in the box and proves to be slightly wrong on every point, and very wrong on some, his evidence on other questions is to be treated with caution" ("The Conversion of Paul," in Foakes-Jackson and Lake, *Beginnings of Christianity*, 5:188–95, quoting 192–95).

[83] On the language of this meeting as indicative of a political decision-making process, see Betz, *Galatians*, 86 n. 273.

[84] By equating the revelation that prompted Paul's visit to Jerusalem (Gal 2:2) with the prophet Agabus's warning about an impending famine (Acts 11:27–28), William O. Walker Jr. has argued that the visit in Gal 2:1–10 has two purposes: to deliver the offering and to deal with the issue of Gentile circumcision ("Why Paul Went to Jerusalem: The Interpretation of Galatians 2:1–5," *CBQ* 54 [1992]: 503–10). It may be more convincing to regard the offering visit in Acts as historically accurate, but chronologically misplaced (e.g., Robert W. Funk, "The Enigma of the Famine Visit," *JBL* 75 [1956]: 130–36).

Perhaps it is enough to remember that even if the apostles' instructions for Paul to "remember the poor" is equated with the Pauline offering, Galatians pretty clearly implies that this obligation was placed upon Paul during his second visit to Jerusalem and that it would be fulfilled *after that visit.*

Not surprisingly, given the difficulty of squeezing Paul's Jerusalem visits in Galatians into the mold of the first two visits in Acts, several scholars have suggested that the visit in Acts 15 (Paul's third visit according to Acts) is best understood as corresponding to Paul's second visit in Galatians. Paul's visit in Acts 15 has the formal and deliberating air of his second visit in Galatians. In Acts, the purpose of this third visit is theological, that is, to decide whether Gentile converts will need to undergo circumcision or not (15:1–6). According to Acts, Paul's arguments against Gentile circumcision won the day and Peter and James sided with Paul in rejecting the need for Gentile circumcision (15:7–11, 13–21). This account conforms quite well to Paul's assessment of the role Peter and James played in acknowledging the truth of his gospel in Gal 2:7–9.

Although it is clearly inaccurate to assert any scholarly consensus on the issue of Pauline chronology, it is accurate to reassert that the primary issue in the debate is the relationship between the Jerusalem visits in Acts and in Paul's letters. Those visits can be easily summarized.

Jerusalem Visits in the Letters	Jerusalem Visits in Acts
Acquaintance (Gal 1:18–23)	Introduction to the apostles (9:26–30)
Conference (Gal 2:1–10)	Famine relief (11:29–30; 12:15)
Offering (Rom 15:25–32)	Apostolic conference (15:1–29)
	Greeting visit (18:22)
	Gentile offering (21:15)

Also, as suggested earlier, the major secondary issue in Pauline chronology is the date for the composition of Galatians. The scholars who draw straight lines across the above chart (i.e., Gal 1:18–23 = Acts 9:26–30 and Gal 2:1–10 = Acts 11–12) necessarily date Galatians before the apostolic conference in Acts 15 and interpret the letter as part of the debate that preceded the conference. The scholars who do not draw straight lines across the above chart often date Galatians after the Jerusalem Conference in Acts 15 and interpret the letter as Paul's reaction to Christian preachers who sought to draw the Galatians toward circumcision and away from the decisions reached at the conference.[85]

---

[85]For recent assessments of Paul's "opponents" in Galatia, see A. E. Harvey, "The Opposition to Paul," in Nanos, *Galatians Debate,* 321–33; Robert Jewett, "The Agitators and the Galatian Congregation," in ibid., 334–47; Nikolaus Walter, "Paul and the Opponents of the Christ-Gospel in Galatia," in ibid., 362–66; John C. Hurd, "Reflections Concerning Paul's 'Opponents' in Galatia," in *Paul and His Opponents* (ed. Stanley E. Porter; Pauline Studies 2; Boston: Brill, 2005), 129–48; and Mark D. Nanos,

Raymond Brown was probably correct to claim that most New Testament scholars identify the visit in Gal 2 with the visit in Acts 15 and therefore date Galatians after the Jerusalem Conference.[86] Even though identifying Paul's second Jerusalem visit in Gal 2 with his third Jerusalem visit in Acts 15 suggests an incongruity between the chronologies of Acts and Galatians, the case for equating these two visits is quite strong. As J. B. Lightfoot's classic commentary on Galatians noted over one hundred years ago: "The *geography* is the same. . . . The *time* is the same. . . . The *persons* are the same. . . . The *subject of dispute* is the same. . . . The *character* of the conference is the same. . . . The *result* is the same. . . . A combination of circumstances so striking is not likely to have occurred twice in a few years."[87] Although this majority opinion of scholarship calls the chronology of Acts into question, even conservative interpreters are often drawn to make this identification. For example, Robert H. Stein, writing in the *Journal of the Evangelical Theological Society*, has concluded that understanding "Galatians 2:1–10 and Acts 15:1–35 [to] refer to the same event therefore best explains the role of Paul during these events."[88]

Therefore, in direct answer to the central question of this chapter, we must conclude that the indications of chronology within Paul's letters can be placed within the Pauline chronology within Acts, albeit it very awkwardly, in the eyes of many scholars. The final question becomes whether one prefers an awkward fit that seems to support the chronological accuracy of Acts or a much more comfortable fit that calls the chronological accuracy of Acts into question. The majority opinion of scholarship supports the notion that a fit that comfortably suits the content of the visits in Galatians and Acts is preferable to a fit that awkwardly suits the constraints of the implied chronology in Acts.

At this point, however, two closing observations are in order. On the one hand, suspicion about, or even rejection of, the accuracy of the chronology in Acts is not equivalent to a wholesale dismissal of the historicity of Acts. Even if the chronology of Paul's travels and visits is not historically accurate, it need not follow that the traditions about what transpired during those travels and visits (e.g., shipwrecks, opposition from silversmiths, preaching in synagogues or public lecture halls) are historically worthless.[89] On the other hand,

---

"Intruding 'Spies' and 'Pseudo-Brethren': The Jewish Intra-Group Politics of Paul's Jerusalem Meeting (Gal 2:1–10)," in ibid., 59–97.

[86] Raymond E. Brown, *An Introduction to the New Testament* (New York: Doubleday, 1997), 477.

[87] J. B. Lightfoot, *St. Paul's Epistle to the Galatians* (London: Macmillan, 1890; repr., Peabody, Mass.: Hendrickson, 1995), 123–24, emphasis Lightfoot's. Also see the equally classic defense of the same position by Kirsopp Lake, "The Apostolic Council of Jerusalem," in Foakes-Jackson and Lake, *Beginnings of Christianity*, 5:159–212.

[88] Robert H. Stein, "The Relationship of Galatians 2:1–10 and Acts 15:1–35: Two Neglected Arguments," *Journal of the Evangelical Theological Society* 17 (1974): 239–42, quoting 242.

[89] Decades ago, Donald T. Rowlingson noted that recognition of Luke's apparent reorganization of the materials in the Gospel of Luke has had little effect on evaluations of the historical significance of the individual pieces of tradition in that

acceptance of the correspondence between the chronology of Paul's two Jerusalem visits in Gal 1–2 and Acts 9–12 does not necessarily require a wholesale acceptance of the historical accuracy of Acts. Even if the chronology of Acts is accurate at these points, it very well may be inaccurate at other points.[90]

---

volume and proffered that a similar reorganization of materials in Acts should likewise have little effect on evaluations of the value of the individual pieces of tradition in Acts ("The Jerusalem Conference and Jesus' Nazareth Visit: A Study in Pauline Chronology," *JBL* 71 [1952]: 69–74). Some scholars have denied the historical accuracy of this first Pauline visit to Jerusalem, while affirming the essential historicity of Acts. For example, the distinguished Lukan and Pauline scholar Joseph A. Fitzmyer rejects the historicity of Paul's famine visit in Acts 11 but still maintains that "the correlation between the Pauline and Lucan data is significant" ("The Pauline Letters and the Lucan Account of Paul's Missionary Journeys," in *SBL Seminar Papers, 1988* (ed. David J. Lull; SBLSP 27; Atlanta: Society of Biblical Literature, 1988), 82–89, quoting 85. Similarly, Pierson Parker argued that Paul's first visit to Jerusalem in Acts is an "error," but that the Pauline chronology throughout the remainder of Acts is correct ("Once More, Acts and Galatians," *JBL* 86 [1967]: 175–82). Donald Fay Robinson argued that Acts 9 and 11 record the same visit to Jerusalem but have split that one visit into two separate visits ("A Note on Acts 11:27–30," *JBL* 63 [1944]: 169–72).

[90] Paul J. Achtemeier, for example, argues that Acts is correct in its chronology for Paul's first two visits to Jerusalem but incorrect in its account of Paul's third visit to Jerusalem. Achtemeier argues that Acts places Paul at the Jerusalem Conference in Acts 15 in spite of the likelihood that Paul was not present at that event (*Quest for Unity*, esp. 58–61). Also see Achtemeier, "Elusive Unity," 1–26.

~ 4 ~

PUTTING PAUL IN HIS PLACE: THE
GRECO-ROMAN WORLD

IN THE last chapter we compared the chronological data in Acts and Paul's letters to determine if those data sets (where Paul went and when he went there) were compatible in these two sources. That project proved to be far less straightforward than it initially appeared. In this chapter, we will examine an even less straightforward, but equally important, aspect of Paul's life: his social location within the Greco-Roman world. In keeping with the restrictive approach of this volume, we will consider only five areas where the depictions of Paul's social location overlap in Acts and the letters: Paul's family (to whom was Paul related?), educational background (to what degree, if any, had Paul been trained in the intellectual traditions of the Greco-Roman world?), pre-Christian religious background (what was the nature of Paul's religious self-identity before he took on his new identity in Christ?), vocation (what revenue-producing activities, besides ministry, did Paul engage in?), and political status (how did Paul view himself in relation to, and how was he viewed by, the political powers and structures of the Roman Empire?).[1] In keeping with the cautious method of this volume, we will first examine the smaller data set from Paul's letters, then examine the larger data set from Acts, and finally compare these two data sets to determine if the smaller data set can be placed within the larger data set.

I. THE PAULINE DATA SET

Paul's Family

Paul's letters provide no evidence about the identity of any members of his family of origin, other than their evident Jewishness (Phil 3:4–6), an

---

[1]John Clayton Lentz suggests that social rank in the Greco-Roman world was based upon five factors: (1) pedigree; (2) education; (3) status as free, freed, or slave; (4) occupation; and (5) wealth (*Luke's Portrait of Paul* [SNTSMS 77; Cambridge: Cambridge University Press, 1993], 14). Because my concern is broader than social rank alone, I have modified his categories.

aspect that will be considered later. However, the Corinthian correspondence reveals an important absence of family in Paul's life. Paul was single when he wrote 1 Corinthians (1 Cor 7:7, 25–31). Paul believed that his singleness enabled him to devote greater time and energy to his ministry (7:32–35) and claimed to possess a gift of celibacy (7:7).[2] Because Paul placed a premium upon his own singleness and imminently expected the *eschaton* (7:25–29), he recommended that other single believers also remain single. But he did not impose the single life upon believers in general (7:28, 36), nor even expect it of the other apostles (9:5).[3] In light of this information, it seems unlikely that Paul ever married, though we cannot be certain.[4] If Paul never married and remained celibate, then he would not have had children.[5] Although Paul mentions both a few of his "relatives" (συγγενής, Rom 16:7, 11; cf. 9:3) and the "mother" that he shared with Rufus (16:13), both expressions are almost certainly metaphorical and reveal nothing about Paul's family of origin.[6]

Paul's Education

Although Paul's letters offer more clues about his educational background than about his family of origin, interpreting the clues about Paul's education nevertheless requires care. Paul's command of languages suggests formal train-

---

[2]On Paul and celibacy, see Dale B. Martin, *The Corinthian Body* (New Haven: Yale University Press, 1999), 209–12; and *Sex and the Single Savior* (Louisville: Westminster John Knox, 2006), 138–39.

[3]By assuming that the other apostles, including Peter, were accompanied by a wife (1 Cor 9:5), Paul's letters appear to conflict with the assumptions of Luke's Gospel (18:28–29). Although Paul's reference presumed that Peter and the other apostles were married and traveled with their wives, the caution from Carolyn Osiek, Margaret Y. MacDonald, and Janet H. Tulloch is well taken when they warn that 1 Cor 9:5 should not be interpreted to preclude the possibility that the apostles' wives were also participating in ministry rather than simply accompanying their husbands as "a 'domestic' supporter of the husband's missionary work" (*A Woman's Place: House Churches in Earliest Christianity* [Minneapolis: Fortress, 2006], 27).

[4]Among the most important studies on Paul's views of marriage and sexuality are David L. Balch, "Paul, Families, and Households," in *Paul in the Greco-Roman World* (ed. J. Paul Sampley; Harrisburg: Trinity Press International, 2003), 258–92; O. Larry Yarbrough, "Paul, Marriage, and Divorce," in ibid., 404–28; and L. Michael White, "Paul and Pater Familias," in ibid., 457–87. Also see the older, but still valuable, Vincent L. Wimbush, *Paul: The Worldly Ascetic* (Macon: Mercer University Press, 1987); and Martin, *Corinthian Body*.

[5]Although Paul was apparently childless himself, his letters have an abundance of language related to children and childhood. He also, uncharacteristically of Greco-Roman culture, frequently characterizes himself with childlike imagery. See Reidar Aasgaard, "Paul as a Child: Children and Childhood in the Letters of the Apostle," *JBL* 126 (2007): 129–59.

[6]See Cranfield, *Romans*, 2:788, 794. On Paul's use of family and adoption metaphors, see Trevor J. Burke, *Adopted into God's Family: Exploring a Pauline Metaphor* (New Studies in Biblical Theology 22; Downers Grove: InterVarsity, 2006); and Reidar Aasgaard, *'My Beloved Brothers and Sisters!' Christian Siblingship in Paul* (JSNTSup 265; New York: T&T Clark, 2004).

ing. Paul was probably bilingual (or even trilingual), and he claimed to have engaged in a life of study. Paul could certainly read and write in Greek (Gal 6:11). Paul's habit of referring to Peter by the Aramaic version of his name, Cephas (1 Cor 1:12; 3:22; 9:5; 15:5; Gal 1:18), may suggest that Paul could also communicate in the Aramaic vernacular of ancient Palestine. Paul's familiarity with Aramaic is also suggested by his emphasis upon his Hebrew heritage because, as Martin Hengel has noted, a " 'Hebrew of the Hebrews' [Phil 3:5] who spoke only Greek would be a strange mixture."[7] Furthermore, Paul insisted that he was a diligent student of the law even in his youth (Gal 1:13–14; Phil 3:5–6), perhaps implying some facility in biblical Hebrew.

When viewed in combination, these facts indicate that Paul had completed at least some formal education, and almost certainly some education in Greek. Even a boy raised within a devout Jewish family would likely have learned Greek in a Greco-Roman style system, which progressed through three levels of education: primary, secondary (grammatical), and tertiary (rhetorical). This education would have begun with basic reading and writing skills at the primary and secondary levels (given the variability of educational structures in the ancient world, these two levels often may have been blended together into a single experience). After mastering grammar, the student would move to the more advanced study of rhetoric at the tertiary level.[8] Paul's ability to write in Greek demonstrates at least a primary education, but his education was unlikely to have stopped at that level.

Yet despite Paul's strong linguistic background, any attempt to infer the precise level of Paul's formal education is complicated by a host of factors. For example, many of Paul's letters have co-authors (e.g., 1 Cor 1:1; 2 Cor 1:1; Phil 1:1; 1 Thess 1:1) or were written out by an amanuensis (Rom 16:22). Even Paul's explicit claim to have written out Galatians and 1 Corinthians with his own hand (Gal 6:11; 1 Cor 16:31) prompts one to wonder both whether or not Paul's personal role in the composition of these letters was an exception to his normal practice and whether or not Paul typically gave a

---

[7] See Martin Hengel in collaboration with Roland Deines, *The Pre-Christian Paul* (trans. John Bowden; Philadelphia: Trinity Press International, 1991), 39. Although Paul appears to have read the Old Testament in LXX Greek, it is possible that he also read Hebrew. On the possibility of a trilingual Paul, see Jan Dochhorn, "Paulus und die polyglotte Schriftgelehrsamkeit seiner Zeit," *ZNW* 98 (2007): 189–212.

[8] On educational systems in the Greco-Roman world, see the classics by H. I. Marrou, *A History of Education in Antiquity* (trans. George Lamb; London: Sheed & Ward, 1956); and Stanley F. Bonner, *Education in Ancient Rome: From the Elder Cato to the Younger Pliny* (London: Methuen, 1977); more recently, Robert A. Kaster, "Notes on 'Primary' and 'Secondary' Schools in Late Antiquity," *TAPA* 113 (1983): 323–46; and A. D. Booth, "The Schooling of Slaves in First-Century Rome," *TAPA* 109 (1979): 11–19. On Paul's education being within a two-stage rather than a three-stage educational system, see Stanley E. Porter, "Paul and His Bible: His Education and Access to the Scriptures of Israel," in *As It Is Written: Studying Paul's Use of Scripture* (ed. Stanley E. Porter and Christopher D. Stanley; SBLSymS; Atlanta: SBL, 2008), 29–40. See also Hengel, *Pre-Christian Paul*, 54–62, on Paul's education.

(perhaps more skilled) co-author or amanuensis a freer hand in shaping his other letters.[9] Even on the assumption that Paul had primary responsibility for the rhetoric in his letters, contemporary assessments of Paul's rhetorical skill vary widely.[10] However, it is probably significant to note that at least some of Paul's readers apparently found his letters more impressive than his presence (2 Cor 10:9–11; cf. 2 Pet 3:15–16).[11] Admittedly, in the adversarial context of the Corinthian correspondence, the "weighty and strong" impression of his letters (2 Cor 10:10) could have resulted more from Paul's harsh tone than from his rhetorical skill—particularly in light of Paul's poor rhetorical showing in comparison with Apollos (1 Cor 1:12; 3:4–6, 22; 4:6). Additionally, even if the letters' strong impressions were due to Paul's perceived rhetorical skills, such rhetorical skill does not necessarily imply formal training. Yet, when all the evidence is weighed, it is probably safe to conclude that Paul had completed a significant (though unspecified) amount of formal education, including presumably some education in rhetoric. Ron Hock has accurately reflected the consensus of scholarship in his conclusion that Paul probably enjoyed the benefits of "not only primary schooling but also secondary and tertiary instruction."[12]

Rather than seeking to establish the precise level of Paul's education, it is probably wiser to follow John M. G. Barclay in seeking to determine the level of Paul's assimilation into the social structures of the Greco-Roman world and the degree of Paul's acculturation into the social values of that society. When the Paul of the letters is examined within these two rubrics, it becomes clear that he is highly assimilated into the Greco-Roman world. He is comfortable living as a minority within the larger Greco-Roman pagan majority. He eats with Gentiles without any reservations and insists that other Jewish Christians

---

[9] On the standard practice of using an amanuensis in the process of drafting and revising letters in antiquity, see E. Randolph Richards, *Paul and First-Century Letter Writing: Secretaries, Composition and Collection* (Downers Grove: InterVarsity, 2004), 59–140. Also see Jerome Murphy-O'Connor, "Co-Authorship in the Corinthian Correspondence," *RB* 100 (1993): 562–79. Paul's insistence that he wrote some letters with his own hands was certainly motivated by his desire to increase the rhetorical impact of that particular letter (C. Keith, "'In My Own Hand': Grapho-Literacy and the Apostle Paul," *Bib* 89 [2008]: 39–58).

[10] For a survey of recent analyses of Paul's rhetoric, see Stanley E. Porter, "Paul of Tarsus and His Letters," in *Handbook of Classical Rhetoric in the Hellenistic Period, 330 B.C.–A.D. 400* (ed. Stanley E. Porter; Leiden: Brill, 1997), 533–85.

[11] The accusation that Paul was not an accomplished speaker (ἰδιώτης τῷ λόγῳ, 2 Cor 11:6) probably referred to his oral more than his written communication. See Furnish, *II Corinthians*, 490.

[12] Ronald L. Hock, "Paul and Greco-Roman Education," in Sampley, *Paul in the Greco-Roman World*, 198–227, quoting 215. Hock's conclusion is consistent with the consensus of contemporary scholarship (e.g., Lauri Thurén, *Derhetorizing Paul: A Dynamic Perspective on Pauline Theology and the Law* [Harrisburg: Trinity Press International, 2000], 35). Opinion is not unanimous, however. R. Dean Anderson has argued that Paul's letters demonstrate no familiarity with ancient rhetorical theory (*Ancient Rhetorical Theory and Paul* [rev. ed.; CBET 18; Leuven: Peeters, 1999]).

do the same (Gal 2:11–14); he is undisturbed by the possibility of eating meat that could have made its way to the marketplace via a pagan temple (Rom 14–15; 1 Cor 8); and he encourages Christian believers to willingly pay taxes to Rome because such authorities are "God's servant" (Rom 13:1–7). He also assumes that some believers are married to unbelievers, and he recommends that they remain within such marriages if possible (1 Cor 7:12–16; cf. 2 Cor 6:14–7:1). Yet Paul's acculturation is less pronounced. Paul makes no attempt to reconcile Greek philosophy and Christian theology in the mode of the later Christian apologists or even in the mode of Jewish thinkers like Philo and the authors of 4 Maccabees or the Wisdom of Solomon.[13] Paul's letters demonstrate no interest in Roman or Greek history and literature generally. In fact, Paul's demonstrated acculturation is slight enough that Barclay is probably correct to assert that Paul demonstrates "no more than a rudimentary knowledge of Greek literature or philosophy [beyond the LXX]."[14] The Paul of the letters—and presumably the pre-Christian Paul—was highly assimilated into the Greco-Roman world, but not highly acculturated to the intellectual heritage of that world. Religiously, Paul was highly resistant to any accommodation to the pervasive idolatry of the Roman world (Rom 1:18–32; 1 Cor 10:14; 1 Thess 1:9),[15] a concern that leads to our next area of inquiry.

Paul's Pre-Christian Religious Background

Scholarly assessments of Paul's pre-Christian religious background have been strongly affected by the horrific events of the Holocaust. Throughout the nineteenth and early twentieth centuries, scholars routinely spoke of Paul rejecting his Jewish heritage in order to adopt a Hellenistic and Gentile perspective as a Christian.[16] More recently, there has been a "significant scholarly reappraisal" of both Paul's Jewish roots and his ongoing relationship to Judaism.[17] Unfortunately, this reappraisal has been unable to establish any

---

[13] On Paul's lack of interaction with mainstream Hellenistic thought in comparison to documents like the Wisdom of Solomon and 4 Maccabees and writers like Aristeas, Aristobulus, and Philo, see John M. G. Barclay, "Paul Among Diaspora Jews," *JSNT* 60 (1995): 89–120.

[14] Barclay, "Paul among Diaspora Jews," 105.

[15] Ibid., 89–120.

[16] E.g., Montgomery J. Shroyer, "Paul's Departure from Judaism to Hellenism," *JBL* 59 (1940): 41–49. Even within this period, a few scholars sought to locate Paul back within a Jewish context, but such scholars typically recognized that they were arguing against the dominant scholarly trends of their day (e.g., Shirley Jackson Case, "The Jewish Bias of Paul," *JBL* 47 [1928]: 20–31; and Samuel Belkin, "The Problem of Paul's Background," *JBL* 54 [1935]: 41–60).

[17] Terence L. Donaldson, "'Riches for the Gentiles' (Rom 11:12): Israel's Rejection and Paul's Gentile Mission," *JBL* 112 (1993): 81–98, here 81. Donaldson appropriately noted that part of this appraisal has been occasioned by "the sobering impact on Christian scholarship of the Holocaust and its aftermath." For a review of post-Holocaust Jewish readings of Paul, see Michael F. Bird and Preston M. Sprinkle, "Jewish Interpretation of Paul in the Last Thirty Years," *CBR* 6 (2008): 35–76.

consensus regarding Paul's pre-Christian religious background. As Wayne
Meeks has noted:

> There has been no dearth of attempts to set Paul against the background of vari-
> ous kinds of Judaism. Now he appears as a "rabbi," again as a representative of
> "Jewish apocalyptic"; perhaps he stands closest to "Jewish mysticism," or even
> to "Jewish Gnosticism." Or his peculiar concerns are simply the result of his
> having been reared in "Hellenistic Judaism." . . . [Paul] writes in fluent Greek;
> his Bible is the Septuagint; he is certainly a "Hellenistic Jew." He is convinced
> that the present, evil age is soon coming to an end; in the meantime he urges the
> children of light not to be like the children of darkness—surely this is "Jewish
> apocalyptic." He has been caught up into the third heaven and seen ineffable
> things—surely, if ever, one can speak of "Jewish mysticism" here?—yet he calls
> himself "in terms of the Law, a Pharisee."[18]

Although Meeks is undoubtedly correct to insist that the scant, but varied, evidence does not allow any narrowly prescribed assessment of Paul's
pre-Christian religious life, the letters do provide some clues about the nature
of Paul's pre-Christian life, particularly regarding his life *as a law-observant
Pharisee, as a person irrevocably identified with the Jewish people, and as a zealous
persecutor of the church.* In speaking of himself, Paul insisted that he was "circumcised on the eighth day, a member of the people of Israel, of the tribe of
Benjamin, a Hebrew born of the Hebrews; as to the law, a Pharisee; as to zeal,
a persecutor of the church; as to righteousness under the law, blameless" (Phil
3:5–6; also see Gal 1:13–14). Unfortunately, our knowledge of first-century
Pharisaic belief and practice is less precise than we would like. Nonetheless,
the evidence seems clear that the Pharisaic movement was largely a lay movement centered in Jerusalem and surrounding Judea, but not among priests.[19]
The references to Paul's past in his letters are consistent with a nonpriestly
origin for Paul and his family. In this regard, it is probably significant that
Paul's accounts of his zealousness as a pre-Christian Jew never include references to attending feasts, festivals, or sacrifices in Jerusalem. In fact, Paul's
letters give no evidence either for his participation in the Jerusalem temple
cult or for his interaction with the Jerusalem priesthood.[20]

---

[18] Wayne A. Meeks, *The First Urban Christians: The Social World of the Apostle
Paul* (New Haven: Yale University Press, 1983), 33. Contrast the skepticism of Meeks
with Martin Hengel's insistence that "knowledge of Saul the *Jew* is a precondition of
understanding Paul the *Christian.* The better we know the former, the more clearly we
shall understand the latter" (*Pre-Christian Paul*, xiii, emphasis Hengel's).

[19] Hengel, *Pre-Christian Paul*, 16; Anthony J. Saldarini, *Pharisees, Scribes and Sadducees in Palestinian Society* (Collegeville, Minn.: Michael Glazier, 1988), 277–97. Saldarini correctly observes that "the evidence that Pharisaic teaching and influence spread
beyond the Palestinian borders is very tenuous" (138); on the evidence for Pharisees
in Galilee, see pp. 291–95.

[20] It should be noted, however, that Friedrich Wilhelm Horn discerns a priestly
influence in Paul's reference to the temple in 1 Cor 3:16; 6:19; 2 Cor 6:16 ("Paulus
und der Herodianische Tempel," *NTS* 53 [2007]: 184–203).

Although the letters seem to distance Paul from priestly and temple influences, they are quite clear that he was a Pharisee of Jewish (as opposed to proselyte) heritage and a cautious observer of the law.[21] Paul's self-identification as a Pharisee appears to be understood primarily in terms of his relationship to the law—"as to the law, a Pharisee" (Phil 3:5). Paul apparently understood one's interpretation of the law to be the primary identity marker for a Pharisee. This understanding is consistent with the witness of Josephus, whose corpus constitutes the only other extant writings from a self-identified Pharisee.[22] Before his encounter with Christ, Paul claimed to have practiced extreme fidelity to the law as the law was understood by the Pharisees—"as to righteousness under the law, blameless" (3:6). Throughout his pre-Christian life as a Pharisee, Paul probably never struggled with obedience to the law.[23] As a Christian, Paul came to believe that believers in Christ were not bound to obey the law.[24]

Although much has been made of Paul the Pharisee, Paul's singular reference to himself as a Pharisee (Phil 3:5) is eclipsed by his repeated references to himself as a Jew more broadly conceived.[25] Paul was circumcised (3:5), was a Hebrew (3:5; 2 Cor 11:22), was an Israelite and a child of Abraham (Rom 11:1; 2 Cor 11:22), and was a member of the tribe of Benjamin (Phil 3:5; Rom 11:1). Paul even claimed to have "advanced in Judaism" beyond his peers (Gal 1:14). While Paul appears to have modified his pre-Christian Pharisaic understanding of the law by reinterpreting the law in light of Christ (Gal 3:21–22) or in terms of love (5:14) and even by sometimes setting aside his own observance of the law (1 Cor 9:20–21), Paul never ceased to regard

---

[21] Hyam Maccoby has been a lone voice in questioning the veracity of Paul's claims to a devout Jewish pedigree (*The Myth Maker: Paul and the Invention of Christianity* [San Francisco: Harper & Row, 1986]; and *Paul and Hellenism* [London: SCM, 1991]). His work has been severely (and appropriately) criticized—even by Maccoby's fellow Jewish interpreters of Paul—as marked by "historical fancy" and "inconsistent argument" (see Amy-Jill Levine, review of Hyam Maccoby, *Paul and Hellenism*, *JQR* 86 [1995]: 230–32, quoting 232).

[22] See Saldarini, *Pharisees, Scribes and Sadducees*, 81–83, 134–37.

[23] Most importantly, see the classic: Krister Stendahl, "The Apostle Paul and the Introspective Conscience of the West," *HTR* 56 (1963): 199–215. Also see Leander E. Keck, "The Quest for Paul's Pharisaism: Some Reflections," in *Justice and the Holy: Essays in Honor of Walter Harrelson* (ed. Douglas A. Knight and Peter J. Paris; Atlanta: Scholars Press, 1989), 163–75.

[24] For a helpful summary of Paul's pre-Christian and Christian views on the law, see Stephen Westerholm, "Sinai as Viewed from Damascus: Paul's Reevaluation of the Mosaic Law," in *The Road from Damascus: The Impact of Paul's Conversion on His Life, Thought, and Ministry* (ed. Richard N. Longenecker; Grand Rapids: Eerdmans, 1997), 147–65. Dieter Lührmann suggests that the *Psalms of Solomon* provide the nearest literary depiction of the type of Pharisaic beliefs that the pre-Christian Paul likely held ("Paul and the Pharisaic Tradition," *JSNT* 36 [1989]: 75–94).

[25] Lentz's caution is perhaps overstated, but still worthy of consideration: "It could be that, in his Letter to the Philippians, Paul was not saying that he was a Pharisee, but only that the party whose views were closest to his views were the Pharisees" (*Luke's Portrait of Paul*, 55).

himself as part of the people of Israel (Rom 11:1; 2 Cor 11:22). Even toward the end of his missionary career, he could refer to the Israelites as "my own people according to the flesh" (Rom 9:3–4).[26] He clearly lamented the Jewish people's general rejection of the Christian message (9:1–3) and perhaps even held them responsible for the death of Jesus and for hindering the spread of his message (1 Thess 2:13–16).[27] Yet, even as a Christian, Paul could still insist: "I myself am an Israelite, a descendant of Abraham, a member of the tribe of Benjamin" (Rom 11:1).[28] Rather than rejecting his pre-Christian Jewish identity and heritage, Paul extended that identity and heritage to include Gentiles by making circumcision "a matter of the heart" (2:28; cf. Phil 3:3) and by making Abraham "the ancestor of all who believe" (Rom 4:11; cf. 4:16; 9:8; Gal 3:7–9, 29). The Christian Paul remained a Jewish Paul; his Christian converts converted to Judaism, but Paul insisted that "a person is not a Jew who is one outwardly, nor is true circumcision something external and physical. Rather, a person is a Jew who is one inwardly, and real circumcision is a matter of the heart—it is spiritual and not literal" (Rom 2:28–29a).

Recognizing Paul's consistent identification with these ancient Jewish kinship groups of Israel (Jacob), Abraham, and Benjamin is particularly important in light of Bruce Malina's and Jerome Neyrey's recognition that some historical reconstructions of Paul's pre-Christian life portray the apostle in anachronistic terms that are saturated with modern individualistic assumptions.[29] Perhaps scholars have overemphasized Paul's Pharisaic commitments and underappreciated Paul's own emphasis upon his Jewishness, more broadly conceived, because Paul's Pharisaic connections are presumed to reflect Paul's individual and personal commitments whereas his connections to his heritage as an Israelite and as a Benjaminite and Abrahamic descendant are presumed to be inherited (and, therefore, less significant and formative). Regardless of what modern assumptions have steered scholarship toward an emphasis upon Paul's Pharisaic background, it is important

---

[26]James D. G. Dunn has plausibly suggested that Paul used the term "Jew" as an ethnic designation that lost its meaning in Christ (Gal 3:28) and the terms "Israel" and "child of Abraham" as religious designations that came to include both ethnic Jews and ethnic Gentiles through Christ ("Who Did Paul Think He Was? A Study of Jewish Christian Identity," *NTS* 45 [1999]: 174–93).

[27]On the possibility that these verses are post-Pauline interpolations, see Daryl Schmidt, "1 Thess 2:13–16: Linguistic Evidence for an Interpolation," *JBL* 102 (1983): 269–79; and Birger Pearson, "1 Thessalonians 2:13–16: A Deutero-Pauline Interpolation," *HTR* 64 (1971): 79–94; *contra* Abraham Smith, "'Unmasking the Powers': Toward a Postcolonial Analysis of 1 Thessalonians," in *Paul and the Roman Imperial Order* (ed. Richard A. Horsley; Harrisburg: Trinity Press International, 2004), 58–65.

[28]Paul's identification with the Jewish people was so profound that throughout his life, Paul probably continued to think predominately in the categories of "Jew and Gentile" as opposed to the categories of "Christians and non-Christians." See Pamela M. Eisenbaum, "Paul, Polemics, and the Problem of Essentialism," *Biblical Interpretation* 13 (2005): 224–38, esp. 237.

[29]Bruce J. Malina and Jerome H. Neyrey, *Portraits of Paul: An Archaeology of Ancient Personality* (Louisville: Westminster John Knox, 1996), 19–20.

to note that the two pre-Christian religious identity markers that changed the most in the wake of Paul's Christian experience (i.e., persecution of the church and obedience to the law) were also the two identity markers most consciously chosen by the pre-Christian Paul. The Jewish identity markers that the Christian Paul emphasized most strongly from his pre-Christian life were the inherited markers of a group identity and not the chosen markers of an individual identity.

All of these observations are important because they help us to understand Paul's conception of himself as a Jew. In his pre-Christian life, Paul saw himself advancing in Judaism beyond his peers in the ways that mattered most to him (Gal 1:14). In his Christian life, he probably rejected or redefined the commitments that had, on the one hand, enabled him to advance within Judaism and that had, on the other hand, hindered Gentile inclusion into the Israelite and Abrahamic faith (that is, commitments to a Pharisaic interpretation of the law and to persecution of the church). At the same time, the Christian Paul continued to see himself as an Israelite and a child of Abraham. In fact, even the Christian Paul was apparently willing to submit himself to the repeated disciplinary actions of Jewish leaders who reportedly gave him "forty lashes minus one" on five separate occasions (2 Cor 11:24).[30] Paul never ceased to respect and identify with the Israelite notion of a perceived literal descent from Abraham and Sarah (Rom 9–11), and he sought only to modify, not to reject, the claims of those who rejoiced at being "Jews by birth and not Gentile sinners" (Gal 2:15). Paul's consistent emphasis upon his status as a Jew has led many interpreters to interpret the life-altering Damascus Road encounter (which provides the originating date for Paul's autobiography in Gal 1:15–16) as the call or commission of a prophet in the Old Testament mode rather than as a conversion.[31]

---

[30] Whipping a person with thirty-nine lashes was a traditional Jewish punishment based on Deut 25:1–3, which forbade more than forty lashes. Only those who were under the authority of the synagogue would be subjected to such punishment. See Meeks, *Urban Christians*, 26; and Furnish, *II Corinthians*, 515–16.

[31] The most important advocate for understanding Paul's encounter as a call is Krister Stendahl ("Call Rather Than Conversion," in *Paul among Jews and Gentiles* [Philadelphia: Fortress, 1976], 7–23) and for understanding Paul's encounter as a conversion is Alan F. Segal (*Paul the Convert: The Apostolate and Apostasy of Saul the Pharisee* [New Haven: Yale University Press, 1990]). Also see Richard V. Peace, *Conversion in the New Testament* (Grand Rapids: Eerdmans, 1999), 17–101; Beverly Roberts Gaventa, *From Darkness to Light: Aspects of Conversion in the New Testament* (OBT 20; Philadelphia: Fortress, 1986), 52–95; Peter T. O'Brien, "Was Paul Converted?" in *The Paradoxes of Paul* (vol. 2 of *Justification and Variegated Nomism*; ed. D. A. Carson, Peter T. O'Brien, and Mark A. Seifrid; Waco: Baylor University Press, 2004), 361–91; Barry Smith, *What Must I Do to Be Saved? Paul Parts Ways with His Jewish Heritage* (Sheffield: Sheffield Phoenix, 2007); and Elsdon, "Was Paul 'Converted' or 'Called'?" Zeba A. Crook (*Reconceptualizing Conversion: Patronage, Loyalty, and Conversion in the Religions of the Ancient Mediterranean* [BZNW 130; Berlin: de Gruyter, 2004]) has argued that the entire debate between a call and a conversion is anachronistic and that Paul's experience in Gal 1:11–17 should be interpreted in terms of the ancient patronage system.

Closely related to the pre-Christian Paul's identity as a devout Jew (and perhaps more narrowly as a devout Pharisee) was his role as a persecutor of the church (1 Cor 15:9; Gal 1:13, 23; Phil 3:6). Although Paul is clear that his persecution of the church was generated by his zeal for the Jewish faith, the precise nature of this persecution remains unclear. On the one hand, in his retelling of the events he speaks of "the church" and "Judaism" as distinct entities (Gal 1:13), and it is exceedingly unlikely that Jews ever had the authority (or inclination) to inflict violence upon non-Jews because of religious differences—not even in Judea (Gal 1:22). Although Paul himself was undoubtedly the victim of mob violence and persecution on several occasions (2 Cor 11:21–12:10), most of Paul's references to persecution, both as a victim (1 Cor 4:12; 2 Cor 4:9; Gal 5:11; 1 Thess 3:4, 7) and as perpetrator (1 Cor 15:9; Gal 1:13, 23; Phil 3:6), do not necessarily imply violence. In one instance, persecution was clearly not violent (Gal 4:29). It is possible that the persecution in which Paul participated was a nonviolent assault against "the faith" as an ideological construct and not a violent assault against the people who practiced that faith (Gal 1:23). As L. J. Lietaert Peerbolte has reminded readers: "It is not very likely . . . that Paul actually used violence [against Christians], and there is no solid proof in his letters to assume this. . . . His opposition to the Jesus movement was directed *against the views* of this movement."[32] On the other hand, violence against those who were perceived to be threats to key Israelite and Jewish practices and institutions was not unprecedented in either the ancient Jewish Scriptures or first-century Judaism. It is possible that Paul's zeal for the law lead him to physical violence.[33]

The key question is: *Over whom could a first-century Jewish leader be realistically expected to exert violent authority?* The answer to that question seems clearly to be "only other Jews." In this respect, it is significant that in recounting his days as a persecutor, Paul was emphatic that he remained "unknown to the churches of Judea" even though he had recently been actively persecuting the church (Gal 1:22–23).[34] Paul's insistence on this point renders it much less likely that his persecution of the church ever moved beyond the realm of an intra-Jewish persecution of Jewish believers within the church. It is highly improbable that any first-century Jew would have been able to violently persecute non-Jewish persons, especially outside of Judea. Such an act would have

---

[32] L. J. Lietaert Peerbolte, *Paul the Missionary* (CBET 34; Leuven: Peeters, 2003), 176, emphasis added. Also see Arland J. Hultgren, "Paul's Pre-Christian Persecutions of the Church: Their Purpose, Locale, and Nature," *JBL* 95 (1976): 97–111. More recently, see J. Ashton, "Why Did Paul Persecute 'the Church of God'?" *Scripture Bulletin* 38 (2008): 61–68.

[33] On the understanding of Paul as a violent persecutor of the church, see Wright, "Paul, Arabia, and Elijah"; and Hengel, *Pre-Christian Paul,* 71–72.

[34] Galatians 1:22 has long been interpreted as evidence against Paul's presence in Jerusalem during the earliest days of Christianity. See Theodor Mommsen, "Die Rechtsverhältnisse des Apostels Paulus," *ZNW* 2 (1901): 81–96; *contra* Hengel, *Pre-Christian Paul,* 23–24.

been criminal—and would have been punished as such by the local Roman authorities. Based on Paul's letters, therefore, Paul's persecution of the church appears to involve either nonviolent confrontations between conflicting belief systems or violent persecution within the Jewish community outside of Judea. Presumably the persecutions Paul himself later suffered were inflicted upon him either by Gentile authorities (or mobs) who perceived him to be violating the *Pax Romana* (Roman peace)[35] or by Jewish leaders whose authority Paul continued to recognize.

In any case, Paul's insistence that he was unknown to the churches of Judea both during his days as a persecutor of the church and even later during the first three years of his Christian life clearly indicates that Paul did not interact with the early Christians in Judea (and presumably Jerusalem) during the earliest years of Christianity (Gal 1:21–23).[36] It would also seem to suggest that Paul, the active persecutor, did not reside in Jerusalem at that time. These inferences raise the question of where the pre-Christian Paul did live and how he related to his fellow Jews. Initially, we must reflect upon Paul's claim to have advanced in Judaism beyond many of his peers (1:13–14). For a Pharisee who wished to rise through the ranks, Jerusalem would certainly have been the place to be. Indeed, with little evidence for the presence of Pharisees outside of Judea, it seems *a priori* unlikely to find a self-proclaimed "zealous" Pharisee residing anywhere else. Still, it is possible, however unlikely, that the pre-Christian Paul had never been to Jerusalem (remember: Paul never mentioned participating in the Jerusalem cult). It is more likely, however, that the pre-Christian Paul had intermittent contact with Jerusalem—enough to establish his credentials as a Pharisee zealous for the law, but not enough to establish a significant acquaintance with Jesus and his earliest followers in Jerusalem.[37]

The larger point at stake in discerning the hometown(s) of the pre-Christian Paul is an understanding of his relationship to his Jewish contemporaries. Calvin Roetzel has made a persuasive case that the Christian Paul existed on the margins of Judaism and that he exploited this marginality to

---

[35] From the Roman perspective, Paul was not being persecuted. He was being prosecuted.

[36] It is unlikely that Paul had ever known the historical Jesus. It has long been recognized that Paul's claim to have once known Christ according to the flesh (2 Cor 5:16) probably means that he once viewed Christ apart from the perspective of Christian faith. See Frank C. Porter, "Does Paul Claim to Have Known the Historical Jesus? A Study of 2 Corinthians 5:16," *JBL* 47 (1928): 257–75; *contra* Hengel, *Pre-Christian Paul*, 63–64; and even earlier, S. MacLean Gilmour, "Paul and the Primitive Church," *JR* 25 (1945): 119–28.

[37] For an argument in favor of Paul's residence in Jerusalem, see W. C. van Unnik, *Tarsus or Jerusalem: The City of Paul's Youth* (trans. George Ogg; London: Epworth, 1962). On Paul's residence outside of Jerusalem (and Judea), see Hengel, *Pre-Christian Paul*, 1–5, 72–74. Also see the older tradition of Tarsus's influence on Paul in T. R. Glover, *Paul of Tarsus* (London: Student Christian Movement, 1925; repr., Peabody, Mass.: Hendrickson, 2002), 5–23.

think in theologically creative ways.[38] Other scholars have maintained that as a Diaspora Jew, Paul existed on the margins of Judaism even before his encounter with Christ and that perhaps Paul was involved in seeking Gentile converts even before becoming a Christian missionary.[39] Although any attempt to discern Paul's pre-Christian attitude toward Gentiles is "more or less intelligent guesswork,"[40] such pre-Christian proselytizing activity is unlikely. Few Jews of Paul's era engaged in any form of proselytizing. Generally speaking, Jewish groups did not discourage interested Gentiles from participating in their synagogues, but active proselytizing was extremely rare.[41] More specifically, if Paul had been engaged in proselytizing before becoming a Christian, then his persecution of the church becomes even less comprehensible. Ultimately, however, the most decisive evidence against the notion of Paul's pre-Christian proselytizing of Gentiles is neither the lack of an analogous practice among Paul's fellow Jews (exceptions do occur) nor even Paul's own persecution of the church. The most decisive evidence against Paul's pre-Christian proselytizing activity is the lack of any suggestion in Paul's letters that his pre-Christian Jewish life included any interest in Gentiles.

Paul's Vocation

Paul's letters never explicitly state Paul's vocation, but they nonetheless contain significant evidence of Paul participating in grueling physical labor (1 Thess 2:9; 1 Cor 4:11). Such Pauline references have generated significant debates on two points: (1) what was Paul's attitude toward his labors? and (2) did Paul experience a downward social dislocation before engaging in such labor? In the late nineteenth and early twentieth centuries, Adolf Deissmann and William Ramsay brought these two questions to the attention of critical scholarship. Ramsay argued that Paul was born into relative privilege and was subsequently reduced to manual labor; Deissmann argued that Paul was reared in poverty and never faced anything other than a future of the physical labors common to the lower social classes in the Roman Empire. Initially, many scholars sided with Deissmann, but in the latter part of the twentieth

---

[38] Roetzel, *Paul: A Jew on the Margins*.

[39] Most recently, see Terence L. Donaldson, "Israelite, Convert, Apostle to the Gentiles: The Origin of Paul's Gentile Mission," in Longenecker, *Road from Damascus*, 62–84.

[40] See A. J. M. Wedderburn, *A History of the First Christians* (New York: T&T Clark, 2004), 79.

[41] See, e.g., Peter Schäfer, *Judeophobia: Attitudes toward the Jews in the Ancient World* (Cambridge: Harvard University Press, 1997), esp. 106–18; Louis H. Feldman, *Jew and Gentile in the Ancient World: Attitudes and Interactions from Alexander to Justinian* (Princeton: Princeton University Press, 1993), esp. 288–341; Irina Levinskaya, *The Book of Acts in Its Diaspora Setting* (BAFCS 5; Grand Rapids: Eerdmans, 1996), 19–50; and Hans Conzelmann, *Gentiles—Jews—Christians: Polemics and Apologetics in the Greco-Roman Era* (trans. M. Eugene Boring; Minneapolis: Fortress, 1992), 135–233.

century, a consensus coalesced around a view similar to Ramsay's originally wealthy, but socially dislocated, Paul.[42]

By the time that Paul wrote his letters, he clearly was accustomed to hard work (1 Thess 2:9; 1 Cor 4:12). Although he does not specify the nature of his work, the general description of his labor is easily recognized as consistent with the artisans who performed much of the urban, nonagricultural labor through the Roman Empire. Such work was laborious, but not unskilled. The life of an artisan was less dismal than many stations within the Greco-Roman world. Although artisans could experience financial insecurity, and they were never far from unaddressed physical needs (e.g., Phil 4:11–12), they could generally expect both to earn enough money to provide for their basic needs and to be more secure than the beggars, day laborers, and unskilled workers below them on the economic ladder.[43]

In fact, artisans were often proud of their professions and they frequently formed voluntary associations with people from similar professions. These associations had a variety of purposes, including social and religious purposes. It is quite plausible to imagine Paul preaching and engaging in Christian evangelism while busily plying his trade. Paul likely could have gathered converts from among his fellow artisans as they interacted in their workshops and vocational associations.[44] In spite of the artisans' comparative advantage when viewed from the perspective of the vast Greco-Roman population below them economically, the idea of being reduced to the physical labor and financial insecurity of an artisan was deeply disconcerting to the comparative few elites higher up on the economic ladder.

One way to answer the question of whether Paul might have belonged to the disenfranchised elite is to consider his attitude toward his work. Hock has argued that Paul's descriptions of his physical toil in 1 Thessalonians and the Corinthian correspondence reflect "the snobbish and scornful attitude so typical of upper class Greeks and Romans."[45] According to Hock, Paul's life as an artisan consisted "of being bent over a workbench like a slave and of

---

[42]The scholarship in relation to Deissmann and Ramsay is ably summarized by Ronald F. Hock ("Paul's Tentmaking and the Problem of His Social Class," *JBL* 97 [1978]: 555–64, esp. 555–58) and in relation to the late twentieth-century consensus by Steven J. Friesen ("Poverty in Pauline Studies: Beyond the So-called New Consensus," *JSNT* 26 [2004]: 323–61). On both, also see Abraham J. Malherbe, *Social Aspects of Early Christianity* (Baton Rouge: Louisiana State University Press, 1977).

[43]See Alison Burford, *Craftsmen in Greek and Roman Society* (Ithaca: Cornell University Press, 1972).

[44]See Ronald F. Hock, "The Workshop as a Social Setting for Paul's Missionary Preaching," *CBQ* 41 (1979): 438–50; Richard S. Ascough, "The Thessalonian Christian Community as a Professional Voluntary Association," *JBL* 119 (2000): 311–28; and idem, *Paul's Macedonian Associations: The Social Context of Philippians and 1 Thessalonians* (WUNT 161; Tübingen: Mohr Siebeck, 2003). Also see Philip A. Harland, *Associations, Synagogues, and Congregations: Claiming a Place in Ancient Mediterranean Society* (Minneapolis: Fortress, 2003).

[45]Hock, "Paul's Tentmaking," 562.

working side by side with slaves; of thereby being perceived by others and by himself as slavish and humiliated; of suffering the artisans' lack of status and so being reviled and abused."[46] Hock argued that Paul viewed his work as an artisan as a humiliation he endured as part of his apostolic calling—a sacrifice made for the sake of the gospel.

More recently, Todd Still has argued that "Paul perceived (his) work as more of a friend than a foe."[47] As Still correctly noted, Hock argued for Paul's sense of "humiliation" and "slavishness" primarily on the basis of 1 Cor 9:19 (where Paul claims to have made himself "a slave to all" so that he could win more people) and 2 Cor 11:7 (where Paul claims to have "humbled" himself so he could preach the gospel "free of charge").[48] Still correctly acknowledged that the elite did look down upon artisans, but he also emphasized both the heavily loaded rhetorical contexts of these passages and Paul's overarching condemnation of the socio-economic divisions within the Corinthian church. In this rhetorical context, for Paul to have denigrated physical labor, even his own physical labor, "would have in effect degraded lower-class Corinthians, the ones for whom he was advocating."[49] Indeed, in the context of the Corinthian correspondence, Paul seems to dignify his physical toils as an artisan because they prevented him from becoming a financial burden upon the Corinthians (1 Cor 9:15–18). In effect, Paul is telling the Corinthians, "see what I put up with for you!"[50] As a general practice, Paul appears to have avoided accepting financial assistance from community members where he was presently preaching. This refusal to accept money from his current congregations was apparently offensive to the believers in Corinth (2 Cor 11:7), but from Paul's perspective it both preempted potential accusations that he was exploiting the goodwill of his converts and freed him from falling into unhelpful patron/client relationships with his converts.[51] In all likelihood, therefore, the Corinthian correspondence's exaggerated rhetoric about the harshness of his physical labor probably represents not so much Paul's disdain for his work as an artisan as his affection for sarcasm throughout these specific letters.[52] Paul generally appears to have remained financially independent from his converts through his work as an artisan (1 Thess 2:9; 1 Cor 9:3–18; 2 Cor 11:8), even though he sometimes allowed

---

[46] Ronald F. Hock, *The Social Context of Paul's Ministry: Tentmaking and Apostleship* (Philadelphia: Fortress, 1980), 67.

[47] Todd D. Still, "Did Paul Loathe Manual Labor? Revisiting the Work of Ronald F. Hock on the Apostle's Tentmaking and Social Class," *JBL* 125 (2006): 781–95, here 794.

[48] Hock, "Paul's Tentmaking," 560–61; and Hock, *Social Context*, 61–65. See the critique in Still, "Did Paul Loathe Manual Labor?" 787–89.

[49] Still, "Did Paul Loathe Manual Labor?" 789.

[50] See Furnish, *II Corinthians*, 506–9.

[51] See Gerd Theissen, *The Social Setting of Pauline Christianity: Essays on Corinth* (trans. John H. Schütz; Philadelphia: Fortress, 1982), 44–49.

[52] On the sarcasm in the Corinthian correspondence, see Jerry W. McCant, *2 Corinthians* (Readings; Sheffield: Sheffield Academic Press, 1999), 13–20.

the converts from his earlier work in other cities to supplement his income (Phil 4:15–17; 2 Cor 11:9).[53]

In regard to his vocation, therefore, we can safely conclude that Paul worked as an artisan and was proud of the fact that the revenue from his labors freed him from becoming financially dependent upon his converts (1 Cor 9:12–18). It is less clear whether or not Paul was proud of his vocation as such or merely of the measure of financial independence that it provided him. In any case, Paul boasted that he never accepted money from the congregations among whom he was presently working. However, even in spite of this boast, Paul did accept money both from congregations he had previously established (Phil 2:25–30; 4:10–20) and from congregations that had been established by others (Rom 15:22–29).

Paul's Political Status and Orientation

The last decade of the twentieth century and the first decade of the twenty-first century saw the emergence of potent political and theological trends that have coalesced to prompt significant revisions to earlier understandings of Paul's political orientation and status. In the realm of geopolitics, the peaceful end to the Cold War and its binary opposition between two superpowers left the United States as the world's sole superpower, a superpower that then waged two wars in oil-rich Arab lands. In the realm of theological discourse, the post-Holocaust "new perspective" on Paul dismantled the notions of first-century Judaism as "legalistic" and of first-century Jews as proponents of "works righteousness."[54] Each of these phenomena created an epiphenomenon in Pauline scholarship. First, during the Cold War, the reigning ideologies allowed first world interpreters to identify the liberal Western democracies with the stabilizing and supposedly civilizing influence of the

---

[53]See Bassler, *God and Mammon*, 63–88.

[54]For a brief introduction to the "new perspective" on Paul, see James D. G. Dunn, "The New Perspective on Paul," in *Jesus, Paul and the Law: Studies in Mark and Galatians* (Louisville: Westminster John Knox, 1990), 183–214. The seminal work of the new perspective is E. P. Sanders, *Paul and Palestinian Judaism* (Minneapolis: Fortress, 1977). The most significant recent critical review of the new perspective and its relationship to earlier critical perspectives is Stephen Westerholm, *Perspectives Old and New on Paul: The "Lutheran" Paul and His Critics* (Grand Rapids: Eerdmans, 2004). Also see A. Andrew Das, *Paul and the Jews* (LPS; Peabody, Mass.: Hendrickson, 2003), esp. 187–96; and Stephen Chester, "When the Old Was New: Reformation Perspectives on Galatians 2:16," *ExpTim* 119 (2008): 320–29. For a particularly insightful investigation into the parallels between this contemporary debate over Pauline interpretation and ancient debate over Pauline interpretation, see Andrew S. Jacobs, "A Jew's Jew: Paul and the Early Christian Problem of Jewish Origins," *JR* 86 (2006): 258–86. It is important to note that Jewish scholars argued against the dominant Christian (primarily Protestant) mischaracterizations of first-century Judaism long before the ascendancy of the new perspective (e.g., M. Friedländer, "The 'Pauline' Emancipation from the Law: A Product of the Pre-Christian Jewish Diaspora," *JQR* 14 [1902]: 265–302; *contra* C. G. Montefiore, "First Impressions of Paul," *JQR* 6 [1894]: 428–74).

Roman Empire and to view the communist regimes of the Soviet Block as the perceived foes of stability and civilization. After the tensions of the Cold War eased and the perceptions of external threats waned, many scholars developed a more self-critical identification with the Roman Empire.

Such post–Cold War—and particularly postcolonial—interpreters often began to view the Roman peace in terms of a superpower's tendency to conquer and dominate rather than to stabilize and civilize. When contemporary first world—and particularly American—interpreters identify parallels between their nation-state's modern hegemony over global affairs and the Roman Empire's ancient hegemony, they now tend to view that hegemony as a symptom of the sinful powers Paul's gospel opposed.[55] Thus, within a few decades, the phenomenon of geopolitical change contributed to an epiphenomenon within Pauline studies: prominent interpretations of Paul's gospel viewed it as a challenge to, rather than legitimation for, the Roman Empire. Second, a theological epiphenomenon conveniently joined forces with this political epiphenomenon. The defunct "old perspective" on Paul had provided a "Judaizing" foe against whom Paul struggled, stereotyped Jewish opponents who sought to extinguish the bright light of the law-free gospel championed by Paul (and his interpreters within the Western democracies). In contrast to Paul's gospel of freedom, these reified Judaizers sought to enslave Gentile Christians to the law in order to force them to earn their salvation through good works. When the "new perspective" on Paul offered a more nuanced and accurate characterization of first-century Judaism, interpreters were left without a proper foe for Paul—and that foe is now often found in the Roman Empire.[56]

These shifts in perspective on ancient antagonisms (Jews vs. Gentiles and the empire vs. subjugated peoples) served as important catalysts for reinterpreting Paul's orientation toward, and thus his status within, the Roman Empire. The unrevised Paul used the peace and stability provided by the empire in order to proclaim his gospel of freedom; the revised Paul offered his message as a direct alternative to the empire's false claims of peace. The many scholars who now view Rome as Paul's chief adversary tend to find this conflict most palpable in Philippians, 1 Thessalonians, and the Corinthian correspondence.

---

[55] See, e.g., the epilogue, "The Lure of a Global Empire," in Crossan and Reed, *In Search of Paul*, 404–13. Also see Robert Jewett, *Paul: The Apostle to America* (Louisville: Westminster John Knox, 1994), esp. 113–27.

[56] On the role of these cultural trends, see Richard A. Horsley, ed., *Paul and Politics* (Harrisburg: Trinity Press International, 2000), 1–16; idem, *Paul and the Roman Imperial Order*, 1–23. Also see Neil Elliott, "Paul and the Politics of Empire: Problems and Prospects," in Horsley, *Paul and Politics*, 17–39; and Elisabeth Schüssler Fiorenza, "Paul and the Politics of Interpretation," in ibid., 40–57. As an illustration of the earlier approach to reading Paul, consider both the benign attitude toward the Roman Empire and the hostility toward "Judaizers" in Bruce, *Apostle of the Heart Set Free*, esp. 22–25; 173–87.

Richard Horsley has been a leading voice in the call for anti-imperial readings of Paul's letters. He has summarized the central tenets of his and related interpretive approaches to Paul in connection with the book of Romans: "Insofar as Paul deliberately used language closely associated with the imperial religion, he was presenting his gospel as a *direct competitor* of the gospel of Caesar. Once this is discerned, then other features of Romans suddenly take on their true political significance."[57] Such readings assume that where the vocabulary of Paul's Christian theology overlapped with that of the imperial cult, Paul was challenging the claims of the empire. These interpretations emphasize the reality that many key Pauline terms such as *gospel, justice, peace,* and *lord* were commonplace within the empire's political soteriology.[58] Until relatively recently, scholars commonly assumed that this overlap in language was insignificant and that the imperial cult, particularly in the Eastern empire (where Paul was most active), involved homage, not worship.[59] However, recent analyses have criticized facile dismissal of the imperial cult and argued that such dismissals are rooted in an anachronistic modern distinction between religion and politics.

Contemporary scholars have come to reject a distinction between religion and politics for the Roman era through a set of interrelated and cross-disciplinary arguments. Using sociological terms, Simon Price insisted: "the imposition of the conventional distinction between religion and politics obscures the basic similarity between politics and religion: both are ways of systematically constructing power."[60] As a matter of historical analysis, Richard Horsley explained:

---

[57] Richard A. Horsley, ed., *Paul and Empire* (Harrisburg: Trinity Press International, 1997), 170, emphasis added. N. T. Wright has correctly observed: "Paul emerges within Horsley's construct as someone opposed not to Judaism but to Caesar's empire. In this light, Sanders does not appear to have gone far enough in opposing the Lutheran model of Paul; Paul may not have had as much of a critique of Judaism as Protestant thought had supposed, but he was still to be understood, in Sanders's model, as fundamentally in dialogue with, and hence in a sense over against, the Jewish tradition, whereas he was in fact first and foremost in confrontation with the Roman world. . . . This emphasis of Horsley and the other contributors [is] easily comprehensible within the sensitivities of a post-Holocaust Western world" ("Paul's Gospel and Caesar's Empire," in Horsley, *Paul and Politics,* 163).

[58] On the overlap of language within Paul's letters and the "soteriology" of the ubiquitous Roman imperial cult, see Horsley, *Paul and Empire,* 1–24. Also see, Wright, "Paul's Gospel and Caesar's Empire," 164–73.

[59] Most importantly, see Arthur Darby Nock, *Essays on Religion and the Ancient World* (ed. Zeph Stewart; Cambridge: Harvard University Press, 1972).

[60] See, e.g., Simon R. F. Price, "Rituals and Power," in Horsley, *Paul and Empire,* 71. It should be noted that more recently, apparently over discomfort with Pauline scholars' emphasis upon the presence and significance of the imperial cult in Asia Minor, Price, a classics scholar, has reminded Pauline scholars that "the world of the Augustan court ideology is very remote from the world of the eastern cities of the Roman empire" ("Response," in Horsley, *Paul and the Roman Imperial Order,* 181).

It is . . . simply anachronistic to think that Paul was founding a religion called Christianity that broke away from a religion called Judaism. Paul's mission and communities would not have appeared as distinctively religious to his contemporaries in the Roman empire. The term he uses for the movement as a whole as well as for particular communities, *ekklēsia*, was primarily political, the term for the citizens' "assembly" of the Greek *polis* (city-state). . . . Paul's assemblies were political as well as religious, somewhat as the Greek *polis* was both political and religious.[61]

In specifically theological terms, Neil Elliott warned:

As soon as we recognize the centrality of the cross of Christ for Paul, the common view that Paul was uninterested in political realities should leave us perplexed. The crucifixion of Jesus is, after all, one of the most unequivocally political events recorded in the New Testament. Behind the early theological interpretations of Jesus' crucifixion as a death "for us," and behind centuries of piety that have encrusted the crucifixion with often grotesque sentimentality, stands the "most nonreligious and horrendous feature of the gospel," the brutal fact of the cross as an instrument of imperial terror.[62]

When read within such sociological, historical, and theological frames of reference, the gospel that Paul proclaimed certainly can be viewed as a direct political challenge to the emperor's gospel. The emperor's gospel proclaimed that peace and justice came only through his lordship; Paul's gospel announced that peace and justice came only through the lordship of Jesus Christ whom the Roman Empire had crucified.[63]

One of the first areas in Paul's letters to be reexamined for its political implications was Paul's discussion of Christ's future *parousia* in 1 Thessalonians. As Abraham Smith has noted, none of Paul's "key terms" in 4:12–5:11 were "politically innocuous."[64] For example, Paul depicted Christ's anticipated return as a *parousia* ("coming" or "presence," 2:19; 3:13; 4:15; 5:23) and the eschatological gathering of the saints as an *apantēsis* ("meeting," 4:17); both terms were closely associated with imperial visits to a city. Even Paul's warning that these events will occur when people say "peace and security" (εἰρήνη καὶ ἀσφάλεια, 5:3) echoes the benefits that the empire claimed to provide its citizens and subjects. According to Smith, such terminology was designed to reject the presence and promises of the emperor and to offer the presence and promises of Christ as their explicit alternative. The pretense of

---

[61] Horsley, *Paul and Empire*, 8.

[62] Neil Elliott, "The Anti-Imperial Message of the Cross," in Horsley, *Paul and Empire*, 167. The phrase which Elliott has enclosed in quotation marks is taken from J. Christiaan Beker, *Paul the Apostle: The Triumph of God in Life and Thought* (Philadelphia: Fortress, 1980), 207.

[63] For the most recent treatment of Paul's gospel as a nonviolent alternative to the violence of the Roman Empire, see Davina C. Lopez, *Apostle to the Conquered: Reimaging Paul's Mission* (Paul in Critical Contexts; Minneapolis: Fortress, 2008).

[64] Abraham Smith, "Unmasking the Powers," 48.

the emperor's lordship is replaced by the reality of Christ's lordship.[65] Similarly, Helmut Koester has suggested that when read against the background of "imperial Roman propaganda," 1 Thessalonians "points to the coming of the Lord as an event that will shatter the false peace and security of the Roman establishment."[66] Indeed, if Paul's depiction of Christ's *parousia* was consciously parodying the pomp and circumstance of an imperial visit to a Roman city, then 1 Thessalonians does provide a potent political challenge to the Roman Empire.

Similar anti-imperial implications can also be found in Philippians and the Corinthian correspondence. Paul's example of the self-abasing Christ, who was "in the form of God" but who set aside such privileges (Phil 2:5–11), can be viewed in contrast to the conduct of the emperor who falsely claimed to be in the form of God and who behaved in a self-exalting fashion.[67] Even Paul's idea that God can bring glory to God's self through Paul's possible Roman execution (Phil 1:15–30)[68] can be regarded as an affirmation that the true God of this world remained sovereign over Rome even when Rome appeared to have matters firmly in hand.[69] Much of the language of Paul's humiliations and struggles in 2 Corinthians also takes on increased significance when read against the background of imperial claims. For example, Paul's insistence that his gospel is victorious over every obstacle even though he does "not wage war according to human standards" (2 Cor 10:3–6) and his claim that his humiliations are ironically enabling him to participate in a "triumphal procession" (2:14–16) may be thinly veiled accusations against the empire's practice of gloating in military conquest and pageantry.[70]

More broadly considered, Paul's widely recognized rejection of the patronage system, particularly as it disrupted the churches in Corinth and

---

[65]Ibid., 48. Also see, J. R. Harrison, "Paul and the Imperial Gospel at Thessaloniki," *JSNT* 25 (2002): 71–96; E. Green, "La *Pax Romana* y el día del Señor—1 Tesalonicenses 5:1–11," *Kairós* 41 (2007): 9–27; and Barbara R. Rossing, *The Rapture Exposed: The Message of Hope in the Book of Revelation* (Cambridge: Westview, 2004), 175–77.

[66]Helmut Koester, "Imperial Ideology and Paul's Eschatology in 1 Thessalonians," in Horsley, *Paul and Empire*, 162. Also see Karl P. Donfried, "The Imperial Cults of Thessalonica and Political Conflict in 1 Thessalonians," in ibid., 215–23; E. Green, "El anuncio del evangelio ante el poder imperial en Tesalónica," *Kairós* 39 (2006): 9–21; and Elliott, "Paul and the Politics of Empire," 24–26.

[67]See Erik M. Heen, "Phil 2:6–11 and Resistance to Local Timocratic Rule: *Isa theō* and the Cult of the Emperor in the East," in Horsley, *Paul and the Roman Imperial Order*, 125–53.

[68]On the possibility that Paul wrote Philippians while contemplating suicide rather than execution, see N. Clayton Croy, " 'To Die is Gain' (Philippians 1:19–26): Does Paul Contemplate Suicide?" *JBL* 122 (2003): 517–31.

[69]See Peter Oakes, "God's Sovereignty over Roman Authorities: A Theme in Philippians," in *Rome in the Bible and the Early Church* (ed. Peter Oakes; Grand Rapids: Baker Academic, 2002), 126–41.

[70]See Neil Elliott, "The Apostle Paul's Self-Presentation as Anti-Imperial Performance," in Horsley, *Paul and the Roman Imperial Order*, 67–88.

Macedonia, can be viewed as a challenge to the emperor who stood at the apex of the patronage system as the empire's ultimate patron.[71]

The potential for uncovering anti-imperial rhetoric in Paul is seemingly limitless. For example, according to Jennifer Wright Knust, Paul's teachings about "sexual virtue and vice" offer a "critique of Roman imperial pretensions";[72] according to Bruce Winter, Paul's criticism of the law is really a criticism of the empire and its pretense of the rule of law;[73] and according to Sze-kar Wan, "the anti-imperial, anti-colonial implications" of Paul's collection for the poor "could not be clearer."[74]

The two principle objections to such readings of Paul underscore (1) Paul's apocalyptic expectation of an imminent end to the present world (e.g., 1 Cor 7:26; 1 Thess 4:12–5:11; Rom 13:12) and (2) his admonition to submit to governing authorities (Rom 13:1–7). The first objection, that Paul's urgent apocalyptic expectation created a disregard for large-scale social and political structures, is assumed in J. Christiaan Beker's claim that Paul had "no conscious emphasis on public relations" and that within Paul's churches, "eschatological expectation motivated Christians to wait for 'the imminent day of salvation' (cf. Rom. 13:11)."[75] Similarly, Marion Soards argued that Paul "cared and spoke little about the structures of this world—after all, they were condemned to pass away."[76] In rebuttal of such claims, it must be recognized that apocalyptic thought was inherently political; the genre of apocalyptic itself arose as a Jewish challenge to a "social setting of imperial domination."[77]

The second objection, which Beker described as Paul's "appeal for subjection to the state" and Paul's "way of describing the state and its officials in the traditional laudatory language of Hellenistic politics" (e.g., Rom 13:1–7), is more difficult to counter.[78] Indeed, Paul insisted: "Let every person be subject to the governing authorities; for there is no authority except from God,

---

[71]See, e.g., John K. Chow, "Patronage in Roman Corinth," in Horsley, *Paul and Empire*, 104–25; Horsley, *Paul and Empire*, 242–52; Horsley, *Paul and Politics*, 72–102; and Efrain Agosto, "Patronage and Commendations, Imperial and Anti-Imperial," in Horsley, *Paul and the Roman Imperial Order*, 103–23.

[72]Jennifer Wright Knust, "Paul and the Politics of Virtue and Vice," in Horsley, *Paul and the Roman Imperial Order*, 173.

[73]Bruce W. Winter, "Roman Law and Society in Romans 12–15," in Oakes, *Rome in the Bible and the Early Church*, 67–102.

[74]Sze-kar Wan, "Collection for the Saints as Anticolonial Acts: Implications of Paul's Ethnic Reconstruction," in Horsley, *Paul and Politics*, 215.

[75]Beker, *Paul the Apostle*, 306, 326. However, Beker also wishes to defend Paul against any charges of advocating a gnostic distinction between the world and the spiritual world to come. See pp. 326–27.

[76]Marion L. Soards, *The Apostle Paul: An Introduction to His Writings and Teachings* (New York: Paulist, 1987), 200.

[77]See Rollin A. Ramsaran, "Resisting Imperial Domination and Influence: Paul's Apocalyptic Rhetoric in 1 Corinthians," in Horsley, *Paul and the Roman Imperial Order*, 94. Also see Elliott, "Anti-Imperial Message of the Cross," 174–77; and Horsley, *Paul and Empire*, 144–45.

[78]Beker, *Paul the Apostle*, 326.

and those authorities that exist have been instituted by God" (13:1). Paul then deduced that whoever resisted the governing authorities was liable to judgment (v. 2) and affirmed that the authorities were "God's servant for your good" (v. 4). Given these convictions, it is small wonder that Paul urged his readers to render honor to whom honor was due and to pay taxes to whom taxes were due (v. 7).[79] Although a number of scholars have offered revisionist readings of this key text, suggesting that Paul's admonitions are actually anti-imperial rhetoric encased in a "protective code" or "hidden transcript," such arguments are hardly convincing.[80] As Bruno Blumenfeld has quipped, Rom 13 reads like "a contribution to a *Festschrift* for Nero."[81] Blumenfeld argued that Paul's pragmatic acceptance of the empire's presence was rooted in classical Hellenistic concepts of justice and kingship. According to Blumenfeld, "In Paul's system, power is not diluted by sharing. Everyone who participates in it [including the emperor] actually *adds* to Christ."[82] Although Blumenfeld's rhetoric may be excessive at points ("Paul loves Rome" and Paul "is the ideological guardian of the processes and structures of imperial power"[83]), he is probably correct to insist that Paul was "conservative" and that Paul saw imperial structures as divinely sanctioned and essential to the spread of the gospel.[84] Even though most Pauline scholars concur—in varying degrees—with Blumenfeld's "conservative" reading of Paul, not all such readings presume a pervasively Hellenistic background behind Paul's perspective. Equally accommodating attitudes toward pagan political structures can be found in the Hebrew Bible and LXX, in Hellenistic Judaism (particularly Philo and Josephus), and in other early Christian writers. Any—or a combination of all—of these sources could have informed Paul's seemingly accommodationist political ethos.[85]

---

[79] Although many scholars have emphasized the empire's demand for Christian believers to offer appropriate honors to the emperor and empire, we should not ignore the empire's willingness to honor its citizens, even openly Christian citizens, when those citizens worked in harmony with the goals of the empire. See Bruce W. Winter, "The Public Honouring of Christian Benefactors: Romans 13.3–4 and 1 Peter 2.14–15," *JSNT* 34 (1988): 87–103.

[80] Dieter Georgi, "God Turned Upside Down," in Horsley, *Paul and Empire*, 157; and Elliott, "Paul and the Politics of Empire," 39. Also see Robert Jewett, "Response: Exegetical Support from Romans and Other Letters," in Horsley, *Paul and Politics*, 65–68; and Neil Elliott, "Romans 13:1–7 in the Context of Propaganda," in Horsley, *Paul and Empire*, 184–204.

[81] Bruno Blumenfeld, *The Political Paul: Justice, Democracy and Kingship in a Hellenistic Framework* (JSNTSup 210; Sheffield: Sheffield Academic Press, 2001), 292. Similarly, Richard J. Cassidy argues that "Paul advocated an approach of full compliance with the demands of the Roman rulers" (*Paul in Chains: Roman Imprisonment and the Letters of Paul* [New York: Herder & Herder, 2001], 16).

[82] Blumenfeld, *Political Paul,* 282, emphasis Blumenfeld's.

[83] Ibid., 282, 283.

[84] Ibid., 276–395, esp. 290.

[85] For the most recent surveys of possible background texts for Paul's attitude toward Roman rule, see Cassidy, *Paul in Chains,* 29–35; and Jewett, *Romans,* 785–87.

Regardless of the background from which Paul drew his ideas concerning the empire, *Paul's outlook on the empire seems to contain a basic incongruity.* On the one hand, Paul's admonishments in Rom 13 call for believers to cooperate with the empire in significant ways. The Paul of Rom 13 is no revolutionary and, as Blumenfeld wisely noted, the Paul of Philippians was probably no revolutionary either—or else his Roman captors almost certainly would not have allowed the Letter to the Philippians see the light of day.[86] On the other hand, it must be admitted that Paul's message could be perceived as a strong challenge to Roman imperial domination. The claims that Paul makes about Christ, justice, peace, worship, and God all run counter to the parallel claims of the empire.[87] Paul's gospel left no room for worship of any being beside or even beneath Christ, and it therefore implies an unequivocal rejection of many of the claims central to imperial ideology and practice. However, such Pauline rejection of the empire was implicit and never explicit. Even though Paul's claims regarding Christ obviously impinged upon well-established imperial claims, a direct challenge to the empire "was not necessarily intended by the author [Paul] or perceived by the audience."[88] In this regard, Ross Saunders is probably correct to conclude that when viewed through Paul's eyes—and certainly when viewed through the logic of his gospel, the claims of the empire and its imperial cult were "blasphemous." Still, Paul never explicitly said so. *Paul's gospel implied a rejection of the empire's ideology and practices, but Paul did not call for this rejection—perhaps Paul never even recognized the need for it.*[89]

The ambiguity of Paul's perspective on the empire is matched by the ambiguity of the empire's perspective on Paul. According to Paul's letters, the empire imprisoned Paul multiple times (e.g., 2 Cor 6:5; 11:13; Rom 16:7; Phlm 1, 9, 13; Phil 1:7, 13–17). Paul's imprisonment was probably a form of military custody in which he was closely guarded—in fact, literally chained to a guard, but still able to participate in many normal activities without facing the absolutely desperate situation of confinement to a Roman prison. Such custody, unlike literal imprisonment, posed little threat to one's immediate

---

On pp. 782–83, Jewett offers reasons for rejecting the proposal that Rom 13:1–7 is an interpolation.

[86]Blumenfeld noted that Paul had to write Philippians "without arousing the suspicions of the very alert Roman praetorian guard [Phil 1:13]. This seems to suggest that the groups he addressed were never perceived as dangerous by the imperial authorities" (*Political Paul,* 291). In addition to his captors, Paul apparently also had close Christian associates who were closely identified with Caesar's household (Phil 4:22).

[87]Stanley E. Porter has plausibly argued that Paul's insistence upon the divine origin of all *just* authorities "directly implie[s] . . . that authorities which were unjust were not authorities at all and to them no obedience was required." "Romans 13:1–7 as Pauline Political Rhetoric," *Filología Neotestamentaria* 6 (1990): 115–39, quoting 137.

[88]Price, "Response," 183.

[89]See Ross Saunders, "Paul and the Imperial Cult," in Porter, *Paul and His Opponents,* 227–38. Also see Peter Oakes, "Re-mapping the Universe: Paul and the Emperor in 1 Thessalonians and Philippians," *JSNT* 27 (2005): 301–22.

health and well-being.[90] In spite of the relative safety of Paul's captive experience, he was keenly aware of the possibility that the empire might eventually execute him (Phil 1:18–26), but even this possibility of execution must be balanced by the fact that Paul was retained and released a number of times (2 Cor 6:5; 11:13; Rom 16:7). Paul's *releases* from custody may be as significant as his imprisonments themselves. Paul's imprisonments demonstrate that someone brought some kind of charges against him, but Paul's releases demonstrate that the Romans must not have regarded the charges against him as particularly credible or significant. If the empire had considered Paul a significant threat, he would not have been released from custody—he would have been executed. Roman "justice" would have dealt swiftly and decisively with any perceived threat to the Roman peace. Paul's letters, therefore, imply that the Romans did not regard Paul as a significant threat. Indeed, Paul's letters suggest that he enjoyed positive relations with at least some of his Roman captors (Phil 1:12–14; 4:22).

The fact of Paul's repeated imprisonments is clear from his letters. However, reasons for his arrests and imprisonments are not. Paul's letters reveal neither the charges against him nor the identity of his accusers. To be sure, his imprisonment did result in his "defense and confirmation of the gospel" (Phil 1:7), but it is unlikely that Paul was imprisoned simply for preaching about Christ. The Roman authorities could not have been acting on any preexisting anti-Christian policies in the cities where Paul preached, because Paul was the first Christian to appear in these cities. Paul's imprisonments, therefore, had to arise from activities specifically associated with him and not from anti-Christian policies in general. Unfortunately, the letters provide no clue to what specific activities landed Paul in Roman custody. Paul's status within the Roman world was, therefore, ambiguous: he was often imprisoned, but also often released. Even while in custody, Paul was allowed both to write letters to his fellow Christians (Phil 1:7; Phlm 1) and to proclaim Christ to his captors (Phil 1:12–14).

Summary of the Pauline Data Set

Paul's letters represent the apostle as a single man who was at home within the Greco-Roman world. He was fluent in oral and written Greek and likely had at least some facility in Aramaic or Hebrew or both. The Paul of the letters was highly assimilated into the Greco-Roman world and negotiated its Gentile and pagan urban environments well. In spite of this assimilation and, it seems likely, the benefits of at least some formal Greek education, the apostle of the letters was not highly acculturated into Greco-Roman society; he demonstrates little interaction with Greek and Roman literature and philosophy. Before becoming a Christian, this Paul, a Jew of Jewish as opposed

---

[90] On the circumstances of Roman custody with respect to Paul, see Cassidy, *Paul in Chains*, 36–43, 69–75, 153–55.

to proselyte origins, persecuted the church and the Christian faith—though perhaps without violence. The Paul of the letters never ceased to identify himself with the Jewish people. Paul's identification with the Jewish people probably even prompted him to accept discipline from his fellow Jews on several occasions. However, this Paul did abandon his Pharisaic commitments (a particularly strict interpretation of the Old Testament law and an especially enthusiastic persecution of the church) after experiencing a revelation of Christ. The Paul of the letters stands out for his pivotal role in bringing the gospel to the Gentiles, but this Paul demonstrates no interest in the Gentiles before his encounter with Christ. The pre-Christian Paul's contact with Jerusalem is uncertain, but his letters provide no evidence of his participation in Jerusalem's temple worship or priestly activities.

The Christian Paul worked as an artisan and took pride in the degree of financial independence that his skills provided him, but not necessarily in the work itself. Paul experienced the financial status appropriate to an artisan, usually—but not always—earning enough to support himself. On occasion, this Paul accepted financial support from Christian congregations, but never from believers in the city where he currently resided. Paul probably wished to avoid any appearance of exploiting those to whom he ministered. The gospel of the Pauline letters implied significant challenges to the structures of the Roman Empire, but the letters never emphasized those challenges or made them explicit. For whatever reasons, the Christian Paul of the letters encouraged compliance with many of the empire's demands (particularly taxation) even though he almost certainly regarded many of the empire's claims to be incompatible with the gospel he proclaimed. The empire to which Paul paid taxes often held him in custody, but also often released him from that custody. The reasons for these imprisonments are never revealed, but the custody never seriously interfered with Paul's preaching and letter writing.

II. The Acts Data Set

Paul's Family

Acts provides little information about Paul's family. However, it does inform the reader that Paul's nephew, the son of Paul's sister, disrupted a murder plot against Paul by speaking to the tribune on Paul's behalf (23:12–22). Paul's nephew is described as a "young man" (νεανίσκος, 23:17), suggesting that he was probably an unmarried male in his twenties or thirties.[91] Paul's sister, if still living, would therefore probably have been in her forties, fifties, or early sixties. Unfortunately, this verse stands alone in Acts—and the rest of

---

[91] On the meaning of νεανίσκος in Acts and more broadly in Greek literature, see F. Scott Spencer, "Wise Up, Young Man: The Moral Vision of Saul and Other νεανίσκοι in Acts," in Phillips, *Acts and Ethics*, 34–48.

the New Testament—in referring directly to a member of Paul's family. Yet even this verse, which demonstrates the existence of Paul's sister and the presence of her son in Jerusalem, provides little other information about Paul's family. Since only Paul's nephew, and not his sister, acted in Paul's behalf, it is unclear whether Paul's sister was in Jerusalem at the time and even whether she was still alive and in contact with her Christian missionary brother.

In earlier discourse, the Paul of Acts claimed to have been raised "in this city" (Acts 22:3), a claim that can be interpreted to suggest that he was raised in Jerusalem (as well as Tarsus).[92] On the basis of this reference to Paul's childhood home and the subsequent reference to his nephew's presence in Jerusalem, some interpreters have suggested that significant portions of Paul's family may have been permanent residents of Jerusalem. Although it is highly plausible to imagine a devout Pharisaic family like Paul's (23:6; 26:5) residing in Jerusalem, this suggestion is difficult to reconcile with Paul's claims both to have been a citizen of the Greek city of Tarsus (21:39) and to have been born as a citizen of Rome (22:28). As will be discussed in more detail later, it is possible—but quite unlikely—that a family of Jerusalem-bound Pharisees would possess citizenship in both Rome and Tarsus.[93] In light of Paul's citizenship claims in Acts, therefore, it is particularly significant to remember that Acts reports Paul's nephew to have been in Jerusalem *during Pentecost* (20:16), a season when many Diaspora pilgrims (potentially including Paul's nephew) would have been visiting Jerusalem.[94] Therefore, even though Acts informs the reader both that Paul had a nephew and that this nephew was in contact with Paul even toward the end of Paul's life, Acts does not allow for any firm inferences about either the residence of Paul's extended family or even the degree to which Paul remained in contact with his (presumably non-Christian) family members.[95]

Paul's Education

Acts provides several clues to Paul's educational background, and the book even makes an explicit claim about Paul's education—that he was trained under Gamaliel (22:3), a leading rabbi of the mid-first century and the grandson of the famed Hillel.[96] Even though the historicity of Paul's claim

---

[92] In Acts 22:3, Paul claims to have been born in Tarsus and raised in "this city." The city in which Paul claimed to have been raised could be either Jerusalem or Tarsus. See Joseph A. Fitzmyer, who takes Jerusalem to be the city of Paul's raising (*Acts*, 704).

[93] No other Pharisee in antiquity is known to have been a citizen of a Greek city. On the extreme improbability of a Pharisaic family being citizens of a Greek city in Asia Minor, see Lentz, *Luke's Portrait of Paul*, 53–55.

[94] See Simon Légasse, "Paul's Pre-Christian Career according to Acts," in *The Book of Acts in Its Palestinian Setting* (ed. Richard Bauckham; BAFCS 4; Grand Rapids: Eerdmans, 1996), 374.

[95] On the possibility that Paul's nephew was also a Christian, see Fitzmyer, *Acts*, 723.

[96] On Gamaliel, see Jacob Neusner, *The Pharisees: Rabbinic Perspectives* (Jersey City: KTAV, 1985), 23–58.

to tutelage under Gamaliel is widely doubted,[97] when read at face value, this claim implies a very privileged Jewish education for the Paul of Acts.[98] Acts also implies a well-educated Paul by characterizing him as bilingual and perhaps trilingual with fluency in Greek (21:37), Aramaic (22:2), and, as a student of Gamaliel, probably Hebrew.[99] The Pauline speeches in Acts likewise implicitly suggest that Paul was well educated. Although Paul's speeches in Acts have been heavily mined for their theological ore, the rhetorical rather than the theological veins are significant for discerning Paul's educational background. When assayed to determine their facility with the conventions of Greco-Roman rhetoric, Paul's speeches in Acts reveal the rhetorical skills of a trained orator, skills commonly acquired in the course of tertiary (as opposed to a less advanced primary or secondary) education.

The Pauline speeches in Acts fall within three rhetorical traditions:[100] deliberative (mission) speeches (to both Jews [13:6–41, 46–47] and Gentiles [14:15–17; 17:22–31]);[101] a farewell speech (20:18–35);[102] and defense speeches (22:1–21; 23:1–6; 24:10–21; 25:2–11; 26:2–29; 28:17–28).[103] Schol-

---

[97] Doubts about the historicity of Paul's study under Gamaliel were commonplace throughout the twentieth century (e.g., Morton S. Enslin, "Paul and Gamaliel," *JR* 7 [1927]: 360–75).

[98] On the possibility of Luke's desire to link Paul with the inclusive tendencies of Hillel as mediated by his grandson Gamaliel, see P. J. Tomson, "Gamaliel's Counsel and the Apologetic Strategy of Luke-Acts," in *The Unity of Luke-Acts* (ed. Joseph Verheyden; BETL 142; Leuven: University Press, 1999), 585–604.

[99] Additionally, although Acts gives no direct evidence of Paul's facility in Latin, H. W. Tajra has argued that the two facts of Paul's Roman citizenship and his extended interactions in Rome imply that the Paul of Acts possessed a mastery of Latin (*The Martyrdom of Paul: Historical and Judicial Context, Traditions, and Legends* [WUNT 67; Tübingen: J. C. B. Mohr, 1994], 2–4).

[100] On the taxonomy of speech types in Acts, see G. Walter Hanson, "The Preaching and Defence of Paul," in *Witness to the Gospel: The Theology of Acts* (ed. I. Howard Marshall and David Peterson; Grand Rapids: Eerdmans, 1998), 295–324.

[101] The deliberative speeches have received a great deal of attention from theologically oriented scholars and less attention from rhetorically oriented critics, but see Philip E. Satterthwaite, "Acts Against the Background of Classical Rhetoric," in *The Book of Acts in Its Ancient Literary Setting* (ed. Bruce W. Winter and Andrew D. Clarke; BAFCS 1; Grand Rapids: Eerdmans, 1993), 337–79, esp. 358–60; John J. Kilgallen, "Acts 17,22b–31—What Kind of Speech Is This?" *Revista Biblica* 110 (2003): 417–24; and Dean Zweck, "The Exordium of the Areopagus Speech, Acts 17.22,23," *NTS* 35 (1989): 94–103.

[102] E.g., Duane F. Watson, "Paul's Speech to the Ephesian Elders (Acts 20.17–38): Epideictic Rhetoric of Farewell," in *Persuasive Artistry: Studies in New Testament Rhetoric in Honor of George A. Kennedy* (ed. Duane F. Watson and George A. Kennedy; Sheffield: JSOT, 1991), 184–208; and John J. Kilgallen, "Paul's Speech to the Ephesian Elders: Its Structure," *ETL* 70 (1994): 112–21.

[103] E.g., Jerome Neyrey, "The Forensic Defense Speech and Paul's Trial Speeches in Acts 22–26: Form and Function," in *Luke-Acts: New Perspectives from the Society of Biblical Literature Seminar* (ed. Charles H. Talbert; New York: Crossroad, 1984), 210–24; Bruce W. Winter, "The Importance of the *Captatio Benevolentiae* in the Speeches of Tertullus and Paul in Acts 24:1–21," *Journal of Theological Studies* 42 (1991): 505–31;

ars have investigated each type of speech in detail with historical, theological, and rhetorical questions in mind.[104] Of course, the speeches were recorded (and probably composed) by Luke, and they advance Luke's narrative and theological agendas.[105] However, our purpose is not to investigate Luke's role in shaping the speeches, but rather to evaluate the net effect of the speeches on the portrayal of Paul in Acts. Our particular concern is to discern if the speeches characterize the Paul of Acts (and by extension the pre-Christian Paul of Acts) as a speaker who was trained in rhetoric. The evidence in this regard is pretty clear. The Paul of Acts demonstrates a mastery of multiple genres of speech. Although Marie-Eloise Rosenblatt's praise for "Paul's rhetorical brilliance" is probably excessive,[106] the results of rhetorical investigations have generally agreed with Richard Pervo's conclusions that the Paul of Acts was "a skilled speaker." As Pervo explains, the Paul of Acts "could draw crowds in barbarous Phrygia, cultured Athens, and a host of places in between," and his defense speeches in particular reveal a "rhetor" skilled in "wit and elocution."[107] His speeches contain the structures and devices expected from a well-trained orator in antiquity, and they largely conform to the directives laid out in the rhetorical handbooks of Paul's day. Paul could even compose a "textbook example" of some common ancient rhetorical forms.[108]

So the Paul of Acts displays competence in rhetoric. Yet as an orator, he does not rise beyond competently trained. As Henry J. Cadbury noted long ago, the premier orators of Paul's day would have viewed Paul's speeches "with scorn," and even the sympathetic, but well-educated, Christian readers of subsequent centuries "found much to apologize for in the crudeness" of

---

and Fred Veltman, "The Defense Speeches in Acts," in *Perspectives on Luke-Acts* (ed. Charles H. Talbert; Edinburgh: T&T Clark, 1978), 243–56.

[104] On the tendencies of biblical scholars to employ theological rather than rhetorical categories when analyzing the speeches, see Conrad Gempf, "Public Speaking and Published Accounts," in Winter and Clarke, *Acts in Its Ancient Literary Setting*, 259–303, esp. 291–98; Richard J. Bauckham, "Kerygmatic Summaries in the Speeches of Acts," in *History, Literature, and Society in the Book of Acts* (ed. Ben Witherington; Cambridge: Cambridge University Press, 1996), 185–217; and Marion L. Soards, *The Speeches in Acts: Their Content, Context, and Concerns* (Louisville: Westminster John Knox, 1994), 1–16.

[105] Luke's role in the composition of the speeches and the importance of the speeches, particularly the defense speeches, to the narrative of Acts has long been widely recognized. See, e.g., Paul Schubert, "The Final Cycle of Speeches in the Book of Acts," *JBL* 87 (1968): 1–16; and, more recently, Earle Hilgert, "Speeches in Acts and Hellenistic Canons of Historiography and Rhetoric," in *Good News in History* (ed. E. L. Miller; Atlanta: Scholars Press, 1993), 83–109; Robert C. Tannehill, "The Narrator's Strategy in the Scenes of Paul's Defense: Acts 21:27–26:32," *Forum* 8 (1992): 255–69; and F. F. Bruce, "The Significance of the Speeches for Interpreting Acts," *Southwestern Journal of Theology* 33 (1990): 20–28.

[106] Marie-Eloise Rosenblatt, *Paul the Accused: His Portrait in the Acts of the Apostles* (Collegeville, Minn.: Liturgical, 1995), 96.

[107] Richard I. Pervo, *Profit with Delight: The Literary Genre of the Acts of the Apostles* (Philadelphia: Fortress, 1987), 75.

[108] Satterthwaite, "Classical Rhetoric," 360.

Paul's speeches.[109] Still, when the rhetorical adequacy of Paul's speeches in Acts is added to his reported education under Gamaliel, the result is a Paul who has enjoyed substantial education in both Jewish law and Greek rhetoric, but not a Paul who was among the true intellectual elite of his day.

When the Paul of Acts is examined under the rubrics of *assimilation, acculturation, and accommodation,* which were introduced earlier,[110] it quickly becomes apparent that this Paul is *highly assimilated* into the Greco-Roman world. He visits many of the leading cities of the empire, even preaching on Mars Hill in Athens (17:16–31) and living for two years in a rented home in Rome (28:30).[111] The Paul of Acts is comfortable interacting with the Roman officers in charge of his custody (22:25–26; 23:17–18; 27:1–11, 31–38) and even speaking before Roman officials (13:6–12; 21:37–39; 22:22–29; 24:10–27; 26:1–32; cf. 18:14). The Paul of Acts even manages to evangelize Sergius Paulus, the Roman consul in Salamis (13:4–12). ("Saul" becomes "Paul" in the middle of his evangelistic appeal to Sergius Paulus. Was Saul assuming the name of his most famous convert?) Paul makes a similar evangelistic appeal to Festus, the Roman governor in Judea. Although Paul was apparently unsuccessful in converting Festus, Festus was so overwhelmed by Paul's appeal that he eventually accused Paul of being driven mad by too much learning (τὰ πολλά σε γράμματα εἰς μανίαν περιτρέπει, 26:24).[112] Paul's rhetorical prowess is demonstrated not only in private and semiprivate situations, but also in public forums. The Paul of Acts can command the attention of vast pagan audiences (17:22–31). He even demonstrates familiarity with classical Greek poets and popular philosophy (17:23, 25).[113]

---

[109] Henry J. Cadbury, "The Speeches in Acts," in Foakes-Jackson and Lake, *Beginnings of Christianity,* 5:424.

[110] Barclay, "Paul among Diaspora Jews," 89–120.

[111] On Paul's rented accommodations in Rome, see Ernst Hansack, " 'Er lebte ... von seinem eigen Einkommen' (Apg 28,30)," *BZ* 19 (1975): 249–53; and David L. Mealand, "The Close of Acts and Its Hellenistic Greek Vocabulary," *NTS* 36 (1990): 583–97.

[112] This interruption of Paul's speech was not a compliment. The emphasis of the comment probably falls on the resulting madness (μανία) rather than the preceding education (γράμματα). Fitzmyer appropriately notes that "Festus is concerned about Paul's mental stability" (*Acts,* 764).

[113] On Paul's echoes of popular Greek philosophy, see Dean Philip Bechard, *Paul Outside the Walls: A Study of Luke's Socio-Geographical Universalism in Acts 14:8-20* (Rome: Pontifical Biblical Institute, 2000), esp. 233–354, 427–31; Karl Olav Sandnes, "Paul and Socrates: The Aim of Paul's Areopagus Speech," *JSNT* 50 (1993): 13–26; Mark D. Given, "The Unknown Paul: Philosophers and Sophists in Acts 17," in *SBL Seminar Papers, 1996* (SBLSP 35; Atlanta: Scholars Press, 1996), 343–51; David L. Balch, "The Areopagus Speech: An Appeal to the Stoic Historian Posidonius against Later Stoics and the Epicureans," in *Greeks, Romans and Christians* (ed. David L. Balch, Everrett Ferguson, and Wayne A. Meeks; Minneapolis: Fortress, 1990), 52–79; Eckhard Plümacher, "The Mission Speeches in Acts and Dionysius of Halicarnassus," in *Jesus and the Heritage of Israel* (ed. David P. Moessner; Philadelphia: Trinity Press International, 1999), 251–66; and N. Clayton Croy, "Hellenistic Philosophies and the Preaching of the Resurrection," *NovT* 39 (1996): 21–39; *contra* Kenneth D. Litwak,

Paul's acculturation to the Greco-Roman world and his awareness of the differences between Jewish and Gentile audiences in Acts are clearly revealed by the adaptations he makes to his missionary sermons as his audiences shift from Jews to Gentiles. In speaking to "Israelites" (13:16), Paul invokes Saul, David, Abraham, and Samuel by name and the Old Testament judges, prophets, and psalmists more generally to gain sympathy and authority for his proclamation of Jesus (13:16–41). The Septuagint provides his central authority in his speeches to Jews (13:33, 34, 41). In speaking to the Gentile "Athenians," Paul draws upon the inscriptions on one of their pagan altars ("to the unknown god," 17:23) and the words of their poets (17:28) to gain sympathy and authority for his proclamation of Jesus.[114] A form of natural theology provides the central authority in his speeches to Gentiles.[115]

In spite of his thorough assimilation into the Gentile world and significant acculturation to that world, the Paul of Acts refuses to accommodate to the pervasive idolatry of that world, and he calls for rejection of pagan idolatry. Paul insists that "we ought not to think that the deity is like gold, or silver, or stone, an image formed by the art and imagination of mortals" (Acts 17:29). His apparent success in turning people from idol worship even arouses the hostility of the local idol makers in Ephesus, who incite a riot against Paul in defense of their industry (19:21–41).

The Paul of Acts is, therefore, *highly educated and deeply assimilated and acculturated* into the Greco-Roman world. He is fluent in the rhetoric of the dominant culture and is regarded as an educated person even by his captors, although he would not rank among its intellectually elite. He is not, however, *accommodating* to its idolatry.

Paul's Pre-Christian Religious Background

Acts reveals three primary characteristics of Paul's pre-Christian life. The pre-Christian Paul of Acts was a Jew and a Pharisee, was a citizen of

---

"Israel's Prophets Meet Athens' Philosophers: Scriptural Echoes in Acts 17,22–31," *Bib* 85 (2004): 199–216.

[114] The exact source of this initial maxim ("in him we live and move and have our being") and the location of this altar both remain unknown. See Pieter van der Horst, "The Unknown God (Acts 17:23)," in *Knowledge of God in the Graeco-Roman World* (ed. R. van den Broek, T. Baarda, and J. Mansfeld; Études préliminaires aux religions orientales dans l'Empire romain; New York: Brill, 1988), 19–42; Kirsopp Lake, "'Your Own Poets,'" in Foakes-Jackson and Lake, *Beginnings of Christianity*, 5:246–50; idem, "The Unknown God," in ibid., 5:240–45; and Michel Gourges, "La Literatura Profana en el Discourse de Atenas (He 17,16–31): ¿Expedient Cerrado?" *Anámnesis* 13, no. 2 (2003): 15–45. The original source of the poetic line ("for we too are his offspring,") is Aratus, a fourth-century B.C.E. Stoic, but the Paul of Acts probably got the line indirectly from Aristobulus, a second-century B.C.E. Jewish writer. See Mark J. Edwards, "Quoting Aratus: Acts 17,28," *ZNW* 83 (1992): 266–69.

[115] See Lynn Allan Kauppi, *Foreign but Familiar Gods: Greco-Romans Read Religion in Acts* (LNTS 277; New York: T&T Clark, 2006).

Rome and a citizen of the Greek city of Tarsus, and was a persecutor of the church.[116] The Paul of Acts—both the pre-Christian and Christian Paul—was clearly Jewish. According to the words placed upon his lips in Acts, Paul studied under Gamaliel, the leading rabbi of his day (22:3). This Paul also described himself as a Jew (21:39), as a Pharisee (26:5), and even as the "son of Pharisees" (23:6). Paul's pre-Christian Pharisaic origins are particularly significant in Acts because Acts indicates that the Pharisees accepted the doctrine of the resurrection, a doctrine the Sadducees rejected (23:6–8). According to Acts, therefore, the Pharisees' belief in the general resurrection made them more open to the Christian message of Jesus' resurrection than the Sadducees. However, Paul's identity in Acts is not strictly sectarian. Throughout his preaching in Acts, Paul identifies himself with the Jewish people generally by speaking of "our ancestral law" (22:3), "our ancestors" (13:17, 32; 24:14; 26:6), and even "my nation" (24:17).[117] Given such self-identification with the Jewish people, it is no surprise that even hostile onlookers identify Paul and Silas as Jews (16:20). What is more, Paul's relationships characterize him as Jewish. The pre-Christian Paul of Acts has direct contact with the high priest and acts under his authority (9:1–2; 22:4–5; 26:10). All of these considerations support Brian Rapske's conclusion:

> By every social measure which a Jew might use, Paul possessed great advantages. His birth credentials were impeccable. He also possessed pristine educational credentials. Not only had he studied with one of the greatest and most influential Pharisees of the century in the Holy City, he had distinguished himself. The political credentials of his pre-Christian years were also significant. Familiar with and having ease of access to the highest levels of Jewish leadership, Paul exercised a persuasive power and inspired sufficient confidence to merit the responsibilities of an authorized agent of the Sanhedrin.[118]

The Christian Paul still desired to be in Jerusalem at Pentecost (20:16) and was willing to subsidize—and even places himself under—a vow that must be concluded in the Jerusalem temple (21:22–26). The Christian Paul was

---

[116]Ben Witherington has argued that the "trinity of Paul's identity" was his identity as a Jew, as a Roman citizen, and as a Christian (*The Paul Quest: The Renewed Search for the Jew of Tarsus* [Downers Grove: InterVarsity, 1998], 52–88). Witherington's analysis is probably correct for the Paul of Acts after chapter 9 (though less certain for the Paul of the letters). In the case of the pre-Christian Paul of Acts, his identity as a Christian was preceded by his identity as a persecutor of the church.

[117]It is probably significant that Paul's final words in Acts separate him from Judaism by referring to "your ancestors," using the second person pronoun to distance himself from Judaism for the only time in Acts (28:25). The shift in pronoun probably symbolizes that the Christian Paul of Acts ultimately abandoned his association with Judaism (see Joseph B. Tyson, *Images of Judaism in Luke-Acts* [Columbia: University of South Carolina Press, 1992], 175–77). Nonetheless, the Paul of our concern here, the pre-Christian Paul, was clearly Jewish.

[118]Brian M. Rapske, *Paul in Roman Custody* (BAFCS 3; Grand Rapids: Eerdmans, 1994), 109. Rapske also speculates that a person of Paul's background and education would probably have been a member of the Sanhedrin itself.

also willing to give alms and offer sacrifice at the Jerusalem temple (24:17). Although called to bear witness to the Gentiles (9:15; 22:21; 26:19–23), the Paul of Acts consistently proclaims his initial messages in the synagogues in the cities he visits (13:5, 14, 43; 14:1; 17:17; 18:4, 19). This "synagogue first" strategy of proclamation continues even after Paul bemoans the Jews' failure to accept his message and announces that he will stop evangelizing the Jews and instead focus his efforts on Gentiles (13:46–47; 18:6).[119]

In addition to being a Jewish Pharisee by family heritage, the Paul of Acts was also *a Roman citizen from birth* (22:28) and *a citizen of the Greek city of Tarsus* (21:39).[120] Such dual citizenship in both Rome and an important Greek city marked Paul off as a person of particular privilege in the first century as even Paul's captors in Acts are well aware.[121] When offered an unceremonious release from their prison in Philippi, Paul and Silas insisted that the magistrates must come and release them in person because they were both Roman citizens (16:35–37). Upon learning that Paul and Silas were Roman citizens, the magistrates became "afraid" and apologized to the missionary pair (16:37–38).[122] Later, in a parallel episode, upon learning that Paul spoke Greek and was a citizen of Tarsus, the Roman tribune in Jerusalem allowed Paul to address the collected assembly (21:37–39). This tribune also became "afraid" upon learning that Paul was a Roman citizen; Paul's floggers even respectfully backed away from him when they learned that he was a Roman citizen (22:25–29).

Paul's Roman citizenship is central to the plot of Acts because his citizenship provides the plot device that fulfills Paul's destiny to proclaim Christ before kings (9:15) and in Rome (19:21; 23:11; 25:25; 28:14, 16). When faced

---

[119] On Paul's mission strategy of going to the Jews in the synagogue before preaching to Gentiles in each city, see Robert C. Tannehill, "Rejection by Jews and Turning to Gentiles: The Pattern of Paul's Mission in Acts," in *Luke-Acts and the Jewish People: Eight Critical Perspectives* (ed. Joseph B. Tyson; Minneapolis: Augsburg, 1988), 83–101.

[120] Opinion regarding the historicity of Paul's dual citizenship ranges from quite optimistic to openly dismissive. For example, Rapske argues that "Paul's claim in Acts to a dual citizenship from birth is entirely defensible" (*Paul in Roman Custody*, 108), while Ernst Haenchen warns that "anyone who takes this conversation [about Paul's dual citizenship] historically embroils himself . . . in sheer impossibilities" (*Acts*, 622).

[121] Légasse, who doubts the accuracy of Paul's citizenship in Tarsus but accepts his Roman citizenship, correctly notes that Luke may well have exaggerated Paul's citizenship status in order to elevate Paul's status in the Greco-Roman world ("Paul's Pre-Christian Career," 366–72). In contrast, Peter van Minnen claims that Paul's Roman citizenship probably derived from his father's or grandfather's status as a freedman ("Paul the Roman Citizen," *JSNT* 56 [1994]: 43–52). Van Minnen does not address whether or not Paul was a citizen of Tarsus.

[122] Andrew C. Clark has suggested that Paul chose to work with Silas because Silas, unlike Barnabas, was a Roman citizen and that the break between Paul and Barnabas was over the legitimacy of the Roman Empire (*Parallel Lives: The Relation of Paul to the Apostles in the Lucan Perspective* [Paternoster Biblical and Theological Monographs; Waynesboro, Ga.: Paternoster, 2001], 312–18).

with accusations from the Jewish leaders, the Paul of Acts took advantage of his right as a Roman citizen and appealed for a hearing before the emperor (25:10–12, 21, 25; 26:32; 28:19). This appeal prompted Paul's journey to Rome for trial, a journey that shapes the rest of the narrative in Acts. Paul's Roman citizenship is, therefore, not an incidental detail within Acts, but is central to the narrative. Paul's Roman citizenship advances the plan of God by enabling Paul to visit Rome and to bear witness before kings.[123]

The pre-Christian Paul of Acts is also *a violent persecutor of the church.* He witnesses and condones the death of Stephen, the first Christian martyr in Acts (7:58–8:2).[124] Immediately after Stephen's death, Paul (Saul) began "ravaging the church," "dragging off men and women," and committing them to prison (8:3). The pre-Christian Paul of Acts breathed "threats and murder" (9:1) against the disciples even before he approached the high priest for the additional authority to persecute those who followed the Way within the Damascus synagogues (9:2). After gaining additional authority from the high priest, the pre-Christian Paul of Acts quickly acquired a reputation among Christians as a virulent persecutor (9:13, 21; 22:19–20), a reputation that both he (22:4; 26:10–11) and the resurrected Christ (9:4–6; 22:8; 26:14–15) recognize to be well deserved.[125] The persecutions of the pre-Christian Paul

---

[123] A. J. M. Wedderburn raises a serious problem for those who reject the historicity of Paul's Roman citizenship: "If one rejects Paul's Roman citizenship, then one must also say whether one thinks that Paul came to Rome and, if so, under what circumstances" (*History of the First Christians,* 83; also see van Minnen, "Paul the Roman Citizen," 45–47). Contrast David Alvarez, who regards both the claims of Roman citizenship and Paul's final journey to Rome as fictions created by Luke ("Pablo, ¿Un Ciudadano Romano?" *Estudio Agustiniano* 33 [1998]: 455–86).

[124] The degree of, and the rationale for, Jewish violence against Christians in the mid-first century are quite unclear. As the extremes, Ernst Bammel argues for widespread Jewish violence against Christians and argues that Acts downplays the true level of violence ("Jewish Activity against Christians in Palestine according to Acts," in *The Book of Acts in Its Palestinian Setting* [ed. Richard Bauckham; BAFCS 4; Grand Rapids: Eerdmans, 1995], 357–64), while Robert M. Price argues that the violence attributed to Paul in Acts falsifies the true nature of the interaction between Jews and Christians in the mid-first century. Price argues that the references to Paul's persecution of Christians are later, historically inaccurate, insertions into Acts ("The Legend of Paul's Conversion," *Journal for the Critical Study of Religion, Ethics and Society* 3 [1998]: 9–22). The consensus position of scholarship is that the violent persecution of Christians in Acts should be read as an embellished account of historical events (e.g., John J. Kilgallen, "Persecution in the Acts of the Apostles," in *Luke and Acts* [ed. Gerald O'Collins and Matthew J. O'Connell; New York: Paulist, 1991], 160; and Légrasse, "Paul's Pre-Christian Career," 379–89). When considering the theme of persecution in Acts, it is wise to remember the particular interest that Acts has in the theme of persecution. As Kilgallen has observed, only chapters 1–3, 10, and 15 do not involve some level of persecution against Christians ("Persecution," 145).

[125] The transformation of Paul from persecutor to preacher is widely recognized as part of Luke's concern to demonstrate how the plan of God triumphs over all resistance. See, e.g., Beverly Roberts Gaventa, "The Overthrown Enemy: Luke's Portrait of Paul," in *SBL Seminar Papers, 1985* (ed. Kent Harold Richards; SBLSP 24; Atlanta: Society of Biblical Literature, 1985), 439–47; and Robert L. Brawley, "Paul in Acts:

were brought to an abrupt end in Acts by an encounter with Christ, an encounter that is narrated in detail (9:1–19) and then reported two additional times in Paul's subsequent defense speeches before Roman officials (22:6–21; 26:12–18). Although the three accounts vary widely in their details, each account portrays Paul as a persecutor of the church.[126] The first two reports of Paul's encounter contain elements of Paul's healing through Ananias's ecclesiastical mediation (9:8–19; 22:11–13), but all three accounts emphasize Paul being commissioned as a witness for Christ to the Gentiles (9:15–16; 22:21; 26:17–20).[127] The accounts' shared emphasis upon Paul's pre-encounter role as a persecutor of the church weighs heavily in favor of reading the encounter in Acts as a conversion rather than solely—or even primarily—a call in the mode of the Old Testament prophets.[128] Granted, Paul is called to proclaim Christ to the Gentiles, but only after turning from his violent persecution of Christ's followers.

Paul's Vocation

In Acts, Paul's vocation is specifically identified as tentmaking (18:3), a trade that he shares with the Jewish Christian couple Aquila and Priscilla (18:2). Although the exact nature of Paul's work as a tentmaker remains unclear, his labors probably revolved around some sort of leather working activity.[129] As discussed earlier, an artisan's wages would not have been substantial. Still, at the end of his ministry, the Paul of Acts claims to have provided for himself and his companions by the work of his own hands: "I worked with my own hands to support myself and my companions" (20:34). Although Paul's hosts in Corinth, Aquila and Priscilla, are said to share a common vocation with him, Acts never records any of Paul's traveling companions engaging in labor of any kind. Barnabas, Paul's traveling companion in Acts 13–15, may have been independently wealthy,[130] but according to Acts, Paul provided

---

Aspects of Structure and Characterization," in *SBL Seminar Papers, 1988* (ed. David J. Lull; SBLSP 27; Atlanta: Society of Biblical Literature, 1988), 90–105.

[126] The first account (Acts 9) emphasizes Paul's healing from blindness; the two later accounts (Acts 22, 26) emphasize Paul's role as a witness more strongly. See David M. Stanley, "Paul's Conversion in Acts: Why the Three Accounts?" *CBQ* 15 (1953): 315–38; Marguerat, "Saul's Conversion"; and Hedrick, "Paul's Conversion/Call."

[127] In the most important investigation of these accounts to date, István Czachesz has argued that commissioning stories in antiquity fell into three categories (institutional, prophetic, and philosophical) and that Paul's commission has echoes of all three categories (*Commission Narratives: A Comparative Study of the Canonical and Apocryphal Acts* [Studies on Early Christian Apocrypha 8; Leuven: Peeters, 2007], esp. 40–89).

[128] For a useful survey of the influence of Paul's conversion narratives on subsequent Christian thought, see Bruce Corley, "Interpreting Paul's Conversion—Then and Now," in Longenecker, *Road from Damascus*, 1–17.

[129] See Hock, *Social Context*, esp. 66–69.

[130] Barnabas, Paul's traveling companion in Acts 13–15, may have come from a wealthy family; Acts 4:36–37 records that he sold a field in order to provide for

economic support for his later traveling companions, including Silas, Timothy, and the narrator of Acts. The Paul of Acts is a tentmaker who takes pride not only in the financial independence that the revenue from his labors provides, but also in his ability to support his fellow missionaries and the poor within the community. The Paul of Acts experiences shipwrecks, beatings, and persecution, but he does not experience unaddressed physical needs for food, clothing, or shelter. In fact, the Paul of Acts has sufficient financial resources that he can claim to "give" rather than "receive" (20:35).

In Acts, Paul, the tentmaker and Christian missionary, is a hardworking and generous artisan.[131] In fact, the degree of Paul's generosity is somewhat surprising for a mere artisan in the Greco-Roman world. Not only can Paul support his fellow missionaries, but upon his arrival in Jerusalem, James assumes that Paul can afford to pay the expenses associated with the fulfillment of a vow for himself and four other persons (21:23–24), and the governor Felix assumes that Paul could afford to offer him a bribe for his freedom (24:26). Paul's apparently flush financial situation in Acts is hardly consistent with the resources typically derived from work as an artisan, a fact that has caused some interpreters to speculate that the Paul of Acts had benefited from inherited wealth.[132] If Paul was a citizen of Tarsus and Rome, his family would almost certainly have possessed significant wealth, and thus his possession of inherited wealth is entirely plausible in light of his claims to dual citizenship. However, in spite of the inherent plausibility of the Paul of Acts benefiting from inherited wealth, he explicitly claims in Acts that his labors, not his inheritance, provided for his own needs, the needs of his traveling companions, and the needs even of some of the poor within the Christian community (20:34–35).

Paul's Political Status and Orientation

Paul's political status and orientation in Acts have attracted considerable attention, in part because, as a citizen of both Tarsus and Rome, the Paul of Acts seems to enjoy an elevated political status, and in part because, even though he is frequently in Roman custody, the Paul of Acts has a complex relationship with the Roman Empire and its authorities. Admittedly, Paul's dual citizenship in Rome and Tarsus is the most crucial mark of his political status, but citizenship is not the only indicator of Paul's elevated political status in Acts. Political power was concentrated in the hands of a relatively

---

the needs of the early believers in Jerusalem. Acts provides no indication that this particular field was Barnabas's sole, or even primary, asset.

[131] The hardworking and generous Paul of Acts is probably a role model for Luke's readers. See Thomas E. Phillips, "Paul as a Role Model in Acts: The 'We'-Passages in Acts 16 and Beyond," in Phillips, *Acts and Ethics*, 49–63.

[132] On Paul's wealth in Acts, see Thomas E. Phillips, *Reading Issues of Wealth and Poverty in Luke-Acts* (Studies in the Bible and Early Christianity 48; Lewiston: Edwin Mellen, 2001), 234–39.

small number of people in the Roman Empire. Political status was acquired only by participating in social networks with politically influential people among the elite governing classes (i.e., the households of the emperor, senators, equestrians, provincial aristocracy, and decurions).[133] In the absence of such interaction, one's only political status within the empire was subject of the emperor. However, given his education, family background, and wealth, as discussed earlier, the pre-Christian Paul of Acts undoubtedly would have had at least some access to such people and networks—particularly among the provincial aristocracy. Access to such networks would have enhanced Paul's political status. Indeed, the strongest evidence that Paul achieved significant political status is found at the end of Acts where Acts reports that the Christian Paul was granted an appeal before the emperor (25:12, 21).

Paul's citizenship alone would not have ensured his right to an audience before the emperor, and it is quite unlikely that Festus—or any other Roman governor—would have bothered to send a provincial artisan like Paul for trial before the emperor without some additional motivation beyond the artisan's mere citizenship.[134] In most cases, only the truly elite were granted an audience with the emperor.[135] Because the Paul of Acts was clearly not part of the elite classes (no elite person would have engaged in tentmaking as did the Paul of Acts), it stands to reason that he somehow secured assistance from powerful friends and patrons among the governing elite. Although Acts implies this patronage, it gives no clear indication whether these patrons were old friends from Paul's pre-Christian days (perhaps they had empathy for an old friend—or old family friend—whom they perceived to have gone off the deep end with this Jesus stuff) or whether these patrons were newer friends from his Christian associations (Acts suggests that some of Paul's converts enjoyed political prominence [13:50], but these people play no reported role in Paul's appeal to the emperor[136]). Regardless of how Paul achieved this status, Jerome Neyrey is probably correct to suggest that the Paul of Acts belonged

---

[133] The best brief introduction to social stratification in the Greco-Roman world and its significance for understanding early Christianity is Ekkehard W. Stegemann and Wolfgang Stegemann, *The Jesus Movement: A Social History of Its First Century* (trans. O. C. Dean; Minneapolis: Fortress, 1999), 53–75.

[134] See Peter Garnsey, *Social Status and Legal Privileges in the Roman Empire* (Oxford: Clarendon, 1970), esp. 76. Matthew Skinner has also emphasized the striking inconsistency between Paul's status as an imprisoned artisan and the respect he receives from Roman officials (*Locating Paul: Places of Custody as Narrative Settings in Acts 21–28* [Academia Biblica; Atlanta: Society of Biblical Literature, 2003], esp. 178–80).

[135] Lentz notes that the people known to have been granted an appeal before the emperor in the first century were "not ordinary citizens [like Paul]," but were people with "high social status and reputation, or personal ties with the emperor" (*Luke's Portrait of Paul*, 151).

[136] On the role of Paul's wealthier, more elite, converts, see David J. Gill, "Acts and Urban Élites," in Gill and Gempf, *Acts in Its Graeco-Roman Setting*, 105–18. Gill argues that Paul's mission enjoyed significant success among the urban elites and that this group provided much of the impetus for the growth of Pauline Christianity.

to the retainer class of the Greco-Roman world, a nonelite class that served as intermediaries between the elite and their clients in lower social classes.[137]

As a member of the retainer class, Paul would not have belonged to the elite itself, but would have been accustomed to interacting with such people and would have derived significant advantages from such interactions. Paul's social location within the retainer class would explain how the artisan-class Paul of Acts could be aware of the etiquette and social customs of the elite and how the artisan-class Paul of Acts could dialogue with elite Roman authorities without exhibiting any fear or social discomfort. Paul's social location within the retainer class (although with an artisan-class vocation[138]) makes sense of Lentz's observations that the Paul of Acts is "at ease with the élite of the empire" and that the Paul of Acts possesses "sufficient influence to gain the favor of the governor [Festus]."[139] An artisan in the retainer class could have had very influential friends in the more elite classes.

It may remain debatable whether the Paul of Acts existed within the higher ranks of the artisan class or whether he enjoyed the more elevated status of the retainer class, but few would debate Alexandru Neagoe's insistence that Acts emphasizes Paul's "socio-religious status" and "the predominantly favorable treatment of Paul by various Roman officials."[140] The key question, therefore, is not whether Paul's political status is elevated in Acts (it is elevated), but rather why Paul's political status is elevated. *Does the elevated political status of the Paul of Acts serve to reinforce a particular political orientation in Acts?*

Paul's elevated political status would have been rare in antiquity (not many people would have had their appeal referred to the emperor). This fact has led some interpreters to suggest that Acts has embellished Paul's political status in order to draw Christianity and the Roman Empire closer together. Scholars have considered this possibility from two vantage points. Some scholars have argued that the depiction of Paul in Acts offered an apology to the Roman Empire in order to demonstrate that the Christian church offered no threat to the empire and its interests.[141] Others have more recently argued that much of the material in Acts would hold no interest at all to Roman officials and that any apologetic purposes would have to run in the other direction—as an apology designed to help skeptical Christians

---

[137]Jerome H. Neyrey, "Luke's Social Location of Paul: Cultural Anthropology and Status of Paul in Acts," in Witherington, *History, Literature, and Society*, 251–79.

[138]Some biblical texts omit the reference to Paul being a tentmaker (e.g., Acts 18:3), perhaps in an effort to avoid the incongruity between Paul's elevated political status in Acts and his lower, artisan class, vocation. See Lentz, *Luke's Portrait of Paul*, 102.

[139]Lentz, *Luke's Portrait of Paul*, 153.

[140]Alexandru Neagoe, *The Trial of the Gospel: An Apologetic Reading of Luke's Trial Narratives* (SNTSMS 116; Cambridge: Cambridge University Press, 2002), 186.

[141]E.g., Cadbury, *Making of Luke-Acts* (2d ed.), 308–15; and Conzelmann, *Theology of St. Luke*, 137–49. More recently, see Robert F. O'Toole, "Luke's Position on Politics and Society in Luke-Acts," in *Political Issues in Luke-Acts* (ed. Richard J. Cassidy; Maryknoll: Orbis, 1983), 1–17.

accept the authority of the Roman Empire and recognize its ability to deal justly with those entrusted to its justice system.[142]

Indeed, many of the interactions between the Paul of Acts and the empire appear to minimize any conflict between the empire and Christian believers. *From a Christian perspective*, it would be appealing to see Roman officials protect Paul during riots instigated by fortune-tellers in Philippi (16:16–40) and by idolmakers in Ephesus (19:23–40). Christians also would likely have delighted in Rome protecting Paul from various Jewish riots and plots (21:31–36; 22:22–29; 23:16–35). *From a Roman perspective*, it would be appealing to see Paul battle against magic, a practice that was illegal within the empire (19:11–20; 16:16–18). Likewise, from a Roman perspective, the fact that Paul was a Roman citizen with the ability to interact respectfully with a wide variety of Roman officials would be very appealing. Any Roman citizen who fought against magic and hobnobbed with local Roman authorities couldn't be all bad in Roman eyes.[143] Whether one was Roman or Christian (and, of course, many people saw themselves as both), one could find much in Acts to place the other in a sympathetic light.

For example, even though some Roman officials were uninterested in Paul and his gospel (18:15–17), others, including a lower-class jailor in Philippi (16:25–34) and an elite proconsul on Cyprus (13:4–12), believed in Paul's message. Paul was even "treated kindly" (φιλανθρώπως) by Julius, the Roman centurion in charge of Paul's custody (27:3). Such examples of kind, believing, protective, and even disinterested interactions between Romans and Christians could have helped alleviate tensions emanating from either Romans or Christians. Moreover, what Acts omits from its presentation is relevant too: Acts reports no conflict between Christians and the empire over the imperial cult and sacrifices to the emperor. This absence in Acts could reflect a strategic skirting of a potentially contentious issue.[144] In any case, it is not unreasonable to view the Paul of Acts as a figure designed to ease tensions between Rome and the church.

Be that as it may, several aspects of Paul's interaction with Rome complicate the matter. Not the least of these are Paul's frequent imprisonments throughout Acts and his implied death at the emperor's hand at the end of Acts. It would be very difficult for Acts to fully exonerate an empire that held

---

[142] E.g., Paul W. Walaskay, *And So We Came to Rome* (SNTSMS 49; Cambridge: Cambridge University Press, 1983); and Schwartz, "End of the Line." Most recently, see Diane G. Chen, *God as Father in Luke-Acts* (SBL 92; New York: Peter Lang, 2006).

[143] On the Rome-friendly political implications of the efforts in Acts to distinguish Christian miracles from the illegal practice of magic, see Hans-Josef Klauck, *Magic and Paganism in Early Christianity: The World of the Acts of the Apostles* (Minneapolis: Fortress, 2003), 63–122. On magic in the ancient world and in the New Testament, see David E. Aune, "'Magic' in Early Christianity and Its Ancient Mediterranean Context: A Survey of Some Recent Scholarship," *Annali di storia dell'esegesi* 24 (2007): 229–94.

[144] Bruce W. Winter, "Acts and Roman Religion: B. The Imperial Cult," in Gill and Gempf, *Acts in Its Graeco-Roman Setting*, 93–103.

Paul in such extended custody,[145] only to eventually execute him (exoneration is even more difficult when one also considers the earlier death of Jesus). Of course, several scholars have correctly observed that Acts portrays the Jewish leadership—not the Romans—as the villains in Paul's imprisonments, persecutions, and eventual death.[146] Although Acts does lay primary blame for the accusations, persecution, and violence against Paul at the feet of the Jewish leaders (14:1; 18:12–13, 19; 21:11; 22:30; 23:12; 26:12, 21), in Paul's case, as in the case of Jesus before him, any Jewish action (other than illegal mob violence) was ultimately subject to Roman control.

Because Paul's implied death raises such problems for those who believe that Acts is seeking to exonerate the empire, some scholars have argued that the absence of a narrative about Paul's death (martyrdom) is more important to the interpretation of Acts than is Paul's implied death. According to such readings, Acts was designed to discourage would-be Christian martyrs from challenging the empire and thereby seeking martyrdom.[147] The implication is clear. If believers leave the empire alone, the empire will leave believers alone. Other scholars have gone even further and argued that the silence about Paul's death at the end of Acts was designed to imply Paul's eventual safe release from Roman custody.[148] Such arguments are, however, unpersuasive. Given the pervasive early Christian traditions about Paul's death in Rome, it is quite unlikely that any early Christian reader would have inferred Paul's release from prison at the end of Acts. Likewise, although Acts does not record Paul's death, would-be martyrs could certainly have been inspired by the Spirit's words that informed Paul that he had been chosen to *suffer* for Christ (Acts 9:16). If the depiction of the Paul of Acts was designed to discourage martyrdom, it would make little sense for Paul to depart for Jerusalem with the words: "I do not count my life of any value to myself. . . . I know that none of you . . . will ever see my face again" (20:24–25). Any persuasive reading of Acts has to deal with the fact of Paul's implied death at the end of Acts, and his death at the hands of the Romans.

In addition to explaining Paul's implied death at the end of Acts, scholars who view Acts as designed to reduce tensions between Christians and Rome must account for the other frequently negative depictions of the empire as Robert Maddox so well summarized:

---

[145]However, John B. Weaver has argued that Paul's lengthy incarcerations in Acts 21–28 serve as a means for the advancement of Paul's gospel and that Paul's release from prison is not a priority for the narrative because the empire's imprisonment of Paul both protects Paul and advances the divine plan for his message (*Plots of Epiphany: Prison-Escape in Acts of the Apostles* [BZNW 131; New York: de Gruyter, 2004], esp. 284–86).

[146]E.g., David P. Moessner, "Paul in Acts: Preacher of Eschatological Repentance to Israel," *NTS* 34 (1988): 96–104; and Conrad Gempf, "Luke's Story of Paul's Reception in Rome," in Oakes, *Rome in the Bible and the Early Church*, 42–65.

[147]E.g., Robert Maddox, *The Purpose of Luke-Acts* (Göttingen: Vandenhoeck & Ruprecht, 1982), esp. 80–82.

[148]E.g., Rapske, *Paul in Roman Custody*, esp. 189–91.

The military magistrates of the colony Philippi by no means treat Paul properly (16:22f., 35–39). Gallio's merit in refusing to countenance a charge against Paul is rather spoiled by his tolerating the disgraceful treatment of Sosthenes right in front of the tribunal (18:12–17). Felix wants a bribe from Paul (24:26). Festus is ready to sacrifice Paul so as to gain favour with the Jews (25:9–11).[149]

Such depictions are not commendable, not even to Roman readers. It is not surprising, therefore, that most recent analyses are more nuanced and see the Paul of Acts as neither selling the empire to Christians nor Christianity to the empire, but rather as a wise believer who has learned both to maintain his witness and to avoid needlessly confronting the empire.[150]

The political status of the Paul in Acts is elevated (perhaps retainer class), but not elite (clearly not governing class). The political orientation of the Paul of Acts is complex. On the basis of his Roman citizenship, Paul sometimes seeks and gains Rome's protection from his accusers (both Jewish and pagan). Sometimes Paul even secures conversions from prominent Roman officials. But Paul's interactions with powerful Romans are not always positive. Romans seek bribes from Paul, are willing to sacrifice him in order to appease his Jewish detractors, and even eventually execute him. The Paul of Acts lives in tension, but not contention, with the Roman Empire.

Summary of the Data Set from Acts

The Paul of Acts came from a family of devout Pharisees. Before becoming a believer, the Paul of Acts was a violent persecutor of the church. Although little can be known about his family of origin, the Paul of Acts had a sister whose son followed Paul's career until nearly the very end of Paul's life. This Paul was highly educated and quite competent in the conventions of Greek rhetoric; he had studied under Gamaliel, the leading rabbi of the age, and was at least bilingual, if not trilingual. The Paul of Acts was not only highly educated, but also deeply assimilated and well acculturated into the Greco-Roman world, even enjoying dual citizenship in Rome and Tarsus. The pre-Christian Paul was well connected with the temple leadership in Jerusalem and even gained authority from the high priest to proceed with

---

[149] Maddox, *Purpose of Luke-Acts,* 95.

[150] For excellent surveys of scholarship on Paul's political orientation in Acts, see Steve Walton, "The State They Were In: Luke's View of the Roman Empire," in Oakes, *Rome in the Bible and the Early Church,* 1–41; and Neagoe, *Trial of the Gospel,* 175–87. In addition to the bibliography provided there, see Matthew L. Skinner, "Unchained Ministry: Paul's Roman Custody (Acts 21–28) and the Sociopolitical Outlook of the Book of Acts," in Phillips, *Acts and Ethics,* 79–95; Heike Omerzu, "Das Imperium schlägt zurück: Die Apologetik der Apostelgeschichte auf dem Prüfstand," *ZNT* 9 (2006): 26–36; Warren Carter, *The Roman Empire and the New Testament: An Essential Guide* (Nashville: Abingdon, 2006), 71–77; and John T. Carroll, "Literary and Social Dimensions of Luke's Apology for Paul," in *SBL Seminar Papers, 1988* (ed. David J. Lull; SBLSP 27; Atlanta: Scholars Press, 1988), 106–18.

his persecutions of the church even beyond Judea. The Christian Paul also participated in worship in the Jewish temple.

The Paul of Acts was called to proclaim Christ's name to Gentiles and even to take the Christian message to kings. Still, in each city that he visited, the Paul of Acts typically preached to Jews in synagogues until his message was rejected. After this rejection, he would proclaim Christ to the Gentiles of the city. The Paul of Acts was frequently persecuted by Jewish leaders, but he never appears to have willingly submitted to their corporal punishment. The Romans protected the Paul of Acts from frequent Jewish-instigated mob violence, legal prosecutions, and even a murder plot. Although the Paul of Acts was a tentmaker by trade and labored as an artisan, he quite possibly belonged to the retainer class in Greco-Roman society. In any case, his education, citizenship, and perhaps wealth distinguished him from most artisans in the empire; Roman officials treated him with unusual respect. On the basis of his Roman citizenship, the Paul of Acts often requested—and received from various Roman officials—protection from detractors, reprieve from physical abuse, and release from prison. Still, the Paul of Acts spent much time in Roman custody and probably lived in tension with, but not opposition to, the Roman Empire. He probably died at the emperor's hand.

III. Comparing the Data Sets

Some aspects of Paul's social location in Acts and in his letters are quite compatible, and many of the differences that do appear can be viewed as complementary rather than contradictory of one another. For example, the single Paul of the letters reports no living family members, while the Paul of Acts interacts with his nephew (his sister's son). The nonreport of Paul's singleness in Acts and the absence of his sister and nephew in the letters are hardly significant in a comparison of the two Pauls. Even the most critical reader must admit that the Paul of Acts may have been single (no spouse is mentioned) and that the Paul of the letters may well have had a sister and nephew (there is no reason to assume that Paul was an only child). The vocation of each Paul is likewise entirely compatible. The laborious tasks performed by the artisan-class Paul of the letters are consistent with the tentmaking attributed to the Paul of Acts. With similar congruence, the pre-Christian Paul of both Acts and the letters was reared as a devout Pharisee and studied the law intensively. Before becoming a zealous Christian missionary to the Gentiles, both Pauls persecuted the church, although the Paul of Acts was probably more prone to violence. As Christians, both Pauls continued to see themselves as heirs to the promises to Abraham and Sarah, and, in that sense, Jewish.

However, not all aspects of Paul's life in Acts and the letters are so clearly reconcilable. Both in general and in many specific ways, the Paul of Acts appears to be more culturally advantaged than the Paul of the letters. In general terms, the Paul of Acts is more acculturated and socially privileged than the Paul of the letters. The Paul of Acts is wealthier. He has financial resources at his disposal and never experiences obvious economic privations as did the Paul of the letters.[151] The Paul of Acts has a more clearly distinguished family pedigree than the Paul of the letters. The Paul of Acts has an impeccable Jewish pedigree, having studied under Gamaliel, the leading rabbi of his day, and having regularly interacted with the chief priests and temple leadership. Although the Paul of the letters claims to have studied the law from his youth, he reports no interaction with temple leadership or Gamaliel even when boasting of his accomplishments within Judaism (Gal 2; Phil 3). The Paul of Acts also possessed a coveted Greco-Roman pedigree as a citizen of both Tarsus and Rome, citizenships that worked to his advantage in legal proceedings. The Paul of the letters never mentions citizenship in either Rome or Tarsus even when discussing the Roman authorities and his own Roman custody (Rom 13; Phil 1).

Both Pauls were well educated by ancient standards, being literate in Greek and perhaps Aramaic and Hebrew as well. Yet the Paul of Acts probably possessed a superior education both as a Jew (having studied under Gamaliel) and as a Greek (having mastered several genres of Greek rhetoric). Although both Pauls are fully assimilated into the Greco-Roman world, the Paul of Acts is more acculturated into the intellectual traditions of that world and can draw upon its literary and cultural repertoire more easily. Neither Paul is accommodating to pagan idolatry, but the Paul of Acts can use idols as a point of departure for Christian preaching (Acts 17), while the Paul of the letters views idolatry as decisive proof of Gentile sin (Rom 1).

Both Pauls also demonstrate a complex and ambiguous relationship with the Roman Empire, but the Paul of Acts, in large measure thanks to his wealth, citizenship, and family pedigree, appears to possess a more elevated political status than the Paul of the letters. The Paul of Acts probably belonged to the retainer class, while the Paul of the letters was a step lower on the social and political hierarchy in the strictly artisan class. This difference would explain why the Paul of Acts comfortably interacts with Roman officials at all levels of Roman administration, while the Paul of the letters demonstrates interaction only with the soldiers who guard him. The Paul of Acts tends to view the Roman officials as political allies who protect him from hostile outsiders (both Jewish and pagan), while the Paul of the letters tends to view the Roman authorities as sovereigns who hold the "sword"—the power of life and death—over him.

These differences in Paul's social location are not insurmountable, particularly if one remembers the different rhetorical goals in Acts and Paul's letters. As Jerome Neyrey appropriately reminds us:

---

[151] Steve Walton argues strongly for the similarity between the Pauline ethos in the Miletus speech (Acts 20) and the Pauline ethos in Paul's letters (particularly 1 Thessalonians), but his analysis fails to appreciate the more flush financial condition of the Paul of Acts (*Leadership and Lifestyle: The Portrait in the Miletus Speech and 1 Thessalonians* [SNTSMS 108; New York: Cambridge University Press, 2000], esp. 199–201).

It is part of Paul's own rhetorical strategy to present himself as weak in public speaking and lacking in rhetoric (1 Cor. 1.17; 2.5), whereas . . . it is characteristic of the Lucan rhetorical argument to present Paul as forensically adept. In his own letters, Paul calls attention to his lack of honor (1 Cor. 4.8–13; 2 Cor. 4.7–12; 11.21–33). In contrast, Luke calls attention at every turn to Paul's honorable status in terms of cities where he lives, his associates and "friends," his citizenship, and the like.[152]

Neyrey is quite correct that the Paul of the letters tends to speak in a rhetoric of self-humiliation even when he claims to boast. He regards his accomplishments in Judaism as "nothing" (Phil 3; Gal 1–2), and he boasts about his "weakness" (2 Cor 10–11). In contrast, the author of Acts plainly views Paul as a hero and makes every effort to speak well of his hero. The Paul of Acts is, therefore, presented by an admirer who has no interest in weakening or humiliating the object of his affection.

Many, perhaps all, of the differences between the social locations of the Paul of the letters and the Paul of Acts can be explained in terms of rhetorical strategies. The rhetorical strategy of Acts seems to be to intensify and elevate Paul's social location. The Paul of the letters persecuted the church; the Paul of Acts persecuted the church with utmost violence—and did so with the direct approval of the high priest. The Paul of the letters had probably studied rhetoric; the Paul of Acts had mastered several genres of rhetoric. The Paul of the letters had studied the law; the Paul of Acts had studied under no less an authority than Gamaliel. The Paul of the letters was at home in the Greek cities of the empire; the Paul of Acts was a citizen of both a Greek city and the empire. The Paul of the letters worked to support himself; the Paul of Acts worked to support himself and his traveling companions—and then even donated funds to the needy within the church. The Paul of the letters was frequently released from custody; the Paul of Acts boldly demanded an apology from the magistrates who wanted to release him from prison. Such examples could continue, but the point seems clear. Acts tends to provide accounts and to emphasize details that would not have served the self-deprecating purposes of the Paul of the letters.

However, in spite of the importance of recognizing the differing rhetorical goals of Acts and the letters, it is also appropriate to acknowledge that several specific aspects of Paul's social location in Acts are probably embellished by the Pauline admirer who gave us the Paul of Acts. In particular, Paul's wealth, citizenships, tutelage under Gamaliel, and commissioning by the high priest—as well as the retainer class social status that Paul probably derived from these advantages—have probably (but not necessarily) been embellished to varying degrees by the author of Acts.

---

[152]Neyrey, "Luke's Social Location of Paul," 279.

⌒ 5 ⌒

FINDING PAUL A PLACE IN THE CHURCH: THE PARTICIPANTS IN THE JERUSALEM CONFERENCE

THE PREVIOUS chapter located Paul within the Greco-Roman world. The next two chapters will locate Paul within the narrower world of early Christianity. Of course, with the possible—but not certain—exceptions of a few New Testament letters such as James, 1 Peter, and Hebrews, Paul's letters are themselves our only primary sources from the first thirty years of the Christian movement. This paucity of evidence is significant, but not debilitating. In keeping with the disciplined method employed throughout this volume, these chapters will neither offer nor presume any sweeping historical reconstructions of earliest Christianity. Instead, these chapters will limit themselves to a single aspect of early Christian social systems—Paul's interactions with other Christians.[1]

As is commonly recognized, any attempt to categorize the diverse traditions within early Christianity is imperiled by the dangers of creating false dichotomies and quaint oversimplifications. However, for the sake of analysis, this chapter will use a single key event within Paul's ministry as decisive

---

[1] Nicholas Taylor has urged New Testament scholars to investigate early Christianity as a series of communities (e.g., Jerusalem, Antioch, Ephesus) and to avoid an undue emphasis upon individual personalities (e.g., Paul, Peter, James). In dialogue with Taylor's advice, I have chosen to organize this chapter and the next chapter around the two most prominent types of communities (the Jerusalem church of the original disciples and Paul's non-Jerusalem churches). However, after adopting Taylor's advice in establishing the perimeters of each chapter, I have abandoned his advice and organized the content within each chapter around key personalities. I have departed from a community centered model within each chapter for three reasons. First, our sources provide more evidence about persons than they do about communities. Second, several people are associated with more than one Christian community. And third, not all of the members of the various Christian communities were completely homogeneous in their interactions with Paul. Although I have adapted Taylor's central methodological urging, I acknowledge the essential accuracy of his claim that Paul maintained a deeper and more stable relationship with the largely unnamed leadership of the Christian community in Antioch than he did with the named leadership of the Christian community in Jerusalem (*Paul, Antioch and Jerusalem: A Study in Relationships and Authority in Earliest Christianity* [JSNTSup 66; Sheffield: Sheffield University Press, 1992]).

for its categorization of Paul's interactions with the diverse traditions and personalities within early Christianity. That decisive event is the Jerusalem Conference in which the leaders of early Christianity gathered to discuss the issue of Gentile inclusion within the church. As discussed in the third chapter of this volume, this conference probably occurred during the visit that Acts reports as Paul's third visit to Jerusalem and that Galatians reports as Paul's second visit to Jerusalem (Acts 15; Gal 2:1–10). This chapter will consider the individuals who are reported to have participated in that event (i.e., Peter, James, John, Barnabas, and Titus). Although the data sets associated with the participants in that event are roughly the same size in both Acts and Paul's letters, this chapter will begin with a consideration of the data set in Paul's letters and then will consider if that data set can be placed within the slightly larger data set of Acts. The next chapter will consider Paul's interactions with the figures within early Christianity who were not reported as participants in the Jerusalem Conference.

I. THE PAULINE DATA SET

In Paul's letters, Paul associates five people (in addition to himself) with the Jerusalem Conference. Those five people are his co-missionaries Barnabas and Titus and the three pillars of the Jerusalem church: Peter, James, and John.

Peter

Given Peter's importance in the gospels,[2] it is little surprise that Paul's letters recognize Peter, whom Paul typically calls by the Aramaic "Cephas," as a central authority within the early church.[3] Note, for example, Paul's reiteration of the slogans of various factions within the Corinthian church: "'I belong to Paul,' or 'I belong to Apollos,' or 'I belong to Cephas,' or 'I belong to Christ'" (1 Cor 1:12; cf. 3:22). Although the reference to the Christ party is probably a rhetorical flourish on Paul's part,[4] Paul's characterization of the community's divisions reveals Peter's reputation as an authority even in Corinth, a city nearly a thousand-mile sea voyage away from Peter's traditional home in Galilee. Although Paul sternly rejected such factionalism

---

[2] For a recent survey of Peter's importance within the gospel traditions, see Richard J. Cassidy, *Four Times Peter: Portrayals of Peter in the Four Gospels and at Philippi* (Collegeville, Minn.: Liturgical, 2007).

[3] The equation between the "Cephas" in Paul's letters and the "Simon Peter" in the gospels and Acts has been called into question by a few scholars (e.g., Donald W. Riddle, "The Cephas-Peter Problem, and a Possible Solution," *JBL* 59 [1940]: 169–80; and more recently Bart D. Ehrman, "Cephas and Peter," *JBL* 109 [1990]: 463–74), but the equation is nonetheless quite firmly established (e.g., Allison, "Peter and Cephas").

[4] *Contra* C. K. Barrett, *A Commentary on the First Epistle to the Corinthians* (Harper's New Testament Commentaries; San Francisco: Harper & Row, 1968), 46–48.

within the Corinthian community (1:10), 1 Corinthians reveals no inclination on Paul's part to oppose Peter or even to directly confront those who demonstrated loyalty to Peter. In fact, the faction that claimed loyalty to Paul himself was in the crosshairs of Paul's assault in 1 Corinthians. Paul asked, "Has Christ been divided? Was Paul crucified for you? Or were you baptized in the name of Paul?" (1 Cor 1:13, emphasis added). Paul offered no corresponding admonition of those who claimed loyalty to Peter. The issue for Paul was factionalism produced by misguided loyalty to one particular authority. As Hans Conzelmann put it, "the object of Paul's attack [in 1 Cor 1–4] is not Peter and his party, but all parties."[5]

Peter's name reappears toward the end of 1 Corinthians. As in Paul's earlier references to Peter, this one reveals no antagonism between Paul and Peter. In fact, Paul drew upon Peter's reputation as an authority to help establish the truth of his own claims about the resurrection. Either unaware or dismissive of the gospel traditions that make Mary Magdalene (Matt 28:1–10; John 20:1–19) or Cleopas and his unnamed companion (Luke 24:13–35) the first persons to see the resurrected Jesus, Paul recorded that the resurrected Christ first appeared to Peter (Cephas),[6] "then to the twelve. Then he appeared to five hundred brothers and sisters at one time. . . . Then he appeared to James, then to all the apostles. Last of all, as to one untimely born, he appeared also to me" (1 Cor 15:5–9). For our purposes, this carefully ordered list of Jesus' post-resurrection appearances reveals two things. First, it shows Paul's awareness that Peter played a central role within the faith as the earliest witness to the resurrection. Second, it shows that Paul did not consider Peter's testimony to be exclusive. Paul also insisted upon the importance of the witness of "the twelve,"[7] some five hundred others, James, and "all the apostles." By placing his reference to "all the apostles" in the penultimate position (just before his own name) in his list of witnesses, Paul revealed his assumption that the circle of apostles transcended the boundaries of both "the twelve" and the twelve plus Paul. In 1 Corinthians 15, therefore, while Paul clearly recognized Peter's central role as a reliable witness to the proclamation of the

---

[5] Conzelmann, *1 Corinthians*, 34.

[6] The earliest texts of Mark record no post-resurrection appearances of Jesus. Rather, a group of women discovers the empty tomb and is told by a heaven-sent messenger to inform "his disciples and Peter" that Jesus is "going before them to Galilee," where they "will see him" (16:1–8). Because the women did not see the resurrected Christ in Mark, Paul's tradition in 1 Cor 15 is more easily reconciled with Mark than with the other gospel traditions. On the Easter story in Paul and in the gospels, see N. T. Wright, *The Resurrection of the Son of God* (vol. 3 of *Christian Origins and the Question of God*; Minneapolis: Fortress, 2003), 312–61, 585–682.

[7] Paul speaks of "the twelve" only here, but his use of the definite article (*the* twelve) suggests that he regarded this body as a distinct and authoritative group in contrast to the other group of five hundred believers whose number is not qualified by an article. Paul does not explicitly state that Peter was included among the twelve, but there is no reason to doubt that Paul regarded Peter as a member of the twelve. See Fee, *First Epistle to the Corinthians*, 729.

resurrection, he also recognized a larger, but undefined, group of apostles. *In any case, 1 Corinthians reveals no tension between Peter and Paul.*

In Galatians, the story changes. In this letter Paul displayed open hostility to those who followed a message that apparently traced its immediate origin to Peter. In fact, Galatians not only reveals tensions between the followers of Peter and Paul (as was probably the case in 1 Corinthians), but even recounts a direct confrontation between the two leaders.[8] Paul insisted that "when Cephas came to Antioch, I opposed him to his face" (Gal 2:11). When assessing such claims, we should remember both that this triumphal version of the conflict was conveyed *by Paul* some time after the incident in question and that Peter's response to Paul's rebuke is not recorded. Perhaps Peter never came to see the issue as Paul did.[9] In any case, Paul's language is shrill throughout Galatians. Paul worried that the Galatians were being led to "a different gospel" and that the purveyors of this alternative message wanted "to pervert the gospel of Christ" (1:6–7). Paul insisted that "if anyone proclaims to you a gospel contrary to what you received [from Paul], let that one be accursed!" (1:9). Of course, it is not clear that Peter himself was actively preaching the message Paul so strongly opposed. Nor is it even clear whether or not those who did preach that message were accurately representing the convictions of Peter. Still, it is clear that the central and recurring themes of Paul's narrative in Gal 1–2 are the independence of *his gospel* and its freedom from any reliance upon Peter and the apostles in Jerusalem for its authority.

In Gal 1–2, Paul claims to have interacted with Peter in person three times. (The second of these meetings presumably occurred at the apostolic conference in Jerusalem.) These three exchanges could be characterized as follows: a brief *casual* contact in Jerusalem about three years after Paul's missionary career began (1:18–19); a more formal, but *conciliatory,* contact again in Jerusalem about fourteen years later (the Jerusalem Conference, 2:1–10); and a *confrontational* contact some time later in Antioch (2:11–14). The significance of this account for reconstructing Pauline chronology was addressed earlier in this volume. In this chapter, the important issues to consider within this account are the relationships between Paul and Peter and between their respective messages. In 1 Corinthians Paul emphasized the continuity of the early Christian message proclaimed by him, Peter, the twelve, James, and "all the apostles" (15:3–8). Paul even seemed to imply the traditional, and perhaps

---

[8] Frank McGuire has suggested that Galatians is pseudonymous and that Peter and Paul never met ("The Posthumous Clash Between Peter and Paul," *Journal of Higher Criticism* 9 [2002]: 161–74). Such claims can be safely ignored.

[9] Bruce Chilton has sarcastically, but accurately, observed that Paul "seems so confident that one might overlook the fact he was the loser in the battle with the representatives of James. It was he, not they, who left the area of Antioch" ("James, Peter, Paul, and the Formation of the Gospels," in *The Missions of James, Peter, and Paul: Tensions in Early Christianity* [ed. Bruce Chilton and Craig A. Evans; NovTSup 115; Boston: Brill, 2005], 7). For a much older reminder of the same reality, see Benjamin W. Bacon, "Peter's Triumph at Antioch," *JR* 9 (1929): 204–23.

dependent, nature of his message by explaining: "I handed on to you as of first importance what I in turn had received" (15:3; cf. 11:23). Although Paul did not explicitly state from whom he had received the message, Paul's outline of the content he had received certainly privileged Peter. Paul recorded four traditions that he received:

> *that* (ὅτι) Christ died for our sins in accordance with the scriptures,
>
> and *that* (ὅτι) he was buried,
>
> and *that* (ὅτι) he was raised on the third day in accordance with the scriptures,
>
> and *that* (ὅτι) he appeared *to Cephas . . .*" (1 Cor 15:3–5, emphasis added).[10]

Although it is difficult, perhaps impossible, to distinguish the traditional material from the Pauline editing of that material,[11] for our present purpose it is sufficient to note that Paul demonstrated no interest in distinguishing the source of his message from the traditions stemming from Peter and the twelve.[12]

Galatians is very different in this regard. Paul contrasted "human approval" with "God's approval" (1:10) and insisted that God "set *me* apart before *I* was born and called *me* . . . to reveal his Son to *me*, so that *I* might proclaim him among the Gentiles" (1:15–16, emphasis added). Although Paul recognized the existence of other apostles in both Galatians and 1 Corinthians, even persons who were apostles before him (Gal 1:17; 1 Cor 15:7–9; Rom 16:7), when recounting the inception of his missionary career he insisted: "I did not confer with any human being, nor did I go up to Jerusalem to those who were already apostles before me . . ." (Gal 1:16–17). Then Paul insisted that his initial contact with Peter occurred three years later and was itself brief, lasting only fifteen days (1:18). According to Paul, his next contact with Peter

---

[10]Paul demonstrates no awareness of the empty tomb tradition. Paul even refers to Jesus being "buried" (θάπτω, 1 Cor 15:4) instead of being laid in a tomb (μνεῖον, Matt 27:60–66; Luke 23:53; Mark 15:46; John 19:41–42). The gospels (and Acts) know Paul's language of burial (e.g., Matt 8:21; 14:12 [cf. Mark 6:29]; Luke 9:59; 16:22; Acts 2:29; 5:6, 9, 10), but avoid using it in reference to Jesus' body. For whatever reason, Paul speaks only of Jesus' post-resurrection appearances, and never of the empty tomb. See Daniel Alan Smith, *The Post-Mortem Vindication of Jesus in the Sayings Gospel Q* (LNTS 338; London: T&T Clark, 2006), 159–66.

[11]For the most recent example of speculation about what content Paul inherited and what modifications Paul may have introduced into these inherited materials, see David M. Moffitt, "Affirming the 'Creed': The Extent of Paul's Citation of an Early Christian Formula in 1 Cor 15,3b–7," *ZNW* 99 (2008): 33–48.

[12]Scholarly assessments of Paul's relations to the twelve have hardly budged in the last hundred years. At the turn of the twentieth century, some scholars characterized this relationship—at least in its early years—as cooperative and mutually supportive (e.g., Shirley Jackson Case, "Paul's Historical Relation to the First Disciples," *AJT* 11 [1907]: 269–86), while others characterized this relationship as consistently troubled and contentious with only fleeting periods of cooperation (e.g., Ezra P. Gould, "St. Paul and the Twelve," *JBL* 18 [1899]: 184–89).

occurred fourteen years later and came about through a divine—not human—summons (a "revelation," 2:2).[13] According to Paul, this second contact (the Jerusalem Conference) with Peter involved more participants, but resulted in no change to Paul's message because "those leaders contributed nothing to me" (2:6). In Paul's account, Peter and the leadership in Jerusalem could contribute nothing to Paul's gospel because Paul's gospel came from God and lacked nothing, as the leaders themselves acknowledged according to Paul's telling of things (2:9).[14] According to Galatians, Paul's third contact with Peter was adversarial because Paul "saw that they [Peter and others] were not acting consistently with the truth of the gospel" (2:14). Consequently, Paul publicly rebuked Peter (2:11, 14).

Regardless of what historical reconstructions one builds around this evidence or what theological implications one draws from it, *one conclusion is clear:* Paul's relationship with Peter as revealed in Paul's letters was uneven. According to Paul's letters, personal contact between Peter and Paul was rare and brief. It ranged from cordial in their first meeting, to supportive in their second meeting, to antagonistic in their final recorded meeting. The contacts between their ideologies were more common and ranged from the Petrine traditions offering strong ideological support for the Pauline position in 1 Cor 15, to Paul being in strong ideological disagreement with the Petrine traditions in Galatians. In 1 Cor 1–4, we see that the followers of Peter and of Paul sometimes clashed even when these leaders were not present or in obvious tension.15

James

Paul's interaction with James, the other prominent leader of Christianity in Jerusalem, was less frequent but also uneven. Recent years have seen a surge of scholarly interest in James, the brother of Jesus, particularly since the discovery of the so-called—and probably fraudulent—"James ossuary."[16]

---

[13] On the divine origin of Paul's gospel in Galatians, see Lyons, *Pauline Autobiography*, 152–56.

[14] Ironically, even in the defense of his own authority, Paul was forced to presume Peter's earlier authority. As James D. G. Dunn has correctly observed, "in trying to assert his [Paul's] independence from Jerusalem, and the directness of his apostleship and gospel from Christ, he cannot escape the fact that previously he had readily acknowledged the authority of the Jerusalem apostles" ("Incident at Antioch," 202). Also see Pheme Perkins, *Peter: Apostle of the Whole Church* (Studies on Personalities of the New Testament; Minneapolis: Fortress, 2000), 111–18.

[15] Perkins has noted that Protestant scholars have tended to emphasize the hostile moments in the relationship between Peter and Paul, while Catholic scholars have tended to emphasize the mutually supportive aspects in the relationship between Peter and Paul (*Peter*, 3–14, 109–18). Both emphases have textual support in Paul's letters, but neither has exclusive support.

[16] Most importantly Hershel Shanks and Ben Witherington, *The Brother of Jesus: The Dramatic Story and Significance of the First Archaeological Link to Jesus and His Family*

Although James is a fascinating figure within early Christianity, most of this scholarship is not relevant to the purposes of this chapter. For our purposes, it is initially significant only to observe that James appears in Paul's letters only in contexts where Peter also appears and that James tends to remain largely in the shadow of Peter either as Peter's colleague or as a force behind Peter's least admirable conduct. Paul mentioned James by name in only two contexts (1 Cor 15:7; Gal 1–2; cf. 1 Cor 9:5).[17]

Paul's reference to James as one of the witnesses to the resurrection can be interpreted as either diminishing or emphasizing James's significance within early Christianity (1 Cor 15:7). On the one hand, James was apparently neither one of the original twelve nor even one of the five hundred who initially saw the risen Christ (15:5–6). Rather, James saw the risen Christ just before "all the apostles" (15:7). Thus, one could infer that Paul regarded James as participating in a second round of christophanies—not as distant from Peter's as was Paul's, but still not among the earliest witnesses. On the other hand, Paul specifically named only two people (besides himself) who saw the resurrected Christ. Therefore, one could infer that these two named witnesses, Peter and James, were particularly important among the larger group of witnesses. Thus, Paul's reference to James in 1 Corinthians is ambiguous. James is distinguished from the other witnesses, but the rationale for that distinction is not clear. One could infer either that Paul distinguished James from the other witnesses in order to emphasize either his inferiority (as a later witness to the resurrection like Paul) or his superiority (as a named witness of particular significance). In any case, according to Paul, James was clearly a trustworthy, perhaps even a distinguished, witness to the resurrection. However, Paul's letters provide no rationale—positive or negative—for distinguishing James from the other witnesses.

Paul's references to James in Galatians, like his reference in 1 Corinthians, do not clearly establish whether or not Paul regarded James as an apostle. In the account of his first visit to Jerusalem, Paul insisted "I did go up

---

(San Francisco: HarperSanFrancisco, 2003); Craig A. Evans, *Jesus and the Ossuaries* (Waco: Baylor University Press, 2003); John Painter, *Just James: The Brother of Jesus in History and Tradition* (2d ed.; Studies on Personalities of the New Testament; Columbia: University of South Carolina Press, 2004); Jodi Magness, "Ossuaries and the Burials of Jesus and James," *JBL* 124 (2005): 121–54; Emile Peuch, "James the Just, or just James? The 'James Ossuary' on Trial," *BAIAS* 21 (2003): 45–53; André Lemaire, "The 'James Ossuary on Trial': A Short Rejoinder," *BAIAS* 22 (2004): 35–36; and A. Ayalon, M. Bar-Matthews, and Y. Goren, "Authenticity Examination of the Inscription on the Ossuary Attributed to James, Brother of Jesus," *Journal of Archaeological Science* 31 (2004): 1185–89. For an excellent review of scholarship on James more generally, see Matti Myllykoski, "James the Just in History and Tradition: Perspectives of Past and Present Scholarship," *CBR* 5 (2006): 73–122; *CBR* 6 (2007): 11–98.

[17]While 1 Cor 9:5 does not name James, it does refer to the "brothers of the Lord," who traveled with their wives in ministry. This reference probably included James and, therefore, informs us that James was probably married. See Painter, *Just James*, 78.

to Jerusalem to visit Cephas and stayed with him fifteen days; but I did not see any other apostle except James the Lord's brother" (Gal 1:18–19). Paul's exception clause is ambiguous and could be translated "I saw none of the other apostles—only James, the Lord's brother" (NIV). Although the weight of the evidence suggests that Paul probably did regard James as an apostle, Paul's grammar leaves room for the possibility either that James's apostleship was not universally recognized within the early church or even that Paul did not regard James as an apostle.[18] Even though Paul's first reference to James in Galatians does not clearly convey his recognition of James's apostleship, Paul's other references to James in Galatians reveal that he clearly acknowledged James's prominence and importance within early Christianity.

Paul mentioned James three times in Galatians (1:19; 2:9, 12). According to Paul, these three contacts all occurred in conjunction with Paul's interaction with Peter. And as was the case in Paul's contacts with Peter, these contacts with James and his ideas can be characterized as casual (1:19), conciliatory (2:9), and confrontational (2:12). In spite of the parallels between the tone of their respective interactions, Paul's interaction with James did not simply mirror his interactions with Peter. According to Galatians, Paul's first interaction with James was largely coincidental. The purpose for Paul's visit to Jerusalem was "to see Peter," and he just happened to see James while in the area (1:18–19). The situation was different when Paul visited Jerusalem the second time for the Jerusalem Conference. In his retelling of this visit, Paul listed James as an "acknowledged pillar" of the Jerusalem church, and even listed James's name before the names of Peter and John (Gal 2:9; cf. *1 Clem.* 5.2). In the intervening time, James's influence within the Jerusalem church—or at least his significance for Paul—appears to have grown.[19] James moved from being a coincidental contact for Paul during his first visit to Jerusalem to being the first person listed as a "pillar" during Paul's second

---

[18]On the interpretation of Paul's exception clause in Gal 1:19, see the debate between L. Paul Trudinger ("'*Heteron de tōn apostolōn ouk eido, ei mē Iakōbon . . .*': A Note on Galatians i.19," *NovT* 17 [1975]: 200–202) and George Howard ("Was James an Apostle?" *NovT* 19 [1977]: 63–64). More recently, see William R. Farmer, "James the Lord's Brother, according to Paul," in Chilton and Evans, *James the Just and Christian Origins*, 133–53; and O'Neill, "Gal. 1:19." Perhaps James D. G. Dunn is correct to suggest that Paul himself was uncertain (or even unconvinced) about James's apostleship (*The Epistle to the Galatians* [BNTC 9; Hendrickson: Peabody, Mass., 1993], 77).

[19]James's increased prominence in Paul's second visit to Jerusalem for the Jerusalem Conference (Gal 2:9) and Peter's later presence in Antioch rather than Jerusalem (2:11) have led some scholars to conjecture that James replaced Peter as the most prominent disciple in Jerusalem and even displaced Peter from leadership in the Jerusalem church. Such analyses find support not only in Galatians, but also in 1 Corinthians, where the reference to Jesus' appearance to James can be regarded as a later Pauline addition to a traditional formula which originally emphasized only Peter and the twelve (15:5–7). See Wilhelm Pratscher, *Der Herrenbruder Jakobus und die Jakobustradition* (FRLANT 139; Göttingen: Vandenhoeck & Ruprecht, 1987), 45–46; Gerd Lüdemann, *Opposition to Paul in Jewish Christianity* (trans. M. Eugene Boring; Minneapolis: Fortress, 1989), 49–51; and Painter, *Just James*, 68–71.

visit to Jerusalem.[20] In Paul's final recorded interaction with James, James did not appear in person, but rather was present only as the source behind Peter's conduct. According to Paul, his public rebuke of Peter occurred after "certain people from James" coaxed Peter away from eating with Gentiles (Gal 2:12). Although Paul did not directly interact with James on this occasion, he claimed to have rebuked Peter for succumbing to the influence of James. By the time of Paul's third interaction with Peter, James had become influential enough to entice Peter away from what Paul regarded as essential to the Christian faith.

From this evidence, therefore, it appears that Paul had only brief, rare, and sometimes incidental contact with James, but that Paul recognized James's role as a witness to the resurrection and as an increasingly prominent authority within the Jerusalem church. It appears that Paul's recognition of James's authority and influence grew between his first and second visit to Jerusalem.[21] In any case, Paul had a sustained ideological conflict with James after their second meeting. Although Paul recognized the prominence of James within the church as a witness to the resurrection and as a pillar of the Jerusalem church, *it is not clear that Paul regarded James as an apostle. Eventually Paul—and probably at least some of his converts—came into significant ideological conflict with James.*

John

The only other resident authority in Jerusalem with whom Paul interacts in the letters was John. Paul's singular reference to John appears in his account of his second visit to Jerusalem when his message was approved in his conciliatory meeting with the pillars of the Jerusalem church. Paul includes John among the Jerusalem pillars, suggesting that Paul recognized John as an authority in the Jerusalem church (Gal 2:9). However, John never became a central figure in any Pauline discussion, and therefore we can only infer that *Paul recognized John as an authority within the Jerusalem church, but probably had minimal direct interaction with him.*[22]

---

[20]David Wenham and A. D. A. Moses have plausibly suggested that James, the brother of Jesus, grew in prominence after the death of the original apostle James (Acts 12:2) and that Paul's account in Galatians reflects the rising prominence of James, the brother of Jesus, after the death of the earlier James ("'There Are Some Standing Here . . .': Did They Become the 'Reputed Pillars' of the Jerusalem Church?" *NovT* 36 [1994]: 146–63).

[21]Protestants and Catholics have traditionally interpreted James's ascendancy within the Jerusalem church differently. Protestants have commonly used the rise of James to undermine Catholic claims about the primacy of Peter, while Catholics have tended to interpret James as only a regional leader of the church in contrast to Peter's universal leadership of the church. See Pierre-Antoine Bernheim, *James, Brother of Jesus* (trans. John Bowden; London: SCM, 1997), 191–222.

[22]R. Alan Culpepper is correct to insist that Gal 2:9 "provides unimpeachable evidence for the role of John, the son of Zebedee, in the leadership of the early church in Jerusalem" (*John: The Son of Zebedee* [Minneapolis: Fortress, 2000], 49).

Barnabas

Whereas Peter, James, and John were residents of Jerusalem, and Paul encountered them briefly, intermittently, and primarily in that setting, Barnabas apparently traveled with Paul, and the two shared a relationship that was apparently both lengthy and significant. Paul even seems to have regarded Barnabas as a fellow apostle. As Paul defended his own apostleship ("Am I not an apostle?" 1 Cor 9:1), he asked "is it only Barnabas and I who have no right to refrain from working for a living?" (9:6). Thus, in this context, it appears that Paul was arguing not only for his own apostolic rights, but also for the apostolic rights of Barnabas. However, in spite of this insistence that he and Barnabas were entitled to the apostolic right of financial compensation, Paul also boastfully claimed that they had not and would not make "use of this right" (9:12).[23] Paul's references to Barnabas in 1 Cor 9 reveal the status that Barnabas possessed in Paul's eyes; Paul's references to Barnabas in Galatians reveal the status that Barnabas apparently enjoyed more broadly within early Christianity.

In Barnabas's other appearance in Paul's letters, Barnabas appears as an equal to Paul—or perhaps even as a senior partner. In his own highly charged retelling of the events surrounding the Jerusalem Conference, Paul's language distinguished his traveling companions very clearly. Paul went to Jerusalem "with Barnabas" and "took Titus along" (Gal 2:1). Barnabas was clearly more prominent than was Titus at the time of the Jerusalem Conference. On the basis of Paul's distinction between the status of his two companions, some interpreters have even speculated that Barnabas was a more prominent member of this entourage than was Paul, or at least more prominent from the perspective of the Jerusalem church and its Galatian sympathizers.[24] In this regard, it is probably significant that Paul listed Barnabas first when he insisted that the leaders in Jerusalem gave "to *Barnabas and me* the right hand of fellowship" (2:9, emphasis added). At the time of the Jerusalem Conference, Paul may well have considered himself—or the Jerusalem leaders may well have considered Paul—a junior partner to Barnabas. Whether Barnabas had ever served as Paul's senior partner—perhaps even his mentor and benefactor—remains unclear in the letters, but what is clear is Paul's disappointment with Barnabas's behavior after the Jerusalem Conference. In detailing the events that led to Paul's rebuke of Peter (2:14), Paul provided a genealogy of error, explaining that people from James led Peter away from eating with Gentiles and that *even Barnabas* was eventually led into this error (2:11–13). Paul seems to have expected such disappoint-

---

[23] A surface reading of Paul's reference to Barnabas in this context would imply that Paul and Barnabas were current colleagues when Paul wrote 1 Corinthians, but most scholars assume that Paul and Barnabas had parted ways long before the composition of 1 Corinthians. See Conzelmann, *1 Corinthians,* 154; and Fee, *First Epistle to the Corinthians,* 404–5.

[24] E.g., Duncan, *Galatians,* 35.

ing behavior from James and was hardly surprised to observe such behavior from Peter, but Paul was shocked and dismayed to see such behavior from Barnabas.

From these discussions, we can therefore learn that according to Paul's letters, Barnabas was a traveling companion of Paul and was quite prominent within early Christianity. (The casual reference to Barnabas in 1 Cor 9:6 attests to this reputation, assuming that Barnabas had not visited the Corinthians personally.) Barnabas was probably even an apostle in Paul's eyes, and it is possible that he was more respected in Jerusalem than was Paul. Barnabas's ties to the Jerusalem church may help to explain why he greatly—and unexpectedly—disappointed Paul in regard to the issue of Gentile inclusion in the church.

Titus

Titus makes several appearances in 2 Corinthians and two appearances in Galatians. The most striking characteristic of Paul's references to Titus is his effusive praise for Titus. Paul identified Titus as a "partner and co-worker" (2 Cor 8:23) and claimed to be unable to rest (2:12–13) until "consoled" by his presence (7:6). Paul was confident that Titus shared his desire to complete his offering among the Corinthians (8:6) and shared Paul's passion for the Corinthians' well-being (8:16). In fact, Paul even challenged the Corinthians to demonstrate that Titus's behavior was in any way subject to reproach (12:18). Although Paul had once been disappointed by his inability to locate Titus in Troas in Asia Minor (2:12–13), Paul gave no indication that this failed connection was due to any failure on Titus's part. In fact, Paul continued to plan future travels with Titus (8:19). According to 2 Corinthians, Titus was a highly trusted Pauline associate, so much so that he could be trusted to travel to the church in Corinth "on his own accord" while "the brother who is famous among the churches" was sent to Corinth with him (8:17–18). Regardless of the identity of this famous, but unnamed, "brother,"[25] it appears that Titus possessed a great deal of autonomy and authority at this point within the Pauline churches. Titus could determine his own travel agenda and was even described as one of the "apostles of the churches" (8:23, translation mine).

The autonomy of Titus in 2 Corinthians stands in contrast to his subordinate status in Galatians where he travels at Paul's discretion. When discussing the Jerusalem Conference, Paul asserted that "I went up again to Jerusalem with Barnabas, taking Titus along with me" (Gal 2:1). Paul's grammar and language are significant. Paul did not take both Titus and Barnabas along with him to Jerusalem; rather Paul went "with Barnabas" and Paul took Titus along. At this point, Paul apparently could decide whether or not Titus would travel with him. What's more, even Paul's boast that Titus remained uncircumcised

---

[25] The famous brother was probably Timothy; see Furnish, *II Corinthians*, 434–35.

was recorded as if Titus had no say in the issue. Paul merely insisted that "even Titus, who was with me, was not compelled to be circumcised, though he was a Greek" (2:3). Although Titus was at the center of the controversy and had a cutting personal interest in the decisions being made in the Galatians narrative, Paul treated Titus almost as an exhibit—albeit Paul's premier exhibit—in the defense of a law-free inclusion of the Gentiles into the church. Titus was important to Paul's case, but Titus is portrayed with little authority of his own in Galatians.[26] *From his appearances in Paul's letters, we learn that Titus was well known and well respected in Pauline circles—probably even as an apostle—and that he traveled widely with Paul from Greece in the west to Jerusalem in the east. Although he was an uncircumcised Gentile, he was present with Paul as Paul's loyal subordinate during the Jerusalem Conference, and he was Paul's most important example of the Gentiles' law-free inclusion into the church.*

Summary of the Pauline Data Set

Paul undoubtedly recognized the prominence of the "pillars"—Peter, James, and John. All three, along with Barnabas and Titus, were recognized authorities within the Pauline churches. Initially, Paul had supportive relationships with all five of these men, although he had only marginal contact with John. Paul defended Barnabas's apostolic rights and probably assumed Titus's apostolic authority, but Paul did not draw upon the authority of Barnabas or Titus to support his own message in the way that he drew upon the authority of Peter and James. Even though Paul drew upon two of the three Jerusalem pillars in support of his own message, he was willing to harshly criticize those pillars and Barnabas, and he was unwilling to defer to their authority as superior to his own.

Paul's relationship with Barnabas was probably more enduring (and probably more endearing) than were his relationships with the Jerusalem pillars. The (traveling) relationship between Paul and Barnabas apparently lasted several years before the pair came into conflict; Paul's long-distance relationship with Peter also extended over several years and was sometimes mutually supportive and sometimes confrontational; Paul's equally long-distance relationship with James was even less supportive than his relationship with Peter, and it was deeply antagonistic at points; and Paul's relationship with John was both long-distance and slight, but not necessarily antagonistic (perhaps it lacked the familiarity needed to breed contempt). Titus appears as Paul's junior associate, possibly as an apostle, but most importantly, as Paul's premier example of the truth of the law-free inclusion of the Gentiles into the church. It is probably significant that Paul viewed both of his co-missionaries at the Jerusalem Conference (Barnabas and Titus) as apostles.

---

[26] Some have argued that Titus *was circumcised,* but only voluntarily so and not under compulsion. Such arguments are unconvincing; see F. F. Bruce, *The Pauline Circle* (Grand Rapids: Eerdmans, 1985), 58–61.

II. THE ACTS DATA SET

In Acts, even as a Christian missionary, Saul (Paul after 13:9) found that many believers were reluctant to trust him and his ideas prior to the Jerusalem Conference. Both because of his personal history as a former persecutor of the church and because of his ideological commitments to a law-free inclusion of Gentiles into the church, the integration of Paul and his ideas into the established Christian communities was possible only through the advocacy of four key authority figures. The work of these advocates crested in the Jerusalem Conference with the final advocacy of Peter and James. Sequentially arranged, the authority figures who helped to integrate Paul and his message into the church in Acts are Ananias, Barnabas, Peter, and James.

Ananias

In spite of Saul's experience on the road to Damascus, the believers in Damascus were not eager to welcome him within their communities. Ultimately, however, God intervened in Saul's behalf and instructed a disciple named Ananias to seek out Saul at the house of Judas and to lay hands on him (Acts 9:11–12). Even Ananias was initially resistant to this divine plan, and he understandably protested: "Lord, I have heard from many about this man, how much evil he has done to your saints in Jerusalem" (9:13). Eventually, however, Ananias overcame his reluctance, visited Saul, and laid hands on him. This "laying on of hands" both healed Saul's Spirit-induced blindness and conveyed to him the Holy Spirit (9:17–18).[27] Following this, Saul was completely integrated into the community through baptism (9:18). The Paul of Acts later retold this story during his defense speech, where his words

---

[27] "Laying on of hands" has three functions in the book of Acts: healing (Acts 28:8; cf. Luke 4:40; Mark 5:23; 6:5; 8:23–25), bestowing the Holy Spirit (Acts 8:17–18; 19:6), and authorizing for distinctive Christian service (sometimes anachronistically translated "ordain," Acts 6:6; 13:3; cf. 1 Tim 4:14; 5:22; 2 Tim 1:6). In this context, Saul is both healed (Acts 9:17) and filled with the Holy Spirit (9:18), but the third function, authorizing for service, is less clear (Sten Lundgren, "Ananias and the Calling of Paul in Acts," *Studia theologica* 25 [1971]: 117–22). Although Ananias is clearly aware of Saul's chosenness for service (9:15), it is unclear if Ananias is empowered to authorize Saul for service. The origin of this practice of laying on of hands is unclear. Precedents within the Old Testament and Jewish practices are often sought (e.g., Everett Ferguson, "Jewish and Christian Ordination," *HTR* 56 [1963]: 13–19; and Majorie Warkentin, *Ordination: A Biblical-Historical View* [Grand Rapids: Eerdmans, 1982], esp. 1–51), but as was long ago noted, none of the Old Testament practices offers clear parallels to the Christian practice (e.g., Henry Preserved Smith, "The Laying-On of Hands," *AJT* 17 [1913]: 47–62). J. K. Parratt, who recognizes the three different functions of the laying on of hands in Acts, has plausibly argued that the central conception behind the practice is the conveyance of a blessing, as in Jesus' blessing of the children in Mark 10:16 and Matt 19:13–15 ("The Laying on of Hands in the New Testament: A Re-examination in Light of the Hebrew Terminology," *ExpTim* 80 [1969]: 210–14).

reasserted that Ananias was the human agent of Paul's healing and baptism (22:12–16). According to Acts, therefore, Ananias was the Christian disciple responsible for Paul's initial integration into the Christian community.[28]

Barnabas

Barnabas, the second Christian leader with whom Saul made contact in Acts, also served an integrative function for Paul. Ananias had introduced Saul to the Christian community in Damascus and helped that community to overcome their fear of Saul; Barnabas served the same intermediary role between Saul and the Jerusalem community.[29] Acts records that "when he [Saul] had come to Jerusalem, he attempted to join the disciples; and they were afraid of him" (9:26). This fear was overcome only when "Barnabas took him, brought him to the apostles, and described for them how on the road he had seen the Lord" (9:27).[30] According to Acts, Saul was then able to go "in and out among them in Jerusalem" (9:28) until his preaching created external animosity toward him in Jerusalem—just as it had in Damascus. In the face of Hellenistic opposition to Saul, a group of believers in Jerusalem sent him back to his hometown of Tarsus (9:30; cf. 9:11). Saul's time (exile?) in Tarsus came to an end only when Barnabas journeyed there and brought Saul back with him to Antioch (11:25–26). While Saul and Barnabas were in Antioch, the Christians there learned that the believers in Jerusalem were suffering under a famine. In response to this famine, the believers in Antioch dispatched Barnabas and Saul to deliver aid to the elders in Judea (11:29–30). According to Acts, Barnabas and Saul distributed that aid throughout Judea, including Jerusalem (12:25).[31]

---

[28] The appearances of the name Ananias in Acts provide clear evidence for why the mere correspondence of names is no guarantee of a correspondence in identity between persons. Acts refers to three different figures named Ananias: an early believer who died along with his wife Sapphira (5:1–11), the disciple just discussed (9:10–19; 22:12), and a Jewish high priest in Jerusalem (23:2; 24:1). In their present contexts in Acts, these three persons are clearly distinguished from one another. However, if the order of their appearances was reversed, it would be impossible to distinguish them with complete confidence.

[29] On Barnabas's role as Paul's mentor in Acts, see Clark, *Parallel Lives*, 294–319. Also see Bruce, *Pauline Circle*, 15.

[30] Jenny Read-Heimerdinger has argued that Barnabas's role as an intermediary between Paul and the apostles is diminished in the familiar Alexandrian text behind most English translations. In her view, the lesser known textual tradition represented by Codex Bezae preserves an even more intense role for Barnabas as an intermediary by inserting Barnabas as the proper choice to replace Judas in Acts 1. She also argues that Codex Bezae preserves earlier and more original traditions than the later traditions preserved in the Alexandrian text and contemporary English translations ("Barnabas in Acts: A Study of His Role in the Text of Codex Bezae," *JSNT* 72 [1998]: 23–66).

[31] This visit to Jerusalem is Paul's so-called "famine visit" as discussed in chapter three of this volume.

In the next scene in Acts, Barnabas was back in Antioch. He apparently enjoyed considerable prominence in that church, for Luke's list of its "prophets and teachers," which is probably ordered from most to least prominent, included Barnabas, Simeon, Lucius, and Saul (Paul) in that order (13:1).[32] While the prophets were together, Acts records that the Holy Spirit said: "Set apart for me Barnabas and Saul for the work to which I have called them" (13:2). The church—or perhaps just the prophets—in Antioch responded by sending Barnabas and Saul on what would become a preaching engagement through the island of Cyprus and the mainland of central Asia Minor (13:4–14:21). Barnabas's name again appears first when he and Saul were sent out to preach (13:2) and in Luke's account of the summons that the proconsul, Sergius Paulus, issued calling Barnabas and Saul to appear before him (13:7). However, in the subsequent narrative, after Acts abandoned the name "Saul" in favor of the name "Paul" (13:9),[33] Paul's name repeatedly appears before Barnabas's name (13:42, 43, 46, 50; 14:1, 23; 15:2, 22). The only exceptions to this "Paul first" tendency in Acts are the one case where Acts designates Paul as one of the apostles ("the apostles Barnabas and Paul," 14:14; cf. 14:4[34])

[32] It is possible to infer the presence of Simeon at the later apostolic conference in Jerusalem. Many ancient manuscripts have James referring to remarks made by "Simeon" rather than "Simon" (Acts 15:14). Although it is possible that the Simeon of Antioch was present at the Jerusalem Conference and even spoke at that event, it is far more likely that James was referring to the comments just offered by Simon Peter (15:7–11). "Simeon" would have been a common way for an Aramaic-speaking person, like James, to refer to Simon Peter, although Acts elsewhere consistently speaks of "Simon" Peter (10:5, 18, 32; 11:13). Perhaps the difference in spelling reflects dependence upon a different, and more Aramaic-influenced, source. See Joseph A. Fitzmyer, *Essays on the Semitic Background of the New Testament* (Missoula: Scholars Press, 1974), 105–12; *contra* Rainer Riesner, "James's Speech (Acts 15:13–21), Simeon's Hymn (Luke 2:29–32), and Luke's Sources," in *Jesus of Nazareth: Lord and Christ* (ed. Joel B. Green and Max Turner; Grand Rapids: Eerdmans, 1994), 263–78.

[33] Some scholars have suspected that the name change from "Saul" to "Paul" in Acts reflects a change in the underlying sources for the respective parts of Acts. However, the issue of the sources is so complex that such inferences should remain chastened. For a recent analysis of the probable sources underlying Acts 15, see Barrett, *Acts*, 1:49–56 and the bibliography provided there.

[34] Acts often speaks of the apostles in the plural (1:2, 26; 2:37, 42, 43; 4:2, 33, 35, 36, 37; 5:2, 12, 17, 18, 22, 26, 27, 29, 40, 41; 6:6; 8:1, 14, 18; 9:27; 11:1; 14:4, 14; 15:2, 4, 6, 22, 23; 16:4; cf. Luke 6:12, 13; 9:10; 11:49; 17:5; 22:14; 24:10), but Acts never uses the singular "apostle." In Acts (and in Luke's Gospel), the apostles appear as a collective body. Acts never speaks of apostleship as an office or calling which one individual possessed apart from participation in the larger body of apostles. The eleven (the original twelve minus Judas) are very important in Acts (1:26; 2:14), and replenishing their number to twelve is a clear priority in the opening of Acts, a priority which is attended to by the selection of Matthias to serve as the twelfth apostle (Acts 1:12–26; cf. Luke 6:13; Acts 6:2). Paul's lack of extended interaction with the twelve may explain part of Paul's ambiguous apostolic status in Acts. As John P. Meier has noted, Luke and Acts assume a "close connection, if not total identification, between the Twelve and the apostles" ("The Circle of the Twelve: Did It Exist during Jesus' Public Ministry?" *JBL* 116 [1997]: 635–72, quoting 641). Also see Philippe H. Menoud,

and the two cases where Acts records Barnabas and Paul interacting with the apostles in Jerusalem (15:12, 25).

This prioritizing of Barnabas's name over Paul's in these contexts is significant first because Acts identifies Paul as one of the apostles only in this one place (after 13:9) where Paul's name is preceded by Barnabas's name (14:14) and second because Barnabas's name always takes precedence over Paul's when Acts records Barnabas and Paul interacting with the established Christian communities in Antioch (11:27–30; 13:1–7) and Jerusalem (15:12, 25). Acts, therefore, not only hesitates to designate Paul as an apostle in his own right apart from Barnabas's co-apostleship,35 but also seems tacitly to recognize Paul's inferiority to Barnabas in the eyes of the preexisting Christian communities in Antioch and Jerusalem. In spite of this apparent slighting of Paul's apostolic status in Acts 11–15, Acts clearly assumes—even emphasizes—Paul's role as a leading Christian preacher and witness.[36] Even when Paul and Barnabas are together in Acts, Paul does nearly all the public speaking (13:10–11, 16–41; 14:9–11). Although Acts gives Paul and Barnabas co-responsibility for all that is said, shouted, reported, and proclaimed (13:46–47; 14:14–18, 21; 15:2, 4, 12), even pagan observers recognize that Paul, like the messenger god Hermes, is the chief speaker for the pair (14:12).

Paul's role as chief speaker is unchallenged outside of Jerusalem. However, when the church in Antioch appointed Paul and Barnabas to discuss the issue of circumcision of Gentile converts with the Jerusalem leadership (15:2–3), Paul's role as chief speaker is mitigated. Upon their arrival in Jerusalem, "the apostles and the elders met together to consider the matter" (Acts 15:6). Peter spoke before the whole assembly (πλῆθος), and then the assembly "listened to Barnabas and Paul" (15:12). It is unclear if Acts 15 portrays two meetings: first, a private meeting with only the apostles and elders present and in which Peter was the primary speaker (15:6–11) and, second, a more public meeting of the "whole assembly" in which Barnabas and Paul were the primary speakers (15:12–21).[37] Regardless of whether Acts 15:11–21 portrays one meeting or two, and regardless of whether Paul and Barnabas were even

"The Addition to the Twelve Apostles according to the Book of Acts," in *Jesus Christ and the Faith* (trans. Eunice M. Paul; Philadelphia: Pickwick, 1978), 133–48.

[35] On Luke's reluctance to designate Paul as an apostle and Luke's probable agenda to place Paul with the narrator of Acts in post-apostolic Christianity, see Phillips, "Paul as a Role Model" and the bibliography provided there; *contra* Andrew C. Clark, "The Role of the Apostles," in Marshall and Peterson, *Witness to the Gospel,* 169–90; and Clark, *Parallel Lives,* 136–49.

[36] On "witness" rather than "apostle" as the most appropriate title for Paul in Acts, see Boyd Mather, "Paul in Acts as a 'Servant' and 'Witness,'" *Biblical Research* 30 (1985): 23–44.

[37] In regard to the sources behind Acts 15, Fitzmyer is certainly correct to suggest that the chapter's "conflated character is widely admitted" (*Acts,* 552). Many scholars, Fitzmyer included, assume that the account in Acts depends upon multiple sources from different points in history and with different perspectives. Unfortunately, not only is the pre-history of the text largely irretrievable, but even the current literary context

present when Peter spoke, the members of the Jerusalem community were content to send their "beloved Barnabas and Paul" back with a letter outlining the decision of the entire Jerusalem church (15:25). For good measure, Judas and Silas were sent along with Barnabas and Paul in order to provide oral confirmation of the written words (15:27). This entourage "delivered the letter" to Antioch, but then Paul and Barnabas parted company after a sharp disagreement over John Mark (15:30, 39).[38] Acts gives only scant attention to Barnabas's subsequent activities (15:39), but records that Paul and his companions continued delivering the Jerusalem-derived letter to other churches (16:1–5).

In spite of their painful and apparently permanent break, Barnabas was very important to Paul's career in Acts. It was Barnabas who introduced Paul to a reluctant Christian community in Jerusalem (9:27), Barnabas who retrieved Paul back to Antioch from his obscurity in Tarsus (11:25–26), Barnabas who accompanied Paul on a famine relief visit to Jerusalem (11:29–30; 12:25), Barnabas who preached with Paul during a major missionary expedition (13:13–14:28), and Barnabas who helped Paul win the Jerusalem church's approval of a relatively law-free gospel (15:1–35). Still, according to Acts, Paul and Barnabas separated after the Jerusalem Conference (15:36–41), and their narrative paths never again intersected in Acts. According to Acts, therefore, Barnabas played an important integrative role in Paul's early ministry but had no contact with Paul during his later ministry.

Peter

Paul's ministry in Acts intersects with Peter far less than it does with Barnabas. According to Acts, Barnabas introduced Paul to "the apostles" shortly after his experience on the road to Damascus (9:27). Although Peter is not named in this reference, one may quite safely infer that Luke's reference to the apostles included Peter. This first reference to Paul's interaction with Peter reveals little about their relationship, because Paul preached in Jerusalem for only a short time before opposition from "the Hellenists" caused him to be "sent off" (ἀποστέλλω) to Tarsus (9:28–30). Paul's only other clearly reported interaction with Peter in Acts occurred at the apostolic conference in Jerusalem (Acts 15). Upon arriving in Jerusalem, Paul and Barnabas were welcomed by the apostles, presumably including Peter (15:2). More importantly, during the initial phase of the conference proceedings, Peter took the opportunity to voice support for Gentile inclusion in the church. Even before

---

remains ambiguous in regard to the presence of Barnabas and Paul in the first part of the meeting with the apostles and elders (15:6–11).

[38] Although Acts attributes Paul's refusal to allow John Mark to travel with them to John Mark's previous abandonment of Paul and Barnabas in Pamphylia (15:38), Painter is probably correct to suggest that Paul was opposed to John Mark's inclusion in the entourage on ideological grounds: John Mark's career began as an emissary from Jerusalem to Antioch (Acts 11:22; see Painter, *Just James*, 51–52).

Paul was given an opportunity to speak (15:7–11), Peter reminded the other apostles and elders: "you know that in the early days God made a choice among you, that *I should be the one* through whom the Gentiles would hear the message of the good news and become believers" (15:7, emphasis added). As the one who had initial charge over the church's Gentile mission, Peter ultimately concluded that God "has made no distinction between them and us [Jews]" (15:9). Peter presumably was also an active voice in supporting the decision of the apostles, the elders, and "the whole church" (15:22; 16:4) when they concluded that the Gentiles should be free from all except minimal requirements of the law—the requirements that Gentiles abstain from fornication, food offered to idols, blood, and things strangled (15:19–20, 28–29).[39]

According to Acts, therefore, Peter probably met Paul briefly while Paul was preaching in Jerusalem shortly after his life-altering encounter on the road to Damascus. Peter and Paul met again at the apostolic conference in Jerusalem where Peter claimed to have prior authority over the Gentile mission and where Peter was supportive of a relatively law-free proclamation to the Gentiles apart from circumcision. Peter was, therefore, instrumental in integrating Paul and his idea of (relatively) law-free Gentile inclusion into the established Christian communities. In fact, according to Acts, Peter was the originator of the (Pauline) idea of Gentile inclusion. Acts records no tensions between Peter and Paul. In fact, Peter was *a major force behind the successful integration of Paul and his ideas into the established Christian communities.*

James

Paul's interaction with James is also brief in Acts. The two first interacted when James announced his decision at the apostolic conference in Jerusalem. James's appearance in the narrative is sudden. The first three persons who helped to integrate Paul into the established Christian communities were briefly introduced into the narrative before they spoke on Paul's behalf. Ananias was introduced via a brief dialogue with God about Paul (9:10–16); Barnabas was pre-introduced as a significant benefactor within the commu-

---

[39]The origin and significance of these particular restrictions on Gentile freedom from the law have been widely debated. The most widely accepted theory is that these restrictions were adapted from the requirements for aliens living within Israel as recorded in Lev 17–18 (e.g., David R. Catchpole, "Paul, James and the Apostolic Decree," *NTS* 23 [1977]: 428–44). Others have suggested that the regulations derive from the covenant with Noah's family in Gen 9 (e.g., Hans-Joachim Schoeps, *Theologie und Geschichte des Judenchristentums* [Tübingen: Mohr Siebeck, 1949], 188–96; on origin and history of the Noahide laws, see David Novak, *The Image of the Non-Jew in Judaism: An Historical and Constructive Study of the Noahide Laws* [Toronto Studies in Theology 14; Lewiston: Edwin Mellen, 1984], 28–35). Still others have suggested that the regulations have no basis in Judaism and the Hebrew Bible traditions, but that they were designed to separate Christian Gentiles from the practices of their pagan neighbors (e.g., A.J. M. Wedderburn, "The 'Apostolic Decree': Tradition and Redaction," *NovT* 35 [1993]: 362–89).

nity (4:36–37); and Peter had the whole of the Third Gospel and Acts 1–8 to introduce him. In contrast, Acts allows James to speak and render important decisions single-handedly with no prior introduction and without as much as a reference to his credentials. Jacob Jervell is undoubtedly correct that James was "an undisputed authority" and "uncontestable figure" for the author of Acts.[40]

As Jervell also notes, the area and character of James's authority are also important. Whereas Peter's speech had defended Gentile inclusion into the church by appealing to the work of the Holy Spirit among Gentiles (15:8), James's defense of Gentile inclusion is rooted in the words of Israel's prophets (15:15–17; cf. Amos 9:11–12). In Acts, therefore, James is the Jerusalem church's authoritative interpreter of scriptural and legal traditions.[41] Speaking after both Peter and Paul, James spoke in the first person singular as if the decision about Gentile inclusion was his alone to make. He declared: "*I* have reached the decision that *we* should not trouble those Gentiles who are turning to God, but *we* should write to them to abstain only from things polluted by idols and from fornication and from whatever has been strangled and from blood" (15:19–20, emphasis added).[42] James's authority in Jerusalem seems unquestioned in Acts. Pierre-Antoine Bernheim rightly suggests that it is only a slight exaggeration to call James "the first pope"—as least to the degree that anyone in the mid-first century deserves that anachronistic designation.[43] As Acts tells the story, the apostles, the elders, and the whole church conducted no debate about the decision handed down by James.

In its present form, Acts implies that the only decision-making role afforded to anyone other than James was the selection of persons to disseminate a letter that detailed the decision reached by James (15:22, 25).[44] Paul was

---

[40] Jacob Jervell, *Luke and the People of God* (Minneapolis: Fortress, 1972), 187.

[41] See Jervell, *Luke and the People of God*, 191–92.

[42] Although most scholars consider this speech by James and all other speeches in Acts to be Lukan creations (e.g., Marion L. Soards, *The Speeches in Acts: Their Content, Context, and Concerns* [Louisville: Westminster John Knox, 1994], esp. 1–17, 92–95), Richard Bauckham has argued that this speech largely reflects the historical words of James and gives witness to his prominence within early Christianity ("James and the Gentiles (Acts 15.13–21)," in Witherington, *History, Literature, and Society*, 154–84).

[43] Bernheim, *James*, 222.

[44] One could plausibly argue that James's speech (Acts 15:13–21) was inserted into a narrative in which he originally played no role. If one reads Acts 15 without James's speech, the narrative reads more consistently. The apostles and elders met (15:6) and Peter, who—unlike James—was an apostle, gave a speech (15:6–11). Then Paul and Barnabas spoke (15:12) and finally the entire assembly gathered to hear the decision reached by the "apostles and elders" (15:22–23), a decision that Paul and his companions were charged with communicating to their fellow believers (15:25–29). Although 15:19 credits James alone with making the decision, James is never mentioned outside of 15:13–21, and the decision-making in the rest of the chapter is portrayed as corporate, involving either the apostles and elders (15:22–23, 28) or the entire community (15:12, 22, 25, 30)—and never James alone as in 15:13–21. James's involvement in 15:13–21 can, therefore, be read as both superfluous to and inconsistent with the rest of the chapter.

among those entrusted with delivering this letter, but even while delegating this duty to Paul, Acts appears to subordinate Paul to the Jerusalem leadership. Acts reports that the letter was handed down from the "apostles and elders" (15:23), a group that apparently did not include Paul. Remember that Paul had been sent to Jerusalem for the specific purpose of conferring with "the apostles and elders" (15:2), not with "the *other* apostles and elders."

As a side note, Paul's relationship to this letter—and to the rest of the letters in Acts—is significant. As just mentioned, Acts gave Paul no role in composing this letter. Instead, Paul served as one of four emissaries who delivered the letter. Even more surprisingly, Acts never credits Paul with writing any letter.[45] This absence of Pauline literary activity is particularly striking in light of Acts' frequent references to the exchange of letters between various persons and groups (9:2; 15:23, 30; 18:27; 20:17; 22:5; 23:25–34; 25:26; 28:21).[46] In the particular case of this letter produced by the apostles and elders in Jerusalem, Paul was excluded not only from participating in its authorship, but also from participating in its oral interpretation. The responsibility of offering oral interpretation was delegated specifically to Judas and Silas and not to Barnabas and Paul (15:27). Although Acts records Paul dutifully delivering the letter that contained the "decisions that had been reached by the apostles and elders who were in Jerusalem" (16:4), according to Acts, Paul never again interacted with most of the elders and apostles who were so important to his early integration into the established Christian communities. Acts never again mentions Ananias, Barnabas, Peter, or any other participant in the Jerusalem Conference except James—and Acts mentions James only once more.

---

[45]Although there have been a few dissenting voices along the way (e.g., William O. Walker, "Acts and the Pauline Corpus Revisited," in *Literary Studies in Luke-Acts* [ed. Richard P. Thompson and Thomas E. Phillips; Macon: Mercer University Press, 1998], 77–86; idem, "Acts and the Pauline Letters," *Forum* 5 [2002]: 105–15), even the best in late twentieth-century critical scholarship on Acts has tended to quickly dismiss the idea that the author of Acts used Paul's letters as a source (e.g., Barrett, *Acts,* esp. xliii; and Fitzmyer, *Acts,* esp. 2:52; cf. Grässer, *Forschungen zur Apostelgeschichte,* 179–87). Even Jacob Jervell, who has repeatedly argued for the necessity of drawing upon Acts for an adequate understanding of Paul (e.g., *Unknown Paul,* 52–76), has avoided suggesting that Acts used Paul's letters as a source. Jervell argued that the author of Acts had a vast array of traditions at hand, but he avoided any suggestion of Luke's use of Paul's letters as a source for Acts (e.g., *Luke and the People of God,* 19–40; and, more recently, *Die Apostelgechichte* [KEK; Göttingen: Vandenhoeck & Ruprecht, 1998], 61–72). This situation has now entirely changed with the publication of Richard I. Pervo's *Dating Acts: Between the Evangelists and the Apologists* (Santa Rosa: Polebridge, 2006). Pervo has clearly shifted the burden of proof back upon those who wish to deny that the author of Acts knew and used Paul's letters. Also see Pervo's *Acts: A Commentary* (Hermeneia; Minneapolis: Fortress, 2008).

[46]Some of these letters are embedded in Acts and others are simply alluded to. On the function of embedded letters in Acts, see Justin R. Howell, "Embedded Letters and Rhetorical αὔξησις," in *Contemporary Studies in Acts* (ed. Thomas E. Phillips; Macon: Mercer University Press, 2009), 154–80.

James reappears during Paul's final visit to Jerusalem in Acts, again functioning as an authoritative interpreter of legal traditions and as a defender of Paul (21:18). Upon this return, Paul was accused of teaching Jews—not Gentiles—to disregard the law, a charge that the James of Acts regarded as false (21:21–24). In order to disprove these charges, James devised a plan to demonstrate Paul's fidelity to the law by having Paul participate in carefully prescribed Jewish practices. James explained to Paul: "We have four men who are under a vow. Join these men, go through the rite of purification with them, and pay for the shaving of their heads. Thus all will know that there is nothing in what they have been told about you, but that you yourself observe and guard the law" (21:23b–24).[47] Although Paul cooperated with the plan (21:26), it ultimately failed, and Paul became the victim of Jewish mob violence (21:27–30).[48] According to Acts, James played no discernible role in any of the subsequent events that transpired around Paul in Jerusalem—neither as Paul's advocate nor as Paul's detractor. According to Acts, in the wake of the plan's failure, Paul was left to face the resulting hardships without any additional discernable support from James.[49]

To summarize, in their first interaction, James validated Paul's message of a relatively law-free Gentile inclusion into the church; in their second interaction, James defended Paul as a faithful and law-observant Jew. In spite of significant differences in the circumstances of each meeting, the function of James's interaction with Paul in both cases in Acts was similar. *James was presented as a faithful observer and interpreter of the law who nevertheless served as an advocate for Paul as a faithful observer of the law and for Paul's idea of a (relatively) law-free mission to the Gentiles as a faithful interpretation of the Jewish Scripture.*[50] In fact, Acts even makes James the central authority behind the integration of Paul and his ideas into the established Christian communities. Acts records no tensions between Paul and James, although Acts does allow James to

---

[47]The exact nature of this vow is unclear, but the James of Acts clearly regards the vow as a Jewish vow that will demonstrate Paul's fidelity to the law. Although the description in Acts is not a clear fit for a Nazirite vow (see Num 6:2–21), Acts is probably nonetheless suggesting that Paul undertook a Nazirite vow. Haenchen is probably correct to suggest that the problem arises from the fact that the author of Acts "appears to have no exact idea of the Nazirite vow" (*Acts*, 543 n. 2; *contra* Witherington, *Acts*, 649).

[48]The ambiguous references to Jews and Jewish believers in this context (Acts 21:20, 21, 27, 28) render it impossible to discern if the Jewish Christians who were originally concerned about Paul's conduct engaged in the violence against Paul or if only non-Christian Jews engaged in the violence. See Richard P. Thompson, "'What Do You Think You Are Doing, Paul?' Synagogues, Accusations, and Ethics in Paul's Ministry in Acts 16–21," in Phillips, *Acts and Ethics*, 64–78.

[49]Porter suggests that the silence in Acts regarding James's involvement in the riot against Paul is designed to conceal the fact that James ultimately turned against Paul (*Paul in Acts*, 172–86).

[50]In this sense, Jervell is correct to describe the James of Acts as the "defender of Paul" (*Luke and the People of God*, 185–207).

conveniently fade from the narrative during the traumatic events surrounding Paul's final visit to Jerusalem.

Summary of the Data from Acts

According to Acts, Paul and his ideas were integrated into the existing Christian communities in Antioch and Jerusalem through the advocacy of four key figures: Ananias, Barnabas, Peter, and James. Ananias baptized Paul and laid hands on him, resulting in his receiving the Holy Spirit. Barnabas introduced Paul and his ideas into the Jerusalem community and retrieved him from narrative obscurity in Tarsus. Barnabas also traveled with Paul and stood with him at the Jerusalem Conference, where Paul interacted with Peter and James—both of whom affirmed Paul and his relatively law-free gospel to the Gentiles. Acts records that Paul came into conflict with Barnabas over personnel issues, but Acts records no tensions between Paul and either Peter or James.

III. Comparing the Data Sets

Having surveyed the data sets that relate to participants in the Jerusalem Conference in both Acts and Paul's letters, we are now in a position to compare those data sets. However, before comparing the details of Paul's interactions with the participants at the Jerusalem Conference, we should note a few interrelated tendencies that will appear intermittently across all of Paul's relationships in Acts and in his letters.

First, leadership functions and theological authority tend to be more concentrated and less diversified in Acts than in Paul's letters. Paul's letters are much more generous with their attribution of the title "apostle" and with its accompanying apostolic authority than is Acts. Acts give limited apostolic status and authority to the twelve and (somewhat sparingly) to Paul and Barnabas; Paul expanded apostleship far beyond the twelve, himself, and Barnabas (e.g., 1 Cor 15:7). Paul even included his Gentile colleague Titus (2 Cor 8:23; cf. Gal 2:3) among the apostles.[51]

Second, Paul tends to portray his gospel, particularly his message of a law-free inclusion of Gentiles into the church, as more independent than does Acts. In his letters, Paul insisted that his message came from God and was in no way inferior to, or dependent upon, the message of the other apostles (Gal 1–2). In Acts, Paul's message may have come from God, but it was validated by a series of Christian leaders who served as Paul's advocates. The most important of these advocates, Peter and James, appear to possess the author-

---

[51] By Pauline reckoning, Andronicus (Rom 16:7), Junia (Rom 16:7), Barnabas (1 Cor 9:1–6), Timothy (1 Thess 1:1; 2:7; cf. 3:2), and Silvanus (1 Thess 1:1; 2:7) may also have been deemed apostles in at least some contexts.

ity either to accept or to reject Paul's message. Of course, both men accepted Paul's message in Acts—Peter did so on the basis of the Spirit's activity, and James did so on the basis of his reading of the Jewish Scriptures (Acts 15). Still, in Acts, the validity of Paul's message was dependent upon its acceptance by Peter and James. In Acts, Paul's very apostleship appears dependent upon his association with Barnabas, who served as his established mentor (14:14; cf. 14:4). In fact, according to Acts, Peter—not Paul—was chosen as the first apostle to the Gentiles (Acts 15:7; cf. Rom 11:13; Gal 1:1–5; 2:8).

Third, relations between Paul and the other recognized authorities of early Christianity tend to be more contentious and uneven in Paul's letters than in Acts. At some points in his letters, Paul drew upon the authority of Peter and James to support his message (e.g., 1 Cor 15:3–7), and he even rebuked those who divided the church by asserting Paul's prominence over Peter (1 Cor 1–3). However, at other points, Paul was openly hostile toward both the ideas and the persons of Peter, James, and even Barnabas (Gal 2:11–14). Acts provides no indication of any tensions at all between Peter and Paul or between James and Paul. Acts records neither the confrontation between Peter and Paul in Antioch (Gal 2:11) nor the tensions between James and Paul that lay behind that confrontation (2:12). Although Acts does record a strong disagreement between Paul and Barnabas (Acts 15:39), it provides a decidedly nontheological origin for the debate. In Acts, Paul and Barnabas disagree over what role—if any—John Mark will play in their continued work (15:37–38); in Paul's letters, Paul and Barnabas disagree over the "hypocrisy" Barnabas practiced by failing to recognize Gentiles as equals (Gal 2:13).

Of course, these three tendencies are deeply interrelated, and one could plausibly argue that any one of the three gives rise to the others. In reality, however, all three tendencies are probably aspects of Luke's idealized view of earliest Christianity. Acts tends to view earliest Christianity as highly unified and harmonious; this unity and harmony tends to be achieved by making all of the characters in Acts rally around the standard held aloft by the original twelve apostles (or the eleven original apostles plus Matthias).[52] The twelve are themselves largely portrayed as a single body that relies upon Peter for its collective voice. These tendencies, which are often labeled "early Catholicism," have been long noted and widely discussed in Lukan studies.[53] My concern in this chapter is not to engage in the ongoing scholarly debate about

---

[52] Kirsopp Lake divided Pauline controversies into four categories: controversies with Jews, controversies with Jewish Christians, controversies with Gentiles, and controversies with Gentile Christians ("Paul's Controversies," in Foakes-Jackson and Lake, *Beginnings of Christianity*, 5:212–23). If these four groups are used as a taxonomy, then Paul's letters probably reflect controversy between Paul and all four groups, with his greatest opposition coming from Jewish Christians, while Acts depicts no significant tensions between Paul and other Christians but extensive conflicts between Paul and the Jews and only slightly less extensive conflicts between Paul and non-Christian Gentiles.

[53] For the classic expression of this position, see Conzelmann, "Luke's Place."

Luke's relationship—or nonrelationship—to early Catholicism, but merely to highlight these tendencies and to note that many of the more specific tendencies we will briefly note are simply aspects of these overarching tendencies.

The following comparison will ask the guiding question of this entire volume: Can the smaller data set gathered from Paul's letters be placed within the typically larger data set from Acts in regard to the respective persons' interactions with Paul? When the data sets allow, this chapter will consider three particularly significant aspects of Paul's relationships to the various people: the locations and occasions of the individual's interactions with Paul (where and under what circumstances did the person interact with Paul?), the individual's role within the Pauline churches (to what degree was the person recognized as an authority within the Pauline churches?), and the character of the individual's relationship with Paul himself (was the relationship mentoring, mutually supportive, or adversarial?).

Of the five people under consideration in this chapter, one, *Ananias*, appears only in Acts and another, *Titus*, appears only in Paul's letters. Ananias's absence from Paul's letters is easily explained by the fact that he appears only at the very earliest stage of Paul's missionary career in Acts (9:10–19). Paul's letters relate events from that very early time in Paul's ministry only in Gal 1–2 where it probably would have worked against Paul's rhetorical strategy to include a reference to Ananias.[54] Paul's overarching concern in the context of that autobiographical material was to demonstrate the independence of his gospel, and any Pauline acknowledgement of Ananias's advocacy role in his early career could have been interpreted as evidence against the independence of Paul's gospel. Thus one could easily conjecture that Paul's account of his early missionary career suppressed Ananias's role in order to bolster Paul's claims to independence from the Jerusalem authorities.

The failure of Acts to mention Titus is more surprising than is the failure of Paul's letters to mention Ananias,[55] especially in light of Titus's importance

---

[54] Paul's failure to mention his blindness is less easily explained. Paul could have used the miracles of his blindness and the recovery of his sight as powerful symbols of his significance within God's plans. Still, Paul's letters make no reference to his blindness and recovery of sight at the time of his original christophany (note Gal 4:13–15). The blindness motif in Acts is, therefore, often regarded as a literary device without historical foundation. See Dennis Hamm, "Paul's Blindness and Its Healing: Clues to Symbolic Intent (Acts 9; 22 and 26)," *Bib* 71 (1990): 63–72; and, more recently, Chad Hartsock, *Sight and Blindness in Luke-Acts: The Use of Physical Features in Characterization* (Biblical Interpretation 94; Boston: Brill, 2008), 184–97.

[55] It is possible, but unlikely, that the Titius Justus in Acts 18:7 is synonymous with the Titus of Paul's letters. The location of each person is similar: Titius Justus resided in Corinth (Acts 18:7) and Titus was a Greek (Gal 2:3). Both were also Gentile (Gal 2:3; Acts 18:7). However, the Titus of Paul's letters was an important Pauline emissary (2 Cor 7:6–16; 8:6–23) and frequent traveler (2:12–13), while the similarly named Titius Justus of Acts was never reported outside of Corinth. These differences, along with differences in the spelling of the names, make identification of these two individuals unlikely. On the textual variants which place Titus in this context in Acts and on the improbability of equating these two persons, see Barrett, *Acts*, 2:868–69.

to both Galatians and 2 Corinthians (2 Cor 2:12–13; 7:6–16; 8:6–23; Gal 2:1–3). Titus's absence from Acts is made even more conspicuous by an important contrast. In Galatians, Titus's uncircumcised inclusion into the church was extremely important to Paul's argument at the Jerusalem Conference. By accepting Titus's uncircumcised condition, Paul argued, the participants in the Jerusalem Conference had validated the inclusion of all Gentiles apart from the law. In Acts, Paul's first action after the Jerusalem Conference was to circumcise Timothy (Acts 16:1–3). Timothy's circumcision will be considered in detail in the next chapter, but at this point it is important to note the contrast between the uncircumcised Titus in Galatians and the circumcised Timothy in Acts. On the one hand, Acts made no reference to the presence of the uncircumcised Titus at the Jerusalem Conference, while Paul chose to emphasize Titus's uncircumcised presence at the event. On the other hand, Paul made no reference to the circumcision of Timothy after the conference, while Acts chose to emphasize Timothy's circumcision immediately after the event.

Unlike Ananias and Titus, *Barnabas* appears in both Acts and Paul's letters. The data set from Acts is significantly larger. Paul's letters place Barnabas in two *locations:* Jerusalem and Antioch (Gal 2:1, 9, 13).[56] Within the data set of Paul's letters, Jerusalem stands apart as the only location where Paul and Barnabas were both clearly present at the same time. In fact, Paul's letters report that Paul and Barnabas twice visited Jerusalem together (Gal 2:1–10). Paul's letters also place Barnabas in Antioch, but only in the company of Peter and emphatically not in the company of Paul (Gal 2:13). According to Paul's letters, the *occasion* for each of these visits to Jerusalem by Paul and Barnabas was to consult with the Jerusalem apostles. Regardless of the undisclosed purpose behind Barnabas's presence with Peter in Antioch, Paul regarded the primary result of this visit to be hypocrisy—Barnabas's betrayal of the message of the Gentiles' inclusion into the church as equals. According to Paul's letters, therefore, the locations and occasions of Barnabas's interaction with Paul and the other apostles were two consultations with the apostles in Jerusalem while in Paul's company and hypocrisy with Peter in Antioch while not in Paul's company.

In spite of Paul's outrage over Barnabas's conduct in Antioch (Gal 2:13), according to Paul's letters, Barnabas enjoyed *a role of considerable authority*

---

[56] Given Paul's references to Barnabas in Galatians (2:1–13) and 1 Corinthians (9:6), one could argue that Barnabas was known to the Pauline believers in those areas. However, Paul's letters do not clearly indicate that Barnabas ever visited either of these areas. The reference to Barnabas in 1 Corinthians is particularly curious because Paul never named Barnabas as one of the many preachers (e.g., Cephas, Apollos, Silvanus, Timothy, Titus) who had taught in Corinth (1 Cor 1–3; 2 Cor 1:19; 8:6–23) and because Acts never locates Barnabas any further west than Asia Minor (13:1–15:41). The reference to Barnabas in the context of 1 Corinthians is, therefore, a particular enigma. Barrett is correct to note that, other than this obscure reference, "we know nothing whatever of any contact he [Barnabas] may have had with Corinth" (*First Epistle to the Corinthians,* 204).

within the Pauline churches. In 1 Corinthians, Paul argued that both he and Barnabas deserved the rights of apostleship, and Paul did so without distinguishing himself as in any way superior to Barnabas (9:6). In Galatians, Paul even mentioned Barnabas's name before his own in this account of their role in the Jerusalem Conference (2:1, 9). These references imply both that Paul, and perhaps the Corinthians, regarded Barnabas as Paul's peer in terms of authority at Corinth and that the readers of Galatians may well have presumed that Barnabas was more prominent than Paul, at least at the time of the Jerusalem Conference. Similarly, according to Paul's letters, the *personal relationship between Paul and Barnabas* appears to have been mutually supportive at least in the early part of Paul's ministry. Later, however, their relationship probably became adversarial in the wake of Paul's disappointment with Barnabas's behavior regarding Gentile inclusion (Gal 2:13). Still, Paul's favorable reference to Barnabas in 1 Corinthians (9:6) even leaves open the possibility that Paul and Barnabas reconciled with one another to some degree after the dispute recorded in Galatians.

Placing the Barnabas data set from Paul's letters within the Barnabas data set from Acts is problematic only in regard to the chronological issues discussed earlier in this volume. The *locations* of Barnabas do not present significant problems by themselves. Acts locates Paul and Barnabas together in *Jerusalem* twice (12:25; 15:2) as do Paul's letters (Gal 2:1–10). Acts also frequently records Barnabas's presence in *Antioch*—even his presence in Antioch without Paul (11:22; cf. 11:26; 13:1–3; 14:21; 15:22–35). Tensions arise between the data sets only when the *occasions* of these visits are also considered. Without revisiting all of the chronological issues discussed earlier, it is sufficient to note that significant chronological problems attach themselves to any consideration of the Jerusalem Conference.[57] However, if chronology is set aside, Jerusalem is a well-documented *location* for interaction between Paul and Barnabas. The two visits of Paul and Barnabas to Jerusalem in Paul's letters can easily be set within the data set from Acts with the second visit to Jerusalem in Paul's letters (Gal 2:1–10) being equivalent to the Jerusalem Con-

---

[57] If one equates Paul's two visits to Jerusalem in Galatians (1:18; 2:1) with Paul's first two visits to Jerusalem in Acts (9:26; 12:25), then one is forced to date Galatians before the Jerusalem Conference. However, understanding Galatians in this manner— and especially understanding Paul's condemnation of Barnabas's hypocrisy as occurring before the Jerusalem Conference— makes it very difficult to understand why Acts portrays Paul and Barnabas acting together at the conference. Richard J. Bauckham recognizes this significant flaw in the early dating of Galatians and, therefore, argues that Paul and Barnabas were split apart when Paul wrote Galatians (Gal 2:13), but that they came back together before the Jerusalem Conference, only to split up again after the conference (Acts 15:39) ("Barnabas in Galatians," *JSNT* 2 [1979]: 61–70). This suggestion of an on-again, off-again relationship between Paul and Barnabas is a historical conjecture with no explicit support in either Acts or Paul's letters. Bauckham's suggestion is less attractive to me than the simpler conclusion that Galatians was written after the Jerusalem Conference as suggested in chapter three of this volume and assumed throughout this chapter.

ference (Acts 15). Barnabas's interaction with Peter in Antioch (Gal 2:11–13) is not recorded in Acts, but this omission is easily explained by an appeal either to Acts' tendency to avoid depicting theological disagreements among its leading characters or to Acts' disinterest in Barnabas (and Peter) after the Jerusalem Conference.

The data set from Paul's letters, regarding *Barnabas's role within the Pauline churches* is comparatively small. Paul recognized Barnabas as an authority, probably even an apostle, and Paul could speak of Barnabas as a peer (1 Cor 9:6). Barnabas had been a leading voice in the interaction between Paul's Gentile churches and the Jerusalem apostles (Gal 2:1–10). As such, Barnabas's conduct toward Gentiles was particularly important to the Pauline churches, and his perceived infidelity to the ideal of Gentile inclusion in the church was particularly disappointing to Paul and quite likely a major factor behind the composition of Galatians (2:11–13). Still, Barnabas's name appears rather infrequently in Paul's letters, occurring only in one ambiguous reference in 1 Corinthians and in a historical narrative in Galatians. According to Paul's letters, therefore, Barnabas was a recognized authority within the Pauline churches, but probably most recognized for his connections to the Jerusalem church. Galatians could even lead one to infer that Barnabas may have been known primarily for his early involvement in Paul's ministry and for his eventual defection from Paul's ministry. This image derived from the Pauline data set fits easily within the data set from Acts where Barnabas helped facilitate Paul's early integration into the established Christian communities (9:26–30; 11:25–30; 13:1–3; 15:2, 12, 22) and where Barnabas engaged in Paul's earliest missionary preaching (13:1–14:28) before separating from the Pauline mission (15:39).[58] Even the prominent role Paul gives Barnabas at the Jerusalem Conference (by placing Barnabas's name first) accords well with Acts (Gal 2:9; Acts 13:2, 7; 14:14; 15:12, 25).

The data set from Paul's letters regarding *Barnabas's personal relationship with Paul* is also easily reconciled with the data set from Acts. Both portray Paul and Barnabas as mutually supportive with one major and significant disruption in their relationship (Gal 2:13; Acts 15:39). Neither data set precludes the possibility of reconciliation between the two, and Paul's reference to Barnabas in the Corinthian correspondence would even seem to encourage serious consideration of that possibility (1 Cor 9:6). Yet the rationale for

---

[58] For a recent and comprehensive study on Barnabas's role within early Christianity, see Markus Öhler, *Barnabas: Die historische Person and ihre Rezeption in der Apostelgeschichte* (WUNT 156; Tübingen: Mohr Siebeck, 2003). Öhler compellingly argues that the historical Barnabas was probably a wealthy Jewish Christian who was prominent in bringing Jewish and Gentile Christianity together, in part by serving as Paul's patron during Paul's early ministry. For a similar treatment which expands this thesis to a larger group of Jewish Christians from Barnabas's home island of Cyprus, see Enique Mena Salas, *"También a los Griegos" (Hch 11,20): Factores del inicio de la misión a los gentiles en Antioquía de Siria* (Plenitudo Temporis; Salamanca: Universidad Pontificia de Salamanca, 2007).

the tensions between Paul and Barnabas is significantly different in Acts and Paul's letters. In Paul's letters, the tensions erupted from an overtly theological origin, Barnabas's perceived hypocrisy. In Acts, the tensions emerged from a decidedly nontheological source, a difference of opinion over the reliability of John Mark.

In Galatians, Paul referred to three "pillars" of the church (2:9), who were present at the Jerusalem Conference: Peter, James, and John. All three appear in Acts. Of the three men, *John* can be dealt with most succinctly. John's lone appearance in Paul's letters is as an attendee of this conference. However, John exerted no discernible influence at the conference. In Acts, John appears several times (1:13; 3:1, 3, 4, 11; 4:1, 3, 7, 13, 19, 23; 8:17, 25; 12:2), but nearly always in conjunction with Peter. Therefore, given both John's consistent presence with Peter in Jerusalem and his consistently silent presence in Peter's shadow throughout the early chapters of Acts, it is not difficult to imagine that John was present in Jerusalem with Peter and James when Paul visited for the Jerusalem Conference (Acts 15:1–29). Acts portrays Jerusalem as a plausible *location* for John. Although Acts does not record John's presence at the Jerusalem Conference, it is reasonable to infer that he was present on that *occasion* along with the other apostles who were present (15:2, 4, 6, 22, 23; 16:4). Both Acts and Paul's letters characterize John's role within the Pauline churches as authoritative, but minimal, and John's personal relationship with Paul as mutually supportive, but also as minimal.

The data sets associated with the other two pillars of the Jerusalem church, Peter and James, are less easily reconciled. According to Paul's letters, *Peter* and Paul interacted directly only in Jerusalem and Antioch (Gal 1:18; 2:1, 9, 11). Acts records Pauline visits to both *locations* on repeated occasions (9:26; 11:25–30; 12:25; 13:1–3; 14:21–28; 15:1–35; 18:22–23; 21:17–23:30). Peter's presence in Jerusalem is likewise well documented in Acts (1:1–8:1, 25; 11:1–18; 12:1–18; 15:2–29). Jerusalem is, therefore, a likely location for Peter to interact with Paul. However, on the basis of Acts, Antioch is a less likely location for interaction between Peter and Paul. Peter spent the bulk of his time in Jerusalem, and his only recorded travels in Acts are to the cities of Lydda, Joppa, and Caesarea (9:32–10:48), all of which were well south of Antioch. In fact, Acts never records Peter's presence in Antioch. More importantly, Acts does not record any *occasion* of Peter and Paul interacting confrontationally. Yet, according to Galatians, Paul's interaction with Peter in Antioch was confrontational (2:11–14). Of course, it is entirely possible (even likely) that Peter visited Antioch at some point, and this visit is not recorded in Acts (particularly because travel between Jerusalem and Antioch was apparently common among early Christians; e.g., 11:19–20, 22, 27; 15:1, 22–23, 30; cf. 6:5), but *Acts records no Petrine visit to Antioch that corresponds to the visit recorded in Galatians.*

The are several points of correspondence between Paul's letters and Acts with regard to the role Peter played in the Pauline churches. Both treat Peter as an authority who was—and appropriately so according to some

Pauline texts—respected within the Pauline churches (1 Cor 1–3; 15:5; Gal 2:9; Acts 15:6–11). However, in Paul's letters, loyalty to Peter caused some tensions among people in the Pauline churches in Corinth and Galatia (1 Cor 1–3; Gal 2:11–14). In keeping with its tendency to emphasize the harmony and unity of the apostolic church, Acts records nothing of the turmoil in Corinth and probably nothing of the turmoil in Galatia.[59] Of course, Acts is almost certainly downplaying the presence of an actual conflict between Peter and Paul, but it is important to note that the difference between Peter's role in Acts and in Paul's letters is more profound than can be explained by a simple tendency on the part of Acts to downplay the inevitable tensions and controversies that existed in the early church.

According to Acts, Peter was the human originator and legitimating authority behind Paul's mission to the Gentiles. Peter was the first person to proclaim that "God shows no partiality" between Jews and Gentiles (10:34), and Peter was the one through whom the Gentiles first received the Spirit (10:44). Peter was proclaiming the gospel to Gentiles even before Barnabas sought out Paul in Tarsus (11:25). When Paul's Gentile mission eventually drew opposition, Peter was the first person to speak out against the opinion that Gentile believers should be circumcised (15:5–11). Significantly, Peter advocated for a law-free Gentile inclusion into the church on the bases of his own insights and his own experiences with the Gentiles, not on the bases of Paul's insights and experiences. According to Acts, Peter claimed that "in the early days God made a choice among you, that I should be the one through whom the Gentiles would hear the message of the good news and become believers" (15:7).

According to his letters, Paul certainly had inherited portions of the Christian message—particularly traditions about the Lord's Supper and the resurrection (1 Cor 11:23–26; 15:3–8)—from other believers, including Peter. But Paul insisted that in regard to Gentile inclusion, his gospel had come directly from God (Gal 1–2). Paul was emphatic both about the divine origin and the legitimating authority of his gospel: "the gospel that was proclaimed by me is not of human origin; for I did not receive it from a human source, nor was I taught it, but I received it through a revelation of Jesus Christ" (1:11–12). Paul insisted that Peter and the leadership in Jerusalem "contributed nothing" to him (2:6) and that he had been "entrusted with the gospel for the uncircumcised, just as Peter had been entrusted with the gospel for the circumcised" (2:7). Although the Paul of the letters did meet with the apostles in Jerusalem, he claimed to be indifferent to their opinions: "what they actually were makes no difference to me; God shows no partiality—those leaders contributed nothing to me" (2:6).[60]

---

[59]A controversy over circumcision like the one which Paul faced in Galatia does appear in Acts, but according to Acts, the controversy was located in Antioch in Syria rather than in Galatia, and it was attributed to "certain individuals" (15:1) rather than to Peter.

[60]On the Stoic origins of Paul's claim of indifference toward authority, see James L. Jaquette, "Paul, Epictetus, and Others on Indifference to Status," *CBQ* 56 (1994): 68–80.

These two views of Peter's role and authority within Paul's churches are difficult to reconcile. The differences cannot be overcome by appeals to omissions or lapses in our sources (as is the case with the nonoverlapping portion of the data sets regarding the locations and occasions of Peter's and Paul's interactions). At a very basic level, Acts claims that the Gentile mission began with Peter, a claim that possesses some historical plausibility but that is difficult to reconcile with Paul's letters. Even more problematically, Acts strongly implies that Paul's Gentile mission required Peter's approval, an implication that Paul most certainly would have rejected.[61] The more adversarial aspects of Peter's role within the Pauline churches as depicted in the letters-derived data set are not easily placed within the larger (but less adversarial) Acts-derived data set.

Paul's letters and Acts also differ in their depictions of the *personal relationship* between Peter and Paul. Acts portrays a relationship that is mutually supportive at every point, particularly at the climatic moment of the Jerusalem Conference (Acts 15). Paul's letters portray a much more complex and uneven relationship. In his discussion of the resurrection, Paul recognizes his debt to Peter's witness and portrays himself almost as an heir to Petrine tradition (1 Cor 15:3–8). In his account of their first meeting, Paul portrays Peter as a supportive senior colleague (Gal 1:18–20), and in his account of the Jerusalem Conference (their second meeting), Paul likewise portrayed Peter as generally supportive of him and his Gentile mission (2:9–10). However, in their final recorded meeting, Paul portrayed their relationship as confrontational (2:11–14). As mentioned earlier, Acts gives no indication of this adversarial encounter. In regard to their personal relations, therefore, the smaller Pauline data set does not fit well within the larger Acts-derived data set. Paul's letters imply an element of personal hostility that is foreign to Acts.

The patterns of Paul's interactions with *James* almost perfectly mirror the patterns of his interactions with Peter in both Acts and Paul's letters. In the letters, Paul portrays James as a trustworthy witness to the resurrection, just like Peter (1 Cor 15:5–7), but also as someone with whom Paul eventually came into intense conflict (Gal 2:12, cf. 1:19). In Acts, Luke portrays Paul and James interacting twice; the first meeting was an unqualified success, and the second meeting was perhaps tense, but not adversarial (15:13; 21:18). These two data sets are approximately the same size, and they overlap at key points, but there are also important areas of nonoverlap (perhaps even incongruity) between the data sets.

The *location* of Paul's direct interaction with James is consistently Jerusalem in both Acts and Paul's letters (Acts 15:2; 21:17; Gal 1:18; 2:1). Even when James's teaching caused Paul problems in Antioch, it was not because James was present in Antioch, but rather because "certain people came from James" (Gal 2:12). In both Acts and Paul's letters, James remained firmly located in Jerusalem.

---

[61] Similarly, see Perkins, *Peter*, 118–20.

The *occasions* of the interactions between Paul and James vary slightly in Acts and the letters. As discussed earlier in this volume, Paul's visit with James in Acts 15 is probably synonymous with the Jerusalem Conference in Gal 2:1–10.[62] The occasion of this visit is easily reconciled in Acts and Paul's letters. However, Acts and Paul's letters each record another visit between Paul and James. According to Galatians, Paul met James both at the Jerusalem Conference and earlier in Paul's career, only three years after his experience on the road to Damascus (1:19). According to Acts, however, the other meeting occurred much later in Paul's career, during his last visit to Jerusalem (21:17–18). When compared, these two data sets are complementary. The early meeting between Paul and James that Galatians records could have occurred during one of Paul's first two visits mentioned in Acts (9:26; 12:25), and their final meeting in Acts probably coincides with the visit Paul anticipated in Romans (15:25), a visit that likely occurred after Paul had written all of his extant letters.[63]

James's role within the Pauline churches is very similar to Peter's. James was a recognized authority in both Paul's letters and Acts. According to Paul's letters, James was a trustworthy witness to the resurrection (1 Cor 15:7) and one of the Jerusalem pillars before whom Paul laid his message for inspection (Gal 2:1). This corresponds well with the portrayal of James in Acts as a leader of the church in Jerusalem (15:13). Acts and Paul's letters also both seem to imply James's growing influence within the Pauline churches. Thus, Paul's first mention of James in Galatians was largely incidental (1:19), whereas his second reference implied a more significant role for James as the first of the named "pillars" (2:9). Similarly, in Acts, James's name didn't even appear until his sudden appearance at the Jerusalem Conference, where he alone possessed the ultimate authority for decision-making (15:19).

Acts and Paul's letters also both portray James as an interpreter of the law and its relevance for Gentiles. However, they disagree significantly on the degree of Paul's satisfaction with James's conclusions about Gentile obedience to the law. In Galatians, Paul characterized James as belonging to the "circumcision faction" (2:12) and twice labeled those who followed that teaching as guilty of "hypocrisy" (2:13). Without mincing words, Paul insisted that those who came under the influence of James "were not acting consistently with the truth of the gospel" (2:14). These Pauline accusations against James find no parallel in Acts. In fact, in Acts, James possessed the authority to impose legal restrictions upon the Pauline churches (15:20). Even toward the end of his ministry, the Paul of Acts willingly obeyed James's advice to show himself as one who would "observe and keep the law" (21:24). The difference here is significant. In Paul's letters, James was an authority alongside Peter and Paul in the case of the resurrection (1 Cor 15:7), or an authority who recognized the truth of Paul's gospel (Gal 2:9), or even an authority who opposed Paul

---

[62] *Contra* Bockmuehl, "Antioch and James the Just."
[63] See chapter three of this volume for a discussion of the problem of Paul's extra visits to Jerusalem in Acts.

(2:12). Still, in Paul's letters, James contributed "nothing" to Paul, and Paul was in no way dependent upon, or subordinate to, James (Gal 2:6–7). In Acts, James decided the legal restrictions that would be incumbent upon Paul's churches (15:19–20) as well as those that would be incumbent upon Paul and those who traveled with him (21:23–26).

The role of James as an authority within Paul's churches is, therefore, significantly different within Acts and Paul's letters. The data sets regarding James's role within the Pauline churches are similar in size, but divergent in content. In Paul's letters, James and those who followed his teachings about the law were perceived as a threat; in Acts, James was portrayed as the premier interpreter of the Jewish law and its application for the churches—both Pauline and non-Pauline.[64] The divergence between the data sets cannot be easily explained by simple appeal to the inevitable incompleteness of the data sets.

Paul's personal relationship with James likewise has significant similarities and dissimilarities in Acts and Paul's letters. Both Acts and Paul's letters record only minimal direct interaction between Paul and James, and neither Acts nor Paul's letters imply any face-to-face conflicts between James and Paul. All of the personal contacts between Paul and James in both Acts and Paul's letters could be fairly characterized as mutually supportive. However, according to Paul's letters, the relationship between James and Paul became adversarial when their ideas clashed over a distance. In Galatians, Paul castigated those who surrendered to the influence of James and his ideas (2:11–14), even suggesting that those who followed such teachings were "foolish" (3:1). Acts gives no indication of this kind of hostility between Paul and James.[65] The data sets regarding the personal relationships between Paul and James are therefore also similar in size but divergent in content.

Finally, a comparison of Paul's relationships to the key figures involved in the Jerusalem Conference and the events leading up to that conference reveals that the data sets from Acts and Paul's letters overlap and cohere considerably at some points, but diverge, sometimes considerably, at other points. Perhaps the data sets do not diverge beyond possible reconciliation (the data sets have considerable omissions and gaps, and they were written under very different circumstances). Still, many interpreters will find it difficult—or even unwise—to reconcile the data sets.

---

[64] It is possible that Paul and James differed more in their understandings of sanctification than in their understandings of salvation. Jacob Neusner has demonstrated that rabbinic systems that emphasized salvation (like Paul) were often welcoming toward Gentiles, while rabbinic systems that emphasized sanctification (like at Qumran—and possibly James's thought) often feared Gentiles as a corrupting influence. See "What, Exactly, Is Israel's Gentile Problem? Rabbinic Perspectives on Galatians," in Chilton and Evans, *Missions*, 276–306.

[65] Painter wonders about the historical possibility that James, "in suggesting that Paul participate in an act of purification in the Temple (Acts 21:20–21), might not have hoped for Paul's arrest" in Jerusalem (*Just James*, 57). Although this history may lie behind the text, even Painter acknowledges that Acts implies no such duplicity on the part of James.

ᴧ 6 ᴨ

FINDING A PLACE IN PAUL'S CHURCHES: PAUL'S ASSOCIATES, HIS CONVERTS, AND APOLLOS

ALTHOUGH THE Jerusalem Conference appears to be pivotal to the history of early Christianity in both Acts and Paul's letters, both sources frequently mention several figures who played no recorded role in the Jerusalem Conference. This chapter will consider the wide variety of Christians that Acts and Paul's letters report interacting with Paul in contexts other than the Jerusalem Conference. For the sake of convenience, these people will be grouped within three categories: Paul's associates, his converts, and the unique case of Apollos. Because the data set from Paul's letters is generally smaller in relation to these figures, this chapter will begin with the letters and ask if the data set from Paul's letters can be placed within the larger data set from Acts.

I. THE PAULINE DATA SET

Pauline Co-workers, Apostles, Emissaries, Co-senders, and Prisoners

Paul clearly regarded himself as an apostle with a direct commission from God (Gal 1:1), and he was unwilling to allow anyone to suggest that his apostolic authority was in any way subordinate to that of the other apostles (particularly those present at the Jerusalem Conference).[1] Paul insisted that he deserved all the rights and privileges that were afforded to other apostles like Peter, including the right to receive financial support from congregations (1 Cor 9:3–7; 1 Thess 2:7).[2] When the Corinthians dared to regard

---

[1] On Paul's insistence upon his apostolic authority, see Lyons, *Pauline Autobiography*, 124–25.

[2] Ernest Best has argued that Paul claimed both to be an apostle and to possess authority in matters of faith and practice, but that Paul did not explicitly link these two claims ("Paul's Apostolic Authority—?" *JSNT* 27 [1986]: 3–25). While Best is correct to emphasize that early Christianity was not highly institutionalized, he fails to appreciate the degree to which Paul associated apostleship and authority. Also see John Howard Schütz, who argues that Paul's perceived authority was a function of

Paul's apostleship as less significant than that of other supposed apostles, Paul sarcastically insisted that "I think that I am not in the least inferior to these super-apostles" (2 Cor 11:5; cf. 12:11).[3] In spite of these and other defenses of his own apostleship (e.g., Gal 1–2; 1 Cor 9; 2 Cor 10–12), Paul recognized the unusual origin of his apostleship. In less confrontational moments, Paul was willing to engage in rhetorical self-deprecation, even characterizing himself as an apostle "untimely born" and as "the least of the apostles" (1 Cor 15:8–9).[4] Still, Paul was convinced that God had called him to be an apostle (15:10), and he no doubt would have quickly recanted—or at least qualified—these self-deprecating remarks if they came to be used to cast doubt or aspersions upon his God-given apostolic authority.

Although Paul's admissions about the unusual origin of his apostleship must be interpreted with caution, such statements do demonstrate Paul's awareness, and the awareness of those around him, that Paul's rise to apostleship was different than was that of the other apostles. Paul had never walked and talked with the historical Jesus, and this fact set him apart from at least the other prominent apostles. It made Paul "untimely born" as an apostle. Paul's status as an apostle was clearly important to him and probably important to many within the churches that he established, but Paul never limited the work of ministry to those he deemed apostles. Paul referred to dozens of people who assisted him in ministry at different times.

For the sake of analysis, those whom Paul recognized as fellow ministers can be divided into four categories. First, Paul named nineteen people—seven women and twelve men—as *co-workers* with him in ministry: Tryphaena and Tryphosa (Rom 16:12); Persis (16:12); Prisca and Aquila (16:3); Stephanas (1 Cor 16:15–16); Urbanus (Rom 16:9); Timothy (16:21); Titus (2 Cor 8:23); Epaphroditus (Phil 2:25); Euodia, Syntyche, and Clement (4:2–3); Philemon (Phlm 2); Mary (Rom 16:6); Mark, Aristarchus, Demas, and Luke (Phlm 24).[5] Little is known about many of these people, particularly those who are men-

---

social legitimacy and that his apostleship was a function of transcendent gift (*Paul and the Anatomy of Apostolic Authority* [New Testament Library; Louisville: Westminster John Knox, 2007]). Similarly, David M. Hay challenges the notion of a cause and effort relationship between apostleship and authority by arguing that Paul understood the gospel as the only legitimate source of authority ("Paul's Indifference to Authority," *JBL* 88 [1969]: 36–44).

[3] The identity of these "super-apostles" is widely debated. Although some interpreters identify these people with Peter and the original twelve, this identification is probably unwise, particularly if these are the same people whom Paul described as "false apostles" (2 Cor 11:13). Their identity remains unclear. See Furnish, *II Corinthians*, 502–5.

[4] Paul's language, ὡσπερεὶ τῷ ἐκτρώματι (1 Cor 15:8), literally means "like an abortion," rather than the euphemistic "as one untimely born," and serves as part of Paul's self-deprecating rhetoric in this context. See Harm W. Hollander and Gijsbert E. van der Hout, "The Apostle Paul Calling Himself an Abortion: 1 Cor. 15:8 within the Context of 1 Cor. 15:8–10," *NovT* 38 (1996): 224–36.

[5] Paul used some form of the word ἐργάζομαι or κοπιάω in his references to these people. The semantic fields of these words overlap greatly; both mean "labor,

tioned only once in the Pauline corpus. Second, Paul named three people as *co-senders* of one or more of his letters: Sosthenes (1 Cor 1:1); Timothy (2 Cor 1:1; Phil 1:1; 1 Thess 1:1; Phlm 1); and Silvanus (1 Thess 1:1). Although Paul allowed Tertius to insert his name as the secretary behind the writing of Romans (16:22), Sosthenes, Timothy, and Silvanus were the only people to be specifically named as co-sender of a Pauline letter.[6] Third, Paul named various *other apostles and emissaries* whose ministries overlapped with Paul's ministry. In addition to Barnabas (1 Cor 9:6; Gal 2:1–13), whom we have already considered, Paul spoke of Adronicus (Rom 16:7), Junia (16:7),[7] Titus (2 Cor 8:23), and (probably in a more limited sense) Epaphroditus (Phil 2:25) as "apostles."[8] Timothy, though not an apostle in Paul's letters, frequently served as Paul's emissary to the congregations that he had established (Phil 2:19–24; 1 Thess 3:4–6; 1 Cor 4:17; cf. 2 Cor 8:6–23), as did the apostle Titus (2 Cor 8:16–23). Fourth, Paul named three people, Junia, Andronicus, and Epaphras, as his *co-prisoners* (Rom 16:7; Phlm 23). Although any prominent member of the Christian community could have been incarcerated in the first century, Paul clearly regarded his own imprisonment as a significant marker of his status as both an apostle and a servant of the gospel (e.g., 2 Cor 11:23; Phlm 1, 9–10, 13, 23; Phil 1:7, 13–17), so his mention of these persons as fellow prisoners was a mark of their distinctive service in Paul's eyes.

When the various lists of the persons Paul named as co-workers, co-senders, emissaries, lesser known apostles, and co-prisoners are compared to one another, it becomes obvious that there is significant overlap between the lists. The categories are heuristic, not absolute, but they do provide some

---

toil or work." See M. Seitz and H.-G. Link, "Burden, Heavy, Labour," *NIDNTT* 1:260–63; and H. C. Hahn, "Work, Do, Accomplish," *NIDNTT* 3:1147–52.

[6]In a probable attempt to augment his authority, Paul claimed that Galatians was being co-sent by "all the members of God's family" (1:2), but Paul named no specific co-sender of the letter.

[7]On Paul's willingness to designate a woman, Junia, as an apostle, see Eldon Jay Epp, *Junia: The First Woman Apostle* (Minneapolis: Fortress, 2005); John Thorley, "Junia, a Woman Apostle," *NovT* 38 (1996): 18–29; and Linda Belleville, "'Ιουνιαν . . . ἐπίσημοι ἐν τοῖς ἀποστόλοις: A Re-examination of Romans 16:7 in Light of Primary Source Materials," *NTS* 51 (2005): 231–49. On the "radical egalitarianism" of the undisputed Pauline letters, see William O. Walker, "The 'Theology of Woman's Place' and the 'Paulinist' Tradition," *Semeia* 28 (1983): 101–12.

[8]Scholars commonly distinguish Titus and Epaphroditus from the other apostles in Paul's letters, claiming that Epaphroditus and Titus were only representatives of local churches (e.g., Furnish, *II Corinthians*, 424–25; and Collange, *Philippians*, 118). This claim is much stronger in the case of Epaphroditus than in the case of Titus—though the issue is not clear-cut in either case. Paul defended his own apostolic status primarily on the bases of his having seen the risen Christ and his having labored in the service of that risen Christ (1 Cor 9:1–3; 15:7–10). There is no reason to assume that his co-workers Titus and Epaphroditus did not also claim to have seen the risen Christ. If they made such claims, they may well have qualified as apostles in Paul's eyes. The best survey of Paul's use of the titles "apostle" and "apostles" remains Rudolf Schnackenburg, "Apostles before and during Paul's Time," in Gasque and Martin, *Apostolic History*, 287–303.

indication of the characteristic identity markers applied to the people around Paul. Most of the people just listed make only one appearance in Paul's letters, so little can be discovered about them beyond their placement within one or more of these categories of Pauline ministry. When our focus moves to the people who make more frequent appearances in Paul's letters, the number of individuals under consideration becomes relatively small.

Seven Pauline associates make repeated appearances in Paul's letters. Six are male and one is female. Four—three men and one woman—appear only twice in Paul's letters. *Silvanus* is listed as a co-sender of 1 Thessalonians (1:1) and is described as one of three preachers who, along with Paul and Timothy, had proclaimed the gospel in Corinth (2 Cor 1:19). While Silvanus was apparently well known in both Greece (Corinth) and Macedonia (Thessalonica)—and Paul clearly recognized him as a fellow preacher—*Epaphroditus* appears only in connection with Philippi, and Paul seems to regard him primarily as an envoy between himself and the Philippians. Paul describes Epaphroditus as the Philippians' minister to Paul's needs (Phil 2:24) and the bearer of the Philippians' gifts to Paul (4:18). Paul clearly regarded Epaphroditus with great respect and fondness (2:27–29), but he also regarded Epaphroditus as one whose rightful place was in Philippi and not at Paul's side as a fellow missionary (2:25–26).[9]

Prisca and Aquila, the other two co-workers mentioned twice in Paul's letters, appear only where he exchanged greetings with the readers of his respective letters. In the first reference, Paul told the Corinthians that "Aquila and Prisca, together with the church in their house, send greetings" (1 Cor 16:19). It appears that Aquila and Prisca were a married couple who sponsored a house church, and, in keeping with the Greco-Roman tradition of *pater familias,* Aquila, the male member of the household, is mentioned first.[10] Paul's other reference to this couple also mentions their role as the sponsors of a house church (Rom 16:5). However, in this letter Paul was not sending greetings from Aquila and Prisca, but rather to "Prisca and Aquila"—listing Prisca first. Here Paul describes the couple as persons "who work with me in

---

[9] Paul's language of the Philippians' sending Epaphroditus to Paul and of Paul's sending Epaphroditus back to the Philippians has led to conjectures about Epaphroditus's intended role in Paul's ministry. It is possible that the Philippians had intended Epaphroditus to join Paul's mission permanently (e.g., B. S. Mackay, "Further Thoughts on Philippians," *NTS* 7 [1961]: 161–70) or that they merely intended him to visit Paul and then return to them (e.g., Hawthorne, *Philippians,* 162).

[10] Paul often mentioned women who were coupled with another person in ministry. Some of these couples were biologically related (e.g., Rufus and his mother, Rom 16:13; Nereus and his sister, 16:15); some were same sex (e.g., Tryphaena and Tryphosa, 16:12; Euodia and Syntyche, Phil 4:2–3); and others appear to be spouses. Admittedly, Paul never explicitly stated that Prisca and Aquila were married, but a marriage relationship seems likely in their case, as well as in the case of Junia and Andronicus (Rom 16:7). On these "missionary couples" and their role within the house churches in the Pauline communities, see Osiek, MacDonald, and Tulloch, *Woman's Place,* 26–29.

Christ Jesus, and who risked their necks for my life, to whom not only I give thanks, but also all the churches of the Gentiles" (16:3–4). It is noteworthy that when Paul spoke primarily of their household, he listed Aquila first, but when he emphasized their Christian service, he mentioned Prisca first. Thus, even though Paul probably shared the traditional assumption that Aquila was the head of the household, Peter Lampe is correct to conclude that Paul probably also assumed that "Prisca was more prominent in community activity than her husband."[11] Paul apparently regarded Prisca as more prominent than Aquila in the limited sphere of their home, but regarded Aquila as more prominent in the broader world of "all the churches of the Gentiles." In any case, Prisca was a significant Christian worker in her own right, and Paul did not regard her ministry as dependent upon or subordinate to her husband's Christian service.

Among all of Paul's co-workers, co-senders, and emissaries, one stands out as clearly the most prominent in Paul's letters: *Timothy*, who is mentioned in every undisputed Pauline letter except Galatians. Timothy was the co-sender of four Pauline letters (Phil 1:1; Phlm 1; 1 Thess 1:1; 2 Cor 1:1), and his name as co-sender of so many Pauline letters—over half of Paul's undisputed letters—bears compelling witness to his importance to both Paul and Paul's churches. This impression of Timothy's importance to Paul's ministry is strengthened by the language Paul used to describe Timothy. Paul told the Philippians that he "had no one else like him [Timothy]" (Phil 2:20). In addition to describing Timothy as a "brother" (ἀδελφός, 2 Cor 1:1; cf. Phlm 1), Paul twice depicted his relationship with Timothy in terms comparable to a father's relationship with a son (Phil 2:22; 1 Cor 4:17). In contrast to his comments about Barnabas, his other close associate, Paul never spoke negatively about Timothy in his preserved letters. In fact, Paul's praise for Timothy was even more effusive than was his praise for Titus. Paul insisted that Timothy had "served" the gospel with Paul (δουλεύω, Phil 2:22), was "doing the work of the Lord" (ἔργον κυρίου ἐργάζεται, 1 Cor 16:10), was a "co-worker for God" (συνεργὸν τοῦ θεοῦ, 1 Thess 3:2; cf. 2 Cor 1:19), and was "faithful in the Lord" (πιστὸν ἐν κυρίῳ, 1 Cor 4:17).[12]

---

[11]Lampe, *From Paul to Valentinus*, 167. Admittedly, throughout Rom 16, Paul reflected the Roman custom of male domination of the household—even to the point of recognizing the non-Christian heads of households in his salutations to the Christian members of their households (e.g., "the family of Aristobulus," Rom 16:10; "the family of Narcissus," Rom 16:11). Still, eight of the thirty-one people mentioned in Rom 16 were women; Paul spoke of four women (Mary, Tryphaena, Tryphosa, and Persis; Rom 16:6, 12) who "worked" (κοπιάω) with him in ministry; and only Mary among all the people mentioned in this chapter is said to be active in ministry in Rome (16:6). For a complete analysis of the greetings in Rom 16, including issues of gender, see Lampe, *From Paul to Valentinus*, 153–83. For a survey of the women who participated in Paul's ministry, see Florence M. Gillman, *Women Who Knew Paul* (Zacchaeus Studies; Collegeville, Minn.: Liturgical, 1992).

[12]Paul's directive regarding Timothy in 1 Cor 16:10–11 ("If Timothy comes, see that he has nothing to fear among you, for he is doing the work of the Lord just as I am; therefore, let no one despise him. Send him on his way in peace") has caused some

In spite of Paul's obviously high regard for Timothy, Paul did not view Timothy as his equal in ministry. The opening of 2 Corinthians clearly reveals Paul's assumption of Timothy's subordinate status: "Paul, an apostle of Christ Jesus by the will of God, and Timothy our brother" (1:1). "Brother" was clearly a title of respect and endearment for Paul; he used the term both to refer to his fellow believers in general (e.g., Rom 1:13; 7:4; 1 Cor 1:10; 3:1; 2 Cor 1:8; 8:1; Gal 1:11; 4:12; Phil 3:1, 17; 1 Thess 2:1, 9 [inclusively translated as "brother and sisters"]) and to refer more narrowly to his co-workers in ministry (e.g., Phlm 1; 1 Cor 16:11–12; 2 Cor 2:13; 8:18; 9:5; 12:18; Phil 1:14; 2:25; Gal 1:2). Thus, while Paul's description of Timothy as a "brother" cannot be interpreted as a pejorative, in the opening of 2 Corinthians Paul nevertheless did use the term to depict Timothy's ministry as something other than apostolic. So although Paul's remarks in 1 Thessalonians can be broadly interpreted to imply Timothy's apostleship (1:1; 2:7), Paul's explicit statements in 2 Corinthians leave little room for doubt: *Paul was an apostle, but Timothy was not.* Malina's recent designation of Timothy as Paul's "closest associate," but nevertheless subordinate partner, has correctly captured the nature of Timothy's relationship to Paul.[13]

According to Paul's letters, Timothy's ministry as Paul's faithful subordinate included representing Paul to the congregations in Macedonia (Philippi and Thessalonica) and Greece (Athens and Corinth) and perhaps elsewhere. Paul told the Philippians that he was unable to visit them, but that he hoped to send Timothy in his stead (Phil 2:19). Paul likewise recounted that he had sent Timothy to Thessalonica from Athens when he was worried about the well-being of that congregation (1 Thess 3:1–5). At Paul's behest, Timothy also visited the church in the Greek city of Corinth on at least one occasion (1 Cor 4:17; 16:10), a city where Timothy was known to have preached along with Paul and Silvanus (2 Cor 1:19).[14] Philippi, Thessalonica, Athens, and Corinth were, of course, all located in the fairly compact geographical

---

interpreters to speculate that Timothy was not well regarded in Corinth. However, as Conzelmann has noted, "what lies behind the emphatic recommendation, we do not know" (*1 Corinthians*, 297). There is no need to assume that the Corinthians had any particular antipathy toward Timothy. In any case, Paul's regard for Timothy remains unquestionable.

[13] Bruce J. Malina, *Timothy: Paul's Closest Associate* (Paul's Social Network—Brothers and Sisters in Faith; Collegeville, Minn.: Liturgical, 2008).

[14] Most scholars assume with Robert W. Funk that Paul preferred to visit his congregations in person and that Paul sent an envoy like Timothy only when a personal visit from Paul was not possible ("The Apostolic Parousia: Form and Significance," in *Christian History and Interpretation: Studies Presented to John Knox* [ed. William R. Farmer, C. F. D. Moule, and Richard R. Niebuhr; Cambridge: Cambridge University Press, 1967], 249–69). However, Margaret M. Mitchell has questioned these assumptions and argued that "envoys were consciously sent by Paul to play a complex and crucial *intermediary role that he could not play,* even if present himself" ("New Testament Envoys in the Context of Greco-Roman Diplomatic and Epistolary Conventions: The Example of Timothy and Titus," *JBL* 111 [1992]: 641–62, quoting 662, emphasis added).

region of Greece and Macedonia, but Timothy likely traveled to other places in the course of his work with Paul. In 1 Corinthians, Paul talked about sending Timothy to Corinth and having Timothy return to him (4:17; 16:11). If 1 Corinthians was written from Ephesus (as appears likely from 16:8),[15] then Timothy probably spent at least some time in Ephesus in Asia Minor. Even if Timothy's presence cannot be definitively demonstrated outside of Macedonia and Greece, his influence can be. In Romans, Paul sent Timothy's greeting to the Romans, demonstrating the Roman Christians' awareness of—and presumably their interest in—Timothy (16:21).[16]

According to Paul's letters, therefore, Timothy was a uniquely trusted brother, a co-worker in the gospel, a co-sender of Pauline letters, and an emissary between Paul and his congregations, but not an apostle. Timothy was active in Greece, Macedonia, and probably Ephesus in Asia Minor. His influence extended even further than Greece, Macedonia, and Asia Minor.

Paul's Converts and Local Congregational Leaders

Paul's references to the participants in local Christian communities are largely incidental and reveal little about the people being mentioned. Occasionally, Paul singled out an individual or a group of individuals with specific instructions. For example, Paul instructed Euodia and Syntyche to set aside their differences for the sake of the gospel (Phil 4:2), and he dedicated the brief letter of Philemon to resolving the tensions between the runaway slave Onesimus and the threesome of Philemon, Apphia, and Archippus (Phlm 2).[17] On other occasions Paul shared the reports he had received from specific people within a congregation. Some of these people are mentioned as formal emissaries. For example, the Corinthians sent Achaicus, Stephanas,

---

[15]For more on the Ephesian origin of 1 Corinthians and Timothy's travels, see Conzelmann, *1 Corinthians*, 3–5.

[16]Although Rom 16 probably was an integral part of the original Letter to the Romans, even the possibility that this chapter was originally an independent letter (to Ephesus) is evidence of Timothy's broader reputation within the Pauline churches. On the integrity of Rom 16 to the book of Romans and on the possibility of an Ephesian origin for Rom 16, see Jewett, *Romans*, 4–18, esp. 8–9.

[17]Philemon is addressed to "Philemon, our dear friend and co-worker, to Apphia our sister, to Archippus our fellow soldier, and to the church in your house" (vv. 1–2). The pronoun indicating ownership of the house is second person singular (σου, v. 2) and could refer to the last person named (Archippus, v. 2) or to the first person named (Philemon, v. 1). Most interpreters assume that the pronoun refers back to Philemon and that the church met in the home which he shared with his wife, Apphia (e.g., Eduard Lohse, *Colossians and Philemon* [trans. William R. Poehlmann and Robert J. Karris; Hermeneia; Philadelphia: Fortress, 1971], 190–91; and Peter T. O'Brien, *Colossians, Philemon* [WBC 44; Waco: Word, 1982], 271–72). However, this interpretation leaves the subsequent reference to Archippus strangely out of place. If the pronoun refers to Archippus, he may have been a prominent minister ("fellow soldier," v. 2) in the house church maintained by Philemon and Archippus, and not the son of the couple as is often supposed.

and Fortunatus to Paul (1 Cor 16:17), and the Philippians sent Epaphroditus to Paul (Phil 2:25–30; 4:18). Other reporting agents, like "Chloe's people" (1 Cor 1:11), apparently served as far less formal sources of information about congregational life. Although Paul sometimes singled out key individuals for specific instructions or mentioned someone as a reporting agent to him, the vast majority of Paul's references to the members of local congregations are simple greetings.

Unfortunately, many of Paul's greetings reveal almost nothing about the person with whom Paul was exchanging greeting. For example, in Rom 16, Paul greeted twenty-six people by name, but fourteen of these names are modified by various expressions that reveal only the individual's Christian faith (e.g., "beloved in Christ," v. 8; "approved in Christ," v. 10; and "chosen in the Lord," v. 13). It is noteworthy, however, that seven of the people greeted in Rom 16 were female (Prisca, v. 3; Mary, v. 6; Junia, v. 6; Tryphaena, v. 12; Tryphosa, v. 12; Persis, v. 12; and Julia, v. 15). In addition to his inclusion of significant numbers of women in his final remarks to the Romans, it is noteworthy that Paul emphasized Epaenetus's stature as the first convert in Asia (16:5) and the stature of Junia and Andronicus as those in the faith before Paul himself was (16:7).

Paul's greetings, not just those that Paul himself offered but also those that others offered by means of Paul's letters, also suggest that many early Christians enjoyed reputations that spread beyond their immediate vicinity. Paul "commended" the deacon Phoebe to the Romans because she was apparently unknown to that Christian community (Rom 16:1–2),[18] but Paul's letters otherwise give the impression that many early Christians were well known to multiple Christian communities. Thus, Paul could send Philemon's household greetings from Epaphras, Mark, Aristarchus, Demas, and Luke under the assumption that the readers of this private letter would recognize these names (Phlm 23–24). Likewise in Rom 16, Paul could extend greetings to the Romans from *Timothy* (v. 21), *Lucius,* (v. 21), *Jason,* (v. 21) *Sosipater* (v. 21), *Gaius* (v. 23), *Erastus* (v. 23), and *Quartus* (v. 23), and in 1 Corinthians, Paul could extend greetings to the Corinthians from Aquila and Prisca (16:19). This frequent exchange of greetings across significant distances suggests that several early Christian leaders were well known throughout the eastern and central Mediterranean.

Two other observations about Paul's interaction with the leaders of local congregations are noteworthy. First, Paul himself baptized at least some of these leaders. In the Corinthian correspondence, Paul diminished his role in baptizing believers, but was still forced to acknowledge that he himself had baptized Crispus, Gaius, and the household of Stephanas (1 Cor 1:14–16).

---

[18]James D. G. Dunn correctly notes that "Phoebe is the first recorded 'deacon' in the history of Christianity," but as Dunn also notes, we know little about the duties, responsibilities, and authority that accompanied this title when Paul penned Romans (*Romans 9–16*, 887).

Second, Paul appears to have been hosted in the homes of some of his converts. Paul mentioned that Gaius was hosting him when he wrote the Letter to the Romans (16:23), and he asked Philemon to prepare a room for his impending visit to Philemon's home (Phlm 22). Although it cannot be proven, it is likely that Paul's description of Phoebe as a "benefactor" to himself and others included hosting the apostle at her home (Rom 16:2).[19]

Apollos

Apollos is a unique individual within Paul's letters. Although he clearly interacted with Paul's communities, he was never treated as either a Pauline associate or convert. Yet, Paul clearly recognized Apollos as an authority within Paul's churches—or at least within the Corinthian church. Apollos's name was evoked in the factionalism that Paul decried in 1 Cor 1–4. On the surface, it is difficult to determine the degree to which Paul held Apollos personally responsible for these divisions. Some interpreters have observed that Paul's sarcastic references to the various parties in Corinth sometimes omit reference to Peter (1 Cor 3:4–6; 4:6), but that they always include the name Apollos (1:12; 3:4–6, 22; 4:6). On the basis of this observation, some interpreters have discerned a subtle Pauline critique of either Apollos or his followers.[20] Such a reading may find additional support in Paul's concluding remarks about the divisions within the Corinthian church. In these comments, Paul specifically claimed to have "applied all this to Apollos and myself" (1 Cor 4:6).

However, two facts mitigate against a supposed antipathy between Paul and Apollos. First, if Paul was hostile toward Apollos, his criticism of Apollos in 1 Corinthians is uncharacteristically subtle for Paul and not nearly as direct as Paul's criticism of his opponents in his other letters (e.g., Phil 3; Gal 1–4; 2 Cor 1–9).[21] Second, toward the end of 1 Corinthians, Paul claimed to have urged Apollos to return to Corinth for a visit (16:12). Although Paul acknowledged that his urgings had been unsuccessful up to that time, his willingness to encourage Apollos to visit Corinth is strikingly different than Paul's admonitions to his other congregations to have nothing to do with his opponents (Phil 3:2; 1 Cor 5:11; Gal 1:9). Of course, Paul's comments in the closing of 1 Corinthians (16:12) do not reveal where Apollos was residing at the time of their interaction (or even whether their interaction was in person

---

[19] On the possibility that Paul was relying upon Phoebe as an advance person and key advocate for his planned visit to Spain, see Robert Jewett, "Paul, Phoebe and the Spanish Mission," in *The Social World of Formative Christianity* (ed. Jacob Neusner and Peder Borgen; Philadelphia: Fortress, 1988), 142–61; *contra* Caroline F. Whelan, "*Amica Pauli*: The Role of Phoebe in the Early Church," *JSNT* 49 (1993): 67–85.

[20] E.g., Donald P. Ker, "Paul and Apollos—Colleagues or Rivals?" *JSNT* 77 (2000): 75–97; and Joop F. M. Smit, "'What Is Apollos? What Is Paul?' In Search for the Coherence of First Corinthians 1:10–4:21," *NovT* 44 (2002): 231–51.

[21] See N. H. Taylor, "Apostolic Identity and Conflicts in Corinth and Galatia," in Porter, *Paul and His Opponents*, 99–127.

or via letter), but they do reveal both that Paul and Apollos maintained contact with one another even when neither was in Corinth and that Apollos's ministry extended beyond Corinth.

It therefore appears that Paul and Paul's congregations regarded Apollos as an authority within Corinth and probably beyond Corinth. It is unclear if Paul and Apollos ever met in person, but they did interact either in person or via letters. Their followers clashed, and Paul strongly disapproved of the resulting factionalism, but it is not readily apparent that Paul and Apollos were ever personally hostile to one another—although Apollos apparently felt free to reject Paul's request to return to Corinth even when Paul "strongly urged" (πολλὰ παρεκάλεσα) Apollos to do so (1 Cor 16:12).

Summary of the Pauline Data Set

According to the data in his letters, Paul engaged in extensive communication with a broad range of early Christian communities and individuals. Paul maintained these communications through personal visits, through letter writing (often with co-senders), and through emissaries who traveled back and forth between Paul and the various churches. All of these persons were male, as was Tertius, Paul's only mentioned scribal assistant. Timothy, Titus, Sosthenes, Silvanus, Achaicus, Stephanas, Fortunatus, and Epaphroditus were among the most prominent Pauline emissaries and co-senders. Timothy undoubtedly was Paul's closest associate. Paul and those around him exchanged greetings with dozens of people through Paul's letters. Philemon, Apphia, and Archippus, who were probably all members of the same family, were the only individuals to have an entire letter specifically and exclusively addressed to them. However, two women, Euodia and Syntyche, were singled out for individual instruction within one letter.

Paul presumed a large—but not clearly defined—number of apostles. The college of apostles in Paul's letters was clearly larger than the twelve plus Paul and probably included Junia, Andronicus, Titus (discussed in the previous chapter), and perhaps even Epaphroditus in addition to Peter and the apostles associated with Jerusalem. Still, for Paul, the ranks of the apostles were closed. Paul considered himself to be the last person called to apostleship. Not even Paul's "son" Timothy was an apostle according to Paul's letters. It is noteworthy, however, that at least one of the apostles, Junia, was female.

According to his letters, Paul maintained a distinction between apostles and non-apostles, but maintained a less clear distinction between what could anachronistically be called ministers and laity. For example, Paul baptized some believers himself, but it is unclear what prerequisites, if any, qualified a person to administer baptism (and the Lord's Supper). Paul credited several people, both men and women, with assisting him in ministry.[22] At many points,

---

[22] Paul's willingness, as discerned from his undisputed letters, to allow both men and women to lead Christian worship and perform other acts of ministry has long been

the mixed-gender list of Paul's co-workers and fellow prisoners overlapped with the exclusively male list of his co-senders and emissaries. At least some of Paul's churches met in homes, and the owners of those homes, both the male and the female owners, appear to have been integral to the leadership of those churches. Several women, including Chloe, Mary, Prisca, Euodia, and Syntyche, appear to have engaged in various ministries with Paul's approval. Phoebe was even singled out for Paul's personal commendation as a deacon.

II. THE ACTS DATA SET

Prophets, Emissaries, and Fellow Travelers

Paul's interaction with authorities of various kinds is quite diverse in Acts. The last chapter examined the key authority figures who effected Paul's integration into the established Christian communities. This chapter will examine several lesser authority figures with whom Paul interacted. These lesser authorities tend to be identified as either prophets, traveling preachers (like Paul), or emissaries between the various Christian communities in Acts. They typically gain authority from a specific and stated source, usually from the Spirit in the case of the prophets (e.g., 11:28; 13:1–2) or from a local community in the case of the various emissaries (e.g., 15:27; 20:1–4) or even from Paul himself (e.g., 17:15; 18:19). In his interactions with these lesser authority figures in Acts, Paul was never forced to rely upon external human advocacy as he was in his interactions with the churches in Jerusalem and in Antioch.

The prominence of these lesser authorities varies widely. Yet nearly all of these characters are mere bit players in Acts. Two prophetic characters, the martyr *Stephen* (22:20; cf. 6:5–8:2) and the preacher *John the Baptist* (13:24–25; cf. Luke 3:15–18), appear only as distant memories for Paul. Some of these figures appear only as names in a list, as in the cases of the prophets of Antioch, *Simeon, Lucius,* and *Manaen,* who—along with Barnabas—determined that Saul should be set aside for particular service (13:1–2). *Agabus,* a prophet from Jerusalem, appears twice to offer Paul advice through the Spirit (11:28; 21:10–14). The four prophesying daughters of Philip the evangelist are not even identified by name; they are mentioned only as a nameless collection (21:8–9).[23] A group of (apparently) Gentile emissaries, *Sopater, Secundus,* and *Tychicus,*

---

recognized. See, e.g., George H. Gilbert, "Women in Public Worship in the Churches of Paul," *BW* 2 (1893): 38–47. More recently, Craig S. Keener, *Paul, Women, and Wives: Marriage and Women's Ministry in the Letters of Paul* (Peabody, Mass.: Hendrickson, 1992).

[23] Acts diminishes the significance of these female prophets by having a male prophet, Agabus, travel from Judea to their home in Caesarea to deliver a prophetic word, a word which apparently eluded the four resident (female) prophets (21:10–11). On these female prophets as both a fulfillment of Joel's prophecy (quoted in Acts 2:17–18) and as "little more than window dressing," see F. Scott Spencer, *Journeying through Acts: A Literary-Cultural Reading* (Peabody, Mass.: Hendrickson, 2004), 207.

appear in the narrative only when Acts reports that they accompanied Paul to Jerusalem (20:1–4). *Judas*, along with *Silas*, appears as Jerusalem's emissary to Antioch (15:22–32),[24] and *Erastus* appears as Paul's emissary to Macedonia (19:22). Other emissaries like *Trophimus* (20:4; 21:27), *Gaius* (19:29; 20:4), and the slightly more prominent *Aristarchus* (19:29; 20:4; 27:2) first appear in a list of similar emissaries and then reappear briefly in an adjacent scene, but still none of these characters ever manages to speak in Acts.[25] In fact, none of the minor characters just considered ever acts on their own initiative. The emissaries do not speak at all; they merely conduct themselves as directed by Paul or the Jerusalem apostles. One of the prophets, Agabus, does manage to speak, but he functions only as a mouthpiece for the Spirit, who provides his words (11:28; 21:10–11; cf. 13:1–2).

Only six of the lesser authority figures in Acts play significant roles as truly self-volitional characters. The first of these characters, *John Mark*, largely serves as what Clifton Black has aptly termed a "foil" in Acts.[26] John Mark is an unreliable young man of Jerusalemite heritage who probably resisted Gentile inclusion. He made his first clearly recognizable appearance in Acts when his mother, Mary, was hosting a prayer gathering during Peter's imprisonment (12:12–13).[27] After emerging from his mother's shadow in Jerusalem (12:12; 13:13), John Mark began traveling with Paul, but clearly as a junior partner in their enterprise. His participation, such as it was, was apparently entirely at the discretion of Paul and Barnabas. Thus, Acts records that Paul and Barnabas "brought with them John, whose other name was Mark" (12:25). When the church in Antioch set Paul and Barnabas apart for Christian work, John Mark was delegated with the distinctly subordinate task of "assisting" (ὑπηρετέω, 13:5) them. While Paul and Barnabas were preaching on the island of Cyprus, John Mark inexplicably left the island and returned to Jerusalem (13:13). Although Acts provides no immediate rationale for John Mark's departure from Paul's and Barnabas's mission, it is probably significant that John Mark separated from the missionaries precisely at the point where Paul's name began taking precedence over Barnabas's name. John Mark's departure appears in the same verse that demotes Barnabas to a mere companion of Paul (13:13).[28]

---

[24] Judas was a common name in first-century Judea, so the Judas in Acts 15 may or may not be the same Judas who first hosted the post–Damascus Road Saul in Jerusalem (9:11).

[25] According to Acts, Aristarchus, the Thessalonian emissary, traveled with Paul back to Rome by ship, while the other emissaries listed in 20:4 disappeared from the narrative after their inhospitable reception in Jerusalem.

[26] C. Clifton Black, *Mark: Images of an Apostolic Interpreter* (Studies on Personalities of the New Testament; Columbia: University of South Carolina Press, 1994), 43.

[27] A few scholars have suggested that John Mark should be identified with the John who accompanied Peter in Acts 3:1, 11 and 4:13, 19. This association is possible, but unlikely. See Black, *Mark*, 26–27.

[28] Acts 13:13 uses the phrase "Paul and his companions" in contrast with the earlier formula "Barnabas and Saul," which privileged Barnabas over Paul (12:24;

John Mark was not mentioned again in Acts until after the apostolic council, when Barnabas wanted to take John Mark with him and Paul as they informed the churches of the decisions reached at the Jerusalem Conference (15:36). Paul objected to including John Mark in their travel plans, characterizing John Mark's departure from Cyprus as desertion (ἀποσπάω, 15:38). The rift between Paul and Barnabas over John Mark was "so sharp that they parted company" (15:39). As a result, Barnabas took John Mark westward to Cyprus, and Paul took Silas northward to Syria and Cilicia (15:39–40). John Mark then fell out of the narrative, as did Barnabas; neither reappears in Acts. Black's summary of John Mark's interaction with Paul in Acts is accurate: "In general, John Mark is cast in an obscure (13:5, 13) or outrightly negative light (15:38–39), arguably owing (in Luke's view) to his reticence or refusal to engage in the Christian mission to Gentiles. Evidently for this reason, in Luke's account, he is the cause of the breakup between Barnabas and Paul (15:39b–40)."[29] When viewed through the eyes of the Paul of Acts, John Mark was unreliable and divisive. In all probability, his commitment to the Gentile mission was also questionable.

If John Mark represents a Jewish believer who was initially resistant to Paul's Gentile mission and with whom Paul was unwilling to work, *Silas* probably represents a Jewish believer who had a fading interest in Paul's Gentile mission and became unwilling to work with Paul. Silas, like John Mark, was a Jewish believer with roots in the Jerusalem church. Unlike John Mark, Silas participated in the Jerusalem Conference and was entrusted with distributing its decree to the churches outside of Jerusalem (Acts 15:22, 27, 32). At this point, when Silas first entered the narrative in Acts, he enjoyed the confidence not only of the Jerusalem believers, but also of Paul. Therefore, after refusing to travel with John Mark and after separating from Barnabas as a result of that refusal, "Paul chose Silas" to travel with him (15:40). Paul and Silas were then quickly joined by the newly circumcised Timothy in Derbe and Lystra (16:1–3). This trio visited the churches in Phrygia and Galatia in Asia Minor (16:6).[30] In Troas, Paul had a vision of a Macedonian man summoning him to preach in Macedonia (16:6–9). In response to this vision, the trio, along with their new traveling partner, the narrator of Acts, "immediately tried to

---

13:2, 7). On this and other explanations for John Mark's departure from Asia Minor, see Black, *Mark*, 34–36.

[29] Black, *Mark*, 43. Also see Painter, *Just James*, 51–52.

[30] John B. F. Miller has plausibly argued that Paul's vision of the Macedonian man contained more ambiguity than is generally recognized. Acts records that Paul and his companions "concluded" (συμβιβάζω, 16:10) that they should travel to Macedonia to preach. Acts implies, therefore, that the vision required interpretation. However, the Spirit in Acts typically speaks directly to people and does not speak through dreams or leave matters open to interpretation as is the case here. Additionally, as Miller notes, Paul's mission in Macedonia was not very successful when compared to his later mission in the non-Macedonian city of Corinth. Perhaps upon reflection, the author of Acts became ambivalent about the wisdom of the interpretation given to the vision. See John B. F. Miller, "Paul's Dream at Troas," in Phillips, *Contemporary Studies in Acts*, 138–53.

cross to Macedonia" (16:10).[31] The narrator traveled with Paul to Philippi (as witnessed by the repeated use of the first person "we" and "us," 16:11, 12, 13, 15, 16, 17). Although Paul's entourage presumably still included Silas and Timothy, Paul is the only member of the group to speak in Philippi (16:14, 18). In spite of his low profile—indeed his complete silence—Silas evidently remained with Paul because Acts singled him out as having been seized, beaten, flogged, and imprisoned with Paul (16:19, 22, 23). Timothy and the narrator fared better than Paul and Silas. They remained unmolested throughout this incident, probably indicating their relative insignificance in the eyes of the mob.

In prison, Paul and Silas engaged in prayer and singing jointly, but Paul alone initiated conversation with their guard (16:28). Still, the jailor responded to both Paul and Silas with the provocative question: "*Sirs*, what must I do to be saved?" (16:30, emphasis added). Although they both answered the question (16:31), and they both "spoke the word of the Lord to him" (16:32), the jailer recognized Paul's leadership role by conveying his superior's instruction to Paul alone (16:36). Paul's insistence that both he and Silas were Roman citizens secured their release (16:37–39). Paul and Silas then traveled to Thessalonica, where Paul again was the only speaker (17:3)—even though the resulting converts "joined Paul and Silas" (17:4). Again, mob violence was aimed at both Paul and the silent Silas (17:5). Their retreat from Philippi lead them to Beroea (17:10), where Paul yet again did all the speaking (17:13). However, when again threatened with violence, Paul went on to Athens alone and left Silas in Beroea with Timothy (17:15).

Acts provides no information about the activities of Silas and Timothy in Beroea after Paul's departure, but records that they rejoined Paul in Corinth where Paul again began preaching in synagogues (18:5, 7). Acts makes no reference to Silas's activities after his arrival in Corinth (18:5). Unlike the earlier episodes in Philippi and Thessalonica, Silas is never mentioned as a co-participant in Paul's Corinthian activities. Acts reports that Paul stayed in Corinth for eighteen months (18:11), but does not mention how long Silas stayed there. Acts reports that the Jews mounted "a united attack on Paul" (18:12), but mentions nothing about an attack on Silas. Paul's opponents in Corinth—unlike his opponents in Philippi, Thessalonica, and Beroea—focused exclusively upon him as if he operated entirely alone. When Paul's Jewish accusers complained about Paul before Gallio, the Roman proconsul of Achaia, they insisted *in the singular* that "*This man* is persuading people . . ." (18:13, emphasis added). This accusation contrasts strongly with the earlier accusations against "these men" (16:20) and "these people" (17:6). In Corinth, unlike in the earlier cities, Paul stood under accusation alone, and when Paul left Corinth, he said farewell to the Corinthians alone (18:18). In Corinth, Silas disappeared from Acts, never to reappear.

---

[31] On the role of the narrator of Acts and his appearance at this point in the narrative, see Phillips, "Paul as a Role Model."

Silas, therefore, appears as a staunch ally of Paul and his gospel in Asia Minor, Philippi, and Thessalonica. Silas even suffered imprisonment with Paul. However, in Corinth, the supportive Silas faded from the pages of Acts. Although Acts never explicitly says so, the break between Paul and Silas may have been as decisive as was the earlier break between Paul and Barnabas. In many ways, Silas was as much of a mismatch for Paul as was John Mark. In Acts, Paul's mission was to take Christ's name to both Jews and Gentiles (9:15; 22:21; 26:17, 23), but *the Silas of Acts seems concerned only about Jews—as does Paul while working with Silas*. It should be noted that Silas first appeared in Acts as the *Jerusalem church's* emissary (15:22, 27, 32) and Paul, while traveling with Silas, behaved like a missionary to the Jews alone. When he was in Asia Minor, Paul circumcised Timothy (16:1–3) and then quickly sought out "a place of prayer" in which to preach (16:13).[32] While at this place of prayer, Paul and Silas made their first convert in Philippi. That convert, Lydia, was a "worshipper of God" (16:14). In Philippi, even their pagan detractors understood that the mission of Paul and Silas was a Jewish mission. In their complaint against Paul and Silas, their Gentile accusers claimed: "These men are disturbing our city; they are Jews" (16:20).[33] In Thessalonica, Paul also engaged in a Jewish mission, preaching in a synagogue "as was his custom" (17:1–2). In Corinth, Silas was by Paul's side in the synagogue (18:4–5), but disappeared from the narrative at the very point when Paul made a decisive break with the Corinthian synagogue—and Paul's break with the synagogue was decisive in Corinth. Paul "shook the dust from his clothes" and said to the Jews: "Your blood be on your own heads! I am innocent. From now on I will go to the Gentiles" (18:6).[34] To make the matter even clearer, Acts immediately followed up on this speech with the narrative comment that Paul "left the synagogue" (18:7). Given Silas's total absence from Acts after this point, one may safely infer that when Paul left the synagogue in Corinth, Silas left Paul.[35]

---

[32] "Place of prayer" presumably implies a Jewish place of prayer. The Paul of Acts never interacts positively with pagan places of worship. It could be that Philippi lacked enough Jewish men and Gentile God-fearers to establish a synagogue *per se*. See Witherington, *Acts*, 491.

[33] The charges made against Paul and Silas, that they were Jews who taught anti-Roman customs (Acts 16:20–21), do not follow from the exorcism which prompted their arrest (16:16–18). Craig S. de Vos appropriately conjectures both that the author of Acts has created charges that Paul and Silas could easily be defended against and that the author of Acts demeaned the motives of Paul's accusers as greedy (16:16, 19) for the same defensive reason ("Finding a Charge That Fits: The Accusation against Paul and Silas at Philippi (Acts 16.19–21)," *JSNT* 74 [1999]: 51–63).

[34] Paul's break with the synagogue (perhaps even with the Jews) in Corinth has been subjected to repeated analyses, in large measure due to its implications for Jewish-Christian relations. On the significance of Paul's rejection of the Corinthian synagogue in relation to the larger narrative of Acts, see Tyson, *Images of Judaism in Luke-Acts*, 141–43 and the literature discussed there.

[35] B. N. Kaye is probably correct that Acts presents Paul's experience with Gentiles while preaching in Athens (17:16–34) as decisive for his own understanding of his mission to Gentiles. According to Kaye's reading of Acts, when Paul rejoined Silas in

Having rejected John Mark as a traveling companion, and having replaced Barnabas with Silas as a traveling companion, and then having lost
Silas's participation in his ministry, Paul adopted *Aquila and Priscilla* as his new
traveling partners when he left Corinth (18:18). Aquila and Priscilla, who Acts
informs us were married (18:2), were introduced into the narrative as Paul's
hosts in Corinth (18:3).[36] Their initial introduction provided no indication of
their role as Christian ministers. They were presented only as Paul's hosts
in Corinth, and, in keeping with the male-dominated culture of the Roman
Empire, Acts mentions Aquila, the senior male member of the household, first.
Acts also informs us that Aquila was a Jew from Pontus, but that he had also
lived in Rome. He and Priscilla were in Rome when the emperor Claudius
expelled the Jews from Rome (18:1–2).[37]

Paul first encountered Aquila and Priscilla in Corinth, where the only
suggestion of the couple's prominence was the fact that Paul took the initiative to find them rather than them seeking out Paul (18:2). Yet even this fact
can easily be explained by the fact that the couple shared a common craft
with Paul, the craft of tentmaking, and Paul wanted to stay with them and
participate in their business (18:3).[38] Paul may have sought them out simply
because he needed a place to live and work, and it made sense for Paul to
begin seeking lodging and employment among those who practiced the same
craft that he did. Regardless of the motivation behind his quest to contact Aquila and Priscilla, Paul was able to continue his ministry while staying at their
home. Interestingly, however, Acts doesn't clarify when Aquila and Priscilla
became believers. One could legitimately infer either that Aquila and Priscilla
were Christians before they met Paul or that they were converted while Paul
resided with them. It is unclear if Paul sought them out because of their shared
faith or simply because of their shared vocation. On the one hand, Acts gives
no indication of a pre-Pauline Christian community in Corinth, a fact that

---

Corinth, Paul had a different understanding of his mission, an understanding which
Silas could not support ("Acts' Portrait of Silas," *NovT* 21 [1979]: 13–27). On the likelihood of a "slightly frosty atmosphere between the two missionaries" at this point in
Acts, see Michael D. Goulder, "Silas in Thessalonica," *JSNT* 48 (1992): 87–106, quoting
102; *contra* Allan Wainwright, "Where Did Silas Go? (And What Was His Connection
with Galatians?)," *JSNT* 8 (1980): 66–70.

[36] The couple's ability to host Paul, along with their extensive travel (Pontus,
Rome, Corinth, and Ephesus according to Acts), has led many scholars to suspect
that the couple owned a thriving business. However, see Lampe's devastating critique
of the notion that a wealthy couple would still have worked as artisans (*From Paul to
Valentinus*, 189–91).

[37] On the edict of Claudius in the late 40s, see Lampe, *From Paul to Valentinus*,
11–16.

[38] Acts seems to imply that both Aquila and Priscilla were artisans in the sewing and leatherworking business. On the role of a woman in such work, see F. Scott
Spencer, "Women of 'the Cloth' in Acts: Sewing the Word," in *A Feminist Companion
to the Acts of the Apostles* (ed. Amy-Jill Levine and Marianne Blickenstaff; Feminist
Companion to the New Testament and Early Christian Writings 9; Cleveland: Pilgrim,
2004), 134–54, esp. 150–53.

argues for Aquila and Priscilla being Pauline converts. On the other hand, Acts does not record Aquila and Priscilla in the brief list of Paul's converts in Corinth (18:7–8), a fact that argues for Aquila and Priscilla being pre-Pauline converts. Regardless of whether or not Aquila and Priscilla were Christians when Paul first sought them out, Acts is clear that Paul acted alone in his efforts to "convince Jews and Greeks" each Sabbath "in the synagogue" (18:4).

The ambiguity surrounding the couple's faith commitments and ministry activities during Paul's stay in Corinth ended with Paul's departure from Corinth. According to Acts, when Paul left Corinth, he was "accompanied by Priscilla and Aquila" (18:18). Yet, upon arriving in Ephesus, Paul again, as in Corinth, went into the synagogue alone to preach (αὐτὸς δὲ εἰσελθών, 18:19). Acts records that when Paul decided to leave Corinth, the Ephesians wanted him to extend his stay there (18:20). But instead of remaining there himself, Paul "left behind" (καταλείπω, 18:19) Priscilla and Aquila. Assuming that Priscilla and Aquila accompanied Paul in order to support his ministry in some capacity (as did Paul's other fellow travelers in Acts), Paul's leaving them behind in Ephesus probably indicates his desire for them to continue his ministry in Ephesus, giving them what C. K. Barrett aptly described as "a free hand to conduct affairs in Ephesus."[39] In this connection, the order of their names—Priscilla followed by Aquila—is probably significant. In the first reference to the couple when the primary concern was their hosting of Paul, Acts mentioned Aquila first (18:2). In the second reference to the couple, when the primary concern was Paul's directive for them to stay in Ephesus, Priscilla was mentioned first (18:18).[40]

This prioritizing of Priscilla's name also occurs in the couple's third and final appearance in Acts, an appearance that firmly establishes their teaching role within the early church. After Paul left Ephesus, Acts records that an Alexandrian Jew named Apollos began teaching in the synagogue there (18:24). Acts records that he "had been instructed in the Way of the Lord . . . though he knew only the baptism of John" (18:25). Apparently Priscilla and Aquila (whose names appear in that order) were still attending the synagogue, because they heard Apollos there, and, being in general sympathy with his message but also sensing its incompleteness, "they took him aside and explained the Way of God to him more accurately" (18:26). This account clearly implies not only Priscilla's and Aquila's status as Christian teachers but also their status as distinguished teachers who could correct false or incomplete teaching. It is particularly noteworthy that Priscilla's name appeared first even when she and her husband were correcting a man who was "eloquent" (ἀνὴρ λόγιος) and "well versed in the scriptures" (δυνατὸς ὢν ἐν ταῖς γραφαῖς, 18:24).[41]

---

[39] Barrett, *Acts*, 2:858.

[40] On the prioritizing of Priscilla's name over Aquila's name, see Gillman, *Women Who Knew Paul*, 54–56.

[41] It is unclear whether this correction took place in the synagogue or in the couple's home. It would have been more in keeping with the customs of the day for Priscilla to speak in the private space of the household than in the public space of the

In Acts, therefore, Aquila and Priscilla were Paul's hosts in Corinth, his traveling companions between Corinth and Ephesus, and distinguished Christian teachers in Ephesus who functioned under Paul's authority. They used that authority to correct the traveling teacher, Apollos. Priscilla was probably a more prominent Christian teacher and companion of Paul than was her husband, Aquila.

Timothy, the last of the lesser authority figures with whom Paul interacts in Acts, had a lengthy, but not particularly close, relationship to Paul. Timothy was already a well-regarded disciple when Paul met him in Lystra, and Paul immediately wanted Timothy to accompany him (16:1–3). Timothy's mother was Jewish, but his father was a Gentile, and Timothy was uncircumcised. Therefore, according to Acts, "because of the Jews who were in those places," Paul circumcised Timothy before they began their journey (16:3). This circumcision, although widely debated in scholarly circles (as we shall discuss later), enabled Timothy to join Paul and Silas as they continued throughout Asia Minor (16:6–18:22).[42] Although Paul and Silas repeatedly appear by name (16:19, 25, 29; 17:1, 4, 5, 10), and the narrator frequently includes himself by speaking in the first person (16:10, 11, 12, 13, 15, 16, 17), Timothy is not mentioned again in Acts until he and Silas are mentioned as remaining behind in Beroea (in Macedonia) (17:14).

The absence of explicit references to Timothy—from his circumcision in Lystra (16:1–3) to Paul's instructions that Silas and Timothy remain in Beroea (17:14–15)—is surprising, but remarkably consistent. Even when Timothy was presumably present in the narrative, his name is absent. For example, when Paul and Silas were arrested in Philippi, apparently while in the company of Timothy and the narrator of Acts, neither Timothy nor the narrator were accosted by the persecuting mob (16:16–24). During the period of Timothy's absence from the narrative, Silas continued to play a significant role in Paul's ministry, but always as Paul's subordinate in the formula of "Paul and Silas" (16:19, 25, 29; 17:1, 4, 5, 10). Interestingly, when Timothy's name reentered the narrative, Silas's name took priority over Timothy's name. "Silas and Timothy" remained behind in Beroea (17:14), and Paul instructed "Silas and Timothy" to rejoin him as soon as possible (17:15). According to Acts, therefore, Silas and Timothy were both subordinate to Paul and took instructions from him, but Silas was the dominant partner in the pair.

---

synagogue, but Acts records only the privacy of the correction ("they took him aside," 18:26) and not the location of the correction. On the significance of place—home or synagogue—and the cultural expectations attached to each, see Osiek, MacDonald, and Tulloch, *Woman's Place*, 33–34. Also see Stegemann and Stegemann, *The Jesus Movement*, 389–407.

[42] The controversial aspects of this circumcision will be revisited later, but at this point it is significant to note that first-century circumcision may have entailed little more than a ceremonial spilling of blood from a small incision in the foreskin, and not the total removal of the foreskin as in later practice. Timothy's discomfort and inconvenience may, therefore, have been minimal. See Malina, *Timothy*, 104–5.

After another brief absence, while Paul was alone in Athens (17:16–34), Timothy reentered the narrative in Corinth. Timothy again appears as the silent subordinate of Silas (18:1, 5), and Timothy's rapid disappearance from the narrative coincides with Silas's disappearance from Paul's ministry in Corinth (as discussed earlier). Therefore, up to this point in Acts, *Timothy appears more as Silas's associate than as Paul's.* Timothy three times appears in tandem with Silas (17:14, 15; 18:5), but never in tandem with Paul. As mentioned earlier, Acts records that Silas and Timothy rejoined Paul in Corinth, but Acts recounts Paul's Corinthian ministry as if Paul were entirely alone in Corinth. Then, when Paul left Corinth, Acts records only two companions, Priscilla and Aquila (18:18). Acts, therefore, seems to imply that Timothy removed himself from Paul's ministry when his mentor Silas removed himself from Paul's ministry.

Timothy, unlike Silas, appeared two more times in Acts. First, Timothy reappeared with Erastus, who appears as Timothy's subordinate in the formula "Timothy and Erastus" (19:22). Here, for the first time, Timothy worked directly under Paul's oversight—but notably only at a distance and with another partner. Paul sent this pair from Ephesus to Macedonia. As is often the case with the minor characters in Acts, the text provides no clear indication of when or how Timothy rejoined Paul's entourage, but the designation of Timothy and Erastus as Paul's "helpers" (διακονούντων) certainly implies their participation in Paul's ministry (19:22). Second, later when Paul returned to Macedonia, he was accompanied by six men from various places in Macedonia and Asia Minor (20:4). All seven of these travelers, except Timothy, are identified with a particular city or region of origin. Whereas Paul's other companions were likely traveling to Rome as representatives of their respective homelands, Timothy's lack of geographical association may suggest that his presence was justified by his status as a Pauline helper and emissary.[43] Regardless of Timothy's status within the group, the group broke up as quickly as it had formed, with Paul and the narrator journeying together to Troas by sea while Timothy and the other six representatives traveled by land and made arrangements to meet Paul in Troas (20:5–6). Although one could infer Timothy's presence with Paul (and the narrator) throughout the subsequent traumatic sea journey from Troas to Jerusalem (19:6–21:17) and throughout the even more traumatic events in Jerusalem (21:17–23:30), nothing in Acts clearly indicates Timothy's presence in the remainder of Acts—even though other members of his entourage of seven are mentioned (21:29; 27:3).

In Acts, therefore, Timothy appears primarily as a junior colleague to Silas (17:14, 15; 18:5) and as an occasional emissary for Paul (19:22). According to Acts, Paul circumcised Timothy in preparation for their journey with Silas, but Timothy never traveled alone with Paul. In the lone instance when Timothy traveled with Paul without Silas, Timothy traveled in a large entourage and was not a particularly close associate of Paul even within this group

---

[43] See Witherington, *Acts,* 603; and Haenchen, *Acts,* 581.

(20:1–6). When this nine-person entourage (including Paul and the narrator of Acts) temporarily broke apart, Timothy (and six others) did not travel with Paul (20:4). In the subsequent narrative, some of Timothy's traveling partners reappeared with Paul (21:29; 27:3), but Timothy did not.

Paul's Converts and Local Congregational Leaders

In addition to the people already considered in this chapter, Acts mentions fourteen people who were Paul's converts, hosts, and sympathizers—or some combination of these three. If the group of converts is narrowed to only those who are explicitly identified as converts to Paul's message in Acts,[44] then the list includes six people: the Roman proconsul on Cyprus, *Sergius Paulus* (13:7); the Philippian God-fearer and dealer in purple, *Lydia* (16:14–15); the presumably Gentile Athenians *Damaris* and *Dionysius* (17:34); the Corinthian synagogue official *Crispus* (18:8); and the nameless Philippian jailer (16:23–26). These converts represent a broad cross section of the Greco-Roman world: men and women; Jews, Gentiles, and semi-Jewish "God-fearers";[45] Roman officials, city functionaries, and artisans. Their reasons for believing were diverse. Some responded to a particularly impressive display of spiritual power on Paul's part (13:7–12; 16:23–26); others responded to Paul's public proclamation (16:13–15; 17:32–34).[46]

Several other people, most of whom were probably also Christian believers and possibly Pauline converts, are mentioned in Acts as Paul's hosts in various cities. Many of these hosts remain nameless in Acts (e.g., 21:7), but several are named, particularly those who were Pauline converts or otherwise notable for their Christian service in Acts. After her conversion, *Lydia* "prevailed" (παραβιάζομαι) upon Paul and his companions to stay in her home (16:14–15). While in Corinth, Paul stayed with Aquila and Priscilla, who would later accompany him in his travels (18:3; cf. 18:18). *Philip*, who was appointed as a deacon by Peter and the twelve in Jerusalem (6:1–7), served as Paul's host in Caesarea when Paul was on his way to Jerusalem for the last time (21:8). Upon his arrival in Jerusalem, Paul was hosted by *Mnason*, a native of Cyprus and a disciple of long-standing (21:15–16). *Jason*, one of Paul's otherwise unknown hosts, was singled out because of the violence inflicted upon him for supporting Paul's ministry. In Thessalonica, Jason was placed

---

[44] Gaventa's classic study of conversion in Acts noted that the mass conversions and lengthy narratives of individual conversions are concentrated in the opening chapters of Acts (*From Darkness to Light*, esp. 96–129). Although her study therefore gives scant attention to the brief notices of conversions which are discussed in this chapter, it provides a helpful introduction to the concern for conversion in Acts.

[45] On the plausibility of Paul targeting God-fearers for conversion, see Crossan and Reed, *In Search of Paul*, 34–41.

[46] On preaching (words) and miracles (spiritual displays) as the two instruments of evangelism in early Christianity, see Ramsay MacMullen, "Two Types of Conversion to Early Christianity," *Vigiliae christianae* 37 (1983): 174–92.

in custody and had his home attacked by a mob because he had "entertained them [Paul's entourage] as guests" (17:5–9). Though most—or perhaps all—of Paul's hosts were Christian believers, not all of them are specifically identified as Christian believers.[47] *Titius Justus* was a God-fearer, but not necessarily a Christian believer, when he hosted Paul in Corinth (18:7). Likewise, *Publius* was a "leading man" on the island of Malta, but probably not a Christian believer, when he hosted Paul. The islanders on Malta, including Publius, respected Paul, particularly for his miraculous powers, and they gave his entourage "many honors," but Acts records no conversions on Malta (28:7–9).

Finally, a few people are portrayed in Acts as generally sympathetic to Paul's message, but not necessarily as followers of his message. Two people in particular are mentioned, both for the unusual circumstances of their interactions with Paul. First, *Sosthenes*, a synagogue official in Corinth, was publicly beaten, both because a mob disapproved of his Pauline sympathies and because Gallio, the proconsul of Achaia, failed to protect him (18:17). Second, *Eutychus* fell asleep during a long-winded sermon by Paul and fell out a window to his death. Fortunately for him, Paul responded to Eutychus's fatal lapse of attention by bringing him back to life—a memorable episode that preserved Eutychus's name in Acts and probably took on metaphorical significance for subsequent readers (20:9–12).[48]

Apollos

Apollos is an unusual character in Acts; he is the only character in Acts who has no direct interaction with the original twelve apostles, the seven deacons, or Paul. Apollos interacted with Paul's colleagues Priscilla and Aquila. Paul interacted with Apollos's ideas (18:24–19:7). But Paul and Apollos never interacted face-to-face in Acts. On both occasions, Apollos's teaching stood in need of correction. In Apollos's earlier appearance, his teaching was corrected—or at least completed—by Priscilla and Aquila in person (18:24–28). In the second and final story related to Apollos, his teaching was corrected by Paul in Apollos's absence. Acts records that Apollos went to Corinth after his encounter with Priscilla and Aquila and that while Apollos was in Corinth, Paul encountered a group of Apollos's converts in Ephesus (19:1). Paul learned that this group was ignorant about the Spirit and knew only

---

[47] On the importance of hospitality in the New Testament, see John Koenig, *New Testament Hospitality: Partnership with Strangers as Promise and Mission* (OBT 17; Philadelphia: Fortress, 1985); and on hospitality in early Christianity more broadly considered, see Amy G. Oden, *And You Welcomed Me: A Sourcebook on Hospitality in Early Christianity* (Nashville: Abingdon, 2001). On the topic of hospitality in Acts, see Andrew E. Arterbury, "The Ancient Custom of Hospitality, the Greek Novels, and Acts," *PRS* 29 (2002): 53–72.

[48] On Eutychus as a metaphor for those who fall asleep morally and cease to hear the word of God, see Andrew Arterbury, "The Downfall of Eutychus," in Phillips, *Contemporary Studies in Acts*, 201–21.

about the baptism of John, ignorance consistent with Apollos's theological error in the previous scene (19:2–3; cf. 18:25). When Paul "laid his hands on them," Apollos's converts received the Spirit (19:6). Although Paul did not directly interact with Apollos in Acts, on the basis of these two back-to-back scenes involving Apollos, one could easily infer that Acts portrays Apollos as a recognized but inadequately informed teacher and authority within the church—a teacher who needed further instruction from the Pauline school.[49]

Summary of the Data Set from Acts

Paul interacts with several lesser authority figures in Acts, including prophets, emissaries, and traveling preachers. Acts presumes that all of these people were Paul's subordinates or perhaps peers in terms of status. Many are mentioned only briefly, but six have substantial interaction with Paul. Of these six, all but one were Jewish—and this one, Timothy, was circumcised so that he could travel with Paul. Of these six, all but one were male—but this lone female, Priscilla, was able to provide doctrinal instruction to a distinguished male preacher. Paul experienced open conflict with one of these six persons in Acts, John Mark, and probably experienced less open conflict with two others, Silas and Timothy. Although it is only an inference, the likely source of the tensions between Paul and these three people was the issue of Gentile inclusion in the church. Both Paul and his most trusted subordinates, Priscilla and Aquila, came into conflict with—and explicitly sought to correct— the teachings of Apollos. Paul also interacted with several other Christians and sympathizers, who functioned as converts, hosts, and emissaries. These persons represented a broad cross section of Greco-Roman society, but none of these figures played a particularly prominent role in Paul's larger ministry.

III. Comparing the Data Sets

Having surveyed the data sets in both Acts and Paul's letters, we are now in a position to compare those data sets. However, before comparing the details of Paul's interactions with the other named Christians in Acts and Paul's letters, we should remind the reader of the three interrelated tendencies discussed in the previous chapter:

---

[49] In an influential essay, Ernst Käsemann argued that the Apollos stories in Acts should be read as a rebuke of the cult of John the Baptist. See his "The Disciples of John the Baptist in Ephesus," in *Essays on New Testament Themes* (trans. W. J. Montague; Philadelphia: Fortress, 1964), 136–48; also see C. K. Barrett, "Apollos and the Twelve Disciples of Ephesus," in *The New Testament Age* (ed. William Weinrich; Macon: Mercer University Press, 1984), 29–40. While these stories certainly do criticize teachings which find their completion in John's baptism, they also criticize Apollos by implication. After all, Apollos is the only person to find the culmination of his message in John's baptism. Elsewhere in Acts, John the Baptist is mentioned without denigration (1:22; 10:37; 11:16). Cf. Johnson, *Acts*, 335.

the tendency for leadership functions and theological authority to be more concentrated and less diversified in Acts than in Paul's letters;

the tendency for Paul to portray his gospel, particularly his message of a law-free inclusion of Gentiles into the church, as more independent than does Acts; and

the tendency for relations between Paul and the other recognized authorities of early Christianity to be more contentious and uneven in Paul's letters than in Acts.

Since the present chapter examines the same issues as the previous chapter (the locations and occasions of the individual's interactions with Paul; the individual's role within the Pauline churches; and the character of the individual's relationship with Paul himself) in relation to similar data sets, these tendencies will figure as prominently in this chapter as they did in the previous chapter.

Converts and Emissaries

Seven names, all masculine, appear in both Paul's letters and Acts as participants in the Pauline mission.[50] It is difficult to draw any firm conclusions about the identities of the persons behind the names because the texts provide so little information; there is no assurance that the overlap in names reflects more than the coincidence of two people having the same name. Two of the names, *Crispus* (Acts 18:8; 1 Cor 1:14) and *Sosthenes* (Acts 18:17; 1 Cor 1:1), appear in both Act's list of Paul's converts in Corinth and the Corinthian correspondence. Two other names, *Aristarchus* (Acts 19:29; 20:4; 27:4; Phlm 24) and *Gaius* (Acts 19:29; 20:4; Rom 16:23; 1 Cor 1:14), appear on the list of emissaries whom Acts reports to have traveled with Paul to Jerusalem and as persons who offer greetings in Paul's letters. One name, *Lucius*, appears among the prophets who sent Barnabas and Paul as emissaries from Antioch and among those who sent their greetings to the Romans through Paul's letter (Acts 13:1; Rom 16:21). The last two names, *Jason* (Rom 16:21; Acts 17:5–9) and *Erastus* (Rom 16:23; 1 Cor 1:14; Acts 19:22), appear in Paul's lengthy exchange of greetings in Rom 16 and briefly in the narrative of Acts (when Jason hosted Paul and his entourage in Thessalonica and when Erastus served as a junior partner to, and emissary with, Timothy).[51]

---

[50] In addition to the people listed in this discussion, one could possibly add Sopater (Acts 20:4) and Sosipater (Rom 16:21), whom some interpreters identify as the same person (e.g., Bruce, *Pauline Circle*, 45, 98).

[51] Although these two men share the name "Erastus," their common identity is not certain. The person in Acts is active in Asia and Macedonia, while the person in Romans is firmly located in Corinth. Still, they are likely to be the same person (see Theissen, *Social Setting*, 76). In any case, it is unlikely that either person should be identified with the person named as a benefactor in the archeological remains in Corinth (Henry J. Cadbury, "Erastus of Corinth," *JBL* 50 [1931]: 42–58).

The limited size of the data sets prohibits any detailed comparisons of the identities behind the names, but the identities behind the names in Acts and Paul's letters likely overlap in five or six of the seven cases. Three of the seven people, Crispus, Sosthenes, and Gaius, are associated with the same city (Corinth) in both Acts and Paul's letters. In all three cases, the men's locations, positive roles within the Pauline churches, and their supportive relationships with Paul correspond in both Acts and Paul's letters. Two of the four remaining people, Erastus and Aristarchus, appear as traveling emissaries in Acts and as those who offer greetings to the readers of Paul's letters. As traveling emissaries, they could have been widely known among the early Christian communities, and so the question of their locations is not particularly germane. However, both men appear to possess some authority (or at least status) within Paul's churches and to have supportive relationships with Paul in both Paul's letters and Acts. The identities behind the last two names, Jason and Lucius, may refer to different people in Acts and Paul's letters. The Jason in Acts was a believer in Thessalonica, while the Jason of Paul's letters offered greetings to the Romans, from Corinth. Of course, Jason could have relocated from Thessalonica in Macedonia to Corinth in nearby Greece (perhaps in response to the persecution he had experienced in Thessalonica; Acts 17:5–9), but the problem of location makes a firm equation between these two men impossible. Still, both "Jasons" have an apparently supportive relationship with Paul, even though nothing can be inferred about the authority of either man. The Lucius in Acts is a prophet in Antioch (13:1), while the Lucius in Paul's letters is not clearly associated with any particular location, although he was probably known in Rome where the letter was being sent and in Corinth where the letter probably originated (Rom 16:21). As was the case with Jason, the locations of Lucius do not seem to coincide in Acts and Paul's letters, but his relationship to Paul and to Paul's congregations is similar even though Acts probably assumes a more stationary "prophet" than do Paul's letters.

When the admittedly limited data sets regarding these seven men are compared, there is striking correspondence between the data sets. In five of the seven cases, the data sets are easily reconciled; in the sixth and seventh cases, the data sets are not irreconcilable, but identification of the persons with the shared name in Acts and in Paul's letters is not assured.

The Prominent Associates of Paul

The data sets of the people in Acts and Paul's letters who had direct interaction with Paul but who were not mentioned in connection with the Jerusalem Conference does not greatly overlap. Only five people—four men and one woman—stand out as prominent associates of Paul in both Acts and Paul's letters: John Mark, Silvanus/Silas, Aquila, Prisc(ill)a, and Timothy. *John Mark* makes a single appearance in Paul's letters. On the surface, this lone appearance is consistent with Paul's low estimation of Mark's performance in Acts. After more sustained consideration, however, the appearance of John

Mark in Philemon (v. 24) raises questions about the occasion of the contact between Paul and John Mark. On the one hand, Paul claimed to write Philemon as an "old man" and as a prisoner (v. 9). On the other hand, Acts placed Paul and Mark together only in the earliest stages of Paul's ministry (12:12, 25; 13:5, 13), while Paul was still young and well before he spent any time in prison. If the Mark of Paul's letters is the same Mark as the Mark of Acts, then the pair must have reconciled after the separation Mark caused between Paul and Barnabas early in Paul's career (Acts 15:37–39). Of course, it is also possible that the Mark of Acts and the Mark of Paul's letters are different individuals, but if they are the same individual then the *occasion* of their interaction does not coincide very well.[52]

Silvanus appears twice in Paul's letters and several times in Acts as *Silas.* Despite the difference between the Latin form of the name (Silvanus) in Paul's letters and the Greek form of the name (Silas) in Acts, the same person undoubtedly stands behind both names (the NIV even translates "Silvanus" as "Silas" in 1 Thess 1:1; 2 Cor 1:19).[53] Silvanus served as Paul's co-sender of 1 Thessalonians (1:1) and as Paul's traveling partner in Thessalonica and beyond (2:1–3:10). In the Corinthian correspondence, Silvanus is mentioned as a participant in Paul's ministry in Corinth (2 Cor 1:19). When this data set is compared with the larger data set in Acts, the *locations and occasions* correspond very well. Acts records Silas as active in both Thessalonica (17:1–9) and Corinth (18:5–11). Earlier we noted the likelihood that Acts probably indicated Silas's silent withdrawal from Paul's Gentile mission during Paul's ministry in Corinth. Even this strategic withdrawal of support for the Pauline mission is consistent with the absence of references to Silvanus in Philippians, Galatians, and Romans. Although Acts records Silas being active with Paul in both Philippi (where Silas was even temporarily taken into custody with Paul; 16:11–40) and Galatia (16:6), it would not have served Paul well to mention Silas in the letters to these communities. In both Philippians and Galatians, Paul strongly castigated those who sought to impose the law on his Gentile converts (Gal 5:2–12; Phil 3:2–11), an imposition that Silas may well have advocated by the time Paul penned these letters if—as Acts may imply—Silas had become disenchanted with Paul's Gentile mission after he and Paul visited these communities. In Romans, Paul proclaimed the same law-free Gentile inclusion as in Galatians and Philippians, and he therefore had no reason to mention anyone (like Silvanus) who dissented from that message. In any of these three letters, a reference to a defector like Silas could only work against Paul's interest. Thus, the locations and occasions of Silas's interactions with Paul—and of Silas's absences from Paul—correspond very closely in Acts and Paul's letters.

---

[52] Black finds the images of Mark in Acts and the Pauline letters irreconcilable and argues that the temptation to blend them should be "resisted" (*Mark*, 66–67).

[53] On the common identity of Silas/Silvanus, see John Gillman, "Silas," *ABD* 6:23; and Bruce, *Pauline Circle*, 23.

The *role Silas played within the Pauline churches* is also similar in both Acts and Paul's letters. First Thessalonians, which is almost certainly one of Paul's earliest letters, portrays Silvanus as Paul's contemporary co-worker— and perhaps co-apostle (1:1; 2:7). Second Corinthians, which Paul wrote later, mentions Silvanus as one of the original missionaries to Corinth, but not necessarily as a contemporary associate of Paul (1:19). In both cases, Silvanus is portrayed as senior to Timothy through the use of the formula "Silvanus and Timothy" (2 Cor 1:19; 1 Thess 1:1). This portrayal of Silvanus as senior to Timothy in Paul's missionary entourage is consistent with the parallel formula of "Silas and Timothy" in Acts (17:14, 15; 18:5). According to both Acts and Paul's letters, Silas/Silvanus was a senior member of Paul's missionary team; he worked in conjunction with Timothy as Timothy's superior in Asia Minor, Macedonia, and Greece; and Silas played no role in the final stages of Paul's ministry, perhaps over his dissatisfaction with Paul's preaching directly to Gentiles with no restrictions based on the law.

In both Acts and Paul's letters, *the personal relationship between Paul and Silas* is mutually supportive in all of the explicit references to the pair. However, both Acts and Paul's letters leave open the possibility that Paul and Silas eventually parted ways over the Gentile mission. Neither Acts nor Paul's letters explicitly record such a break, but the strategic silences allow for that inference. Still, Paul never expressed direct disappointment—or even condemnation—of Silas as he did with Peter, James, and Barnabas (Gal 2:11–14). In both data sets, Silas was a loyal, but disappearing, associate of Paul. He was clearly subordinate to Paul in Paul's letters, and less clearly subordinate in Acts.

The pair of *Aquila and Priscilla/Prisca* includes the only female who was a prominent associate of Paul in both Acts and Paul's letters. The names Aquila and Prisc(ill)a always appear together in Acts and Paul's letters. Although Paul refers to the female member of the pair as Prisca, and Acts refers to her as Priscilla, the common identity of the couple in Paul's letters and Acts is firmly established.[54] Prisc(ill)a and Aquila have accurately been described as "movers and shakers in Pauline circles."[55] Acts depicts the couple as having lived in Pontus in Asia Minor and in Rome and as being active in the Pauline churches in Ephesus and Corinth (18:1–21, 24–28). Paul's letters (assuming the Ephesian origin of 1 Corinthians; 16:8) depict the couple as active in the churches in Ephesus and Rome (Rom 16:3; 1 Cor 16:19). Paul's conveyance of their greetings to the Corinthians would also suggest that the couple was known to the Christians in Corinth (1 Cor 16:19). Thus, both Acts and

---

[54] There are several textual variants associated with the couple's appearances in both Acts and Paul's letters, but these variants demonstrate no clear patterns and, perhaps surprisingly, no distinguishable tendency to diminish the prominence of Priscilla/Prisca. See Dominka A. Kurek-Chomycz, "Is There an 'Anti-Priscan' Tendency in the Manuscripts? Some Textual Problems with Prisca and Aquila," *JBL* 125 (2006): 107–28.

[55] Osiek, MacDonald, and Tulloch, *Woman's Place*, 32.

Paul's letters locate Priscilla and Aquila as active or at least known among the churches across the northeast Mediterranean—Rome in Italy, Corinth in Greece, and Ephesus in Asia Minor. As Osiek, MacDonald, and Tulloch concluded: "With respect to geographical *locations* and movements of the couple from place to place, scholars have had little difficulty in harmonizing the material in Acts with what is known from Paul's letters."[56] Because the Pauline references to the couple appear only in the exchange of greetings, it is not possible to definitively establish the original *occasions* of the relationships behind the greetings.

Although the greetings in Paul's letters provide few details about *the role of Prisca and Aquila within the Pauline churches*, they do reveal three significant facts about the couple. The couple sponsored a church in their home (1 Cor 16:19); the couple were co-workers with Paul (Rom 16:3); and Prisca was probably more renowned as a Christian worker than was her husband. Prisca's prominence over Aquila within the Pauline mission is demonstrated by the different order of the names in Paul's references. When speaking of their home, Paul listed Aquila first; when speaking of their ministry, Paul mentioned Prisca first. As Paul's co-workers, the couple—or at least Prisca—was respected within the Pauline churches, and probably possessed some authority. This letters-derived image of the couple as respected Pauline co-workers fits well within the larger data set in Acts. Acts even coincides with Paul's letters in the surprising characterization of Priscilla as a more prominent Pauline associate than her husband Aquila.[57] In Acts, as in Paul's letters, Aquila's name appears first when the text discussed the couple's home and property (18:1–3), but Priscilla's name appears first when the couple is engaged in missionary travels with Paul (18:18) and in Christian instruction (18:26).[58] Although the couple possessed the authority to correct the teachings of Apollos in Acts (18:26) and Paul thought it wise to include their greetings to the Corinthian church (1 Cor 16:19), the couple never rose to the level of co-sender of any

---

[56] Ibid., 30, emphasis added. William O. Walker extends this compatibility to the point of arguing that the depiction of Priscilla and Aquila in Acts is derived from the material in Paul's letters ("The Portrayal of Aquila and Priscilla in Acts: The Question of Sources," *NTS* 54 [2008]: 479–95).

[57] Priscilla's prominence in Acts is particularly significant in light of the tendency of Acts to ignore the other women who are depicted as Paul's co-workers in the letters (e.g., Junia, Phoebe, Syntyche, Euodia, Mary, Chloe).

[58] Bruce has argued that Priscilla's name sometimes appeared before Aquila's name because Priscilla may have come from a higher social class than Aquila (*Pauline Circle*, 44–46). However, the prominence of Aquila's name in reference to the couple's home and vocation is important evidence against Bruce's claim. If Priscilla was from a higher social class than Aquila, Aquila undoubtedly would have moved into Priscilla's home and her name would be listed first as the home's original owner. The unavoidable conclusion is that Paul's letters and Acts mentioned Prisc(ill)a first when discussing the couple's ministry simply because she was the more prominent minister—an historical fact that not even the post-Pauline church's gender bias against women could suppress.

Pauline letter. *The couple's personal relationship with Paul* is mutually supportive in both Acts and Paul's letters, though Paul's role as their mentor is clearer in the larger data set of Acts.

Unlike the data sets for the rest of Paul's associates (except Titus, who was discussed in the previous chapter), the data set for *Timothy* is significantly smaller within Acts than it is within Paul's letters. Consequently, this comparison will begin with the smaller data set from Acts. In Acts, Paul first encountered Timothy in Lystra (in Asia Minor); then Timothy was Paul's companion throughout much of Asia Minor (including Phrygia and Galatia) and Macedonia (including Philippi and Thessalonica) before separating from Paul in Beroea (still in Macedonia, 16:1–17:14). Timothy later rejoined Paul in Corinth in Greece after Paul had traveled to Athens alone (17:16–18:5). Acts does not record how long Paul and Timothy were together in Corinth, but Acts seems to imply that Paul left Corinth without Timothy (18:18). However, Acts also implies that Paul and Timothy remained in contact, because Paul later dispatched Timothy and Erastus to Macedonia from Ephesus (19:22). The final location of Timothy's interaction with Paul was again Macedonia, where he, Paul, and several others prepared for a trip to Jerusalem (20:4), a trip that Timothy presumably made with Paul, though Acts never again mentions Timothy. According to Acts, therefore, the *locations* of Timothy's interactions with Paul were throughout Asia Minor, Macedonia, Greece, and possibly Judea. The *occasions* of Timothy's interactions with Paul were during Paul's initial missionary activities in Macedonia and Greece (16:1–17:15), during two of Paul's return trips to Ephesus and Troas in Asia Minor (18:5; 19:22), and during the preparation for, and the early stages of, Paul's final visit to Jerusalem (19:22; 20:4).

Timothy's role within the Pauline churches is not particularly prominent in Acts. Most of Timothy's appearances with Paul occur in the company of Silas, who was apparently Timothy's more prominent mentor; when the pair are mentioned together, Silas's name routinely appears before Timothy's. Timothy served as Paul's emissary only once in Acts, and then only in the company of an associate (19:22). Timothy's travels with Paul's entourage during Paul's final trip to Jerusalem were his only travel experiences with Paul in Silas's absence, so Timothy's role within this large group is ambiguous. When the group separated between land travelers and sea travelers, Timothy was not among Paul's fellow sea voyagers. On the basis of this separation, one could plausibly infer either that Timothy was entrusted with leading the landlocked delegation to its intended reunion with Paul in Troas or that Timothy lacked the prominence to be included in Paul's personal entourage. In either case, Timothy lacks many of the key markers of authority in Acts: Timothy never speaks. Unlike Barnabas and Silas, Timothy never even shares credit for the words that Paul speaks. Additionally, Timothy never makes a decision in Acts—not even regarding his own circumcision. Also, unlike Barnabas and Silas, Timothy is never persecuted with Paul. Again in contrast to Barnabas and Silas, Timothy never traveled alone with Paul in Acts. The Timothy of

Acts did serve as a Pauline emissary, but only once. Paul sent Timothy and Erastus from Ephesus to Macedonia, but the primary purpose of this visit was not for Timothy to preach, but rather for Timothy to prepare for Paul's impending visit to Macedonia (19:21–22). Timothy and his companion, the minor-league Erastus, who appeared nowhere else in Acts, are depicted in Acts as little more than Paul's personal servants, as "two of those who ministered to him [Paul]" (δύο τῶν διακονούντων αὐτῷ, 19:22 NASB). Timothy's role as an emissary seems more preparatory (like an ancient advance man) than authoritative (like a fellow missionary).

Timothy's personal relationship with Paul is likewise diminished in Acts. Paul first encountered Timothy while Paul and Silas were disseminating the decisions made at the Jerusalem Conference. Acts reports that Timothy already had a positive reputation among the believers and that Paul wanted Timothy to join his entourage (16:1–2). Yet, in spite of both Paul's initial interest in Timothy and Timothy's willingness to undergo adult circumcision as a concession to the Jewish sensitivities in the area, Paul's subsequent relationship with Timothy was never really close in Acts. Timothy's circumcision at Paul's hand implies the inception of a mentoring relationship, but Timothy's invisibility at the subsequent stops on Paul's itinerary argues against any mentoring relationship between Paul and Timothy. In fact, Timothy's frequent appearances with Silas (17:14, 15; 18:5) give the impression that Timothy was being mentored more by Silas than by Paul. Timothy spent more time together with Silas in Acts than with Paul, and, perhaps most tellingly, Timothy disappeared from Paul's side in Corinth at the same time that Silas disappeared. Timothy's two reappearances in Acts still do not portray a particularly close relationship between him and Paul. In fact, Timothy did not even travel with Paul between Corinth and Troas (19:22; 20:4). In light of such considerations, it seems that Timothy may have begun a mentoring relationship with Paul in Acts, but Timothy quickly adopted Silas rather than Paul as his primary mentor.

The relationship between Paul and Timothy is not depicted as hostile in Acts, but the newly circumcised Timothy may well have shared Silas's disdain for Paul's law-free inclusion of the Gentiles. It is probably significant that Timothy apparently withdrew from Paul's entourage when Paul left the synagogue with such harsh words in Corinth (18:6–7) and that Timothy reappeared in Paul's company only as Paul was planning his trip to Jerusalem to repair the damaged relations between him and the Jerusalem church.

This data set from Acts can be placed within the data set from Paul's letter, but the fit is awkward at several points—perhaps exceedingly awkward at a few points. Because Timothy is mentioned in six of the seven undisputed letters of Paul, the *locations* of Timothy's interactions with Paul in Acts are easily placed within the large data set of locations in Paul's letters. Paul's letters clearly demonstrate that Timothy was known in Philippi (Phil 1:1; 2:19–24), Thessalonica (1 Thess 1:1; 3:1–6), Corinth (1 Cor 4:17; 16:10; 2 Cor 1:1, 19), Rome (Rom 16:21), and probably various parts of Asia Minor (Phlm 1;

1 Cor 4:17; 16:10). Again, because the data set in Paul's letters is so large, the data set of the *occasions* of Paul's and Timothy's interactions in Acts is also easily placed within the data set from Paul's letters. Paul's letters indicate that Timothy was active with Paul and Silvanus/Silas in founding the Corinthian church (Acts 18:5; 2 Cor 1:19) and that Timothy continued to serve as an emissary between Paul and the Macedonian churches in Philippi and Thessalonica (Acts 19:22; Phil 1:1; 2:19–24; 1 Thess 1:1; 3:1–6).

The only significant surprise in terms of locations and occasions is Paul's failure to mention Timothy in his Letter to the Galatians. Acts implies that Timothy was with Paul when Paul's entourage passed through Galatia (16:6), so it stands to reason that the Galatians knew Timothy. Timothy's unexpected absence in Galatians—the only undisputed Pauline letter that does not mention Timothy—is particularly significant in light of Acts' claim that Paul circumcised Timothy (16:3). In Galatians, Paul insisted that his other trusted associate, Titus, was allowed to remain uncircumcised (2:3). Even more importantly, Paul insisted: "Listen! I, Paul, am telling you that if you let yourselves be circumcised, Christ will be of no benefit to you" (5:2). Paul's circumcision of Timothy in Acts is very difficult to reconcile with these words.[59] The occasion of Paul's circumcision of Timothy in Acts is an awkward fit within the data set from the letters.

The awkwardness of fit between the data sets becomes even more pronounced when one considers *Timothy's role within the Pauline churches.* Timothy was much more active both quantitatively and qualitatively on Paul's behalf in the letters-derived data set than in the Acts-derived data set, and this difference appears to be due to more than the difference in size between the two data sets. In Acts, Timothy's role is diminished in terms of presence and authority—he possesses no apparent authority and exerts no clear influence. He appears primarily as a silent companion of Silas, and secondarily as a very

---

[59] Some scholars have suggested that Timothy and Titus were in fact the same person and that Acts has revised Paul's account in Galatians and made Paul practice exactly what he forbids in Galatians; that is, the Paul of Acts allowed—but did not *compel* (ἀναγκάζω, Gal 2:3)—Timothy/Titus to be circumcised (e.g., Richard G. Fellows, "Was Titus Timothy?" *JSNT* 81 [2001]: 33–58; and William O. Walker, "The Timothy-Titus Problem Reconsidered," *ExpTim* 92 [1981]: 231–35). Other scholars argue that Timothy and Titus were different people and that Paul circumcised Timothy but not Titus. Such interpretations often appeal to Acts' claim that Timothy's mother was Jewish and to 1 Cor 9:19–23 as Paul's justification for circumcising Timothy. According to such arguments, Paul was probably acting in defiance of his typical practice when he circumcised Timothy, but he was merely behaving as a Jew among the Jews in order to save some (e.g., Witherington, *Acts*, 472–77). It remains unclear whether or not Paul would have compromised on the question of circumcision (even though Galatians does not reveal the slightest spirit of compromise), but the issues of Timothy's Jewish mother and of his presumed Jewish identity through maternal descent are complicated by the fact that the notion of maternal Jewish descent was probably a later development within Judaism (Shaye J. D. Cohen, "Was Timothy Jewish (Acts 16:1–3)? Patristic Exegesis, Rabbinic Law, and Matrilineal Descent," *JBL* 105 [1986]: 251–68; cf. Christopher Bryan, "A Further Look at Acts 16:1–3," *JBL* 107 [1988]: 292–94).

junior personal assistant to Paul. Acts also implies that Timothy's primary allegiances were to the Jerusalem church and its objective of preserving a Jewish identity for the church. In keeping with this pro-Jerusalem pattern of practice, the Timothy of Acts allowed himself to be circumcised; he left the Pauline mission (along with Silas, his Jerusalem-oriented mentor) when Paul left the synagogue in Corinth; and he rejoined the Pauline mission only when Paul began to pursue a strategy for returning to Jerusalem and mending his ruptured relations with the Jerusalem leaders.

This image of Timothy as Silas's closest associate in Acts betrays a significantly different emphasis in Acts than in Paul's letters. In Paul's letters, Timothy is the most trusted guardian—and the most decisive interpreter—of Paul's ideas. According to Paul's letters, Timothy spoke both *with Paul* when they were together and *for Paul* when they were apart (1 Cor 4:17; 16:10; 2 Cor 1:19; 1 Thess 3:1–5). Timothy was uniquely trusted by the Paul of the letters (Phil 2:19–24) and was even responsible for co-sending four of Paul's letters (Phlm 1; Phil 1:1; 1 Thess 1:1; 2 Cor 1:1). While Timothy's role within the Pauline churches is not entirely irreconcilable in Acts and Paul's letters, the role assigned to Timothy in Acts is greatly diminished in comparison with his role in Paul's letters. Although it is not impossible to place the data set from Acts within the much larger data set from the letters, the overall impression conveyed by each data set diverges significantly.

The data sets likewise diverge regarding *Timothy's personal relationship with Paul.* In Acts, Timothy was mentored by Silas and was treated as a junior assistant to Paul. In Paul's letters, Timothy was Paul's "son" (1 Cor 4:17; Phil 2:22). Acts gives the impression of a Timothy with loyalties closer to Silas and the Jerusalem leadership than to Paul. Paul's letters leave no room to infer tensions between Paul and Timothy or Timothy's closeness to—and perhaps preference for—Silas.

In both Acts and Paul's letters, *Apollos* is known to Paul and at least some of Paul's churches.[60] Neither source implies that Apollos and Paul had extensive personal contact, but the *locations* of their influence do overlap. Paul's letters record that Apollos had visited Corinth and established a network of followers there before moving on to some other undefined location (1 Cor 1:12; 3:4–6, 12; 4:6; 16:12). In Acts, Apollos was active in Ephesus and had established a network of followers there before moving on to Corinth (18:24–19:7). Therefore, Acts and Paul's letters both record the presence and influence of Apollos in Corinth, but only Acts clearly indicates Apollos's presence in Ephesus. Still, nothing in Paul's letters precludes the possibility of

---

[60] In one very important early manuscript of Acts, Sinaiticus, and in several other less significant manuscripts, this person's name is "Apelles," while Paul consistently uses "Apollos." However, given the overlap in the activities of this person, there is little doubt that both authors are referring to the same person (see G. D. Kilpatrick, "Apollos-Apelles," *JBL* 89 [1970]: 77). The one occurrence of "Apelles" in Paul's letters, a person whom Paul greeted in Rom 16:10, is presumably not the same person as "Apollos" (see Peter Lampe, "Apelles," *ABD* 1:275).

Apollos having been active in Ephesus (perhaps even when Paul wrote 1 Corinthians from there; see 1 Cor 16:8, 12). These locations are easily reconcilable if one allows for the probability that their divergences and omissions are coincidences resulting from the limitations of our data. The *occasions* of Paul's and Apollos's respective visits to Corinth are also easily reconciled in Acts and Paul's letters. According to Acts, Apollos visited Corinth after Paul did (18:19–21; 18:24–19:7), an itinerary that coincides well with Paul's implied order to their respective visits to Corinth (1 Cor 3:6).

Apollos's role within the Pauline churches is similar, but not identical, in Acts and Paul's letters. In Acts, Apollos's followers in Ephesus stood in need of Paul's instruction to complete and correct their immature and misguided faith (19:1–7). In Paul's letters, Apollos's followers in Corinth were engaged in community divisions Paul sought to quell (1 Cor 1–3). In both cases—albeit in different cities—Apollos is recognized as an authority in the Pauline churches, but an authority whose teachings are not identical to Paul's. In Paul's letters, the differences between the teachings of Paul and Apollos were regarded as less significant in Paul's eyes than was the disunity the followers of Paul and Apollos (and Peter) allowed to develop on account of those differences. In Acts, Apollos's teachings are regarded as incomplete and in need of correction by Paul's associates (18:24–28) and by Paul himself (19:1–7). The content of Apollos's teaching is, therefore, more directly criticized in Acts.

In spite of Apollos's troublesome role within the Pauline churches, neither Acts nor Paul's letters record any obvious conflict in the *personal relations between Paul and Apollos.* Interestingly, neither data set explicitly states that Paul and Apollos ever met face to face. In Acts, Paul's associates, Priscilla and Aquila, interacted with Apollos in person in Ephesus (18:24–28), but Paul interacted only with Apollos's lingering influence there—after Apollos had left Asia Minor for Corinth (19:1–7). In Paul's letters, his converts in Corinth had personally encountered Apollos and his teaching, but it is unclear that Paul had done so (Paul's interaction with Apollos as recorded in 1 Corinthians may well have taken place through third parties or letters; see 1 Cor 16:12). In his letters, Paul expressed no personal dismay with Apollos and never explicitly blamed Apollos for the discord at Corinth. Paul even granted Apollos credit with having watered the seed of the gospel that Paul had planted (1 Cor 3:4–6). Perhaps most importantly, Paul even urged Apollos to return to Corinth (16:12), an invitation that, though rejected by Apollos, demonstrated Paul's continued confidence in Apollos's ministry. With no personal interaction recorded between Paul and Apollos in Acts, one cannot reasonably infer the presence of ill-will from the narrative silence. According to Acts, Paul served as a mentor at a distance to Apollos, both through the intermediary role of Priscilla and Aquila in instructing Apollos and through Paul's own role in instructing the followers of Apollos in Ephesus.

Two pieces of data, Apollos's rejection of Paul's request in Paul's letters and Paul's mentorship at a distance in Acts, are particularly significant. Although both Acts and Paul's letters imply a mutually supportive relationship between Paul and Apollos, the relationship in the letters is probably more of a relationship between equals (Apollos can refuse a Pauline request), and the relationship in Acts is probably more of a relationship between the mentor Paul and his subordinate Apollos. Again, the two data sets are not irreconcilable, but their emphases do diverge.

Thus, a comparison of Paul's relationships to other Christians as inferred from the data sets in Acts and in Paul's letters reveals that the data sets are often quite compatible, but also are sometimes quite divergent—like the other data sets considered in this volume. The sizeable gaps and omissions within each data set notwithstanding, the data sets often lend themselves to divergent interpretations. However, the data sets do not diverge beyond all possible interpretive reconciliation. Some interpreters will wish to reconcile the data sets by interpreting each set only in light of the other set. Other interpreters will find it difficult—or even unwise—to reconcile the divergences between the data sets.

CONCLUSION

IN THE introduction to this volume, I predicted that many equally skilled and perceptive readers would come to very different conclusions after reading my comparisons of the Paul of Acts and the Paul of the letters. Although I suspect that some readers have already reached some quite firm conclusions of their own about the relationship between the two Pauls, I also suspect that many—perhaps most—readers will agree with the distinguished Pauline scholar Leander Keck, who suggested that "the Paul who emerges from the letters and Acts is a richly diverse figure, about whom no easy conclusions can be reached concerning his historical shape or theological legacy."[1] In spite of my own assent to the essential truth of Keck's observation, the time has come for me to filter the brackish waters of Pauline studies and offer my own tentative conclusions about the relationship between the Paul of Acts and the Paul of the letters.

Because I have provided summaries at the end of each chapter, I will not reiterate the specific findings of the previous chapters. Rather, I wish to return to the twofold project I laid out for this volume in the introduction: *1) to help my readers both to understand and perhaps establish for themselves the lines of demarcation between the Paul of Acts and the Paul of the letters* and *2) to compare the Pauls who reside on each side of these lines of demarcation*. In the introduction, I warned that it is not easy either to discern the degree to which the Paul of Acts and the Paul of the letters are the same character or to discern the degree to which they are two clearly distinguishable characters. In the subsequent chapters, I tried to bring discipline to the comparison first by independently examining the data sets in Acts and the data sets in Paul's letters and then by comparing those two independent data sets to one another with the ultimate goal of determining if the smaller data set (from Paul's letters) could be comfortably placed within the larger data set (from Acts). In some cases (e.g., Paul's visits to Macedonia and Paul's vocation), I found that the smaller set from Paul's letters can be comfortably placed within the larger data from Acts. In other cases (e.g., Paul's visits to Jerusalem and Paul's relationship with James), I found that the two data sets cannot be *easily* reconciled. (Although some scholars continue to argue that the data sets

---

[1] Keck, "Images of Paul," 341.

can be reconciled, few scholars would argue that the reconciliation of these data sets is *easily* achieved.)

Throughout this volume, I tried to focus very closely upon the raw data in Acts and Paul's letters. Since my primary goal has been to acquaint my readers with the primary data sets from Acts and Paul's letters in order to facilitate the readers' comparison of the Paul of Acts and the Paul of the letters, I avoided, as much as possible, offering or consciously relying upon large theoretical constructs for orientation. Instead, I tried to provide a sense of the scholarly considerations that were relevant to the data sets and their comparison, without offering original solutions to the long-familiar problems associated with reconstructing Paul's life. However, I did emphasize both the scholarly trend toward separating the Paul of Acts from the Paul of the letters and also the importance of one's interpretation of the frequency and purpose of Paul's visits to Jerusalem. In keeping with both of these emphases in the third chapter, I mildly endorsed a Pauline chronology that equated Paul's visit to Jerusalem in Gal 2 with his visit to Jerusalem in Acts 15 (describing both as the "Jerusalem Conference"). As I explained in that chapter, that endorsement is shared by most—but by no means all—New Testament scholars. When I endorsed that majority opinion of scholarship, I did not explore the full implications of that decision in any detail. In these final pages, I now wish to briefly consider the major implications of that interpretive decision to equate Paul's Jerusalem visit in Galatians with his Jerusalem visit in Acts 15.

Documents like Acts and Paul's letters have many purposes (uses for which their authors created them) and effects (uses to which their readers put them). Biblical scholars in the late twentieth and early twenty-first centuries have hotly debated where the normative value of the Christian Scriptures should be found, whether in their purposes, in their effects, or both.[2] While I don't wish to enter into that debate here, I do want to consider some possible purposes and effects of Acts and Paul's letters. I will offer my considerations in three stages. First, I will explain why I regard one's interpretation of Gal 2 and Acts 15 as *the pivotal issue* for interpreting the relationship between the Paul of Acts and the Paul of the letters. Second, I will also explore what I regard as *the most important effect* of critical scholarship's tendency to interpret Gal 2 and Acts 15 as referring to the same event. That effect is to create a Paul of the letters who needs to be rehabilitated by Acts. Third, I will offer some tentative reflections about what I believe could have been *some Lukan purposes* behind the depiction of Paul in Acts.

First, let me explain why I regard one's interpretation of Acts 15 and Gal 2 to be the central issue for relating the Paul of the letters to the Paul of Acts. As discussed at length in the third chapter of this volume, and intermittently throughout, Paul provided an extended retrospective on his interaction with

---

[2]See my article, "Reading Theory and Biblical Interpretation for Postmodern Wesleyans," *Wesleyan Theological Journal* 35, no. 2 (Fall 2000): 32–48; repr. in *Acts in Diverse Frames of Reference* (Macon: Mercer University Press, forthcoming).

the Jerusalem apostles only in Gal 1–2, where Paul recounted two visits to Jerusalem. Yet, Acts recorded five Pauline visits to Jerusalem. As also explained earlier, the interpretive problem is not primarily a matter of reconciling the number of Paul's visits to Jerusalem in each source, but rather is a matter of deciding whether Paul's second visit to Jerusalem in Galatians (2:1–10) corresponds to his third visit to Jerusalem in Acts (15:1–29).

Of course, many interpreters regard Gal 2 and Acts 15 as a key test case for determining the historical accuracy of Acts, but the implications of this question are much broader than a simple determination regarding the historical reliability or unreliability of Acts. If Gal 2 and Acts 15 are not referring to the same event (i.e., the Jerusalem Conference), then the events Paul narrated in Gal 2 presumably occurred during Paul's second visit to Jerusalem in Acts (11:29–30; 12:24–25). If this is the case, then the implications are profound. In this scenario, which situates the writing of Galatians before the conference, the confrontation between Peter and Paul (Gal 2:11–14) would probably have occurred between Paul's second and third visits to Jerusalem in Acts, and Galatians would probably have been written in the time frame between Acts 11 and Acts 15. Acts 15 would then be read as an account of the reconciliation between Peter and Paul after the disagreement recorded in Galatians (2:11–14). Consequently, the contentious relationship between Peter and Paul in Galatians becomes an anomaly within their relationship and not the beginning of a decisive break between the two.

This implied reconciliation between Peter and Paul has important implications for one's larger understanding of Paul's place within early Christianity. To begin with, this scenario implies a Paul who was *more accepted* by the Jerusalem church than is commonly assumed in critical scholarship. This reconciled Paul becomes a Paul who is embraced by the Jerusalem church and whose conflicts with the Jerusalem church over Gentile inclusion were ultimately resolved to everyone's satisfaction in Paul's lifetime. Additionally, this scenario also implies a Paul who was *more accepting* of the Jerusalem church than is commonly assumed in critical scholarship. This reconciled Paul becomes a Paul who was willing to accept at least minimal legal restrictions upon the Gentiles as a condition for their inclusion within the church (Acts 15:19–20, 28–29; 21:25). *This reconciled Paul is a Paul who leans in the direction of Acts,* and Galatians comes to be regarded as arising from Paul's momentary outrage and not from the core of his central and abiding theological convictions.

Although much could be said in defense of this reconciled Paul, let me now reiterate—for the plausible reasons discussed earlier—that the majority of scholarly interpreters have rejected this reconciled Paul and instead have equated the events in Gal 2 and Acts 15. Consequently, most scholars date Paul's composition of Galatians after the events discussed in Acts 15.[3] *The*

---

[3] Admittedly, most of these scholars regard the legal restrictions in Acts 15:19–20, 28–29 and 21:25 as Lukan inventions which Paul would never have accepted. See, e.g., Fitzmyer, *Acts,* 552–53.

effect of this scholarly trend has been to envisage a Paul of the letters who leans away from Acts. With a Paul of the letters who leans in this direction, Galatians comes to be regarded as a reflection of the central and abiding core of Paul's theological convictions.

The predominance of this trend to envisage an "historical Paul"—a Paul of the letters alone—who leans away from the Paul of Acts can be illustrated by two contrasting quotations that I. Howard Marshall offered decades ago to summarize the state of then contemporary scholarship concerning the Paul of the letters and the Paul of Acts:

> "Yes, he [the Paul of Acts] is the real Paul, seen in retrospect through the eyes of a friend and admirer." (F. F. Bruce)[4]

> "The problem of the Lucan Paul in its briefest form is that the Paul of the Epistles is a different Paul." (Robert Brawley)[5]

Although these assessments are diametrically opposed, it is worth noting that Bruce's quote came from the conclusion to his article, while the quote from Brawley came from the introduction to his article. A generation ago, Brawley could already assume that the Paul of the letters and the Paul of Acts were incongruous figures and he could proceed from that assumption; Bruce was on the defensive and was impelled to prove what could not be assumed—the congruity between the Paul of the letters and the Paul of Acts.[6]

The current state of critical scholarship is much the same: those who wish to defend the congruity between the Paul of Acts and the Paul of the letters are in the minority and on the defensive. As Stanley Porter recently observed, many scholars presume "what appears to be several of the assured results of scholarship—that the book of Acts is anything but primarily a historical document, and that its depiction of Paul is at odds with that of the Pauline letters."[7] Porter, who, like Marshall, rejects the validity of these presuppositions, nevertheless acknowledges that these presuppositions may reflect "the consensus of modern scholarship."[8] This is not to say that "the history of research has made it abundantly clear that the attempt to harmonize the historical Paul with the Paul of Luke-Acts has come to a radical end," as Beker believes.[9] Dissenting voices—even strong and eloquent dissenting

---

[4]F. F. Bruce, "Is the Paul of Acts the Real Paul?" *BJRL* 58 (1976): 305, quoted in I. Howard Marshall, "Luke's View of Paul," *SJT* 33 (1990): 41.

[5]Robert L. Brawley, "Paul in Acts: Lucan Apology and Conciliation," in Talbert, *Luke-Acts: New Perspectives*, 129, quoted in Marshall, "Luke's View of Paul," 41.

[6]It is probably noteworthy that even the contemporary practice of separating the disputed Pauline letters from considerations of Paul's life and relationships (as I have done) no doubt heightens the disparity between the Paul of Acts and the Paul of the (undisputed) letters.

[7]Porter, *Paul in Acts*, 188.

[8]Ibid., 189.

[9]See J. Christiaan Beker, "Luke's Paul as the Legacy of Paul," in *SBL Seminar Papers, 1993* (ed. Eugene H. Lovering Jr.; SBLSP 32; Atlanta: Society of Biblical Litera-

voices—continue to offer cogent appeals for serious reconsideration of the scholarly consensus. Still, as an advocate like Beker and a detractor like Porter have both noted, the consensus of scholarship assumes both that the struggles between Paul and the Jerusalem church did not end with the Jerusalem Conference (as Acts implies) and that interpreters can be seriously misled if they rely upon Acts to bolster their readings of Paul's letters.

Second, I want to reflect upon what I perceive to be the primary effect of this consensus on New Testament scholarship, as the second stage of my consideration. *I contend that the primary effect of critical scholarship's strong tendency to separate the Paul of Acts from the Paul of the letters has been to create an "historical Paul" (the Paul of the letters) who needed to be rehabilitated by Acts if he was to be accepted in the post-Pauline churches.*

If, as most scholars believe, Galatians was written after the Jerusalem Conference, it follows that the relationship between the Jerusalem leadership and the "historical Paul" climaxed disastrously shortly after the Jerusalem Conference in the hostile confrontation between Peter and Paul in Antioch (Gal 2:11–14). In the consensus view, Paul fired off the hostile Letter to the Galatians in the wake of that confrontation because he believed that Peter had violated the agreements reached at the Jerusalem Conference (Acts 15; Gal 2:1–10). This Paul never reconciled with Peter and the Jerusalem leadership, and he subsequently came into frequent conflict with these leaders over the ongoing significance of the law for Gentiles. Yet, even this Paul of consensus scholarship continued to desire the approval of the Jerusalem leadership for his churches; he even sought that approval through an offering for Jerusalem (1 Cor 16:1–3; 2 Cor 8–9; Gal 2:10; Rom 15:25–28). When viewed through the eyes of the consensus Paul, this offering, Paul's final attempt at reconciliation with the Jerusalem leadership, had only meager hopes for success (Rom 15:30–31). As commonly conceived, this Paul was right to suspect trouble in Jerusalem, and his hostile reception there brought about his eventual death in Rome.

Of course, scholars add various nuances to this basic story, but this narrative—Jerusalem Conference, conflict with Peter in Antioch, much missionary activity with intermittent conflict with the Jerusalem leadership, and finally an unsuccessful visit to Jerusalem for the offering—summarizes the "facts" of the life of the "historical Paul" of the letters and understood by the scholarly consensus.

If this narrative is accepted, its effect is to create an historical Paul whose legacy would have desperately needed rehabilitation in the post-Pauline churches of the late first century, particularly in the eastern empire. The Paul of consensus scholarship is a Paul who would have had no enduring legacy in the eastern empire. In Arabia, he was a failure; in Jerusalem, he was rejected

---

ture, 1993), 511–19, quoting 511. Beker further speculated that any lingering attempts to reconcile the Paul of Acts with the Paul of the letters were motivated by theological concerns for the unity of the canon and not by honest historical analysis.

by James; in Antioch, he fought with Peter; and, most importantly of all, in Asia Minor, he was known only through the combative letter to the Galatians and the theologically innocuous letter to Philemon. This Paul would have had every reason to be ignored, or even distrusted, everywhere east of the Aegean Sea. When viewed from the perspective of those in this eastern part of the empire, the consensus Paul would have been known almost exclusively for his confrontation with the Jerusalem church—a view reinforced by Paul's own words in Galatians.

In the consensus view, Paul clearly would have needed some rehabilitation if he were to be accepted in the east—as even he seemed to understand. As he was going back to Jerusalem, as it were with his tail between his legs, and with his churches' reluctant bribe in his hands, he would have been forced to admit to the Romans that there was nowhere left for him to preach in the eastern Mediterranean (Rom 15:23). This Paul hoped that his churches' offering to Jerusalem would repair his damaged relations with the Jerusalem church. Ominously, however, none of the churches in Asia Minor had chosen to participate in the offering; Paul could report only that the churches from Achaia (Greece) and Macedonia had participated in his offering (Rom 15:26). Some contend that the Galatians had abandoned Paul and his offering (Gal 2:10); perhaps they had simply not found Paul's letter compelling, and they sided with Paul's opponents in Galatia.

This brings us to the third point of my considerations. *Could the rehabilitation of Paul have been one of Luke's major purposes for writing Acts?* Critical scholars are increasingly coming to argue that one of the major purposes of Acts was the rehabilitation of Paul for its late first- or early second-century readers.[10]

According to the consensus viewpoint in critical Acts scholarship, the historical Paul, as reflected in the letters, had become increasingly unpopular in the east toward the end of his life and had died before establishing a new presence in Spain in the west (as he had planned). Paul's only pocket of loyal followers were along the western coast of the Aegean in Philippi, Thessalonica, and Corinth—and even these followers were becoming infested with Petrine influences during Paul's lifetime (1 Cor 1–4; Phil 3). After Paul's death, one can only imagine that the influence of Peter had grown. Given this scenario, the purpose for the book of Acts was to take a disreputable Paul and rehabilitate him for subsequent generations. The author of Acts would have inherited a Paul who was a pretender to apostleship, a would-be leader of the Gentile church who was rejected and rebuked by virtually all of the key leaders of early Christianity—James, Peter, Barnabas, and Silas—and by all of the key

---

[10]Prominent recent examples of this trend include Joseph B. Tyson, *Marcion and Luke-Acts: A Defining Struggle* (Columbia: University of South Carolina Press, 2006); "Wrestling with and for Paul," in Phillips, *Contemporary Studies in Acts,* 13–28; and Richard I. Pervo, *Dating Acts; Acts: A Commentary;* and "Acts in the Suburbs of the Apologists," in Phillips, *Contemporary Studies in Acts,* 29–46.

Christian communities in the eastern empire—Jerusalem, Antioch, Ephesus, and probably Rome in the west. This Paul refused to make any concessions regarding Gentiles in the manner of Peter and James.[11] This Paul would have had only two relatively young followers and associates, the Gentile Titus and the near-Gentile Timothy—neither of whom ever walked and talked with the historical Jesus as did Peter and James.

The author of Acts sought to rehabilitate a Paul who was a social embarrassment. In a world characterized by hierarchy and *pater familias*, this Paul had not only made overly grandiose claims about his own authority, but had also allowed far too many unqualified—or at least suspect—people lead congregations. This inherited Paul of the letters was even willing to recognize Gentiles like Titus and females like Junia as apostles—to say nothing of his recommendation of Phoebe the female deacon. This Paul was completely undistinguished both politically and intellectually by the standards of the eastern empire. He was often reduced to accepting—and sometimes even seeking—money from his former converts and from relative strangers.

According to the contemporary scholarly consensus, the author of Acts wrote his book in large measure to rehabilitate the Paul of the letters. Socially, the author of Acts gave Paul a more impressive pedigree, granting him citizenship in both Rome and Tarsus, placing him at the feet of the famed Gamaliel, and making him both an accomplished rhetorician and a devotee of philosophy and poetry. The author of Acts even boosted Paul's financial status and enabled him to practice generosity toward those in need. Even more importantly, the author of Acts rehabilitated Paul's place in the church by placing him firmly under the authority of the Jerusalem church, especially Peter and James. The author of Acts gave his Paul a much closer relationship to the Jerusalem church than the historical Paul had experienced. This rehabilitated Paul of Acts visited Jerusalem more often than the Paul of the letters had and never came into conflict with any of the leaders of the Jerusalem church. This rehabilitated Paul recognized James's authority to interpret the Old Testament law for the Gentile church and gladly announced the decisions that James handed down—things the historical Paul would never have done!

This rehabilitated Paul of Acts not only subjected himself to the Jerusalem authorities, but he even made sure that his associates did so as well. According to Acts, the ever-loyal Timothy of Paul's letters was subjected to circumcision by Paul's hand, even though the Paul of the letters had warned that Christ would be of "no benefit" to Gentiles who accepted circumcision (Gal 5:2). Even so, the rehabilitated Paul of Acts saw Timothy's loyalty shift from Paul to the more Jerusalem-oriented Silas. As for the Gentile apostle Titus, he

---

[11] Paul's view of the law and the various other views of the law in early Christianity are more complex than suggested here. However, few scholars would deny that the early church divided its task of evangelism into two missions, one focused on Jews and another focused on Gentiles. For a helpful taxonomy of how various groups viewed these two missions and their relationships to one another, see Painter, *Just James*, 73–78.

simply dropped out of the story of the rehabilitated Paul of Acts. Barnabas remained in the story, but as Paul's senior colleague—perhaps as the one who justified Paul's own inclusion among the apostles (Acts 14:14). In spite of Barnabas's apostolic status, the Paul of Acts still managed to disagree with him, but only over John Mark's reliability and not over Barnabas's alleged hypocrisy. The message of this rehabilitated Paul of Acts meshed so perfectly with the message of the Jerusalem apostles that the Paul of Acts never came into conflict with any major figure within early Christianity except Apollos. Even his disagreement with Apollos was not threatening to Paul's reputation because Apollos was never reported to have had any contact with the Jerusalem church and its leaders. The Paul of Acts could correct Apollos because Apollos was even further from the Jerusalem church's tutelage and influence than was Paul. Indeed, even a woman like Priscilla could correct Apollos.

To summarize, the timing and significance of the Jerusalem Conference is the defining issue for evaluating the relationship between the Paul of Acts and the Paul of the letters. According to the consensus of contemporary critical scholarship, this conference occurred before the composition of Galatians and, therefore, its significance was immense, for it represented the last point at which Paul and the Jerusalem church existed in relative harmony. Shortly after the conference, Paul came to believe that Peter had betrayed the agreements made at the conference—and indeed that Peter had betrayed the very gospel itself. Thus the majority of scholars draw a sharp distinction between the historical Paul—the Paul of the letters—and the Paul of Acts, who was constructed to rehabilitate Paul's damaged image for the post-Pauline churches.

Our close examination of the data sets of the Pauline letters and the book of Acts has served to substantiate the belief of the majority of scholars that the portraits of Paul contained in the two data sets are distinct—and somewhat incongruous—characters. Thus I must concur with the conclusion that the Paul of Acts is indeed a rehabilitated version of the Paul of the letters, a Paul who was recast in terms more attractive to the church of the late first or early second century.

BIBLIOGRAPHY

Aageson, James W. *Paul, the Pastoral Epistles, and the Early Church.* LPS. Peabody, Mass.: Hendrickson, 2008.

Aasgaard, Reidar. *'My Beloved Brothers and Sisters!' Christian Siblingship in Paul.* JSNTSup 265. New York: T&T Clark, 2004.

———. "Paul as a Child: Children and Childhood in the Letters of the Apostle." *JBL* 126 (2007): 129–59.

Achtemeier, Paul J. "An Elusive Unity: Paul, Acts, and the Early Church." *CBQ* 48 (1986): 1–26.

———. *The Quest for Unity in the New Testament Church: A Study in Paul and Acts.* Philadelphia: Fortress, 1987.

Agosto, Efrain. "Patronage and Commendations, Imperial and Anti-Imperial." Pages 103–23 in *Paul and Roman Imperial Order.* Edited by Richard A. Horsley. Harrisburg: Trinity Press International, 2004.

Allison, Dale C. "Peter and Cephas: One and the Same." *JBL* 111 (1992): 489–95.

Alvarez, David. "Pablo, ¿Un Ciudadano Romano?" *Estudio Agustiniano* 33 (1998): 455–86.

Anderson, R. Dean. *Ancient Rhetorical Theory and Paul.* Rev. ed. CBET 18. Leuven: Peeters, 1999.

Arterbury, Andrew E. "The Ancient Custom of Hospitality, the Greek Novels, and Acts." *PRS* 29 (2002): 53–72.

———. "The Downfall of Eutychus." Pages 201–21 in *Contemporary Studies in Acts.* Edited by Thomas E. Phillips. Macon: Mercer University Press, 2009.

Ascough, Richard S. *Paul's Macedonian Associations: The Social Context of Philippians and 1 Thessalonians.* WUNT 161. Tübingen: Mohr Siebeck, 2003.

———. "The Thessalonian Christian Community as a Professional Voluntary Association." *JBL* 119 (2000): 311–28.

Ashton, J. "Why Did Paul Persecute 'the Church of God'?" *Scripture Bulletin* 38 (2008): 61–68.

Aune, David E. "'Magic' in Early Christianity and Its Ancient Mediterranean Context: A Survey of Some Recent Scholarship." *Annali di storia dell'esegesi* 24 (2007): 229–94.

Ayalon, A., M. Bar-Matthews, and Y. Goren. "Authenticity Examination of the Inscription on the Ossuary Attributed to James, Brother of Jesus." *Journal of Archaeological Science* 31 (2004): 1185–89.

Bacon, Benjamin W. "Acts versus Galatians: The Crux of Apostolic History." *AJT* 11 (1907): 454–74.

———. "Peter's Triumph at Antioch." *JR* 9 (1929): 204–23.

Balch, David L. "The Areopagus Speech: An Appeal to the Stoic Historian Posidonius against Later Stoics and the Epicureans." Pages 52–79 in *Greeks, Romans and Christians.* Edited by David L. Balch, Everrett Ferguson and Wayne A. Meeks. Minneapolis: Fortress, 1990.

———. "Paul, Families, and Households." Pages 258–92 in *Paul in the Greco-Roman World.* Edited by J. Paul Sampley. Harrisburg: Trinity Press International, 2003.

Bammel, Ernest. "Jewish Activity against Christians in Palestine according to Acts." Pages 357–64 in *The Book of Acts in Its Palestinian Setting.* Edited by Richard Bauckham. BAFCS 4. Grand Rapids: Eerdmans, 1995.

Barclay, John M. G. "Paul among Diaspora Jews." *JSNT* 60 (1995): 89–120.

———. "Paul's Story: Theology as Testimony." Pages 133–56 in *Narrative Dynamics in Paul.* Edited by Bruce W. Longenecker. Louisville: Westminster John Knox, 2002.

Barnett, Paul. *The Second Epistle to the Corinthians.* NICNT. Grand Rapids: Eerdmans, 1997.

Barrett, C. K. *The Acts of the Apostles.* 2 vols. ICC. Edinburgh: T&T Clark, 1994–1998.

———. "Apollos and the Twelve Disciples of Ephesus." Pages 29–40 in *The New Testament Age.* Edited by William Weinrich. Macon: Mercer University Press, 1984.

———. *A Commentary on the First Epistle to the Corinthians.* Harper's New Testament Commentaries. San Francisco: Harper & Row, 1968.

———. *Luke the Historian in Recent Study.* London: Epworth, 1961.

Bassler, Jouette M. *God and Mammon: Asking for Money in the New Testament.* Nashville: Abingdon, 1991.

Bauckham, Richard J. "Barnabas in Galatians." *JSNT* 2 (1979): 61–70.

———. "James and the Gentiles (Acts 15.13–21)." Pages 154–84 in *History, Literature, and Society in the Book of Acts.* Edited by Ben Witherington. Cambridge: Cambridge University Press, 1996.

———. "Kerygmatic Summaries in the Speeches of Acts." Pages 185–217 in *History, Literature, and Society in the Book of Acts.* Edited by Ben Witherington. Cambridge: Cambridge University Press, 1996.

Baum, Armin D. "Paulinismen in den Missionsreden des lukanischen Paulus: Zur inhaltlichen Authentizität der *oratio recta* in der Apostelgeschichte." *ETL* 82 (2006): 405–36.

Baur, Ferdinand Christian. *Paul, the Apostle of Jesus: His Life and Work, His Epistles and His Doctrines: A Contribution to the Critical History of Primitive Christianity.* 2 vols. London: Williams & Norgate, 1873. Repr., Peabody, Mass.: Hendrickson, 2003. Translation of Paulus, der Apostel Jesu Christi: Sein Leben und Wirken, seine Briefe und seine Lehre.

Ein Beitrag zu einer kritischen Geschichte des Urchristenthums. 2 vols. Stuttgart: Becher & Müller, 1845.

Bechard, Dean Philip. *Paul Outside the Walls: A Study of Luke's Socio-Geographical Universalism in Acts 14:8–20.* Rome: Pontifical Biblical Institute, 2000.

Becker, Jürgen. *Paul: Apostle to the Gentiles.* Louisville: Westminster John Knox, 1993.

Beecher, Willis J. "Paul's Visits to Jerusalem." *BW* 2 (1893): 434–43.

Beker, J. Christiaan. *Heirs of Paul.* Minneapolis: Fortress, 1991.

———. "Luke's Paul as the Legacy of Paul." Pages 511–19 in the *SBL Seminar Papers,* 1993. Edited by Eugene H. Lovering Jr. SBLSP 32. Atlanta: Society of Biblical Literature, 1993.

———. *Paul the Apostle: The Triumph of God in Life and Thought.* (Philadelphia: Fortress, 1980), 207. Quoted in Neil Elliot, "The Anti-Imperial Message of the Cross," in *Paul and Empire* (ed. Richard A. Horsley; Harrisburg: Trinity Press International, 1997), 167.

———. "Paul the Theologian: Major Motifs in Pauline Theology." *Int* 43 (1989): 352–65.

Belkin, Samuel. "The Problem of Paul's Background." *JBL* 54 (1935): 41–60.

Belleville, Linda. "'Ιουνιὰν . . . ἐπίσημοι ἐν τοῖς ἀποστόλοις: A Re-examination of Romans 16:7 in Light of Primary Source Materials." *NTS* 51 (2005): 231–49.

Bercovitz, J. Peter. "Paul and Thessalonica." Proceedings of the Eastern Great Lakes and Midwest Biblical Societies 10 (1990): 123–35.

———. "Two Letters Chronologies." PEGLBS 9 (1989): 178–94.

Bernheim, Pierre-Antoine. *James, Brother of Jesus.* Translated by John Bowden. London: SCM, 1997.

Best, Ernest. *The First and Second Epistles to the Thessalonians.* BNTC. London: A & C Black, 1972.

———. "Paul's Apostolic Authority—?" *JSNT* 27 (1986): 3–25.

Betz, Hans Dieter. *2 Corinthians 8 and 9.* Edited by George W. MacRae. Hermeneia. Philadelphia: Fortress, 1985.

———. *Galatians: A Commentary on Paul's Letter to the Churches in Galatia.* Hermeneia. Minneapolis: Fortress, 1979.

Bird, Michael F. and Preston M. Sprinkle. "Jewish Interpretation of Paul in the Last Thirty Years." *CBR* 6 (2008): 35–76.

Black, C. Clifton. *Mark: Images of an Apostolic Interpreter.* Studies on Personalities of the New Testament. Columbia: University of South Carolina Press, 1994.

Blaiklock, E. M. "The Acts of the Apostles as a Document of First Century History." Pages 41–54 in *Apostolic History and the Gospel: Biblical and Historical Essays Presented to F. F. Bruce.* Edited by W. Ward Gasque and Ralph P. Martin. Exeter: Paternoster, 1970.

Blumenfeld, Bruno. *The Political Paul: Justice, Democracy and Kingship in a Hellenistic Framework.* JSNTSup 210. Sheffield: Sheffield Academic Press, 2001.

Bockmuehl, Markus. "Antioch and James the Just." Pages 155–98 in *James the Just and Christian Origins.* Edited by Bruce Chilton and Craig A. Evans. NovTSup 98. Boston: Brill, 1999.

Bokser, Baruch M. "Unleavened Bread and Passover, Feasts of." Pages 755–65 in vol. 4 of *ABD.* Edited by D. N. Freedman. 6 vols. New York: Doubleday, 1992.

Bonner, Stanley F. *Education in Ancient Rome: From the Elder Cato to the Younger Pliny.* London: Methuen, 1977.

Booth, A. D. "The Schooling of Slaves in First-Century Rome." *TAPA* 109 (1979): 11–19.

Bowen, Clayton R. "Paul's Collection and the Book of Acts." *JBL* 42 (1923): 49–58.

Brawley, Robert L. "Paul in Acts: Aspects of Structure and Characterization." Pages 90–105 in the *SBL Seminar Papers, 1988.* Edited by David J. Lull. SBLSP 27. Atlanta: Society of Biblical Literature, 1988.

———. "Paul in Acts: Lucan Apology and Conciliation." In *Luke-Acts: New Perspectives from the Society of Biblical Literature Seminar,* 129. Edited by Charles H. Talbert. New York: Crossroad, 1984. Quoted in I. Howard Marshall, "Luke's View of Paul," *SJT* 33 (1990): 41.

Breytenbach, Cilliers. *Paulus und Barnabas in der Provinz Galatien: Studien zu Apostelgeschichte 13f.; 16,6; 18,23 und den Adressaten des Galaterbriefes.* AGJU 38. New York: Brill, 1996.

Brown, Raymond E. *An Introduction to the New Testament.* New York: Doubleday, 1997.

Bruce, F. F. "The Acts of the Apostles: Historical Record or Theological Reconstruction?" *ANRW* 25.3:2570–2603. Part 2, *Principat,* 25.3. Edited by H. Temporini and W. Haase. New York: de Gruyter, 1984.

———. *The Acts of the Apostles: The Greek Text with Introduction and Commentary.* 3d ed. Grand Rapids: Eerdmans, 1990.

———. *The Book of Acts.* Rev. ed. NICNT. Grand Rapids: Eerdmans, 1988.

———. "Chronological Questions in the Acts of the Apostles." *BJRL* 68 (1986): 273–95.

———. *Commentary on the Book of Acts: The English Text with Introduction, Exposition, and Notes.* NICNT. Grand Rapids: Eerdmans, 1954.

———. *The Epistle to the Galatians: A Commentary on the Greek Text.* New International Greek Testament Commentary. Grand Rapids: Eerdmans, 1982.

———. "Galatians Problems: 1. Autobiographical Data." *BJRL* 51 (1969): 292–309.

———. "Galatians Problems: 2. North or South Galatia?" *BJRL* 52 (1970): 243–66.

———. "Galatians Problems: 3. The 'Other Gospel.'" *BJRL* 53 (1971): 253–71.

———. "Galatians Problems: 4. The Date of the Epistle." *BJRL* 54 (1973): 250–67.

———. "Is the Paul of Acts the Real Paul?" *BJRL* 58 (1976): 305. Quoted in I. Howard Marshall, "Luke's View of Paul," *SJT* 33 (1990): 41.

————. *The New Testament Documents: Are They Reliable?* 5th ed. Downers Grove: InterVarsity, 1960.

————. *Paul: Apostle of the Heart Set Free.* Grand Rapids: Eerdmans, 1977.

————. *The Pauline Circle.* Grand Rapids: Eerdmans, 1985.

————. "The Significance of the Speeches for Interpreting Acts." *Southwestern Journal of Theology* 33 (1990): 20–28.

————. "St. Paul in Macedonia." *BJRL* 61 (1979): 337–54.

Bryan, Christopher. "A Further Look at Acts 16:1–3." *JBL* 107 (1988): 292–94.

Buck, Charles H. "The Date of Galatians." *JBL* 70 (1951): 113–22.

Bumstead, Arthur. "The Present Status of Criticism." *BW* 17 (1901): 355–60.

Burfeind, Carsten. "Paulus in Arabien." *ZNW* 95 (2004): 129–30.

Burford, Alison. *Craftsmen in Greek and Roman Society.* Ithaca: Cornell University Press, 1972.

Burke, Trevor J. *Adopted into God's Family: Exploring a Pauline Metaphor.* New Studies in Biblical Theology 22. Downers Grove: InterVarsity, 2006.

Cadbury, Henry J. *The Book of Acts in History.* New York: Harper, 1955.

————. "Erastus of Corinth." *JBL* 50 (1931): 42–58.

————. *The Making of Luke-Acts.* London: SPCK, 1927.

————. *The Making of Luke-Acts.* 2d ed. London: SPCK, 1958. Repr., Peabody, Mass.: Hendrickson, 1999.

————. "The Speeches in Acts." Pages 402–27 in vol. 5 of *The Beginnings of Christianity: Part 1. The Acts of the Apostles.* Edited by F. J. Foakes-Jackson and Kirsopp Lake. 5 vols. London: Macmillan, 1920–1933.

Cadoux, C. J. "A Tentative Synthetic Chronology of the Apostolic Age." *JBL* 56 (1937): 177–91.

Campbell, Douglas A. "An Anchor for Pauline Chronology: Paul's Flight from 'The Ethnarch of King Aretas' (2 Corinthians 11:32–33)." *JBL* 121 (2002): 279–302.

Carroll, John T. "Literary and Social Dimensions of Luke's Apology for Paul." Pages 106–18 in *SBL Seminar Papers, 1988.* Edited by David J. Lull. SBLSP 27. Atlanta: Scholars Press, 1988.

Carter, Warren. *The Roman Empire and the New Testament: An Essential Guide.* Nashville: Abingdon, 2006.

Case, Shirley Jackson. "The Jewish Bias of Paul." *JBL* 47 (1928): 20–31.

————. "Paul's Historical Relation to the First Disciples." *AJT* 11 (1907): 269–86.

Cassidy, Richard J. *Four Times Peter: Portrayals of Peter in the Four Gospels and at Philippi.* Collegeville, Minn.: Liturgical, 2007.

————. *Paul in Chains: Roman Imprisonment and the Letters of Paul.* New York: Herder & Herder, 2001.

Catchpole, David R. "Paul, James and the Apostolic Decree." *NTS* 23 (1977): 428–44.

Chen, Diane G. *God as Father in Luke-Acts.* Studies in Biblical Literature 92. New York: Peter Lang, 2006.

Chester, Stephen. "When the Old Was New: Reformation Perspectives on Galatians 2:16." *ExpTim* 119 (2008): 320–29.

Chilton, Bruce. "James, Peter, Paul, and the Formation of the Gospels." Pages 3–28 in *The Missions of James, Peter, and Paul: Tensions in Early Christianity.* Edited by Bruce Chilton and Craig A. Evans. NovTSup 115. Boston: Brill, 2005.

———. *Rabbi Paul: An Intellectual Biography.* New York: Doubleday, 2004.

Chow, John K. "Patronage in Roman Corinth." Pages 104–25 in *Paul and Empire.* Edited by Richard A. Horsley. Harrisburg: Trinity Press International, 1997.

Clark, Andrew C. *Parallel Lives: The Relation of Paul to the Apostles in the Lucan Perspective.* Paternoster Biblical and Theological Monographs. Waynesboro, Ga.: Paternoster, 2001.

———. "The Role of the Apostles." Pages 169–90 in *Witness to the Gospel: The Theology of Acts.* Edited by I. Howard Marshall and David Peterson. Grand Rapids: Eerdmans, 1998.

Clarke, Kent D. "The Problem of Pseudonymity in Biblical Literature and Its Implications for Canon Formation." Pages 440–68 in *The Canon Debate.* Edited by Lee Martin MacDonald and James A. Sanders. Peabody, Mass.: Hendrickson, 2002.

Clarke, W. K. Lowther. "The Acts of the Apostles in Recent Criticism." *Theology* 4 (1922): 69–81, 314–22.

Cohen, Shaye J. D. "Was Timothy Jewish (Acts 16:1–3)? Patristic Exegesis, Rabbinic Law, and Matrilineal Descent." *JBL* 105 (1986): 251–68.

Collange, Jean-François. *The Epistle of Saint Paul to the Philippians.* Translated by A. W. Heathcote. London: Epworth, 1979.

Conzelmann, Hans. *1 Corinthians: A Commentary on the First Epistle to the Corinthians.* Edited by George W. MacRae. Translated by James Leitch. Hermeneia. Philadelphia: Fortress, 1975.

———. *Acts of the Apostles: A Commentary on the Acts of the Apostles.* Hermeneia. Edited by Eldon Jay Epp and Christopher R. Matthews. Translated by J. Limburg, A. Thomas Krabel, and Donald H. Juel. Hermeneia. Philadelphia: Fortress, 1987.

———. *Gentiles—Jews—Christians: Polemics and Apologetics in the Greco-Roman Era.* Translated by M. Eugene Boring. Minneapolis: Fortress, 1992.

———. "Luke's Place in the Development of Earliest Christianity." Pages 298–316 in *Studies in Luke-Acts.* Edited by J. Louis Martyn and Leander E. Keck. Nashville: Abingdon, 1966. Repr., Philadelphia: Fortress, 1980.

———. *The Theology of St. Luke.* Translated by Geoffrey Buswell. San Francisco: Harper & Row, 1960.

Corley, Bruce. "Interpreting Paul's Conversion—Then and Now." Pages 1–17 in *The Road from Damascus: The Impact of Paul's Conversion on His Life, Thought, and Ministry.* Edited by Richard N. Longenecker. Grand Rapids: Eerdmans, 1997.

Cranfield, C. E. B. *A Critical and Exegetical Commentary on the Epistle to the Romans.* 2 vols. ICC 32. Edinburgh: T&T Clark, 1975–1979.

Crook, Zeba A. *Reconceptualizing Conversion: Patronage, Loyalty, and Conversion in the Religions of the Ancient Mediterranean.* BZNW 130. Berlin: de Gruyter, 2004.

Crossan, John Dominic, and Jonathan L. Reed. *In Search of Paul: How Jesus's Apostle Opposed Rome's Empire with God's Kingdom.* San Francisco: HarperSanFrancisco, 2004.

Croy, N. Clayton. "Hellenistic Philosophies and the Preaching of the Resurrection." *NovT* 39 (1996): 21–39.

———. " 'To Die is Gain' (Philippians 1:19–26): Does Paul Contemplate Suicide?" *JBL* 122 (2003): 517–31.

Culpepper, R. Alan. *John: The Son of Zebedee.* Minneapolis: Fortress, 2000.

Czachesz, István. *Commission Narratives: A Comparative Study of the Canonical and Apocryphal Acts.* Studies on Early Christian Apocrypha 8. Leuven: Peeters, 2007.

Das, A. Andrew. *Paul and the Jews.* LPS. Peabody, Mass.: Hendrickson, 2003.

Díaz Rodelas, Juan Miguel. "Pablo en Jerusalén: Los Datos de Gálatas." *Estudios bíblicos* 64 (2006): 485–95.

Dibelius, Martin. *Studies in the Acts of the Apostles.* Edited by Heinrich Greeven. Translated by Mary Ling. New York: Scribners, 1956.

Dihle, Albrecht. *Greek and Latin Literature of the Roman Empire: From Augustus to Justinian.* New York: Routledge, 1994.

Dochhorn, Jan. "Paulus und die polyglotte Schriftgelehrsamkeit seiner Zeit." *ZNW* 98 (2007): 189–212.

Donaldson, Terence L. "Israelite, Convert, Apostle to the Gentiles: The Origin of Paul's Gentile Mission." Pages 62–84 in *The Road from Damascus: The Impact of Paul's Conversion on His Life, Thought, and Ministry.* Edited by Richard N. Longenecker. Grand Rapids: Eerdmans, 1997.

———. " 'Riches for the Gentiles' (Rom 11:12): Israel's Rejection and Paul's Gentile Mission." *JBL* 112 (1993): 81–98.

Donfried, Karl P. "The Imperial Cults of Thessalonica and Political Conflict in 1 Thessalonians." Pages 215–23 in *Paul and Empire.* Edited by Richard A. Horsley. Harrisburg: Trinity Press International, 1997.

Downs, David J. "Paul's Collection and the Book of Acts Revisited." *NTS* 52 (2006): 50–70.

Duncan, George S. *The Epistle of Paul to the Galatians.* Moffatt New Testament Commentary. New York: Harper & Brothers, 1934.

Dunn, James D. G. *The Epistle to the Galatians.* BNTC 9. Hendrickson: Peabody, Mass., 1993.

———. "The Incident at Antioch (Gal 2:11–18)." Pages 199–234 in *The Galatians Debate: Contemporary Issues in Rhetorical and Historical Interpretation.* Edited by Mark D. Nanos. Peabody, Mass.: Hendrickson, 2002.

———. "The New Perspective on Paul." Pages 183–214 in *Jesus, Paul and the Law: Studies in Mark and Galatians.* Louisville: Westminster John Knox, 1990.

———. "The Relationship between Paul and Jerusalem according to Galatians 1 and 2." *NTS* 28 (1982): 461–78.

———. *Romans 9–16.* WBC 38b. Waco: Word, 1988.

———. "Who Did Paul Think He Was? A Study of Jewish Christian Identity." *NTS* 45 (1999): 174–93.

Edwards, Mark J. "Quoting Aratus: Acts 17,28." *ZNW* 83 (1992): 266–69.

Ehrman, Bart D. "Cephas and Peter." *JBL* 109 (1990): 463–74.

Eisenbaum, Pamela M. "Paul, Polemics, and the Problem of Essentialism." *Biblical Interpretation* 13 (2005): 224–38.

Elliot, Neil. "The Anti-Imperial Message of the Cross." Pages 167–83 in *Paul and Empire.* Edited by Richard A. Horsley. Harrisburg: Trinity Press International, 1997.

———. "The Apostle Paul's Self-Presentation as Anti-Imperial Performance." Pages 67–88 in *Paul and the Roman Imperial Order.* Edited by Richard A. Horsley. Harrisburg: Trinity Press International, 2004.

———. "Paul and the Politics of Empire: Problems and Prospects." Pages 17–39 in *Paul and Politics.* Edited by Richard A. Horsley. Harrisburg: Trinity Press International, 2000.

———. "Romans 13:1–7 in the Context of Propaganda." Pages 184–204 in *Paul and Empire.* Edited by Richard A. Horsley. Harrisburg: Trinity Press International, 1997.

Elsdon, Ron. "Was Paul 'Converted' or 'Called'? Questions of Methodology." *Proceedings of the Irish Biblical Association* 24 (2001): 16–48.

Enslin, Morton S. "Paul and Gamaliel." *JR* 7 (1927): 360–75.

Epp, Eldon Jay. *Junia: The First Woman Apostle.* Minneapolis: Fortress, 2005.

Evans, Craig A. *Jesus and the Ossuaries.* Waco: Baylor University Press, 2003.

Farmer, William R. "James the Lord's Brother, according to Paul." Pages 133–53 in *James the Just and Christian Origins.* Edited by Bruce Chilton and Craig A. Evans. NovTSup 98. Boston: Brill, 1999.

Fee, Gordon D. *The First Epistle to the Corinthians.* NICNT. Grand Rapids: Eerdmans, 1987.

———. "ΧΑΡΙΣ in II Corinthians I.15: Apostolic Parousia and Paul—Corinth Chronology." *NTS* 24 (1978): 533–38.

Feldman, Louis H. *Jew and Gentile in the Ancient World: Attitudes and Interactions from Alexander to Justinian.* Princeton: Princeton University Press, 1993.

Fellows, Richard G. "Was Titus Timothy?" *JSNT* 81 (2001): 33–58.

Ferguson, Everett. "Jewish and Christian Ordination." *HTR* 56 (1963): 13–19.

Fitzmyer, Joseph A. *The Acts of the Apostles.* AB 31. New York: Doubleday, 1998.

———. *Essays on the Semitic Background of the New Testament.* Missoula: Scholars Press, 1974.

———. "The Pauline Letters and the Lucan Account of Paul's Missionary Journeys." Pages 82–89 in the *SBL Seminar Papers, 1988.* Edited by David J. Lull. SBLSP 27. Atlanta: Society of Biblical Literature, 1988.

———. *Romans.* AB 33. New York: Doubleday, 1993.

Friedländer, M. "The 'Pauline' Emancipation from the Law: A Product of the Pre-Christian Jewish Diaspora." *JQR* 14 (1902): 265–302.

Friesen, Steven J. "Poverty in Pauline Studies: Beyond the So-called New Consensus." *JSNT* 26 (2004): 323–61.

Funk, Robert W. "The Apostolic Parousia: Form and Significance." Pages 249–69 in *Christian History and Interpretation: Studies Presented to John Knox.* Edited by William R. Farmer, C. F. D. Moule, and Richard R. Niebhur. Cambridge: Cambridge University Press, 1967.

———. "The Enigma of the Famine Visit." *JBL* 75 (1956): 130–36.

Furnish, Victor Paul. *II Corinthians.* AB 32A. Garden City: Doubleday, 1984.

———. "On Putting Paul in His Place." *JBL* 113 (1994): 3–17.

Garnsey, Peter. Social Status and Legal Privileges in the Roman Empire. Oxford: Clarendon, 1970.

Gasque, W. Ward. "A Fruitful Field: Recent Study of the Acts of the Apostles." *Int* 42 (1988): 117–30.

———. *A History of the Interpretation of the Acts of the Apostles.* Tübingen: J. C. B. Mohr, 1975. Repr., Peabody, Mass.: Hendrickson, 1989.

Gaventa, Beverly Roberts. *From Darkness to Light: Aspects of Conversion in the New Testament.* OBT 20. Philadelphia: Fortress, 1986.

———. "Galatians 1 and 2: Autobiography as Paradigm." *NovT* 28 (1986): 309–26.

———. "The Overthrown Enemy: Luke's Portrait of Paul." Pages 439–47 in the *SBL Seminar Papers, 1985.* Edited by Kent Harold Richards. SBLSP 24. Atlanta: Society of Biblical Literature, 1985.

Gempf, Conrad. "Luke's Story of Paul's Reception in Rome." Pages 42–65 in *Rome in the Bible and the Early Church.* Edited by Peter Oakes. Grand Rapids: Baker Academic, 2002.

———. "Public Speaking and Published Accounts." Pages 259–303 in *Acts in Its Ancient Literary Setting.* Edited by Bruce W. Winter and Andrew D. Clarke. BAFCS 1. Grand Rapids: Eerdmans, 1993.

Georgi, Dieter. "God Turned Upside Down." Pages 36–46 in *Paul and Empire.* Edited by Richard A. Horsley. Harrisburg: Trinity Press International, 1997.

———. *Remembering the Poor: The History of Paul's Collection for Jerusalem.* Nashville: Abingdon, 1965.

Gilbert, George H. "Women in Public Worship in the Churches of Paul." *BW* 2 (1893): 38–47.

Gill, David J. "Acts and Urban Élites." Pages 105–18 in *The Book of Acts in Its Graeco-Roman Setting.* Edited by David J. Gill and Conrad Gempf. BAFCS 2. Grand Rapids: Eerdmans, 1994.

Gillman, Florence M. *Women Who Knew Paul.* Zacchaeus Studies. Collegeville, Minn.: Liturgical, 1992.

Gillman, John. "Silas." Page 23 in vol. 6 of *ABD.* Edited by D. N. Freedman. 6 vols. New York: Doubleday, 1992.

Gilmour, S. MacLean. "Paul and the Primitive Church." *JR* 25 (1945): 119–28.

Given, Mark D. "The Unknown Paul: Philosophers and Sophists in Acts 17." Pages 343–51 in the *SBL Seminar Papers, 1996.* SBLSP 35. Atlanta: Scholars Press, 1996.

Glancy, Jennifer A. "Boasting of Beatings (2 Corinthians 11:23–25)." *JBL* 123 (2004): 99–135.

Glover, T. R. *Paul of Tarsus.* London: Student Christian Movement, 1925. Repr., Peabody, Mass.: Hendrickson, 2002.

Gould, Ezra P. "St. Paul and the Twelve." *JBL* 18 (1899): 184–89.

Goulder, Michael. "Silas in Thessalonica." *JSNT* 48 (1992): 87–106.

———. *St. Paul versus St. Peter: A Tale of Two Missions.* Louisville: Westminster John Knox, 1994.

———. "Vision and Knowledge." *JSNT* 56 (1994): 53–71.

Gourges, Michel. "La Literatura Profana en el Discourse de Atenas (He 17,16–31): ¿Expedient Cerrado?" *Anámnesis* 13.2 (2003): 15–45.

Grässer, Erich. *Forschungen zur Apostelgeschichte.* WUNT 137. Tübingen: Mohr Siebeck, 2001.

Green, E. "El anuncio del evangelio ante el poder imperial en Tesalónica." *Kairós* 39 (2006): 9–21.

———. "La *Pax Romana* y el día del Señor—1 Tesalonicenses 5:1–11." *Kairós* 41 (2007): 9–27.

Green, Joel B. "Festus, Porcius." Pages 94–95 in vol. 2 of *ABD*. Edited by D. N. Freedman. 6 vols. New York: Doubleday, 1992.

Griffith-Jones, Robin. *The Gospel according to Paul: The Creative Genius Who Brought Jesus to the World.* San Francisco: HarperSanFrancisco, 2004.

Guthrie, Donald. "Recent Literature on the Acts of the Apostles." *Vox evangelica* 2 (1963): 33–49.

Haacker, Klaus. "Die Gallio-Episode und die Paulinische Chronologie." *BZ* 16 (1972): 252–55.

Haenchen, Ernst. *The Acts of the Apostles: A Commentary.* Translated by R. McL. Wilson. Philadelphia: Westminster, 1971.

———. "The Book of Acts as Source Material for the History of Earliest Christianity." Pages 258–78 in *Studies in Luke-Acts.* Edited by J. Louis Martyn and Leander E. Keck. Nashville: Abingdon, 1966. Repr., Philadelphia: Fortress, 1980.

Hahn, Ferdinand. "Der gegenwärtige Stand der Erforschung der Apostelgeschichte: Kommentare und Aufsatzbände 1980–85." *Theologische Revue* 82 (1986): 117–90.

Hahn, H. C. "Work, Do, Accomplish." Pages 1147–52 in vol. 3 of *New International Dictionary of New Testament Theology.* 4 vols. Edited by Colin Brown. Grand Rapids: Zondervan, 1971.

Hamm, Dennis. "Paul's Blindness and Its Healing: Clues to Symbolic Intent (Acts 9; 22 and 26)." *Bib* 71 (1990): 63–72.

Hansack, Ernst. "'Er lebte . . . von seinem eigen Einkommen' (Apg 28,30)." *BZ* 19 (1975): 249–53.

Hanson, G. Walter. "The Preaching and Defence of Paul." Pages 295–324 in *Witness to the Gospel: The Theology of Acts.* Edited by I. Howard Marshall and David Peterson. Grand Rapids: Eerdmans, 1998.

Harding, Mark. "On the Historicity of Acts: Comparing Acts 9.23–5 with 2 Corinthians 11.32–3." *NTS* 39 (1993): 518–38.

Harland, Philip A. *Associations, Synagogues, and Congregations: Claiming a Place in Ancient Mediterranean Society.* Minneapolis: Fortress, 2003.

Harnack, Adolf von. *The Date of Acts and of the Synoptic Gospels.* Volume 4 of *New Testament Studies.* Translated by J. R. Wilkinson. Crown Theological Library 33. New York: G. P. Putnam's, 1911.

———. *Luke the Physician: The Author of the Third Gospel and the Acts of the Apostles.* Volume 1 of *New Testament Studies.* Translated by J. R. Wilkinson. Crown Theological Library 20. New York: G. P. Putnam's, 1908.

Harrer, G. A. "Saul Who Also Is Called Paul." *HTR* 33 (1940): 19–33.

Harrison, J. R. "Paul and the Imperial Gospel at Thessaloniki." *JSNT* 25 (2002): 71–96.

Hartsock, Chad. *Sight and Blindness in Luke-Acts: The Use of Physical Features in Characterization.* Biblical Interpretation 94. Boston: Brill, 2008.

Harvey, A. E. "The Opposition to Paul." Pages 321–33 in *The Galatians Debate: Contemporary Issues in Rhetorical and Historical Interpretation.* Edited by Mark D. Nanos. Peabody, Mass.: Hendrickson, 2002.

Hawthorne, Gerald F. *Philippians.* Revised and enlarged by Ralph P. Martin. WBC 43. Nashville: Thomas Nelson, 2004.

Hay, David M. "Paul's Indifference to Authority." *JBL* 88 (1969): 36–44.

Hedrick, Charles W. "Paul's Conversion/Call: A Comparative Analysis of the Three Reports in Acts." *JBL* 100 (1981): 415–32.

Heen, Erik M. "Phil 2:6–11 and Resistance to Local Timocratic Rule: *Isa theō* and the Cult of the Emperor in the East." Pages 125–53 in *Paul and the Roman Imperial Order.* Edited by Richard A. Horsley. Harrisburg: Trinity Press International, 2004.

Hemer, Colin J. "Acts and Galatians Reconsidered." *Themelios* 2 (1977): 81–88.

———. *The Book of Acts in the Setting of Hellenistic History.* Edited by Conrad H. Gempf. WUNT 49. Tübingen: Mohr Siebeck, 1989.

———. "Luke the Historian." *BJRL* 60 (1977): 28–51.

Hengel, Martin, and Anna Maria Schwemer. *Paul Between Damascus and Antioch: The Unknown Years.* Translated by John Bowden. Louisville: John Knox Westminster, 1997.

Hengel, Martin, and Roland Deines. *The Pre-Christian Paul.* Translated by John Bowen. Philadelphia: Trinity Press International, 1991.

Hester, James D. "Epideictic Rhetoric and Persona in Galatians 1 and 2." Pages 181–96 in *The Galatians Debate: Contemporary Issues in Rhetorical and Historical Interpretation.* Edited by Mark D. Nanos. Peabody, Mass.: Hendrickson, 2002.

Hilgert, Earle. "Speeches in Acts and Hellenistic Canons of Historiography and Rhetoric." Pages 83–109 in *Good News in History.* Edited by E. L. Miller. Atlanta: Scholars Press, 1993.

Hock, Ronald F. "Paul and Greco-Roman Education." Pages 198–227 in *Paul in the Greco-Roman World.* Edited by J. Paul Sampley. Harrisburg: Trinity Press International, 2003.

———. "Paul's Tentmaking and the Problem of His Social Class." *JBL* 97 (1978): 555–64.

———. *The Social Context of Paul's Ministry: Tentmaking and Apostleship.* Philadelphia: Fortress, 1980.

———. "The Workshop as a Social Setting for Paul's Missionary Preaching." *CBQ* 41 (1979): 438–50.

Hollander, Harm W. and Gijsbert E. van der Hout. "The Apostle Paul Calling Himself an Abortion: 1 Cor. 15:8 within the Context of 1 Cor. 15:8–10." *NovT* 38 (1996): 224–36.

Horn, Friedrich Wilhelm. "Paulus und der Herodianische Tempel." *NTS* 53 (2007): 184–203.

Horsley, Richard A., ed. *Paul and Empire.* Harrisburg: Trinity Press International, 1997.

———. *Paul and Politics.* Harrisburg: Trinity Press International, 2000.

———. *Paul and the Roman Imperial Order.* Harrisburg: Trinity Press International, 2004.

Horst, Pieter van der. "The Unknown God (Acts 17:23)." Pages 19–42 in *Knowledge of God in the Graeco-Roman World.* Edited by R. van den Broek, T. Baarda, and J. Mansfeld. Études préliminaires aux religions orientales dans l'Empire romain. New York: Brill, 1988.

Howard, George. "Was James an Apostle?" *NovT* 19 (1977): 63–64.

Howell, Justin R. "Embedded Letters and Rhetorical αὔξησις." Pages 154–80 in *Contemporary Studies in Acts.* Edited by Thomas E. Phillips. Macon: Mercer University Press, 2009.

Hultgren, Arland J. "Paul's Pre-Christian Persecutions of the Church: Their Purpose, Locale, and Nature." *JBL* 95 (1976): 97–111.

Hunkin, J. W. "British Work on the Acts." Pages 396–433 in vol. 2 of *The Beginnings of Christianity: Part 1. The Acts of the Apostles.* Edited by F. J. Foakes-Jackson and Kirsopp Lake. 5 vols. London: Macmillan, 1920–1933.

Hurd, John C. "Reflections Concerning Paul's 'Opponents' in Galatia." Pages 129–48 in *Paul and His Opponents.* Edited by Stanley E. Porter. Pauline Studies 2. Boston: Brill, 2005.

Hyldahl, Niels. "Historische und theologische Beobachtungen zum Galterbrief." *NTS* 46 (2000): 425–44.

Jacobs, Andrew S. "A Jew's Jew: Paul and the Early Christian Problem of Jewish Origins." *JR* 86 (2006): 258–86.

Jaquette, James L. "Paul, Epictetus, and Others on Indifference to Status." *CBQ* 56 (1994): 68–80.

Jervell, Jacob. *Die Apostelgechichte*. KEK. Göttingen: Vandenhoeck & Ruprecht, 1998.

———. *Luke and the People of God*. Minneapolis: Fortress, 1972.

———. *The Unknown Paul: Essays on Luke-Acts and Early Christian History*. Minneapolis: Augsburg, 1984.

Jewett, Robert. "The Agitators and the Galatian Congregation." Pages 334–47 in *The Galatians Debate: Contemporary Issues in Rhetorical and Historical Interpretation*. Edited by Mark D. Nanos. Peabody, Mass.: Hendrickson, 2002.

———. *A Chronology of Paul's Life*. Philadelphia: Fortress, 1979.

———. *Paul: The Apostle to America*. Louisville: Westminster John Knox, 1994.

———. "Paul, Phoebe and the Spanish Mission." Pages 142–61 in *The Social World of Formative Christianity*. Edited by Jacob Neusner and Peder Borgen. Philadelphia: Fortress, 1988.

———. "Response: Exegetical Support from Romans and Other Letters." Pages 58–71 in *Paul and Politics*. Edited by Richard A. Horsley. Harrisburg: Trinity Press International, 2000.

———. *Romans*. Hermeneia. Minneapolis: Fortress, 2007.

Johnson, Luke Timothy. *The Acts of the Apostles*. Sacra pagina 5. Collegeville, Minn.: Liturgical, 1992.

Joubert, Stephan. *Paul as Benefactor: Reciprocity, Strategy and Theological Reflection in Paul's Collection*. WUNT 124. Tübingen: Mohr Siebeck, 2000.

Kaestli, Jean-Daniel. "Luke-Acts and the Pastoral Epistles: The Thesis of a Common Authorship." Pages 110–26 in *Luke's Literary Achievement: Collected Essays*. Edited by C. M. Tuckett. JSNTSup 116. Sheffield: Sheffield Academic Press, 1995.

Karris, Robert J. *What Are They Saying about Luke and Acts?* New York: Paulist, 1979.

Käsemann, Ernst. "The Disciples of John the Baptist in Ephesus." Pages 136–48 in *Essays on New Testament Themes*. Translated by W. J. Montague. Philadelphia: Fortress, 1964.

Kaster, Robert A. "Notes on 'Primary' and 'Secondary' Schools in Late Antiquity." *TAPA* 113 (1983): 323–46.

Kauppi, Lynn Allan. *Foreign but Familiar Gods: Greco-Romans Read Religion in Acts*. LNTS 277. New York: T&T Clark, 2006.

Kaye, B. N. "Acts' Portrait of Silas." *NovT* 21 (1979): 13–27.

Keck, Leander E. "Images of Paul in the New Testament." *Int* 43 (1989): 341–51.

———. "The Quest for Paul's Pharisaism: Some Reflections." Pages 163–75 in *Justice and the Holy: Essays in Honor of Walter Harrelson*. Edited by Douglas A. Knight and Peter J. Paris. Atlanta: Scholars Press, 1989.

Keener, Craig S. *Paul, Women, and Wives: Marriage and Women's Ministry in the Letters of Paul*. Peabody, Mass.: Hendrickson, 1992.

Keith, C. "'In My Own Hand': Grapho-Literacy and the Apostle Paul." *Bib* 89 (2008): 39–58.

Ker, Donald P. "Paul and Apollos—Colleagues or Rivals?" *JSNT* 77 (2000): 75–97.

Kilgallen, John J. "Acts 17,22b–31—What Kind of Speech Is This?" *Revista Biblica* 110 (2003): 417–24.

———. "Paul's Speech to the Ephesian Elders: Its Structure." *ETL* 70 (1994): 112–21.

———. "Persecution in the Acts of the Apostles." Pages 143–60 in *Luke and Acts*. Edited by Gerald O'Collins and Matthew J. O'Connell. New York: Paulist, 1991.

Kilpatrick, G. D. "Apollos-Apelles." *JBL* 89 (1970): 77.

Klauck, Hans-Josef. *Magic and Paganism in Early Christianity: The World of the Acts of the Apostles*. Minneapolis: Fortress, 2003.

Knox, John. *Chapters in a Life of Paul*. New York: Abingdon-Cokesbury, 1950.

———. *Chapters in a Life of Paul*. Rev. ed. Revised and edited by Douglas R. A. Hare. Macon: Mercer University Press, 1987.

———. "Chapters in a Life of Paul—A Response to Robert Jewett and Gerd Lüdemann." Pages 341–64 in *Colloquy of New Testament Studies: A Time for Reappraisal and Fresh Approaches*. Edited by Bruce C. Corley. Macon: Mercer University Press, 1983.

———. "'Fourteen Years Later': A Note on the Pauline Chronology." *JR* 16 (1936): 341–49.

———. "On the Meaning of Galatians 1:15." *JBL* 106 (1987): 301–4.

———. "The Pauline Chronology." *JBL* 58 (1939): 15–29.

———. "Reflections." Pages 107–113 in *Cadbury, Knox, and Talbert: American Contributions to the Study of Acts*. Edited by Mikeal C. Parsons and Joseph B. Tyson. Atlanta: Scholars Press, 1992.

Knust, Jennifer Wright. "Paul and the Politics of Virtue and Vice." Pages 155–73 in *Paul and the Roman Imperial Order*. Edited by Richard A. Horsley. Harrisburg: Trinity Press International, 2004.

Koenig, John. *New Testament Hospitality: Partnership with Strangers as Promise and Mission*. OBT 17. Philadelphia: Fortress, 1985.

Koester, Helmut. "Imperial Ideology and Paul's Eschatology in 1 Thessalonians." Pages 158–66 in *Paul and Empire*. Edited by Richard A. Horsley. Harrisburg: Trinity Press International, 1997.

Kümmel, Werner Georg. "Current Theological Accusations Against Luke." Translated by William C. Robinson. *Andover Newton Quarterly* 16 (1975): 131–45.

Kurek-Chomycz, Dominka A. "Is There an 'Anti-Priscan' Tendency in the Manuscripts? Some Textual Problems with Prisca and Aquila." *JBL* 125 (2006): 107–28.

Lake, Kirsopp. "The Apostolic Council of Jerusalem." Pages 159–212 in vol. 5 of *The Beginnings of Christianity: Part 1. The Acts of the Apostles*. Edited by F. J. Foakes-Jackson and Kirsopp Lake. 5 vols. London: Macmillan, 1920–1933.

————. "The Chronology of Acts." Pages 445–74 in vol. 5 of *Beginnings of Christianity*.

————. "The Conversion of Paul." Pages 188–95 in vol. 5 of *Beginnings of Christianity*.

————. "Paul's Controversies." Pages 212–23 in vol. 5 of *Beginnings of Christianity*.

————. "The Unknown God." Pages 240–45 in vol. 5 of *Beginnings of Christianity*.

————. "'Your Own Poets.'" Pages 246–50 in vol. 5 of *Beginnings of Christianity*.

Lampe, Peter. "Apelles." Page 275 in vol. 1 of *ABD*. Edited by D. N. Freedman. 6 vols. New York: Doubleday, 1992.

————. *From Paul to Valentinus: Christians at Rome in the First Two Centuries*. Edited by Marshall D. Johnson. Translated by Michael Steinhauser. Minneapolis: Fortress, 2003.

Légasse, Simon. "Paul's Pre-Christian Career according to Acts." Pages 365–90 in *The Book of Acts in Its Palestinian Setting*. Edited by Richard Bauckham. BAFCS 4. Grand Rapids: Eerdmans, 1996.

Lemaire, André. "The 'James Ossuary on Trial': A Short Rejoinder." *BAIAS* 22 (2004): 35–36.

Lentz, John Clayton. *Luke's Portrait of Paul*. SNTSMS 77. Cambridge: Cambridge University Press, 1993.

Leppä, Heikki. "Reading Galatians with and without the Book of Acts." Pages 255–63 in *The Intertextuality of the Epistles: Explorations of Theory and Practice*. Edited by Thomas L. Brodie, Dennis R. MacDonald, and Stanley E. Porter. Sheffield: Sheffield Phoenix, 2006.

Levine, Amy-Jill. Review of Hyam Maccoby, *Paul and Hellenism*. *JQR* 86 (1995): 230–32.

Levinskaya, Irina. *The Book of Acts in Its Diaspora Setting*. BAFCS 5. Grand Rapids: Eerdmans, 1996.

Lightfoot, J. B. *St. Paul's Epistle to the Galatians*. London: Macmillan, 1890. Repr. Peabody, Mass.: Hendrickson, 1995.

Litwak, Kenneth D. "Israel's Prophets Meet Athens' Philosophers: Scriptural Echoes in Acts 17,22–31." *Bib* 85 (2004): 199–216.

Lohse, Eduard. *Colossians and Philemon*. Translated by William R. Poehlmann and Robert J. Karris. Hermeneia. Philadelphia: Fortress, 1971.

Lopez, Davina C. *Apostle to the Conquered: Reimaging Paul's Mission*. Paul in Critical Contexts. Minneapolis: Fortress, 2008.

Lüdemann, Gerd. *Early Christianity according to the Traditions in Acts: A Commentary*. Translated by John Bowden. Minneapolis: Fortress, 1987.

————. *Opposition to Paul in Jewish Christianity*. Translated by M. Eugene Boring. Minneapolis: Fortress, 1989.

————. *Paul, Apostle to the Gentiles: Studies in Chronology*. Translated by F. Stanley Jones. Philadelphia: Fortress, 1984.

Lührmann, Dieter. "Paul and the Pharisaic Tradition." *JSNT* 36 (1989): 75–94.

Lundgren, Sten. "Ananias and the Calling of Paul in Acts." *Studia theologica* 25 (1971): 117–22.

Lyons, George. *Pauline Autobiography: Toward a New Understanding.* SBLDS 73. Atlanta: Scholars Press, 1985.

Maccoby, Hyam. *The Myth Maker: Paul and the Invention of Christianity.* San Francisco: Harper & Row, 1986.

———. *Paul and Hellenism.* London: SCM, 1991.

Mackay, B. S. "Further Thoughts on Philippians." *NTS* 7 (1961): 161–70.

MacMullen, Ramsay. "Two Types of Conversion to Early Christianity." *Vigiliae christianae* 37 (1983): 174–92.

Maddox, Robert. *The Purpose of Luke-Acts.* Göttingen: Vandenhoeck & Ruprecht, 1982.

Magness, Jodi. "Ossuaries and the Burials of Jesus and James." *JBL* 124 (2005): 121–54.

Malas, William H. Jr. "The Literary Structure of Acts: A Narratological Investigation of Its Arrangement, Plot and Primary Themes." PhD diss., Union Theological Seminary and Presbyterian School of Christian Education, 2001.

Malherbe, Abraham J. *Social Aspects of Early Christianity.* Baton Rouge: Louisiana State University Press, 1977.

Malina, Bruce J. *Timothy: Paul's Closest Associate.* Paul's Social Network—Brothers and Sisters in Faith. Collegeville, Minn.: Liturgical, 2008.

Malina, Bruce J., and Jerome H. Neyrey. *Portraits of Paul: An Archaeology of Ancient Personality.* Louisville: Westminster John Knox, 1996.

Manen, W. C. van "A Wave of Hypercriticism." *ExpTim* 9 (1898): 205–11, 257–59, 314–19.

Marguerat, Daniel. "Saul's Conversion (Acts 9, 22, 26) and the Multiplication of Narrative in Acts." Pages 127–55 in *Luke's Literary Achievement.* Edited by Christopher M. Tuckett. JSNTSup 116. Sheffield: Sheffield Academic Press, 1995.

———. "Wie historisch ist die Apostelgeschichte?" *ZNT* 9 (2006): 44–51.

Marrou, H. I. *A History of Education in Antiquity.* Translated by George Lamb. London: Sheed & Ward, 1956.

Marshall, I. Howard. *1 and 2 Thessalonians.* NCBC 52–53. Grand Rapids: Eerdmans, 1983.

———. "Acts in Current Study." *ExpTim* 155 (2003): 49–52.

———. *The Acts of the Apostles.* New Testament Guides. Sheffield: JSOT Press, 1992.

———. *The Acts of the Apostles: An Introduction and Commentary.* Tyndale New Testament Commentaries. Grand Rapids: Eerdmans, 1978.

———. *Luke: Historian and Theologian.* Grand Rapids: Zondervan, 1970.

———. "Recent Study of the Acts of the Apostles." *ExpTim* 80 (1969): 4–8.

Martin, Dale B. *The Corinthian Body.* New Haven: Yale University Press, 1999.

———. *Sex and the Single Savior.* Louisville: Westminster John Knox, 2006.

Martin, Ralph P. *2 Corinthians.* WBC 40. Waco: Word, 1986.

———. *Philippians.* Rev. ed. NCBC 50. Grand Rapids: Eerdmans, 1980.

Mather, Boyd. "Paul in Acts as a 'Servant' and 'Witness.'" *Biblical Research* 30 (1985): 23–44.

Mattill, A. J. "Luke as a Historian in Criticism since 1840." PhD diss., Vanderbilt University, 1959.

McCant, Jerry W. *2 Corinthians.* Readings. Sheffield: Sheffield Academic Press, 1999.

McDonough, Sean M. "Small Change: Saul to Paul, Again." *JBL* 125 (2006): 390–91.

McGiffert, A. C. "The Historical Criticism of Acts in Germany." Pages 363–95 in vol. 2 of *The Beginnings of Christianity: Part 1. The Acts of the Apostles.* Edited by F. Foakes-Jackson and Kirsopp Lake. 5 vols. London: Macmillan, 1922. Repr., Grand Rapids: Baker, 1966.

McGuire, Frank. "The Posthumous Clash Between Peter and Paul." *Journal of Higher Criticism* 9 (2002): 161–74.

McRay, John. *Paul: His Life and Teaching.* Grand Rapids: Baker Academic, 2003.

Mealand, David L. "The Close of Acts and Its Hellenistic Greek Vocabulary." *NTS* 36 (1990): 583–97.

Meeks, Wayne A. *The First Urban Christians: The Social World of the Apostle Paul.* New Haven: Yale University Press, 1983.

Meier, John P. "The Circle of the Twelve: Did It Exist during Jesus' Public Ministry?" *JBL* 116 (1997): 635–72.

Menoud, Philippe H. "The Addition to the Twelve Apostles according to the Book of Acts." Pages 133–48 in *Jesus Christ and the Faith.* Translated by Eunice M. Paul. Philadelphia: Pickwick, 1978.

Miller, John B. F. "Paul's Dream at Troas." Pages 138–53 in *Contemporary Studies in Acts.* Edited by Thomas E. Phillips. Macon: Mercer University Press, 2009.

Minnen, Peter van. "Paul the Roman Citizen." *JSNT* 56 (1994): 43–52.

Mitchell, Margaret M. "New Testament Envoys in the Context of Greco-Roman Diplomatic and Epistolary Conventions: The Example of Timothy and Titus." *JBL* 111 (1992): 641–62.

Moessner, David P. "Paul in Acts: Preacher of Eschatological Repentance to Israel." *NTS* 34 (1988): 96–104.

Moffatt, James. "Wellhausen and Harnack on the Book of Acts." *ExpTim* 19 (1908): 250–52.

Moffitt, David M. "Affirming the 'Creed': The Extent of Paul's Citation of an Early Christian Formula in 1 Cor 15,3b–7." *ZNW* 99 (2008): 33–48.

Mommsen, Theodor, "Die Rechtsverhältnisse des Apostels Paulus." *ZNW* 2 (1901): 81–96.

Montefiore, C. G. "First Impressions of Paul." *JQR* 6 (1894): 428–74.

Moody, Dale. "A New Chronology for the Life and Letters of Paul." *PRS* 3 (1976): 249–72.

Morgan, Robert. "Biblical Classics: II. F. C. Baur: Paul." *ExpTim* 90 (1978): 4–10.

Murphy-O'Connor, Jerome. "Co-Authorship in the Corinthian Correspondence." *RB* 100 (1993): 562–79.

————. *Paul: A Critical Life.* New York: Oxford University Press, 1996.

————. "Paul and Gallio." *JBL* 112 (1993): 315–17.

————. *Paul: His Story.* Oxford: Oxford University Press, 2004.

————. "Paul in Arabia." *CBQ* 55 (1993): 732–37.

————. *St. Paul's Corinth: Texts and Archaeology.* 3d ed. Collegeville, Minn.: Liturgical, 2002.

Myllykoski, Matti. "James the Just in History and Tradition: Perspectives of Past and Present Scholarship." *CBR* 5 (2006): 73–122; *CBR* 6 (2007): 11–98.

Nanos, Mark D. "Intruding 'Spies' and 'Pseudo-Brethren': The Jewish Intra-Group Politics of Paul's Jerusalem Meeting (Gal 2:1–10)." Pages 59–97 in *Paul and His Opponents.* Edited by Stanley E. Porter. Pauline Studies 2. Boston: Brill, 2005.

Neagoe, Alexandru. *The Trial of the Gospel: An Apologetic Reading of Luke's Trial Narratives.* SNTSMS 116. Cambridge: Cambridge University Press, 2002.

Neusner, Jacob. *The Pharisees: Rabbinic Perspectives.* Jersey City: KTAV, 1985.

————. "What, Exactly, Is Israel's Gentile Problem? Rabbinic Perspectives on Galatians." Pages 276–306 in *The Missions of James, Peter, and Paul: Tensions in Early Christianity.* Edited by Bruce Chilton and Craig Evans. NovTSup 115. Boston: Brill, 2005.

Neyrey, Jerome. "The Forensic Defense Speech and Paul's Trial Speeches in Acts 22–26: Form and Function." Pages 210–24 in *Luke-Acts: New Perspectives from the Society of Biblical Literature Seminar.* Edited by Charles H. Talbert. New York: Crossroad, 1984.

————. "Luke's Social Location of Paul: Cultural Anthropology and Status of Paul in Acts." Pages 251–79 in *History, Literature, and Society in the Book of Acts.* Edited by Ben Witherington. Cambridge: Cambridge University Press, 1996.

Nickle, Keith F. *The Collection: A Study in Paul's Strategy.* Studies in Biblical Theology 48. Naperville, Ill.: Alec R. Allenson, 1966.

Nock, Arthur Darby. *Essays on Religion and the Ancient World.* Edited by Zeph Stewart. Cambridge: Harvard University Press, 1972.

Novak, David. *The Image of the Non-Jew in Judaism: An Historical and Constructive Study of the Noahide Laws.* Toronto Studies in Theology 14. Lewiston: Edwin Mellen, 1984.

Oakes, Peter. "God's Sovereignty over Roman Authorities: A Theme in Philippians." Pages 126–41 in *Rome in the Bible and the Early Church.* Edited by Peter Oakes. Grand Rapids: Baker Academic, 2002.

————. "Re-mapping the Universe: Paul and the Emperor in 1 Thessalonians and Philippians." *JSNT* 27 (2005): 301–22.

O'Brien, Peter T. *Colossians, Philemon.* WBC 44. Waco: Word, 1982.

————. "Was Paul Converted?" Pages 361–91 in *The Paradoxes of Paul.* Vol. 2 of *Justification and Variegated Nomism.* Edited by D. A. Carson, Peter T. O'Brien, and Mark A. Seifrid. Waco: Baylor University Press, 2004.

Oden, Amy G. *And You Welcomed Me: A Sourcebook on Hospitality in Early Christianity.* Nashville: Abingdon, 2001.

Ogg, George. *Chronology of the Life of Paul.* London: Epworth, 1968.

Öhler, Markus. *Barnabas: Die historische Person and ihre Rezeption in der Apostelgeschichte.* WUNT 156. Tübingen: Mohr Siebeck, 2003.

Omerzu, Heike. "Das Imperium schlägt zurück: Die Apologetik der Apostelgeschichte auf dem Prüfstand." *ZNT* 9 (2006): 26–36.

O'Neill, J. C. "The History and Pre-History of a Text: Gal. 1:19." *Irish Biblical Studies* 21 (1999): 40–45.

Osborne, Robert E. "Paul and the Wild Beasts." *JBL* 85 (1966): 225–30.

————. "St. Paul's Silent Years." *JBL* 84 (1965): 59–65.

Osiek, Carolyn, Margaret Y. MacDonald, and Janet H. Tulloch. *A Woman's Place: House Churches in Earliest Christianity.* Minneapolis: Fortress, 2006.

O'Toole, Robert F. "Luke's Position on Politics and Society in Luke-Acts." Pages 1–17 in *Political Issues in Luke-Acts.* Edited by Richard J. Cassidy. Maryknoll: Orbis, 1983.

Painter, John. *Just James: The Brother of Jesus in History and Tradition.* 2d ed. Studies on Personalities of the New Testament. Columbia: University of South Carolina Press, 2004.

Parker, Pierson. "Once More, Acts and Galatians." *JBL* 86 (1967): 175–82.

Parratt, J. K. "The Laying on of Hands in the New Testament: A Re-examination in Light of the Hebrew Terminology." *ExpTim* 80 (1969): 210–14.

Parsons, Mikeal C. "Bibliography of John Knox." Pages 115–30 in *Cadbury, Knox, and Talbert: American Contributions to the Study of Acts.* Edited by Mikeal C. Parsons and Joseph B. Tyson. Atlanta: Scholars Press, 1992.

Parsons, Mikeal C., and Martin M. Culy. *Acts: A Handbook on the Greek Text.* Waco: Baylor University Press, 2003.

Peace, Richard V. *Conversion in the New Testament.* Grand Rapids: Eerdmans, 1999.

Pearson, Birger. "1 Thessalonians 2:13–16: A Deutero-Pauline Interpolation." *HTR* 64 (1971): 79–94.

Peerbolte, L. J. Lietaert. *Paul the Missionary.* CBET 34. Leuven: Peeters, 2003.

Perkins, Pheme. *Peter: Apostle of the Whole Church.* Studies on Personalities of the New Testament. Minneapolis: Fortress, 2000.

Pervo, Richard I. *Acts: A Commentary.* Hermeneia. Minneapolis: Fortress, 2008.

————. "Acts in the Suburbs of the Apologists." Pages 29–46 in *Contemporary Studies in Acts.* Edited by Thomas E. Phillips. Macon: Mercer University Press, 2009.

————. *Dating Acts: Between the Evangelists and the Apologists.* Santa Rosa: Polebridge, 2006.

————. *Profit with Delight: The Literary Genre of the Acts of the Apostles.* Philadelphia: Fortress, 1987.

Peuch, Emile. "James the Just, or just James? The 'James Ossuary' on Trial." *BAIAS* 21 (2003): 45–53.

Phillips, Thomas E. *Acts in Diverse Frames of Reference.* Macon: Mercer University Press, forthcoming.

———. "The Genre of Acts: Moving Toward a Consensus?" *CBR* 4 (2006): 365–96.

———. "Paul as a Role Model in Acts: The 'We'-Passages in Acts 16 and Beyond." Pages 49–63 in *Acts and Ethics.* Edited by Thomas E. Phillips. NTM 9. Sheffield: Sheffield Phoenix, 2005.

———. *Reading Issues of Wealth and Poverty in Luke-Acts.* Studies in the Bible and Early Christianity 48. Lewiston: Edwin Mellen, 2001.

———. "Reading Theory and Biblical Interpretation for Postmodern Wesleyans." *Wesleyan Theological Journal* 35, no. 2 (Fall 2000): 32–48. Repr. in *Acts in Diverse Frames of Reference.*

Phillips, Thomas E., ed. *Contemporary Studies in Acts.* Macon: Mercer University Press, forthcoming.

Plümacher, Eckhard. "Acta-Fortschung 1974–82." *Theologische Rundschau* 48 (1984): 105–69.

———. "The Mission Speeches in Acts and Dionysius of Halicarnassus." Pages 251–66 in *Jesus and the Heritage of Israel.* Edited by David P. Moessner. Philadelphia: Trinity Press International, 1999.

Porter, Frank C. "Does Paul Claim to Have Known the Historical Jesus? A Study of 2 Corinthians 5:16." *JBL* 47 (1928): 257–75.

Porter, Stanley E. "The Genre of Acts and the Ethics of Discourse." Pages 1–15 in *Acts and Ethics.* Edited by Thomas E. Phillips. NTM 9. Sheffield: Sheffield Phoenix, 2005.

———. "Paul and His Bible: His Education and Access to the Scriptures of Israel." Pages 29–40 in *As It Is Written: Studying Paul's Use of Scripture.* Edited by Stanley E. Porter and Christopher D. Stanley. SBLSymS. Atlanta: SBL, 2008.

———. *Paul in Acts.* LPS. Peabody, Mass.: Hendrickson, 2001.

———. "Paul of Tarsus and his Letters." Pages 533–85 in *Handbook of Classical Rhetoric in the Hellenistic Period, 330 B.C.–A.D. 400.* Edited by Stanley E. Porter. Leiden: Brill, 1997.

———. "Pauline Authorship and the Pastoral Epistles: Implications for Canon." *Bulletin for Biblical Research* 5 (1995): 105–23.

———. "Romans 13:1–7 as Pauline Political Rhetoric." *Filología Neotestamentaria* 6 (1990): 115–39.

———. "The Theoretical Justification for Application of Rhetorical Categories to Pauline Literature." Pages 100–122 in *Rhetoric and the New Testament: Essays from the 1992 Heidelberg Conference.* Edited by Stanley E. Porter and Thomas H. Olbricht. JSNTSup 90. Sheffield: JSOT, 1993.

Powell, Mark Allan. "Luke's Second Volume: Three Basic Issues in Contemporary Studies of Acts." *Trinity Seminary Review* 13 (1991): 69–81.

Pratscher, Wilhelm. *Der Herrenbruder Jakobus und die Jakobustradition.* FRLANT 139. Göttingen: Vandenhoeck & Ruprecht, 1987.

Price, Robert M. "The Legend of Paul's Conversion." *Journal for the Critical Study of Religion, Ethics and Society* 3 (1998): 9–22.

Price, Simon R. F. "Response." Pages 175–83 in *Paul and the Roman Imperial Order.* Edited by Richard A. Horsley. Harrisburg: Trinity Press International, 2004.

———. "Rituals and Power." Pages 47–71 in *Paul and Empire.* Edited by Richard A. Horsley. Harrisburg: Trinity Press International, 1997.

Ramsaran, Rollin A. "Resisting Imperial Domination and Influence: Paul's Apocalyptic Rhetoric in 1 Corinthians." Pages 89–101 in *Paul and the Roman Imperial Order.* Edited by Richard A. Horsley. Harrisburg: Trinity Press International, 2004.

Ramsay, William M. *The First Christian Century.* London: Hodder & Stoughton, 1911. Repr., Boston: Elibron, 2005.

———. *St. Paul the Traveller and Roman Citizen.* 3d ed. London: Hodder & Stoughton, 1897. Repr., Grand Rapids: Baker, 1979.

Rapske, Brian M. "Acts, Travel and Shipwreck." Pages 1–47 in *The Book of Acts in Graeco-Roman Setting.* Edited by David W. J. Gill and Conrad Gempf. BAFCS 2. Grand Rapids: Eerdmans, 1994.

———. *Paul in Roman Custody.* BAFCS 3. Grand Rapids: Eerdmans, 1994.

Read-Heimerdinger, Jenny. "Barnabas in Acts: A Study of His Role in the Text of Codex Bezae." *JSNT* 72 (1998): 23–66.

Reed, Jeffrey H. "Philippians 3:1 and the Epistolary Hesitation Formulas: The Literary Integrity of Philippians, Again." *JBL* 115 (1996): 63–90.

Rese, Martin. "Zur Lukas-Diskussion seit 1950." *Jahrbuch der theologischen Hochschule Bethel* 9 (1967): 62–67.

Richards, E. Randolph. *Paul and First-Century Letter Writing: Secretaries, Composition and Collection.* Downers Grove: InterVarsity, 2004.

Riddle, Donald W. "The Cephas-Peter Problem, and a Possible Solution." *JBL* 59 (1940): 169–80.

———. *Paul, Man of Conflict: A Modern Biographical Sketch.* Nashville: Abingdon, 1940.

Riesner, Rainer. "James's Speech (Acts 15:13–21), Simeon's Hymn (Luke 2:29–32), and Luke's Sources." Pages 263–78 in *Jesus of Nazareth: Lord and Christ.* Edited by Joel B. Green and Max Turner. Grand Rapids: Eerdmans, 1994.

Robertson, A. T. *Luke the Historian in Light of Research.* New York: C. Scribner's Sons, 1920.

Robinson, Donald Fay. "A Note on Acts 11:27–30." *JBL* 63 (1944): 169–72.

Roetzel, Calvin J. *Paul: A Jew on the Margins.* Louisville: Westminster John Knox, 2003.

———. *Paul: The Man and the Myth.* Minneapolis: Fortress, 1999.

Roloff, Jürgen. *Die Apostelgeschichte.* Das Neue Testament Deutsch 5. Göttingen: Vandenhoeck & Ruprecht, 1981.

Rosenblatt, Marie-Eloise. *Paul the Accused: His Portrait in the Acts of the Apostles.* Collegeville, Minn.: Liturgical, 1995.

Rossing, Barbara R. *The Rapture Exposed: The Message of Hope in the Book of Revelation.* Cambridge: Westview, 2004.

Rowlingson, Donald T. "The Jerusalem Conference and Jesus' Nazareth Visit: A Study in Pauline Chronology." *JBL* 71 (1952): 69–74.

Salas, Enique Mena. *"También a los Griegos" (Hch 11,20): Factores del inicio de la misión a los gentiles en Antioquía de Siria.* Plenitudo Temporis 9. Salamanca: Universidad Pontificia de Salamanca, 2007.

Saldarini, Anthony J. *Pharisees, Scribes and Sadducees in Palestinian Society.* Collegeville, Minn.: Michael Glazier, 1988.

Sampley, J. Paul. " 'Before God, I Do Not Lie' (Gal. 1.20): Paul's Self-Defence in the Light of Roman Legal Praxis." *NTS* 23 (1976–1977): 477–82.

———. "The Second Letter to the Corinthians: Introduction, Commentary, and Reflections." Pages 1–180 in vol. 11 of *The New Interpreter's Bible.* Edited by Leander Keck et. al. 12 vols. Nashville: Abingdon, 2000.

Sanders, E. P. *Paul and Palestinian Judaism.* Minneapolis: Fortress, 1977.

Sanders, J. N. "Peter and Paul in the Acts." *NTS* 2 (1955–1956): 133–43.

Sanders, Jack T. "The Jewish People in Luke-Acts." Pages 51–75 in *Luke-Acts and the Jewish People: Eight Critical Perspectives.* Edited by Joseph B. Tyson. Minneapolis: Augsburg, 1988.

———. "Paul's 'Autobiographical' Statements in Galatians 1–2." *JBL* 85 (1966): 335–43.

Sandnes, Karl Olav. "Paul and Socrates: The Aim of Paul's Areopagus Speech." *JSNT* 50 (1993): 13–26.

Satterthwaite, Philip E. "Acts Against the Background of Classical Rhetoric." Pages 337–79 in *The Book of Acts in Its Ancient Literary Setting.* Edited by Bruce W. Winter and Andrew D. Clarke. BAFCS 1. Grand Rapids: Eerdmans, 1993.

Saunders, Ross. "Paul and the Imperial Cult." Pages 227–38 in *Paul and His Opponents.* Edited by Stanley E. Porter. Pauline Studies 2. Boston: Brill, 2005.

Schäfer, Peter. *Judeophobia: Attitudes toward the Jews in the Ancient World.* Cambridge: Harvard University Press, 1997.

Schmidt, Daryl. "1 Thess 2:13–16: Linguistic Evidence for an Interpolation." *JBL* 102 (1983): 269–79.

Schnabel, Eckhard J. *Paul and the Early Church.* Volume 2 of *Early Christian Mission.* Downers Grove: InterVarsity, 2004.

Schnackenburg, Rudolf. "Apostles before and during Paul's Time." Pages 287–303 in *Apostolic History and the Gospel: Biblical and Historical Essays Presented to F. F. Bruce.* Edited by W. Ward Gasque and Ralph P. Martin. Exeter: Paternoster, 1970.

Schnelle, Udo. *Apostle Paul: His Life and Theology.* Translated by M. Eugene Boring. Grand Rapids: Baker, 2003.

Schoeps, Hans-Joachim. *Theologie und Geschichte des Judenchristentums.* Tübingen: Mohr Siebeck, 1949.

Schubert, Paul. "The Final Cycle of Speeches in the Book of Acts." *JBL* 87 (1968): 1–16.

Schüssler Fiorenza, Elisabeth. "Paul and the Politics of Interpretation." Pages 40–57 in *Paul and Politics*. Edited by Richard A. Horsley. Harrisburg: Trinity Press International, 2000.

Schütz, John Howard. *Paul and the Anatomy of Apostolic Authority.* New Testament Library. Louisville: Westminster John Knox, 2007.

Schwartz, Daniel R. "The End of the Line: Paul in the Canonical Book of Acts." Pages 3–24 in *Paul and the Legacies of Paul.* Edited by William S. Babcock. Dallas: SMU Press, 1991.

Segal, Alan F. *Paul the Convert: The Apostolate and Apostasy of Saul the Pharisee.* New Haven: Yale University Press, 1990.

Seitz, M. and H.-G. Link. "Burden, Heavy, Labour." Pages 260–63 in vol. 1 of *New International Dictionary of New Testament Theology.* Edited by Colin Brown. 4 vols. Grand Rapids: Zondervan, 1971.

Shanks, Hershel, and Ben Witherington. *The Brother of Jesus: The Dramatic Story and Significance of the First Archaeological Link to Jesus and His Family.* San Francisco: HarperSanFrancisco, 2003.

Shroyer, Montgomery J. "Paul's Departure from Judaism to Hellenism." *JBL* 59 (1940): 41–49.

Skinner, Matthew. *Locating Paul: Places of Custody as Narrative Settings in Acts 21–28.* Academia Biblica. Atlanta: Society of Biblical Literature, 2003.

———. "Unchained Ministry: Paul's Roman Custody (Acts 21–28) and the Sociopolitical Outlook of the Book of Acts." Pages 79–95 in *Acts and Ethics.* Edited by Thomas E. Phillips. NTM 9. Sheffield: Sheffield Phoenix, 2005.

Slingerland, Dixon. "Acts 18:1–17 and Luedemann's Pauline Chronology." *JBL* 109 (1990): 686–90.

———. "Acts 18:1–18, the Gallio Inscription, and Absolute Pauline Chronology." *JBL* 110 (1991): 439–49.

Smit, Joop F. M. "'What Is Apollos? What Is Paul?' In Search for the Coherence of First Corinthians 1:10–4:21." *NovT* 44 (2002): 231–51.

Smith, Abraham. "'Unmasking the Powers': Toward a Postcolonial Analysis of 1 Thessalonians." Pages 47–66 in *Paul and the Roman Imperial Order.* Edited by Richard A. Horsley. Harrisburg: Trinity Press International, 2004.

Smith, Barry. *What Must I Do to Be Saved? Paul Parts Ways with His Jewish Heritage.* Sheffield: Sheffield Phoenix, 2007.

Smith, Daniel Alan. *The Post-Mortem Vindication of Jesus in the Sayings Gospel Q.* LNTS 338. London: T&T Clark, 2006.

Smith, Henry Preserved. "The Laying-On of Hands." *AJT* 17 (1913): 47–62.

Soards, Marion L. *The Apostle Paul: An Introduction to His Writings and Teachings.* New York: Paulist, 1987.

———. *The Speeches in Acts: Their Content, Context, and Concerns.* Louisville: Westminster John Knox, 1994.

Spencer, F. Scott. *Journeying through Acts: A Literary-Cultural Reading.* Peabody, Mass.: Hendrickson, 2004.

———. "Wise Up, Young Man: The Moral Vision of Saul and Other νεανίσκοι in Acts." Pages 34–48 in *Acts and Ethics.* Edited by Thomas E. Phillips. NTM 9. Sheffield: Sheffield Phoenix, 2005.

———. "Women of 'the Cloth' in Acts: Sewing the Word." Pages 134–54 in *A Feminist Companion to The Acts of the Apostles.* Edited by Amy-Jill Levine and Marianne Blickenstaff. Feminist Companion to the New Testament and Early Christian Writings 9. Cleveland: Pilgrim, 2004.

Stanley, David M. "Paul's Conversion in Acts: Why the Three Accounts?" *CBQ* 15 (1953): 315–38.

Stegemann, Ekkehard W. and Wolfgang Stegemann. *The Jesus Movement: A Social History of Its First Century.* Translated by O. C. Dean. Minneapolis: Fortress, 1999.

Stein, Robert H. "The Relationship of Galatians 2:1–10 and Acts 15:1–35: Two Neglected Arguments." *Journal of the Evangelical Theological Society* 17 (1974): 239–42.

Stendahl, Krister. "The Apostle Paul and the Introspective Conscience of the West." *HTR* 56 (1963): 199–215.

———. "Call Rather Than Conversion." Pages 7–23 in *Paul among Jews and Gentiles.* Philadelphia: Fortress, 1976.

Sterling, Gregory E. "Images of Paul at the End of the First Century." *ZNW* 99 (2008): 74–98.

Still, Todd D. "Did Paul Loathe Manual Labor? Revisiting the Work of Ronald F. Hock on the Apostle's Tentmaking and Social Class." *JBL* 125 (2006): 781–95.

Suhl, Alfred. "Der Beginn der selbständigen Mission des Paulus: Ein Beitrag zur Geschichte des Urchristentums." *NTS* 38 (1992): 430–47.

Tajra, H. W. *The Martyrdom of Paul: Historical and Judicial Context, Traditions, and Legends.* WUNT 67. Tübingen: J. C. B. Mohr, 1994.

Tannehill, Robert C. "The Narrator's Strategy in the Scenes of Paul's Defense: Acts 21:27–26:32." *Forum* 8 (1992): 255–69.

———. "Rejection by Jews and Turning to Gentiles: The Pattern of Paul's Mission in Acts." Pages 83–101 in *Luke-Acts and the Jewish People: Eight Critical Perspectives.* Edited by Joseph B. Tyson. Minneapolis: Augsburg, 1988.

Tatum, Gregory. *New Chapters in the Life of Paul: The Relative Chronology of His Career.* Catholic Biblical Quarterly Monograph Series 41. Washington, D.C.: Catholic Biblical Association, 2006.

Taylor, Justin. "The Ethnarch of King Aretas at Damascus: A Note on 2 Cor 11, 32–33." *RB* 99 (1992): 719–28.

Taylor, Nicholas H. "Apostolic Identity and Conflicts in Corinth and Galatia." Pages 99–127 in *Paul and His Opponents.* Edited by Stanley E. Porter. Pauline Studies 2. Boston: Brill, 2005.

———. "The Composition and Chronology of Second Corinthians." *JSNT* 44 (1991): 67–87.

————. *Paul, Antioch and Jerusalem: A Study in Relationships and Authority in Earliest Christianity.* JSNTSup 66. Sheffield: Sheffield University Press, 1992.

Theissen, Gerd. *The Social Setting of Pauline Christianity: Essays on Corinth.* Translated by John H. Schütz. Philadelphia: Fortress, 1982.

Thompson, Richard P. "'What Do You Think You Are Doing, Paul?' Synagogues, Accusations, and Ethics in Paul's Ministry in Acts 16–21." Pages 64–78 in *Acts and Ethics.* Edited by Thomas E. Phillips. NTM 9. Sheffield: Sheffield Phoenix, 2005.

Thorley, John. "Junia, a Woman Apostle." *NovT* 38 (1996): 18–29.

Thurén, Lauri. *Derhetorizing Paul: A Dynamic Perspective on Pauline Theology and the Law.* Harrisburg: Trinity Press International, 2000.

Tomson, P. J. "Gamaliel's Counsel and the Apologetic Strategy of Luke-Acts." Pages 585–604 in *The Unity of Luke-Acts.* Edited by Joseph Verheyden. BETL 142. Leuven: University Press, 1999.

Toussaint, Stanley D. "The Chronological Problem of Galatians 2:1–10." *Bibliotheca sacra* 120 (1963): 334–40.

Trudinger, L. Paul. "'*Heteron de tōn apostolōn ouk eido, ei mē Iakōbon . . .*': A Note on Galatians i.19." *NovT* 17 (1975): 200–202.

Tyson, Joseph B. *Images of Judaism in Luke-Acts.* Columbia: University of South Carolina Press, 1992.

————. "John Knox and the Acts of the Apostles." Pages 55–80 in *Cadbury, Knox, and Talbert: American Contributions to the Study of Acts.* Edited by Mikeal C. Parsons and Joseph B. Tyson. Atlanta: Scholars Press, 1992.

————. "The Legacy of F. C. Baur and Recent Studies of Acts." *Forum* 4 (2001): 125–44.

————. *Luke, Judaism, and the Scholars: Critical Approaches to Luke-Acts.* Columbia: University of South Carolina Press, 1999.

————. *Marcion and Luke-Acts: A Defining Struggle.* Columbia: University of South Carolina Press, 2006.

————. "Wrestling with and for Paul." Pages 13–28 in *Contemporary Studies in Acts.* Edited by Thomas E. Phillips. Macon: Mercer University Press, 2009.

Unnik, W. C. van. *Tarsus or Jerusalem: The City of Paul's Youth.* Translated by George Ogg. London: Epworth, 1962.

Veltman, Fred. "The Defense Speeches in Acts." Pages 243–56 in *Perspectives on Luke-Acts.* Edited by Charles H. Talbert. Edinburgh: T&T Clark, 1978.

Vielhauer, Philipp. "On the 'Paulinism' of Acts." Translated by Wm. C. Robinson Jr. and Victor Paul Furnish. Pages 33–50 in *Studies in Luke-Acts.* Edited by J. Louis Martyn and Leander E. Keck. Nashville: Abingdon, 1966. Repr., Philadelphia: Fortress, 1980.

————. "Zum 'Paulinismus' der Apostelgeschichte." *Evangelische Theologie* 10 (1950–1951): 1–15.

Vos, Craig S. de "Finding a Charge That Fits: The Accusation against Paul and Silas at Philippi (Acts 16.19–21)." *JSNT* 74 (1999): 51–63.

Vos, Johan S. "Paul's Argumentation in Galatians 1–2." Pages 169–80 in *The Galatians Debate: Contemporary Issues in Rhetorical and Historical Interpretation.* Edited by Mark D. Nanos. Peabody, Mass.: Hendrickson, 2002.

Wainwright, Allan. "Where Did Silas Go? (And What Was His Connection with Galatians?)." *JSNT* 8 (1980): 66–70.

Walaskay, Paul W. *And So We Came to Rome.* SNTSMS 49. Cambridge: Cambridge University Press, 1983.

Walker, William O. "Acts and the Pauline Corpus Revisited." Pages 77–86 in *Literary Studies in Luke-Acts.* Edited by Richard P. Thompson and Thomas E. Phillips. Macon: Mercer University Press, 1998.

———. "Acts and the Pauline Letters." *Forum* 5 (2002): 105–15.

———. "The Portrayal of Aquila and Priscilla in Acts: The Question of Sources." *NTS* 54 (2008): 479–95.

———. "The 'Theology of Woman's Place' and the 'Paulinist' Tradition." *Semeia* 28 (1983): 101–12.

———. "The Timothy-Titus Problem Reconsidered." *ExpTim* 92 (1981): 231–35.

———. "Why Paul Went to Jerusalem: The Interpretation of Galatians 2:1–5." *CBQ* 54 (1992): 503–10.

Walter, Nikolaus. "Paul and the Opponents of the Christ-Gospel in Galatia." Pages 362–66 in *The Galatians Debate: Contemporary Issues in Rhetorical and Historical Interpretation.* Edited by Mark D. Nanos. Peabody, Mass.: Hendrickson, 2002.

Walton, Steve. *Leadership and Lifestyle: The Portrait in the Miletus Speech and 1 Thessalonians.* SNTSMS 108. New York: Cambridge University Press, 2000.

———. "The State They Were In: Luke's View of the Roman Empire." Pages 1–41 in *Rome in the Bible and the Early Church.* Edited by Peter Oakes. Grand Rapids: Baker Academic, 2002.

Wan, Sze-kar. "Collection for the Saints as Anticolonial Acts: Implications of Paul's Ethnic Reconstruction." Pages 191–215 in *Paul and Politics.* Edited by Richard A. Horsley. Harrisburg: Trinity Press International, 2000.

Warkentin, Marjorie. *Ordination: A Biblical-Historical View.* Grand Rapids: Eerdmans, 1982.

Watson, Duane F. "Paul's Speech to the Ephesian Elders (Acts 20.17–38): Epideictic Rhetoric of Farewell." Pages 184–208 in *Persuasive Artistry: Studies in New Testament Rhetoric in Honor of George A. Kennedy.* Edited by Duane F. Watson and George A. Kennedy. Sheffield: JSOT, 1991.

Weaver, John B. *Plots of Epiphany: Prison-Escape in Acts of the Apostles.* BZNW 131. New York: de Gruyter, 2004.

Wedderburn, A. J. M. "The 'Apostolic Decree': Tradition and Redaction." *NovT* 35 (1993): 362–89.

———. *A History of the First Christians.* New York: T&T Clark, 2004.

———. "Paul's Collection: Chronology and History." *NTS* 48 (2002): 95–110.

Wenham, David and A. D. A. Moses. "'There Are Some Standing Here . . .': Did They Become the 'Reputed Pillars' of the Jerusalem Church?" *NovT* 36 (1994): 146–63.

Westerholm, Stephen. *Perspectives Old and New on Paul: The "Lutheran" Paul and His Critics.* Grand Rapids: Eerdmans, 2004.

———. "Sinai as Viewed from Damascus: Paul's Reevaluation of the Mosaic Law." Pages 147–65 in *The Road from Damascus: The Impact of Paul's Conversion on His Life, Thought, and Ministry.* Edited by Richard N. Longenecker. Grand Rapids: Eerdmans, 1997.

Whelan, Caroline F. "*Amica Pauli*: The Role of Phoebe in the Early Church." *JSNT* 49 (1993): 67–85.

White, John L. *The Apostle of God: Paul and the Promise of Abraham.* Peabody, Mass.: Hendrickson, 1999.

———. "Paul and Pater Familias." Pages 457–87 in *Paul in the Greco-Roman World.* Edited by J. Paul Sampley. Harrisburg: Trinity Press International, 2003.

Wimbush, Vincent L. *Paul: The Worldly Ascetic.* Macon: Mercer University Press, 1987.

Winter, Bruce W. "Acts and Food Shortages." Pages 59–78 in *The Book of Acts in Its Graeco-Roman Setting.* Edited by David W. Gill and Conrad Gempf. BAFCS 2. Grand Rapids: Eerdmans, 1999.

———. "Acts and Roman Religion: B. The Imperial Cult." Pages 93–103 in *The Book of Acts in Its Graeco-Roman Setting.* Edited by David J. Gill and Conrad Gempf. BAFCS 2. Grand Rapids: Eerdmans, 1994.

———. "Gallio's Ruling on the Legal Status of Early Christianity (Acts 18:14–15)." *Tyndale Bulletin* 50 (1999): 213–24.

———. "The Importance of the *Captatio Benevolentiae* in the Speeches of Tertullus and Paul in Acts 24:1–21." *Journal of Theological Studies* 42 (1991): 505–31.

———. "The Public Honouring of Christian Benefactors: Romans 13.3–4 and 1 Peter 2.14–15." *JSNT* 34 (1988): 87–103.

———. "Roman Law and Society in Romans 12–15." Pages 67–102 in *Rome in the Bible and the Early Church.* Edited by Peter Oakes. Grand Rapids: Baker Academic, 2002.

Witherington, Ben, III. *The Acts of the Apostles: A Socio-Rhetorical Commentary.* Grand Rapids: Eerdmans, 1998.

———. *The Paul Quest: The Renewed Search for the Jew of Tarsus.* Downers Grove: InterVarsity, 1998.

Wright. N. T. *The Climax of the Covenant.* Edinburgh: T&T Clark, 1991.

———. "Paul, Arabia, and Elijah (Galatians 1:17)." *JBL* 115 (1996): 683–92.

———. "Paul's Gospel and Caesar's Empire." Pages 160–83 in *Paul and Politics.* Edited by Richard A. Horsley. Harrisburg: Trinity Press International, 2000.

———. *The Resurrection of the Son of God.* Vol. 3 of Christian Origins and the Question of God. Minneapolis: Fortress, 2003.

Yarbrough, O. Larry. "Paul, Marriage, and Divorce." Pages 404–28 in *Paul in the Greco-Roman World.* Edited by J. Paul Sampley. Harrisburg: Trinity Press International, 2003.

Zeitlin, Solomon. "Paul's Journeys to Jerusalem." *JQR* 57 (1967): 171–78.

Zweck, Dean. "The Exordium of the Areopagus Speech, Acts 17.22,23." *NTS* 35 (1989): 94–103.

INDEX OF MODERN AUTHORS

INDEX OF SUBJECTS

INDEX OF SCRIPTURE REFERENCES

238   *Index of Scripture References*